Page 85: This is the first character in the name of the *yakuza* Eigorō. In the context of the name, it is pronounced *ei*, but standing alone it is read as *sakae* and means "prosperity, to prosper." In the Edo period, peasants and other low-ranking individuals did not have a family name, just a single given name. Often, as has Eigorō in this case, they would take the name of where they lived or another identifier. Eigorō uses his personal name combined with the name of the town where he lives (Ōmaeda-no-hama) to create the name Ōmaeda-no-Eigorō (literally, Eigorō of Ōmaeda).

Page 137: A staple of Japanese popular-culture ninja lore is that any ninja who leaves the clan—a *nukenin*—will be hunted down to the ends of the earth and killed by his fellows. Whether this is a fictional construct or has a historical basis, this is the "*shinobi* code" that Tōgō refers to.

Page 166: The Ryūkyūs are today's Okinawa archipelago. The Ryūkyū Kingdom was an influential trading nation strategically positioned between Japan, China, and southeast Asia with its own dialect and culture. It was occupied by Satsuma *han* troops in 1609 and turned into a puppet state. The islands were finally incorporated into post-Tokugawa Japan as Okinawa Prefecture in 1879.

Page 223: Shinja-daishō is one of the more unusual deities in Japanese Buddhism. Shinja-daishō (also rendered as *Jinja-daishō* and other variations) was a Hindu deity who found his way into Japanese esoteric Buddhism and some popular Buddhist sects. He is often depicted in religious art in the company of the historical Xuanzang (AD 602–664), a Chinese monk of the Tang Dynasty who journeyed to India (then called *Tenjiku*) to bring Buddhist sutras back to China in the early days of Buddhism's spread into northeast Asia. Xuanzang's multivolume account of his travels, *Records from the Regions West of the Great Tang Empire*, is a priceless historical record of that era. However, Xuanzang is best known today as the monk who travels to China in the fantastical Ming Dynasty epic *Journey to the West*, more popularly known as *Monkey*. In earlier folk retellings of Xuanzang's journey preceding the publication of *Journey to the West*, Shinja-daishō appears to Xuanzang when he is lost in the desert without water on his way to India, saving the monk's life and making it possible for him to complete his journey.

FOOTNOTES

Page 19: Two separate spy apparatuses reported to the *rōjū* senior councilors and to the *wakadoshiyori* junior councilors. The Hattori clan historically reported to the *rōjū*. The semifictional Ushikudonki here report to junior councilors.

Page 26: The Jōdō-shū Pure Land Sect Buddhist temple Zōjōji in central Edo became the family temple of the Tokugawa after the first *shōgun*, Tokugawa Ieyasu, moved to the city and made it his capital in 1603. Partly destroyed in World War II, Zōjōji has been rebuilt and today is a popular tourist destination near the foot of Tokyo Tower.

Page 28: Today's Hamarikyu Gardens, on the Tokyo waterfront.

Page 29: Kan'eiji temple still stands today next to Tokyo's popular Ueno Park.

Page 30: Sign at the entrance to the Yushima Seido Confucius Temple. Confucianism was first introduced to Japan in the sixth century but did not become the official guiding philosophy of the Tokugawa shogunate until the reign of the dynamic third *shōgun*, Tokugawa Iemitsu (1604–1651), the father of the weak and ineffective Tokugawa Ietsuna (1641–1680), who reigns at the time this story is set.

Page 32: Samegabashi was near today's Tōgū-gosho palace, the residence of the crown prince. Edo Castle and many other Tokugawa properties were turned over to the imperial family after the shogunate's fall and imperial restoration in 1868.

Page 32: The Niō-mon gate, destroyed by US firebombing raids in 1945, was reborn after World War II as the Hōzōmon gate of Asakusa Kannon Temple, one of Tokyo's most popular tourist spots.

Page 76: In this scene, we see that Tōgō is letting Daigoro's hair grow out. Prior to this scene Daigoro wore a *keshibōzu*, a common cut to start giving boys at about four years old. At around six, a boy's hair was allowed to grow out further, although still not as long as when they became a teenager, and not yet adding in the shaven forehead required for men.

Page 77: The historical Ōmaeda Eigorō was one of the most famous Edo-period gambling house operators and *yakuza* bosses. He eventually went on to control most of the gangs in the region around Edo, the premodern center for *yakuza*. Ōmaeda Eigorō lived from 1793 to 1874, more than a century after this story is set, living into the early years of the modern Meiji period.

Page 79: The *kiai* battle cry of the Jigen-ryū sword school, founded by the historical Tōgō Shigekata (also called Tōgō Chūi). Jigen-ryū calls for defeating your enemy with an unblockable first stroke.

TO PAGE 246

新・子連れ狼

LONE WOLF

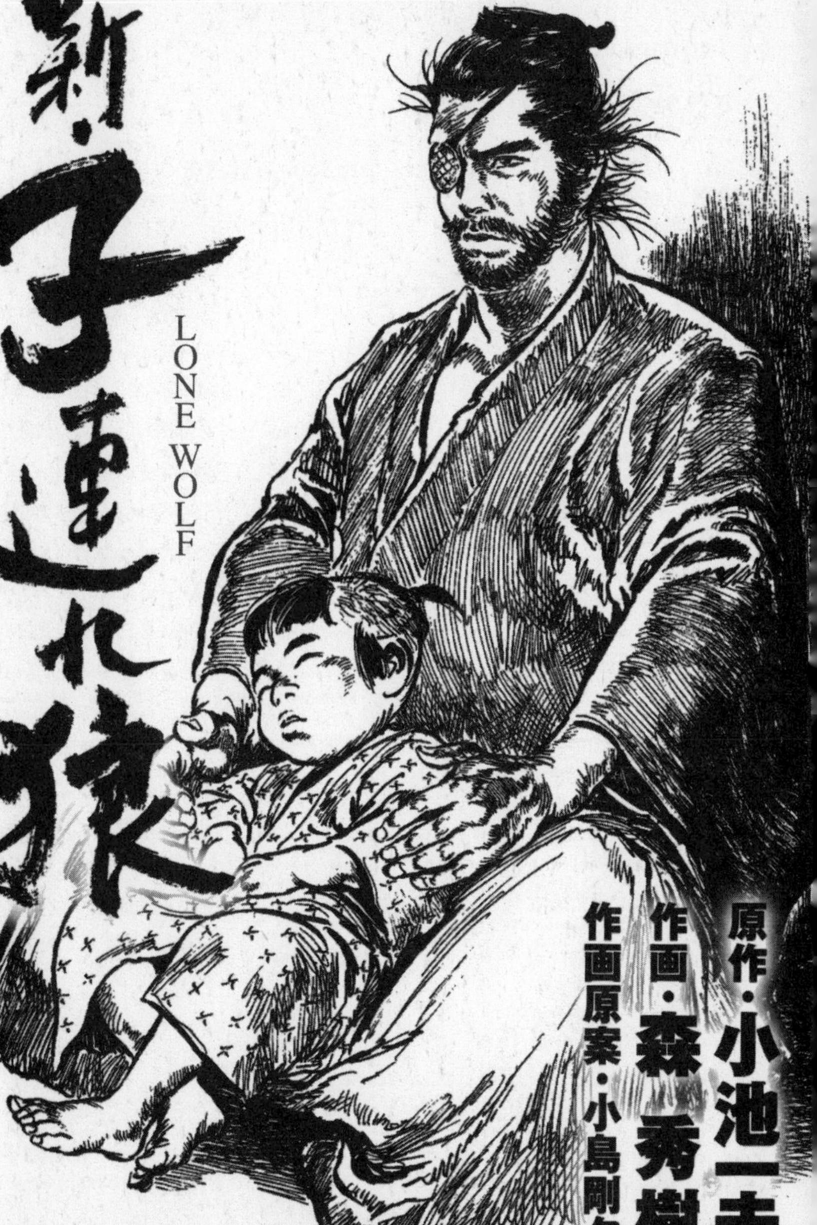

原作・小池一夫
作画・森秀樹
作画原案・小島剛夕

A NOTE TO READERS

NEW LONE WOLF AND CUB is a carefully researched re-creation of Edo-period Japan. To preserve the flavor of the work, we have chosen to retain terms of the period that have no direct equivalents in English. Japanese is written in a mix of Chinese ideograms and a syllabic writing system, resulting in numerous words with multiple meanings. In the glossary, you may encounter these words. A Japanese reader seeing the different ideograms would know instantly which meaning is intended, but these synonyms can cause confusion when Japanese is spelled out in our alphabet.

Some characters in this series come from the Satsuma region of Japan, an area with its own distinctive dialect. Some common words in this dialect have been left untranslated to better give the impression of this dialect being spoken. These terms are defined in the glossary. Other characters in the story come from places or cultural strata (country folk, gangsters) for which there is no direct translation to identify these characteristics. Here they are given corresponding Americanized speech patterns to highlight these traits.

TABLE OF CONTENTS
(Volume Seven)

5	No Staff to Lean On, Part 1
21	No Staff to Lean On, Part 2
37	No Staff to Lean On, Part 3
53	No Staff to Lean On, Part 4
69	No Staff to Lean On, Part 5
85	No Staff to Lean On, Part 6
101	No Staff to Lean On, Part 7
117	No Staff to Lean On, Part 8
133	No Staff to Lean On, Part 9
149	No Staff to Lean On, Part 10
165	No Staff to Lean On, Part 11
181	No Staff to Lean On, Part 12
197	No Staff to Lean On, Part 13
213	No Staff to Lean On, Part 14
229	No Staff to Lean On, Part 15
245	Footnotes
247	Glossary

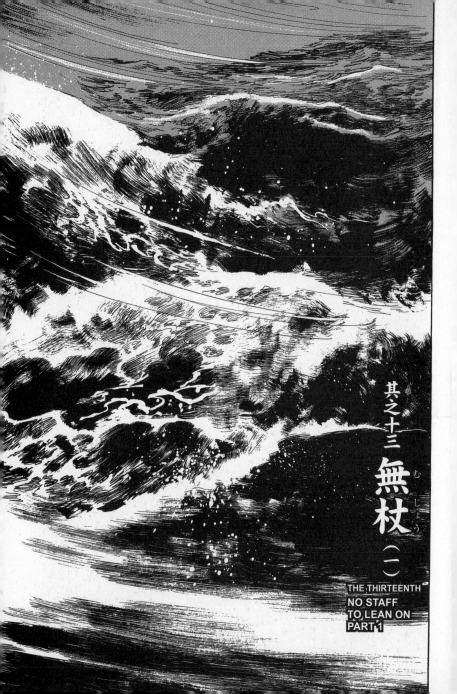

其之十三 無杖（一）

THE THIRTEENTH
NO STAFF
TO LEAN ON
PART 1

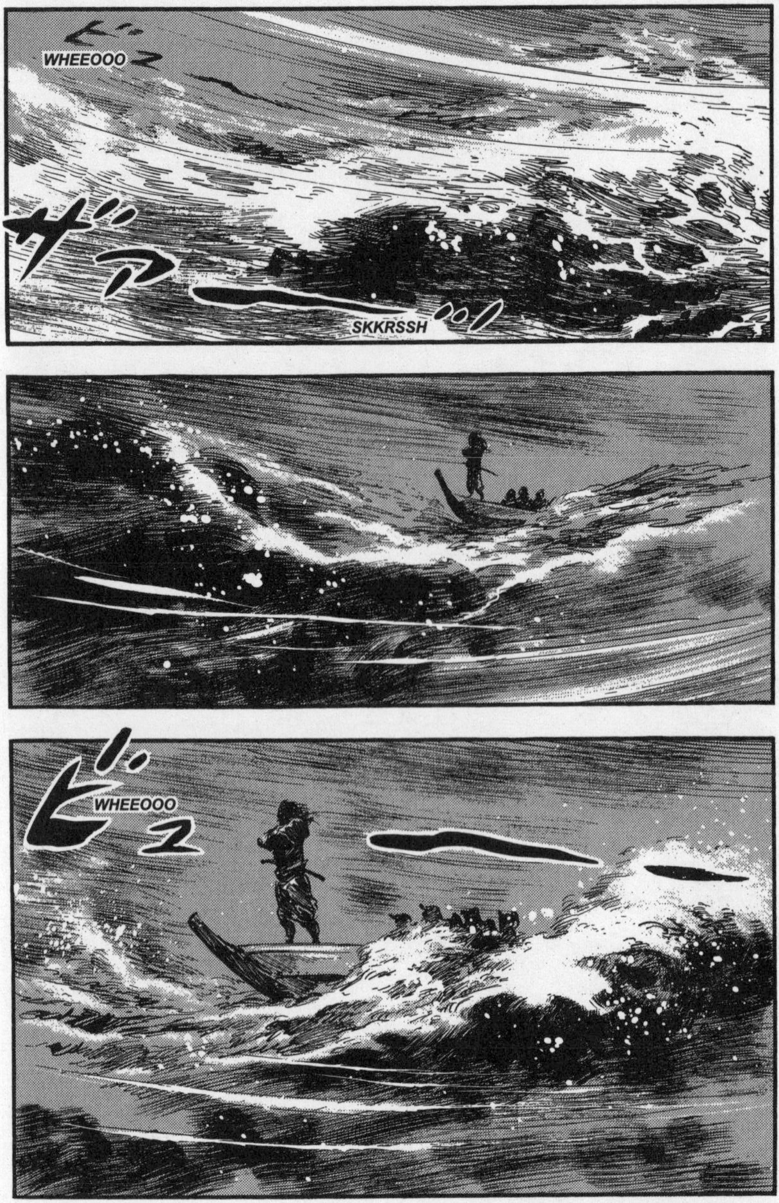
ビュ
WHEEOOO
ザァーッ
SKKRSSH
ビューー
WHEEOOO

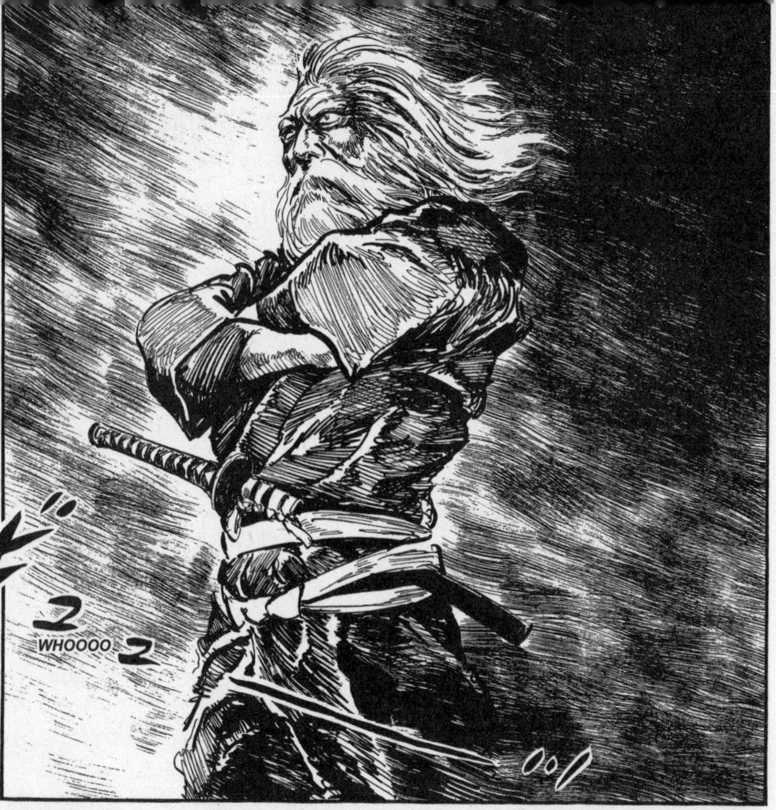
WHOOOO
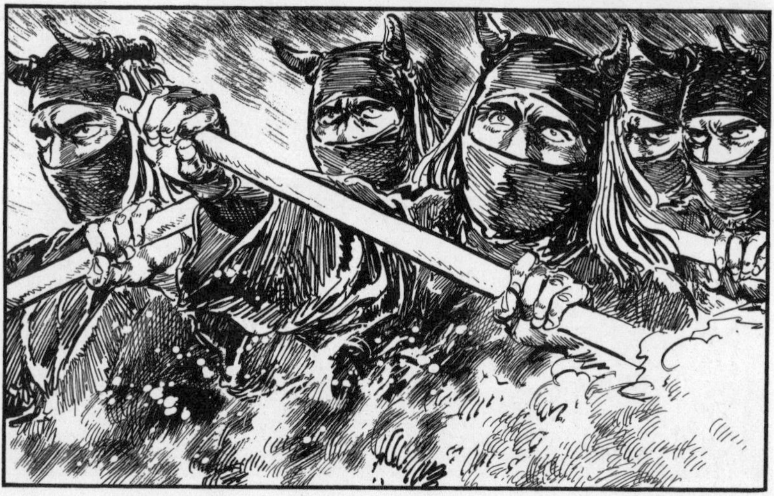

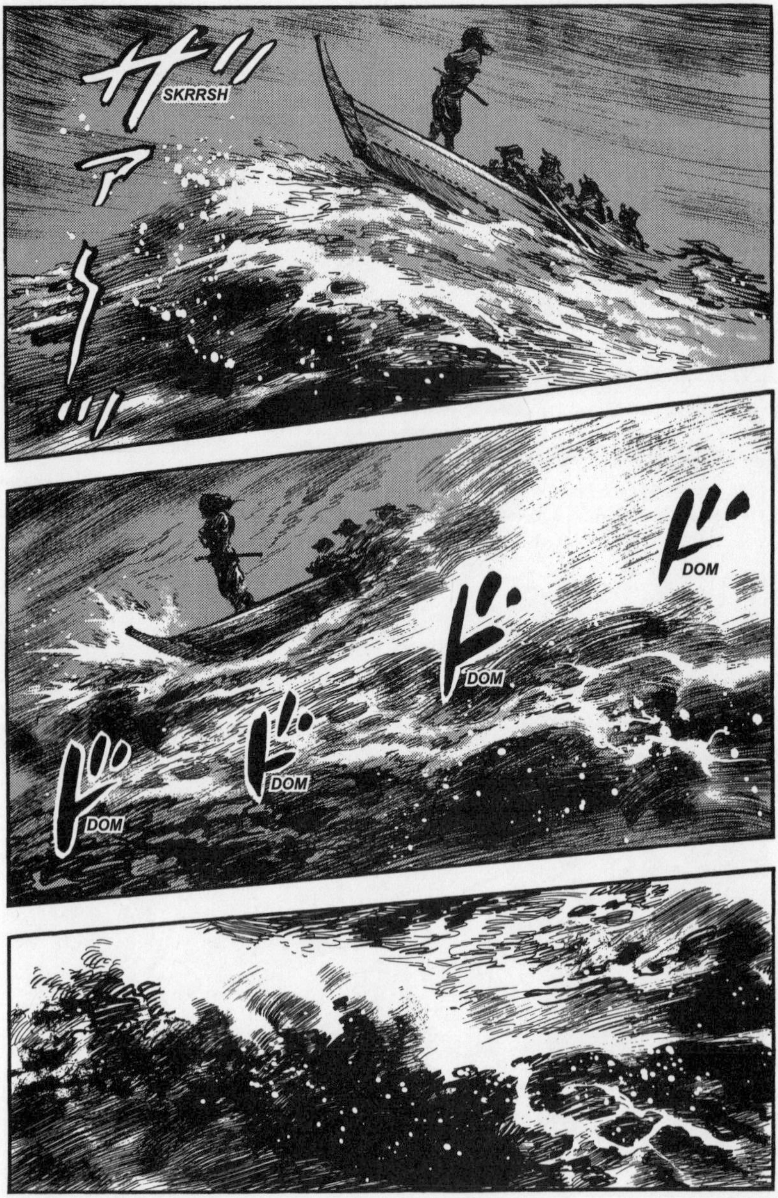
SKRRSH
DOM
DOM
DOM
DOM

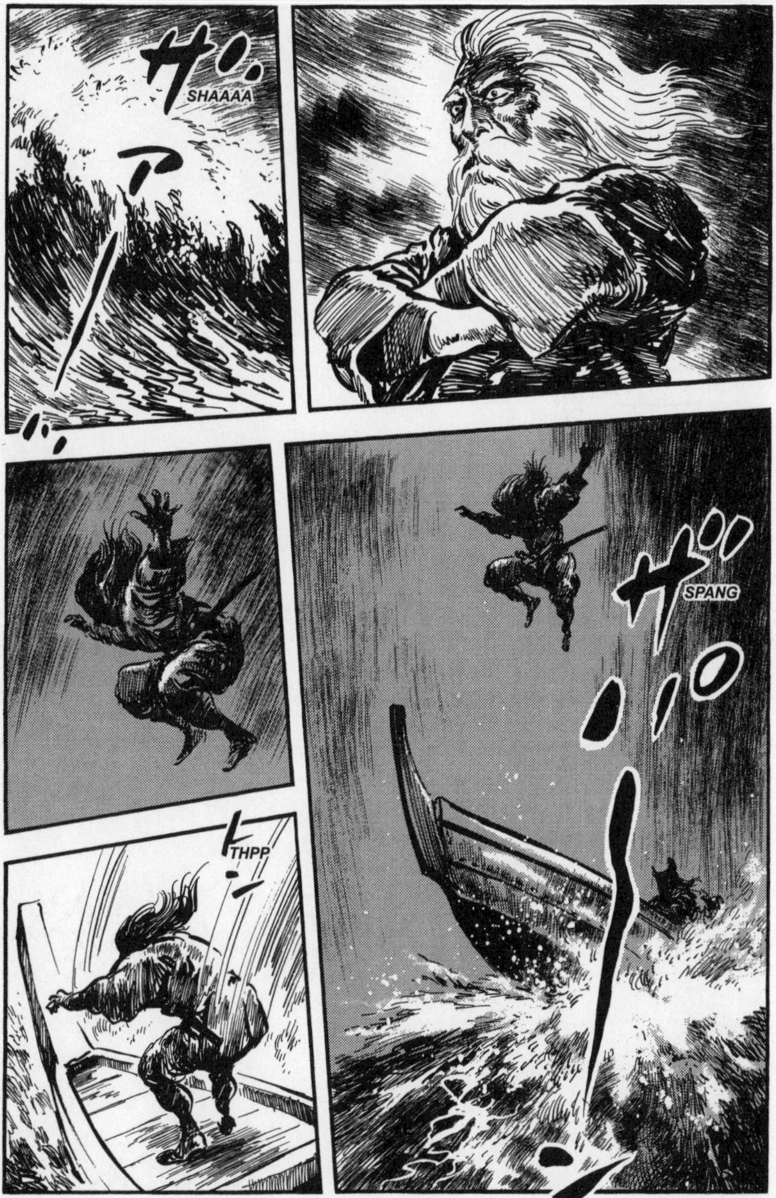
SHAAAA
SPANG
THPP

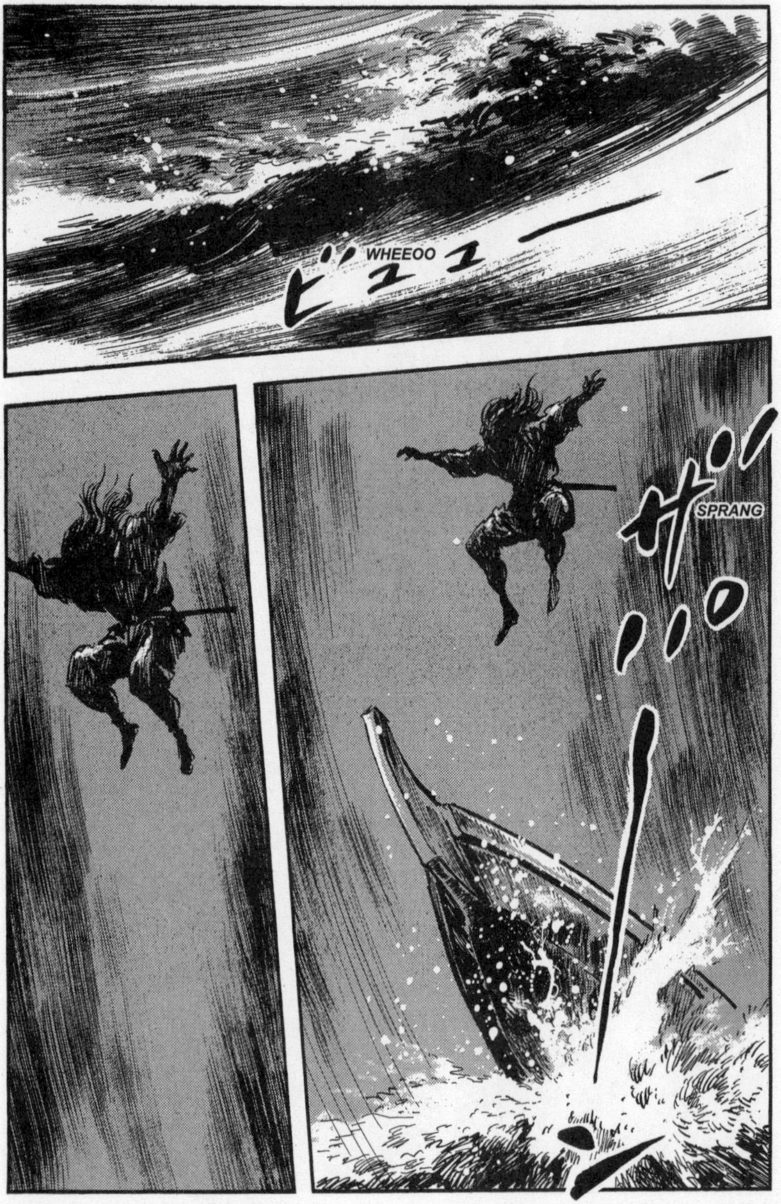
WHEEOO
SPRANG

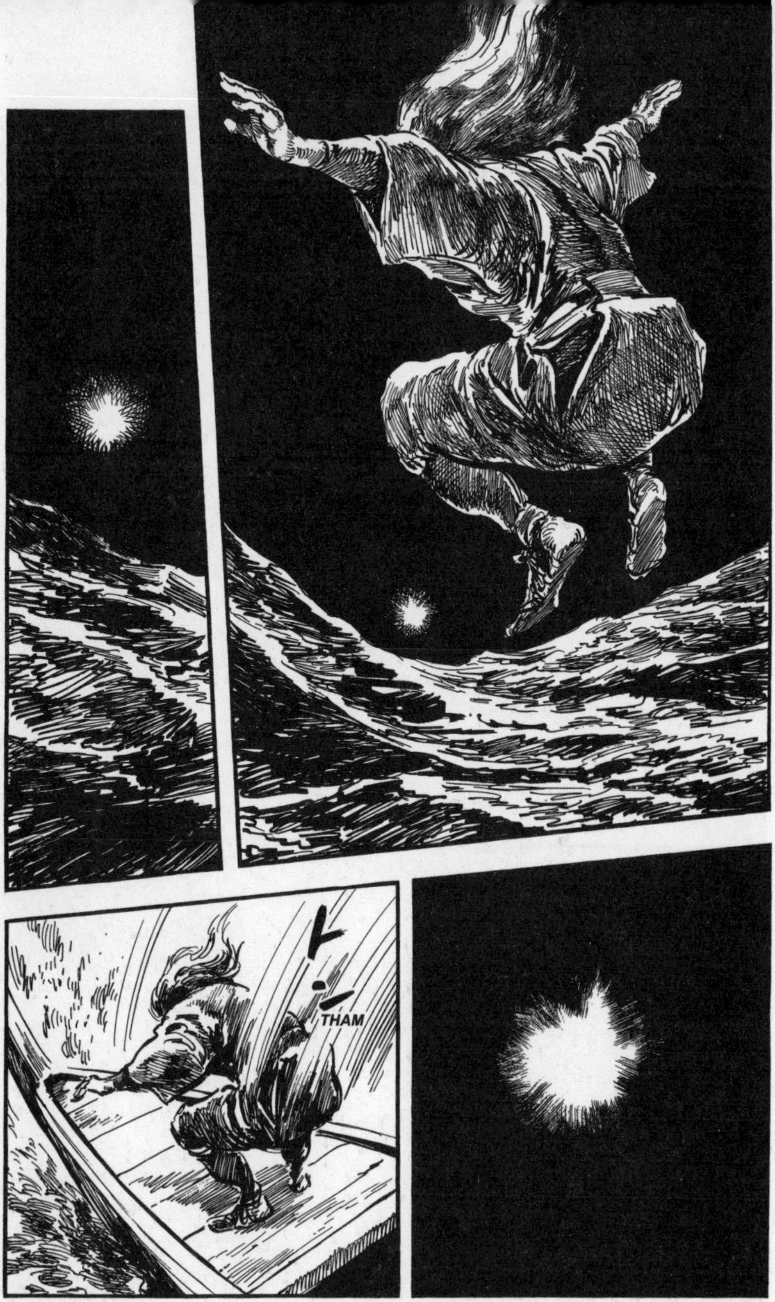
THAM

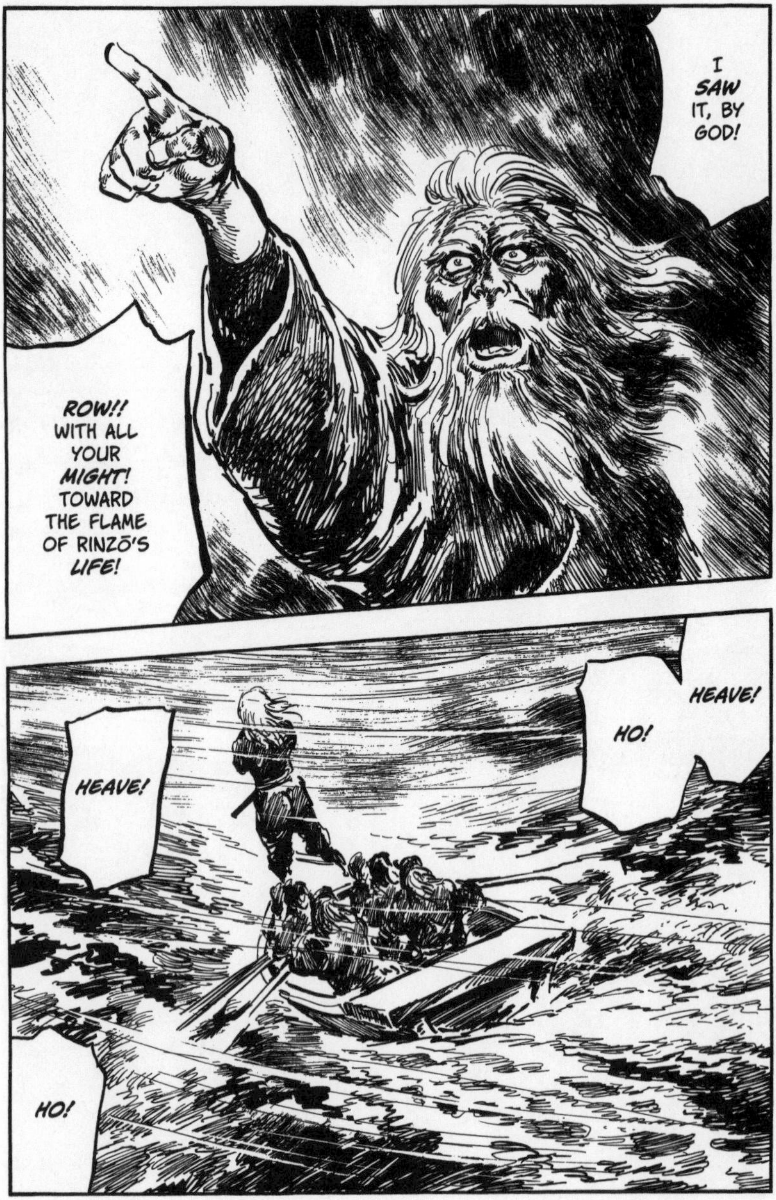
I SAW IT, BY GOD!
ROW!! WITH ALL YOUR MIGHT! TOWARD THE FLAME OF RINZŌ'S LIFE!
HEAVE!
HO!
HEAVE!
HO!

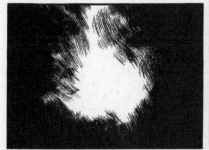

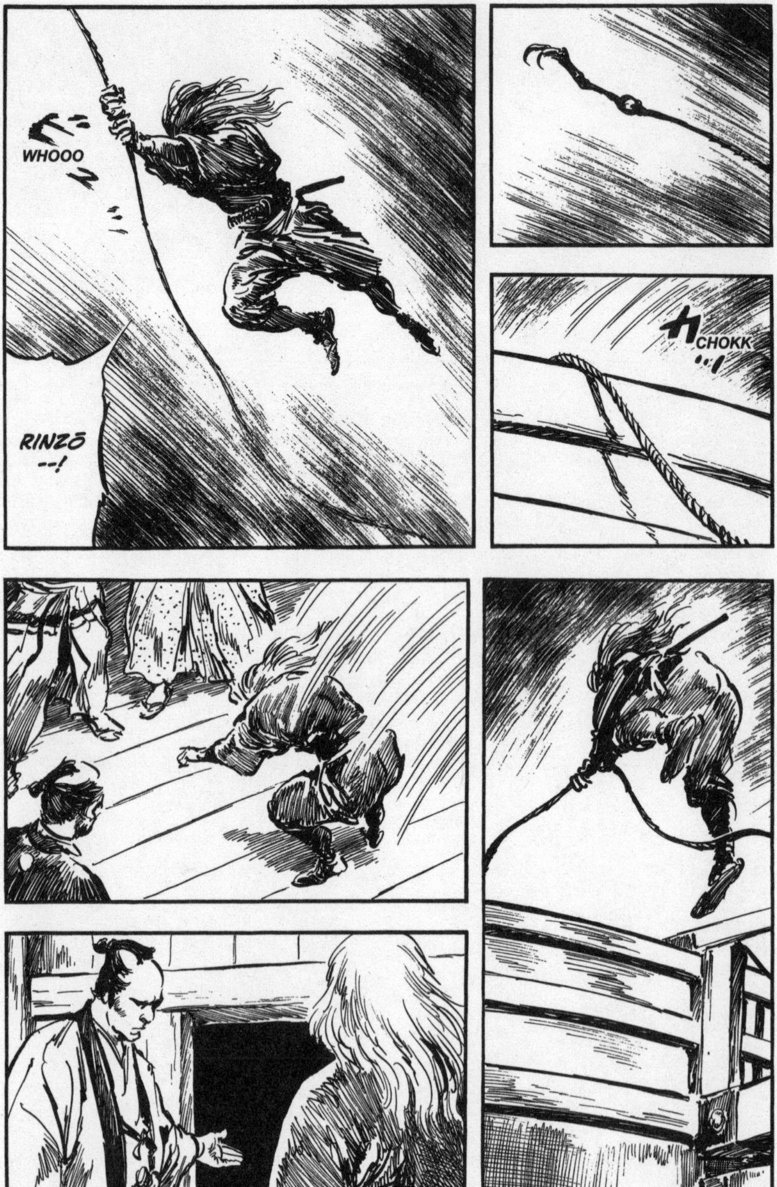
CHOKK
WHOOO
RINZŌ --!

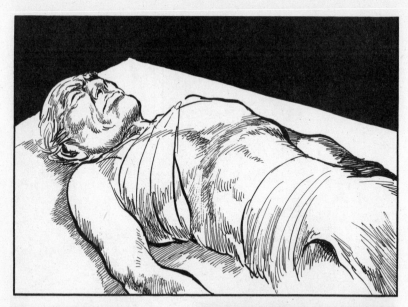

OSA!!

RINZŌ!

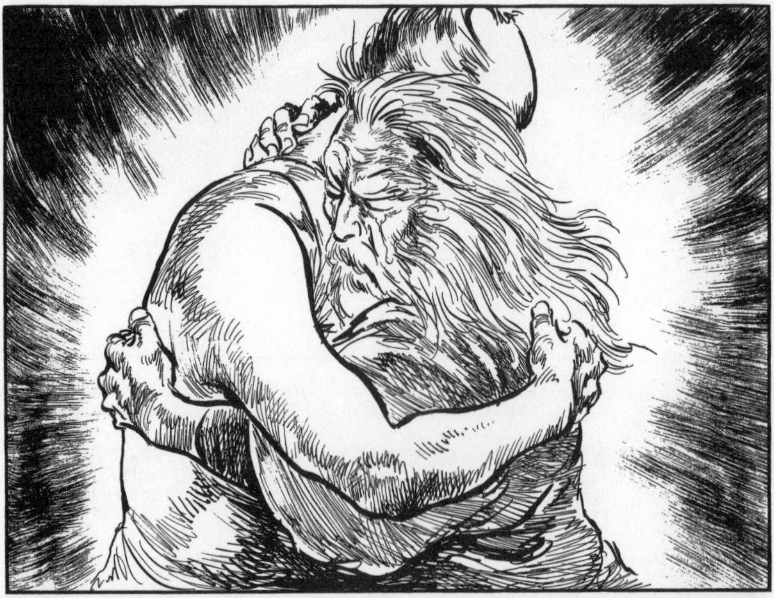

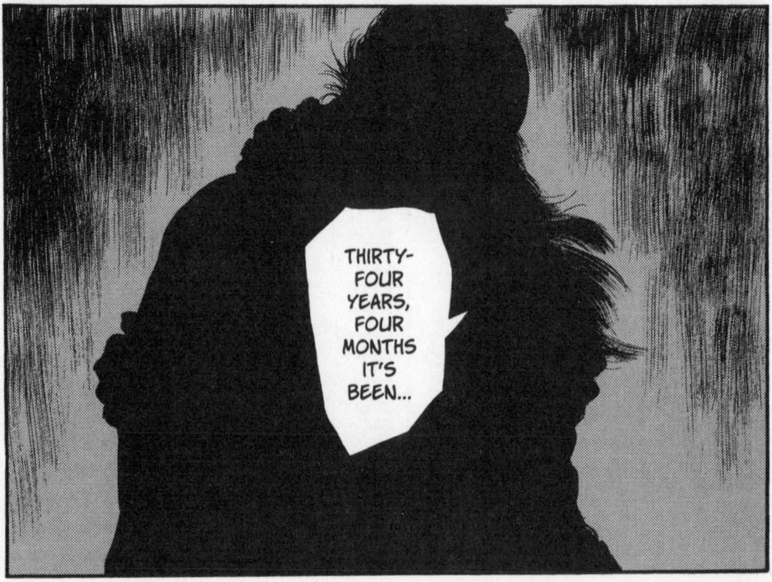
THIRTY-FOUR YEARS, FOUR MONTHS IT'S BEEN...

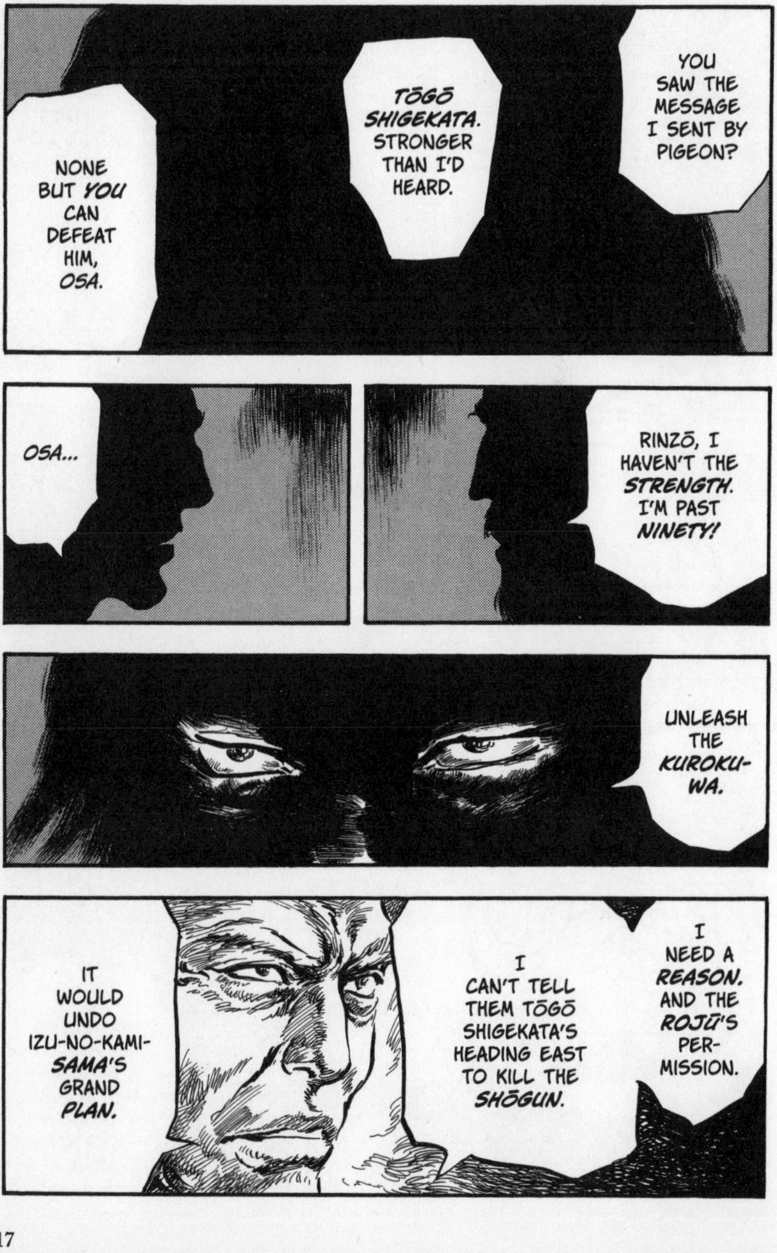
YOU SAW THE MESSAGE I SENT BY PIGEON?
TŌGŌ SHIGEKATA. STRONGER THAN I'D HEARD.
NONE BUT YOU CAN DEFEAT HIM, OSA.
RINZŌ, I HAVEN'T THE STRENGTH. I'M PAST NINETY!
OSA...
UNLEASH THE KUROKUWA.
I NEED A REASON. AND THE ROJŪ'S PERMISSION.
I CAN'T TELL THEM TŌGŌ SHIGEKATA'S HEADING EAST TO KILL THE SHŌGUN.
IT WOULD UNDO IZU-NO-KAMI-SAMA'S GRAND PLAN.

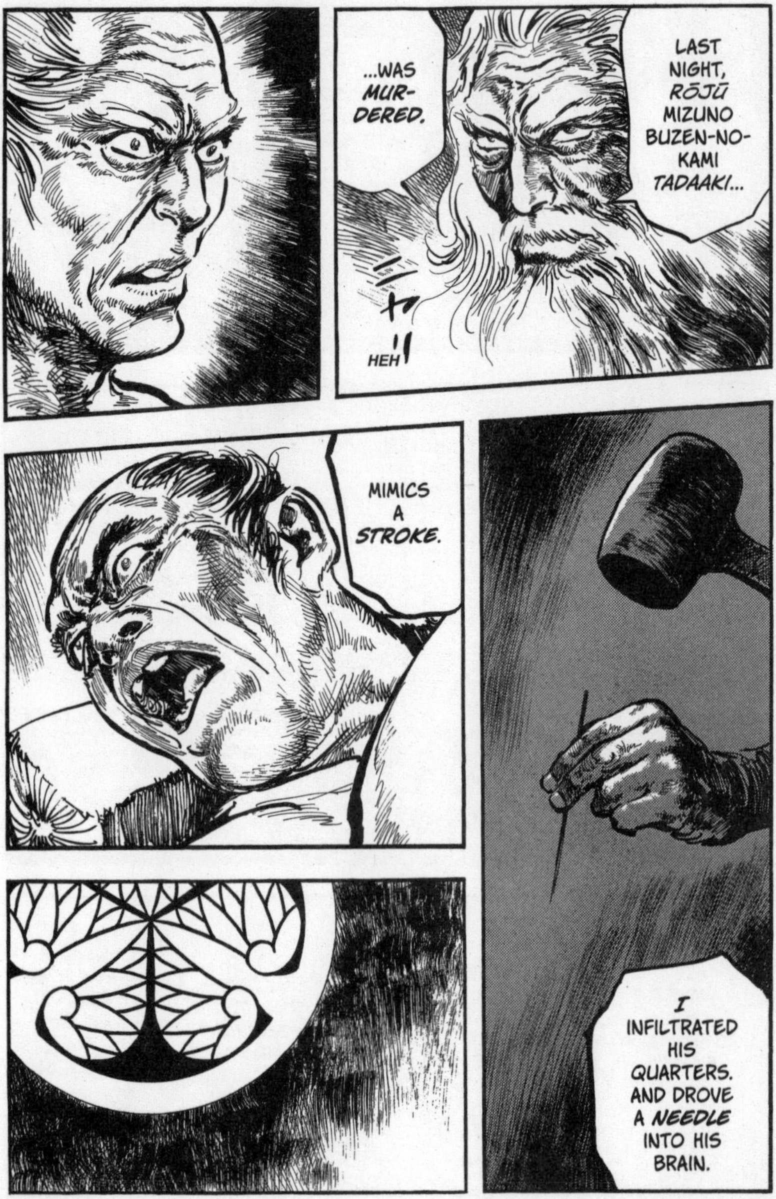
LAST NIGHT, RŌJŪ MIZUNO BUZEN-NO-KAMI TADAAKI...
...WAS MURDERED.
HEH
I INFILTRATED HIS QUARTERS. AND DROVE A NEEDLE INTO HIS BRAIN.
MIMICS A STROKE.

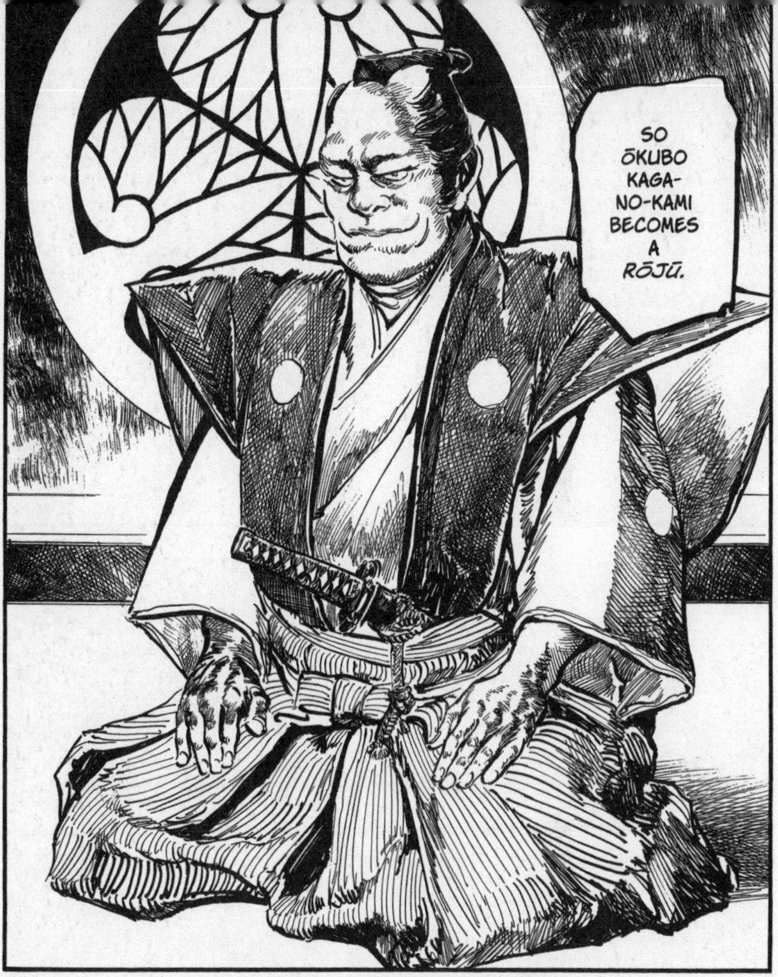
SO ŌKUBO KAGA-NO-KAMI BECOMES A *RŌJŪ*.

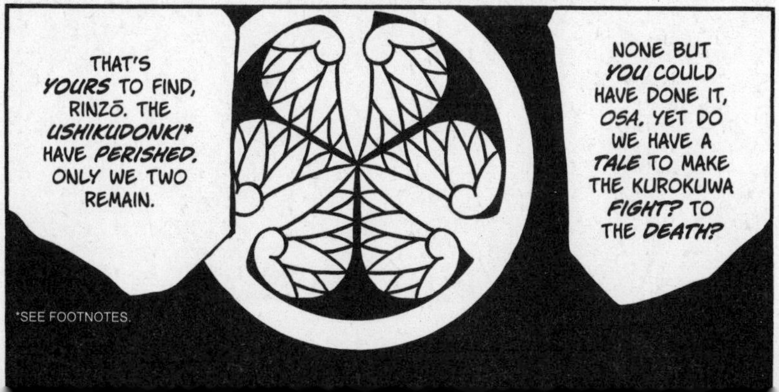
NONE BUT *YOU* COULD HAVE DONE IT, *OSA*. YET DO WE HAVE A *TALE* TO MAKE THE KUROKUWA *FIGHT?* TO THE *DEATH?*
THAT'S ***YOURS*** TO FIND, RINZŌ. THE *USHIKUDONKI** HAVE *PERISHED*. ONLY WE TWO REMAIN.

*SEE FOOTNOTES.

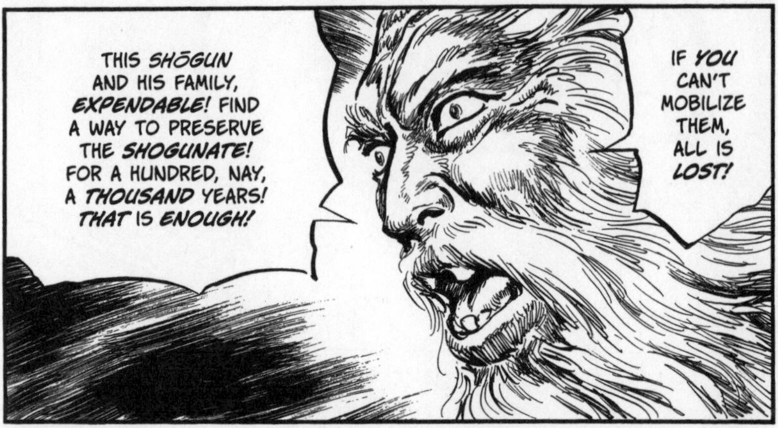
IF YOU CAN'T MOBILIZE THEM, ALL IS LOST!
THIS SHŌGUN AND HIS FAMILY, EXPENDABLE! FIND A WAY TO PRESERVE THE SHOGUNATE! FOR A HUNDRED, NAY, A THOUSAND YEARS! THAT IS ENOUGH!

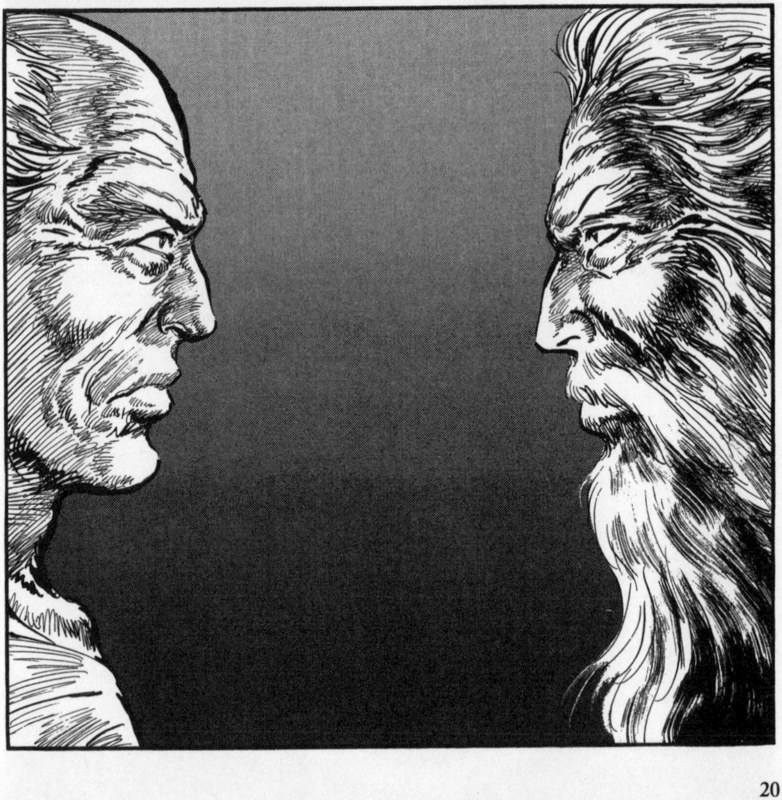

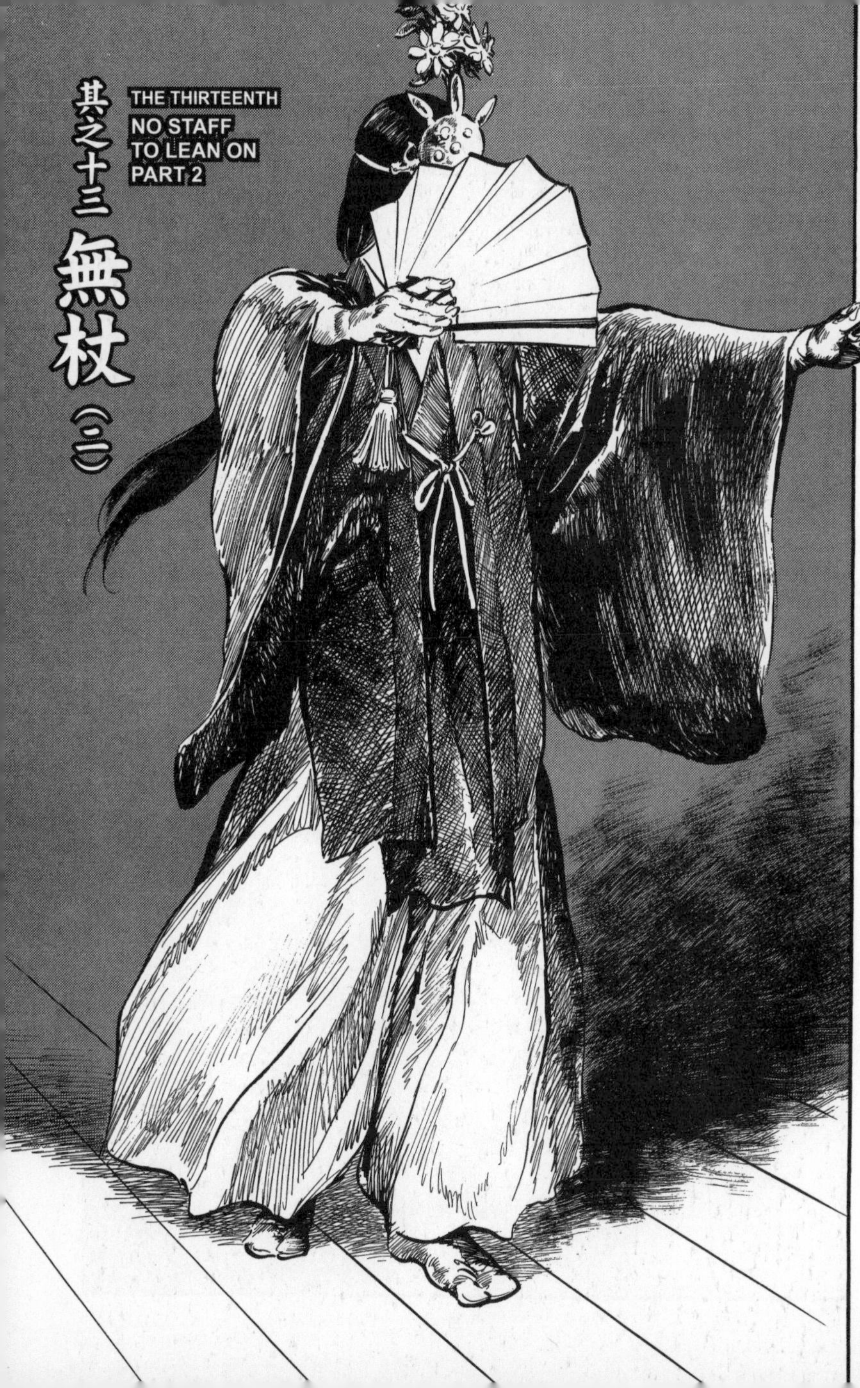
其之十三 無杖（二）
THE THIRTEENTH
NO STAFF
TO LEAN ON
PART 2

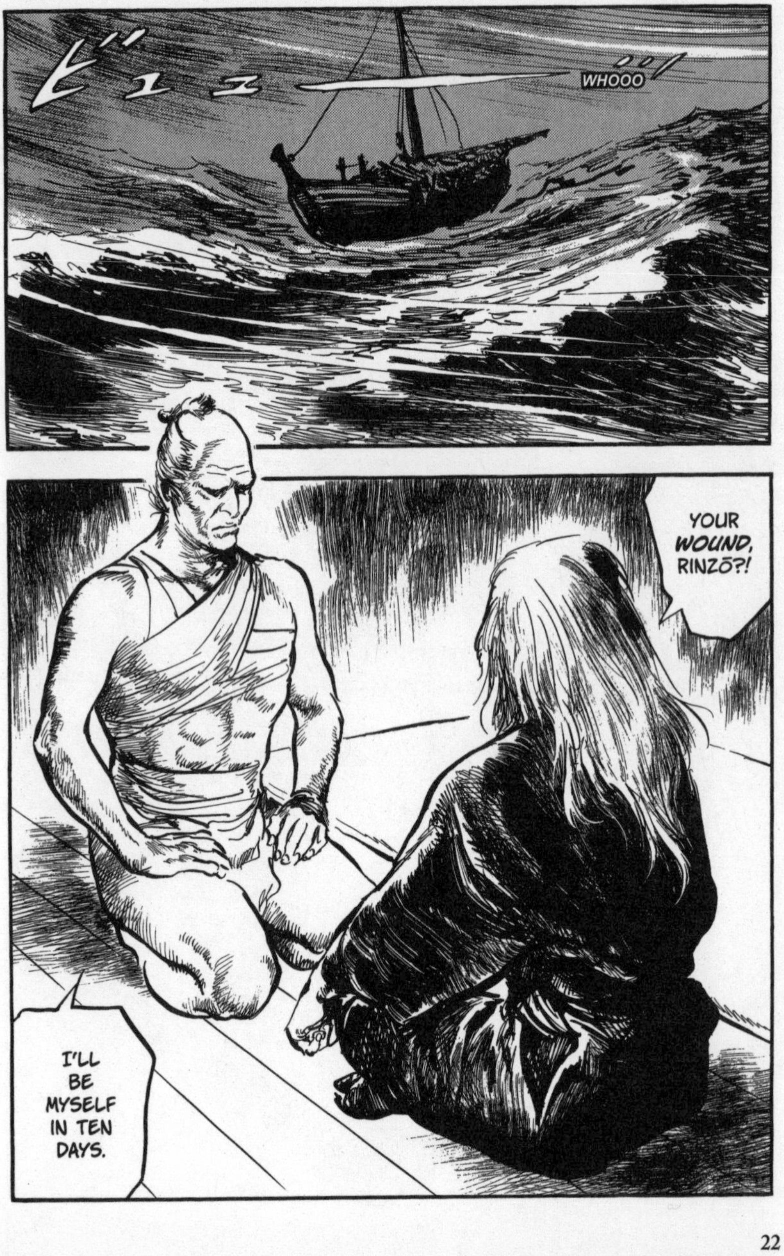
WHOOO
YOUR WOUND, RINZŌ?!
I'LL BE MYSELF IN TEN DAYS.

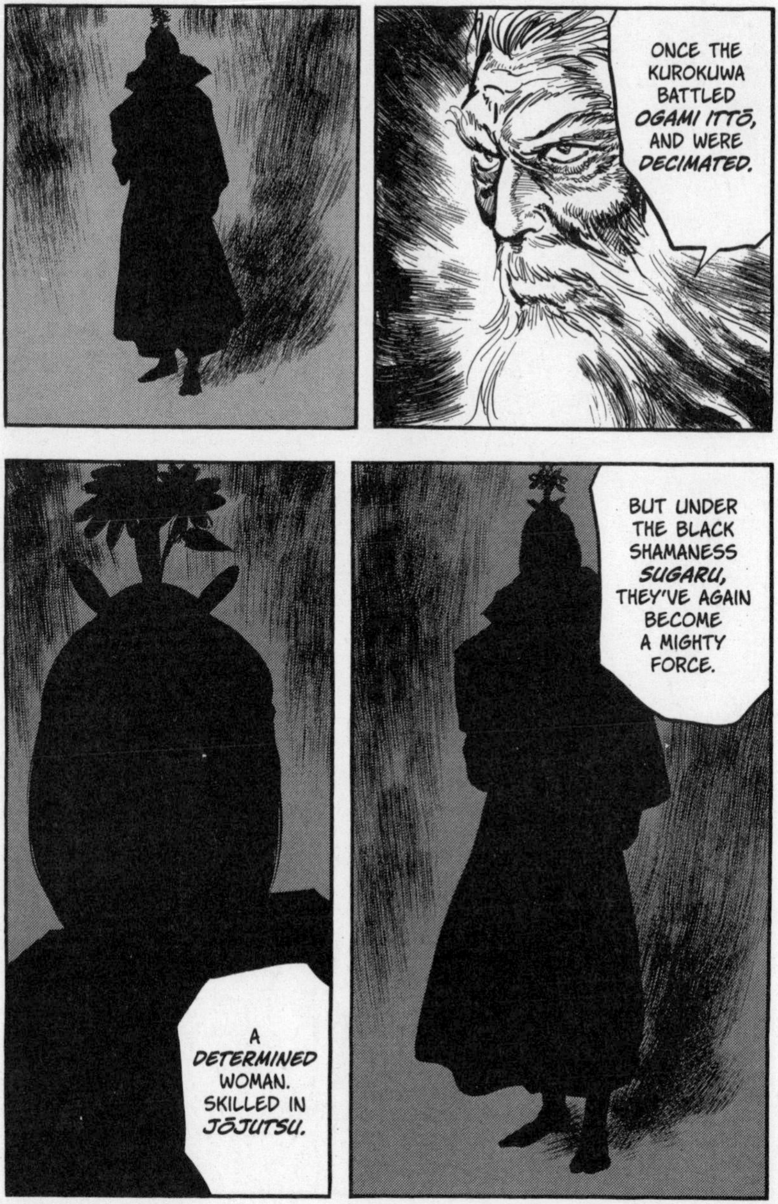
ONCE THE KUROKUWA BATTLED *OGAMI ITTŌ,* AND WERE *DECIMATED.*
BUT UNDER THE BLACK SHAMANESS *SUGARU,* THEY'VE AGAIN BECOME A MIGHTY FORCE.
A *DETERMINED* WOMAN. SKILLED IN *JŌJUTSU.*

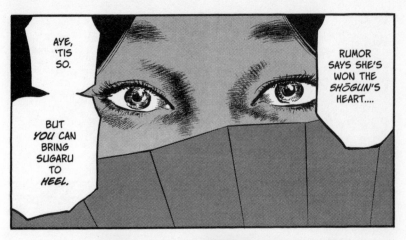

RUMOR SAYS SHE'S WON THE SHŌGUN'S HEART....
AYE, 'TIS SO.
BUT YOU CAN BRING SUGARU TO HEEL.
ONE WAY OR ANOTH-ER....
A DRUG. AFUYŌ BY NAME.
I PLANNED TO GIVE IT TO TŌGŌ IF ALL ELSE FAILED, BUT NOW...
HAVE YOU TESTED IT?!
NOT YET...
TEST IT ON ME!

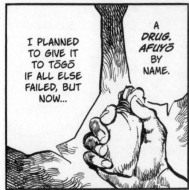

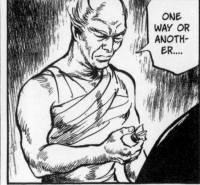

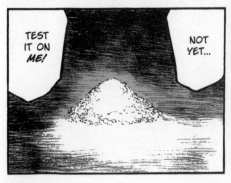

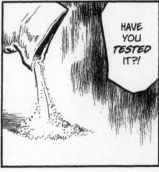

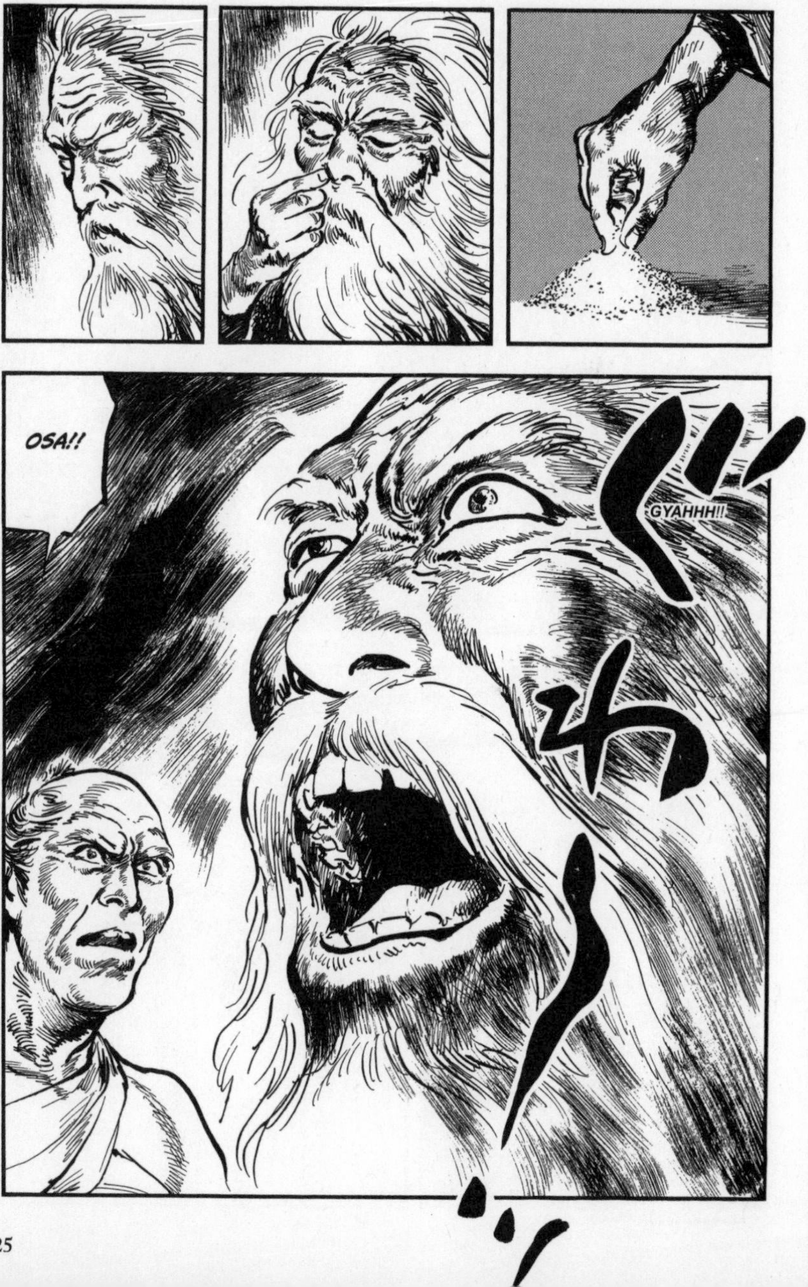
GYAHHH!!
OSA!!

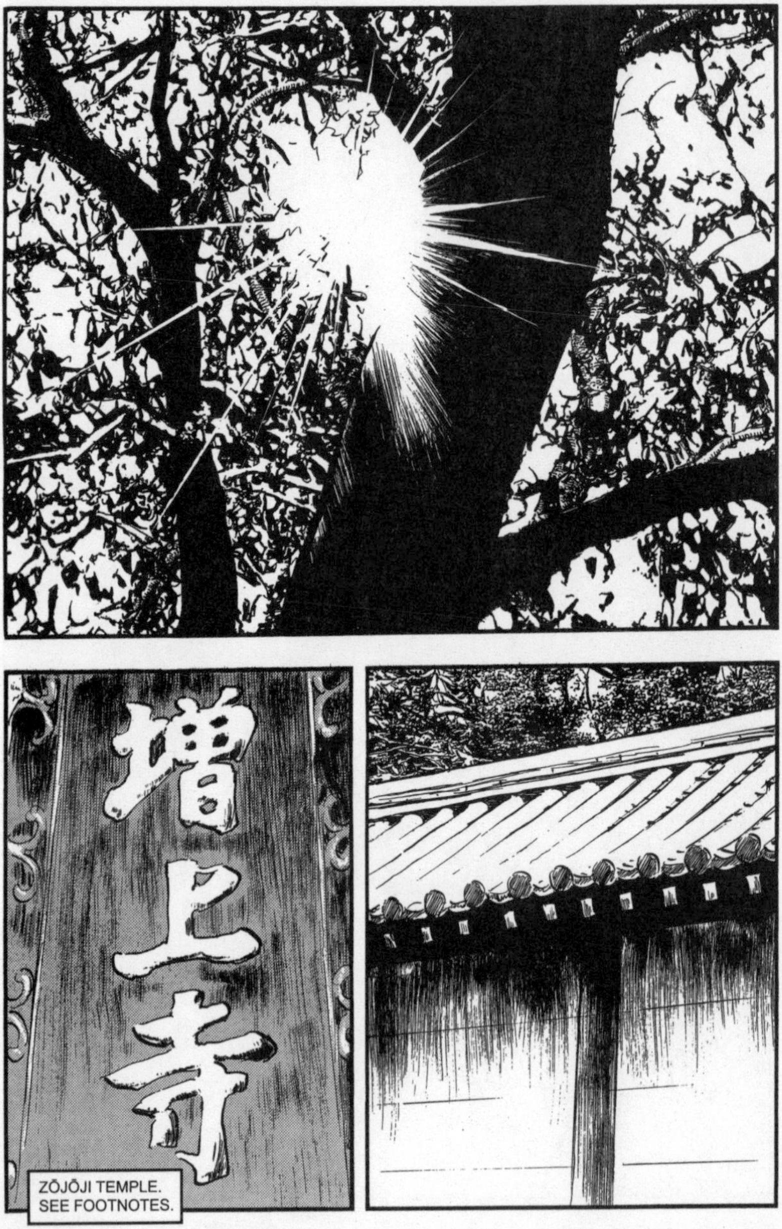
增上寺
ZŌJŌJI TEMPLE.
SEE FOOTNOTES.

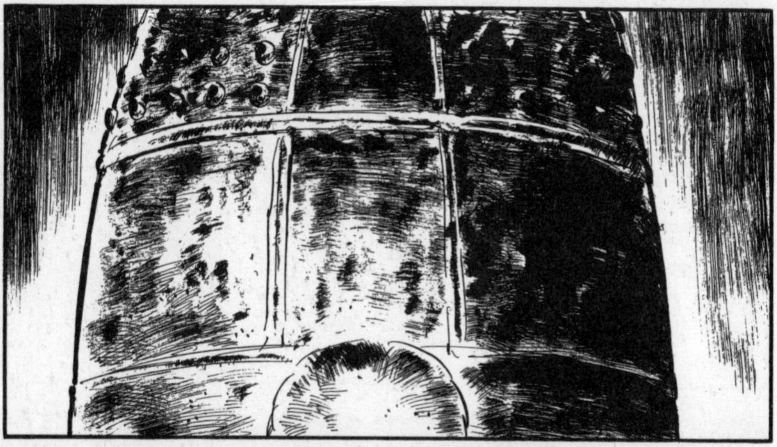
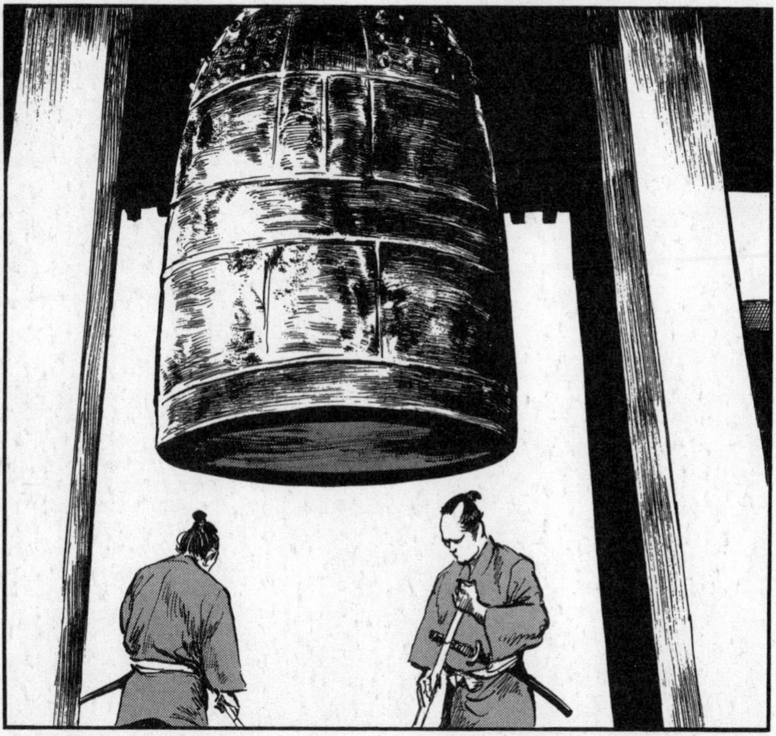

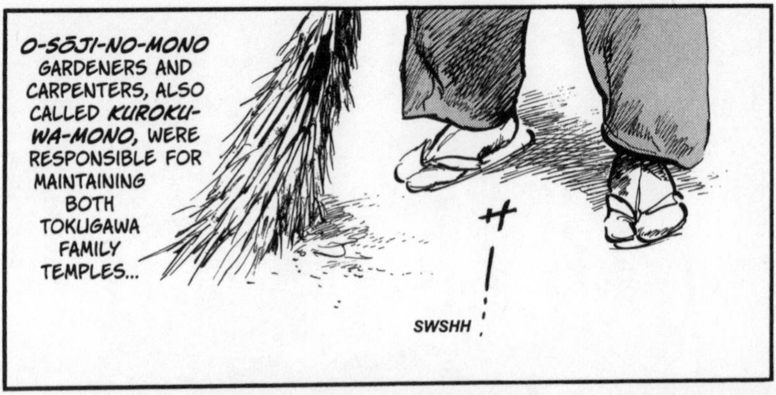
O-SŌJI-NO-MONO GARDENERS AND CARPENTERS, ALSO CALLED KUROKU-WA-MONO, WERE RESPONSIBLE FOR MAINTAINING BOTH TOKUGAWA FAMILY TEMPLES...
SWSHH

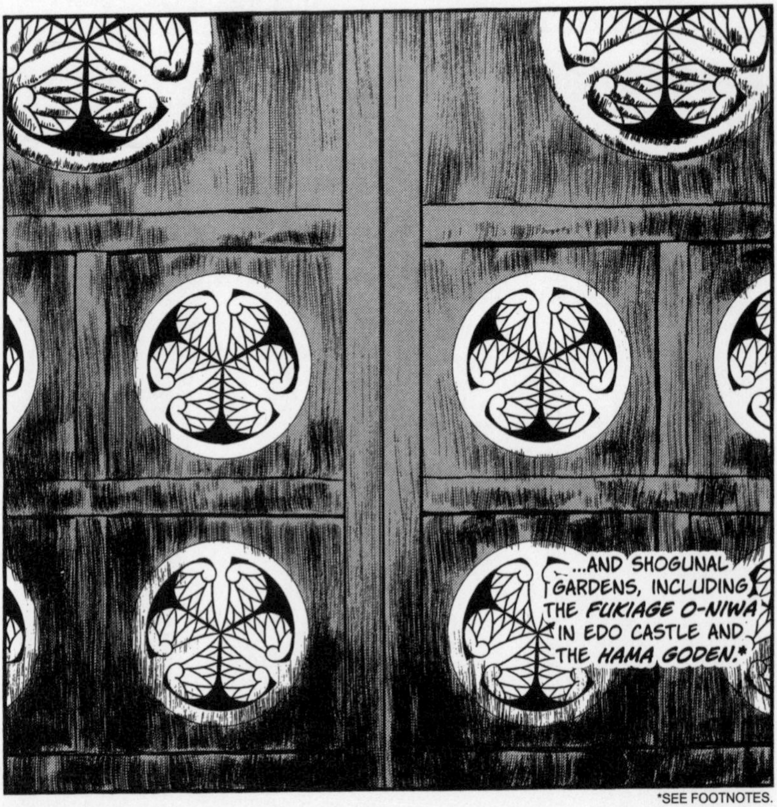
...AND SHOGUNAL GARDENS, INCLUDING THE FUKIAGE O-NIWA IN EDO CASTLE AND THE HAMA GODEN.*

*SEE FOOTNOTES.

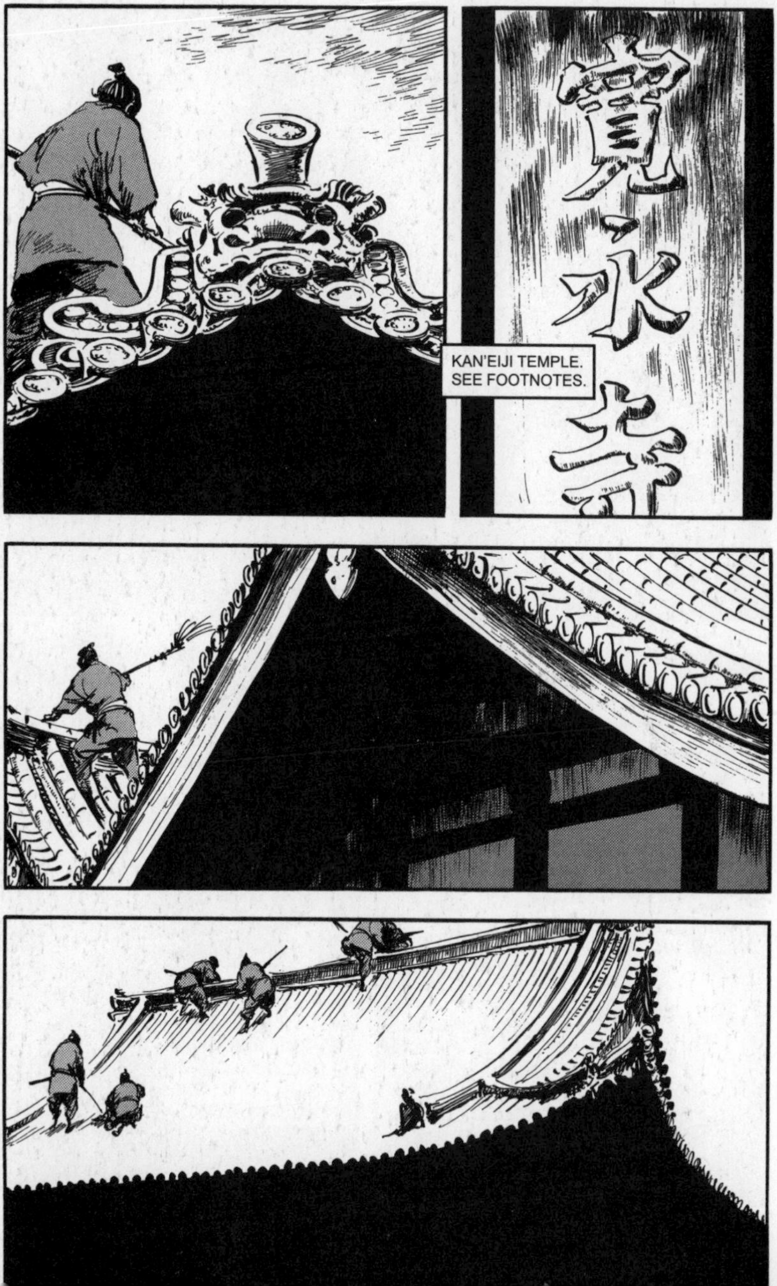
寛永寺
KAN'EIJI TEMPLE.
SEE FOOTNOTES.

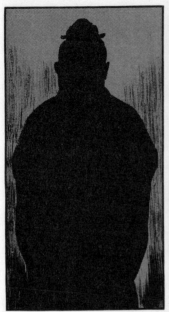

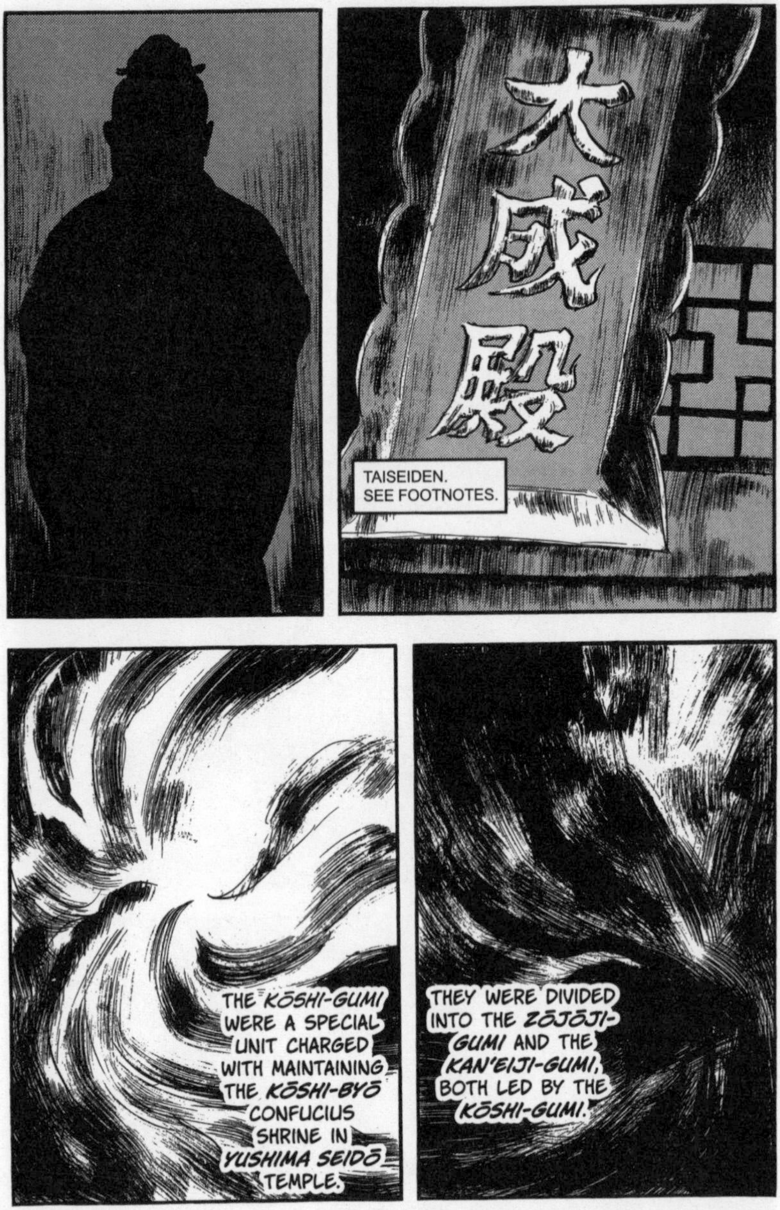
大成殿
TAISEIDEN.
SEE FOOTNOTES.
THEY WERE DIVIDED INTO THE ZŌJŌJI-GUMI AND THE KAN'EIJI-GUMI, BOTH LED BY THE KŌSHI-GUMI.
THE KŌSHI-GUMI WERE A SPECIAL UNIT CHARGED WITH MAINTAINING THE KŌSHI-BYŌ CONFUCIUS SHRINE IN YUSHIMA SEIDŌ TEMPLE.

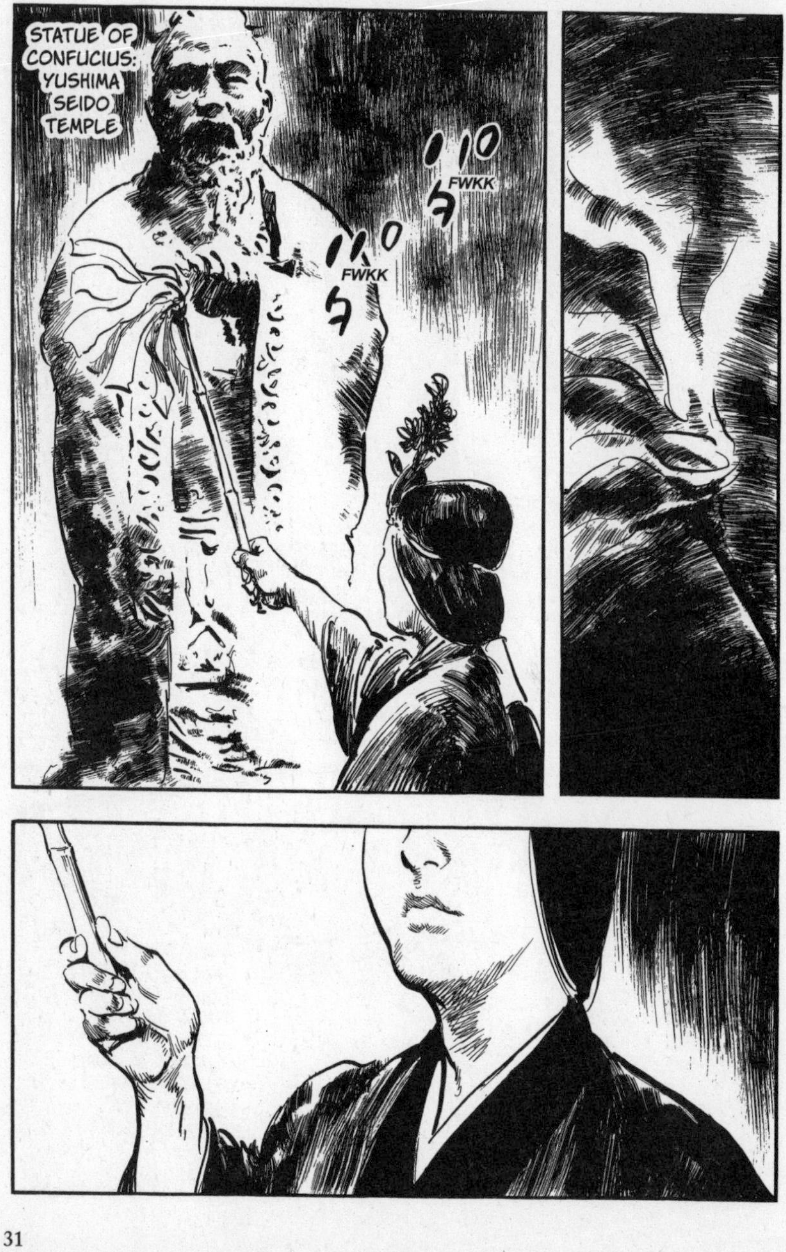
STATUE OF CONFUCIUS: YUSHIMA SEIDO TEMPLE
FWKK
FWKK

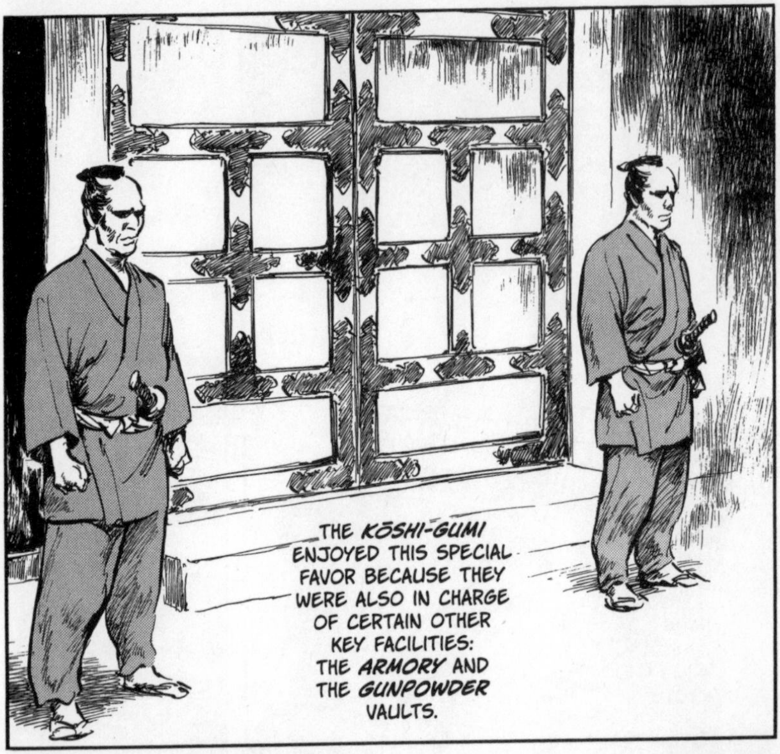
THE *KŌSHI-GUMI* ENJOYED THIS SPECIAL FAVOR BECAUSE THEY WERE ALSO IN CHARGE OF CERTAIN OTHER KEY FACILITIES: THE *ARMORY* AND THE *GUNPOWDER* VAULTS.

12

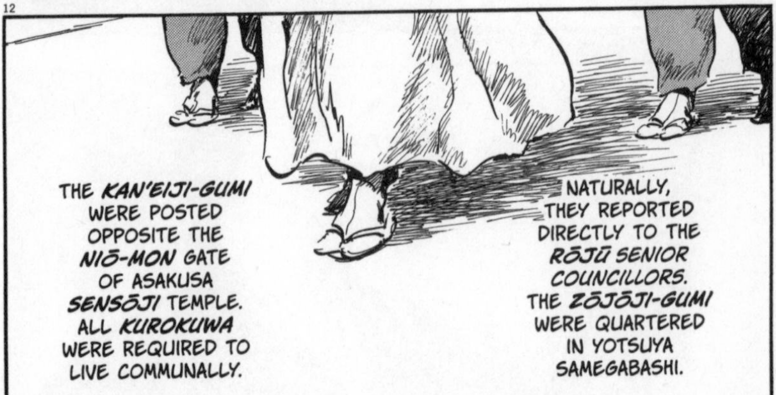
NATURALLY, THEY REPORTED DIRECTLY TO THE *RŌJŪ* SENIOR *COUNCILLORS*. THE *ZŌJŌJI-GUMI* WERE QUARTERED IN YOTSUYA SAMEGABASHI.
THE *KAN'EIJI-GUMI* WERE POSTED OPPOSITE THE *NIŌ-MON* GATE OF ASAKUSA *SENSŌJI* TEMPLE. ALL *KUROKUWA* WERE REQUIRED TO LIVE COMMUNALLY.

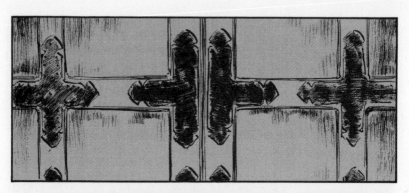

KREEEK

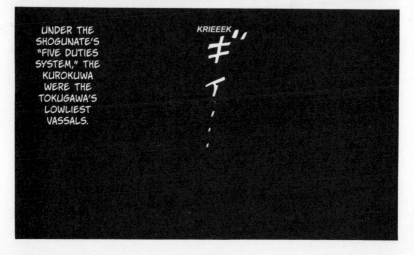

UNDER THE SHOGUNATE'S "FIVE DUTIES SYSTEM," THE KUROKUWA WERE THE TOKUGAWA'S LOWLIEST VASSALS.

KRIEEEK

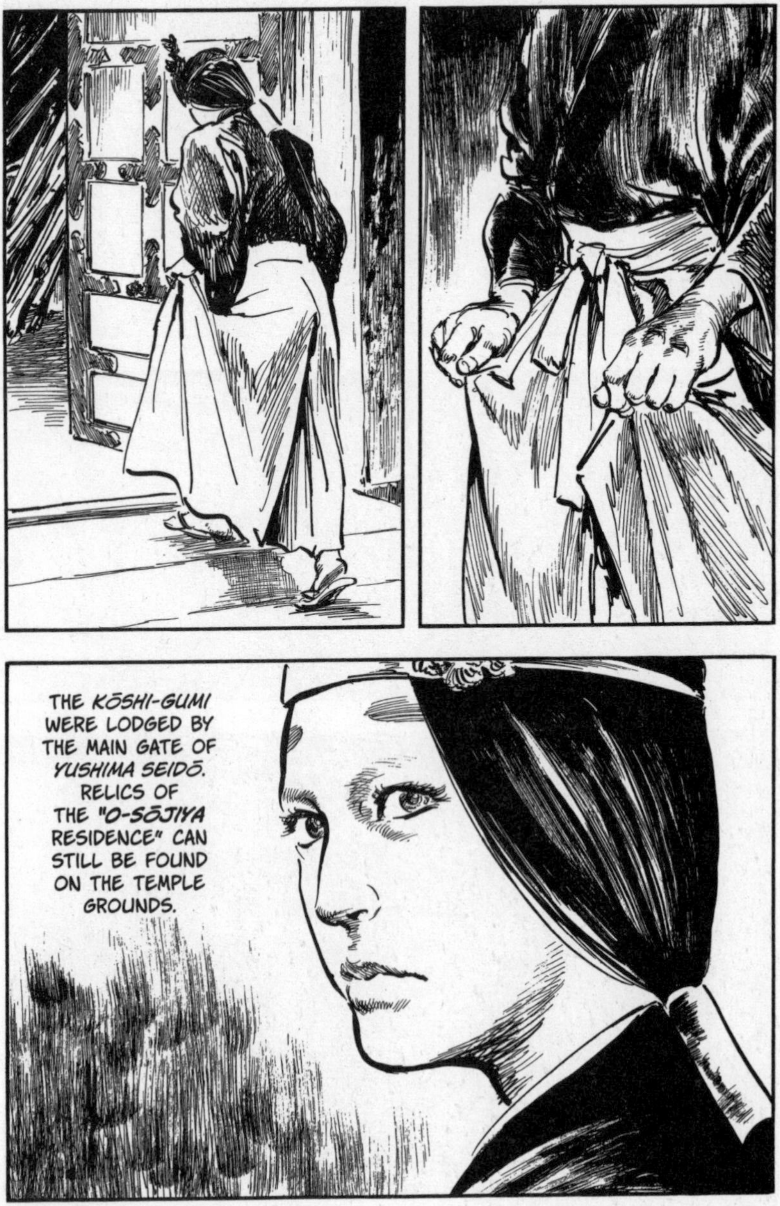
THE *KŌSHI-GUMI* WERE LODGED BY THE MAIN GATE OF *YUSHIMA SEIDŌ*. RELICS OF THE "*O-SŌJIYA* RESIDENCE" CAN STILL BE FOUND ON THE TEMPLE GROUNDS.

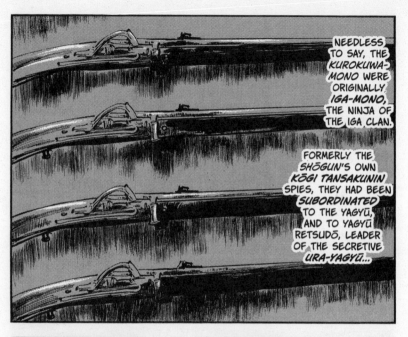

NEEDLESS TO SAY, THE *KUROKUWA-MONO* WERE ORIGINALLY *IGA-MONO*, THE NINJA OF THE IGA CLAN.

FORMERLY THE *SHŌGUN'S* OWN *KŌGI TANSAKUNIN* SPIES, THEY HAD BEEN *SUBORDINATED* TO THE YAGYŪ, AND TO YAGYŪ RETSUDŌ, LEADER OF THE SECRETIVE *URA-YAGYŪ*...

BUT *NOW* THEY HAD REGAINED THEIR POWER, WORKING IN LEAGUE WITH THE *"NEKOZA,"* THE *O-NIWABAN* SPIES OF THE SHOGUNATE.

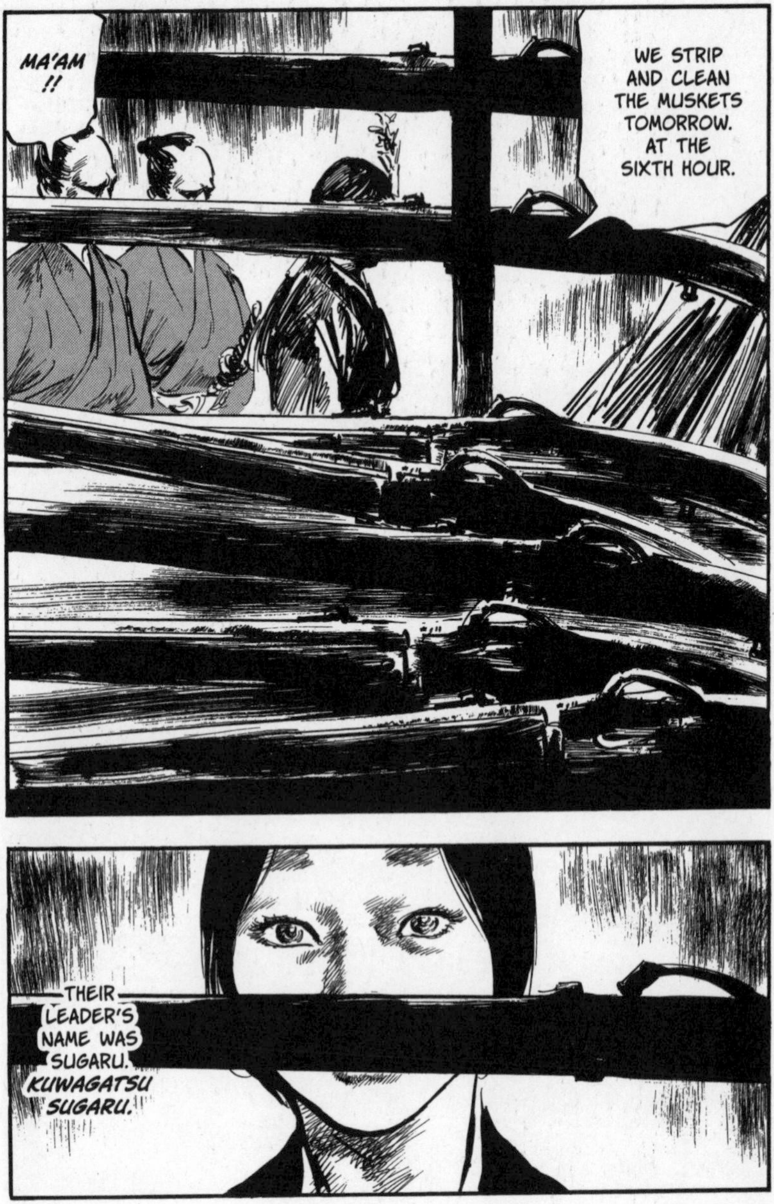
WE STRIP AND CLEAN THE MUSKETS TOMORROW. AT THE SIXTH HOUR.
MA'AM !!
THEIR LEADER'S NAME WAS SUGARU.
KUWAGATSU SUGARU.

其之十三 無杖（三）

THE THIRTEENTH
NO STAFF TO LEAN ON
PART 3

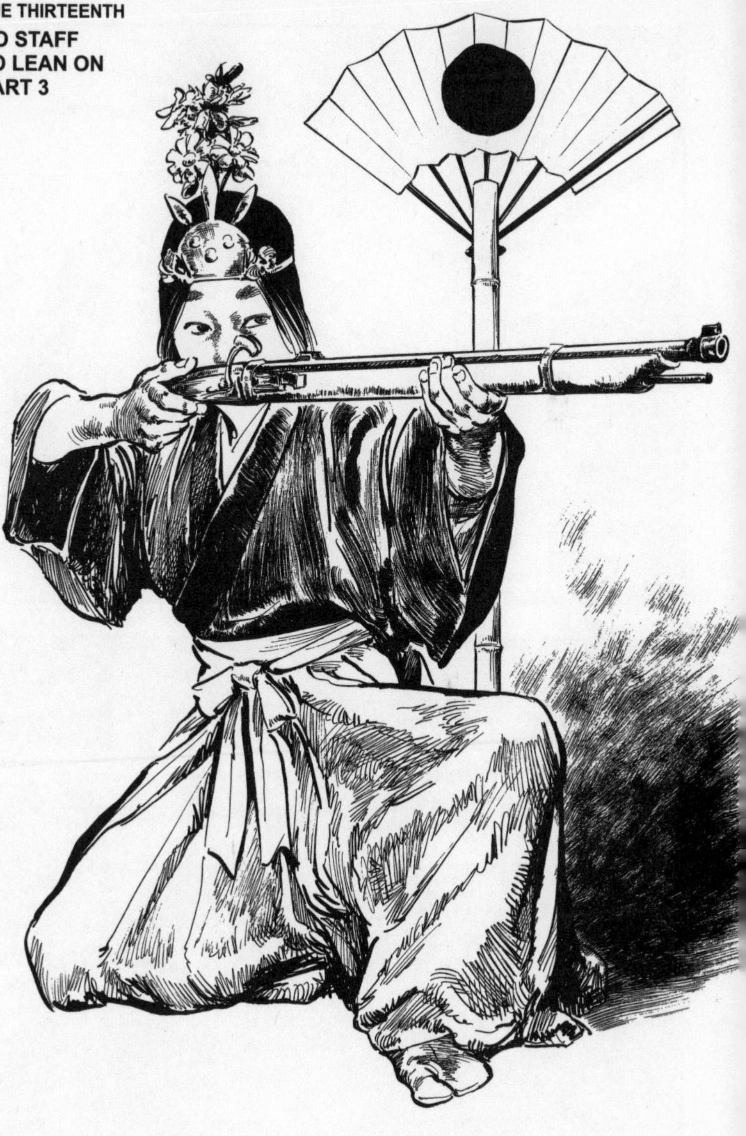

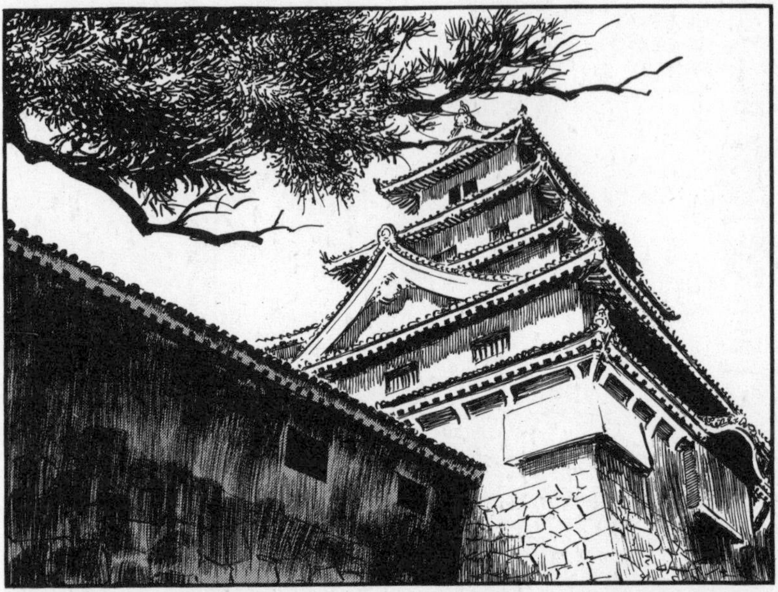
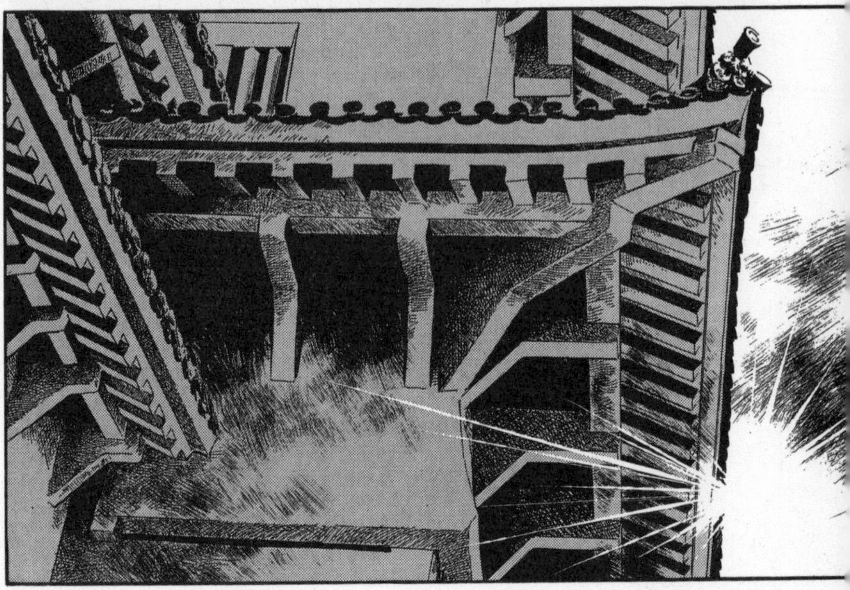

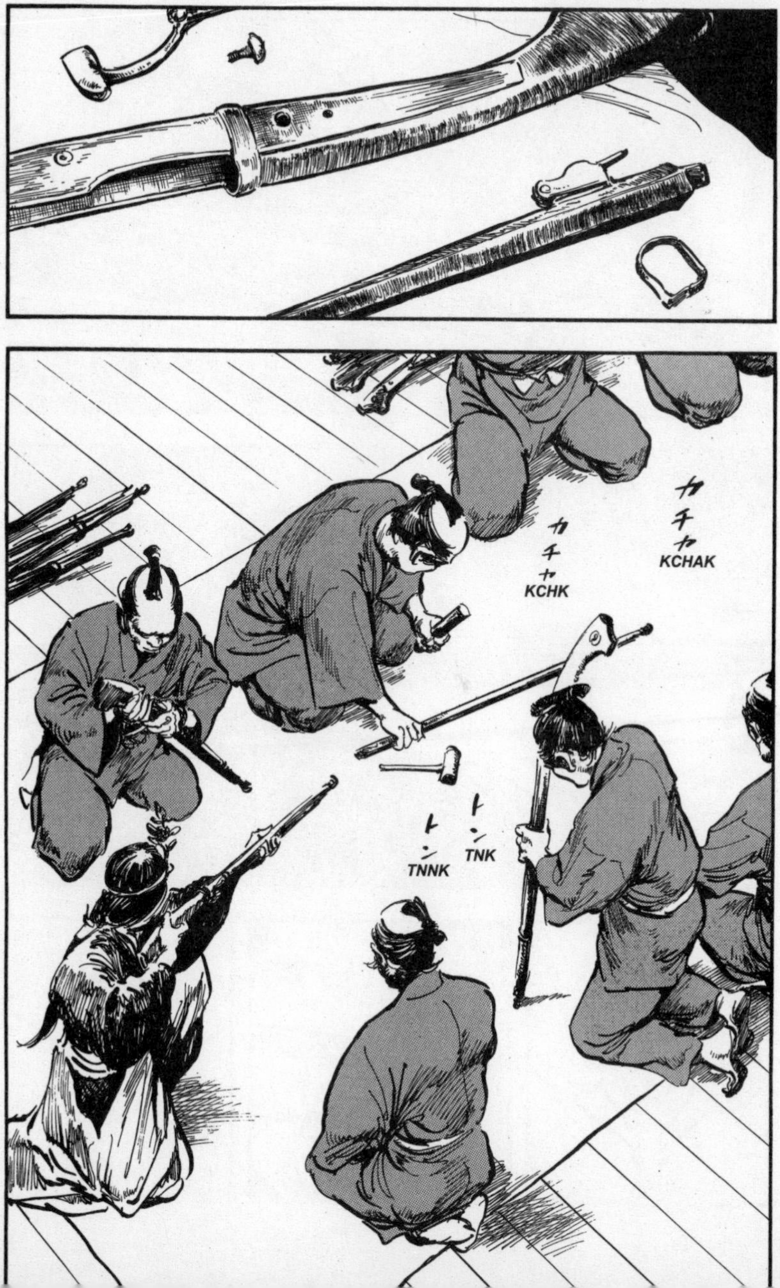

カチャ
KCHAK
カチャ
KCHK
トン
TNK
トン
TNNK

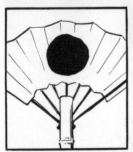

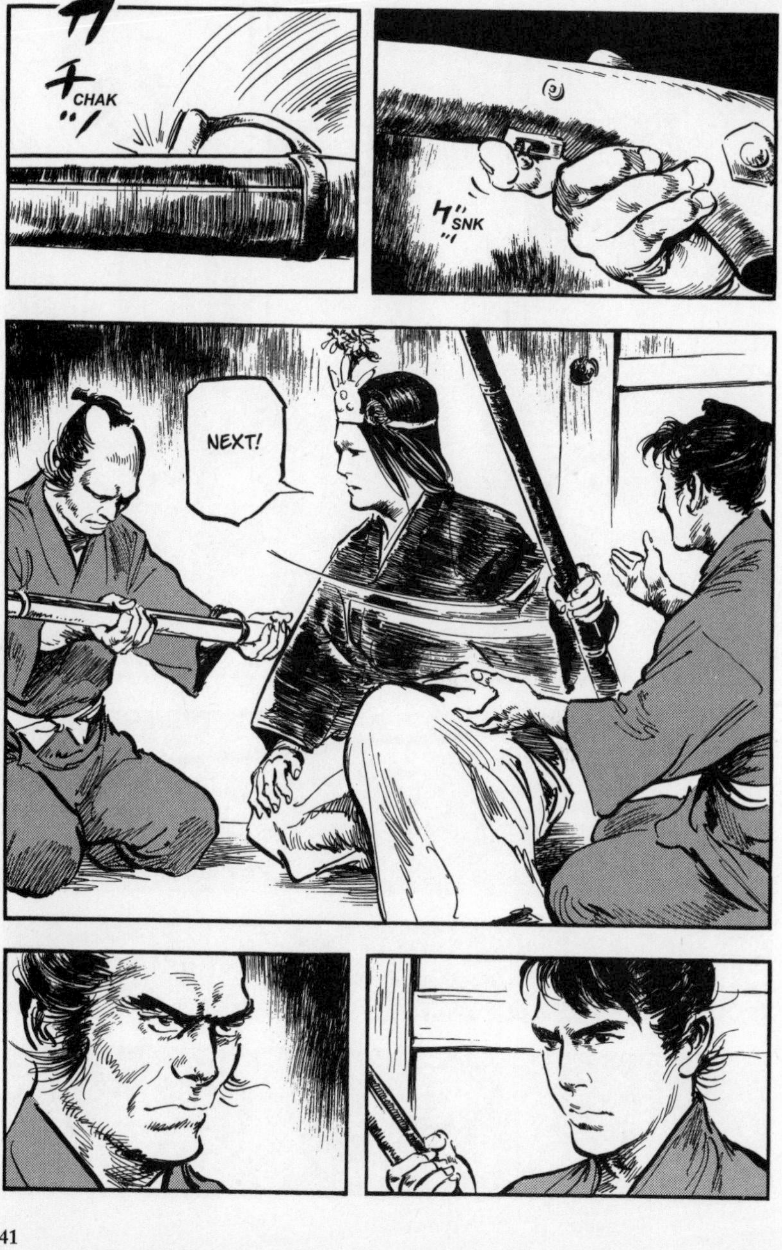
グッ
SNK
ガチッ
CHAK
NEXT!

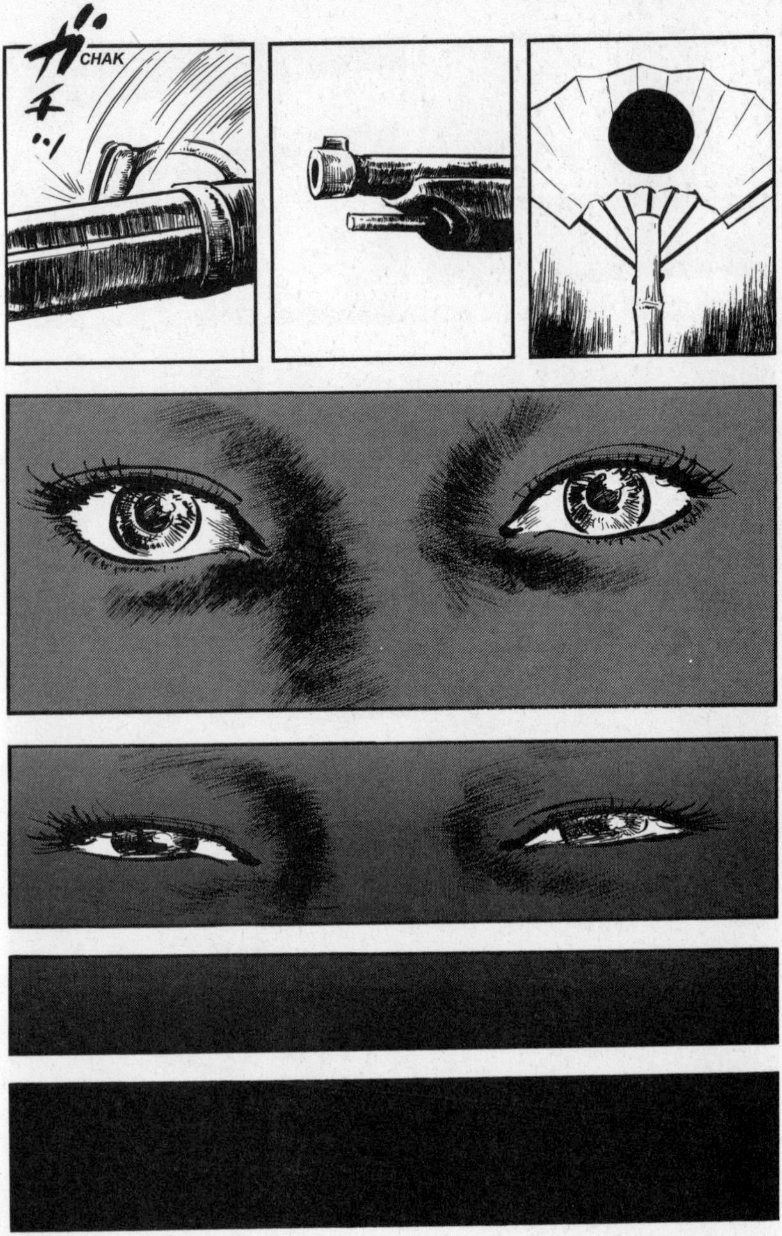
ガチッ
CHAK

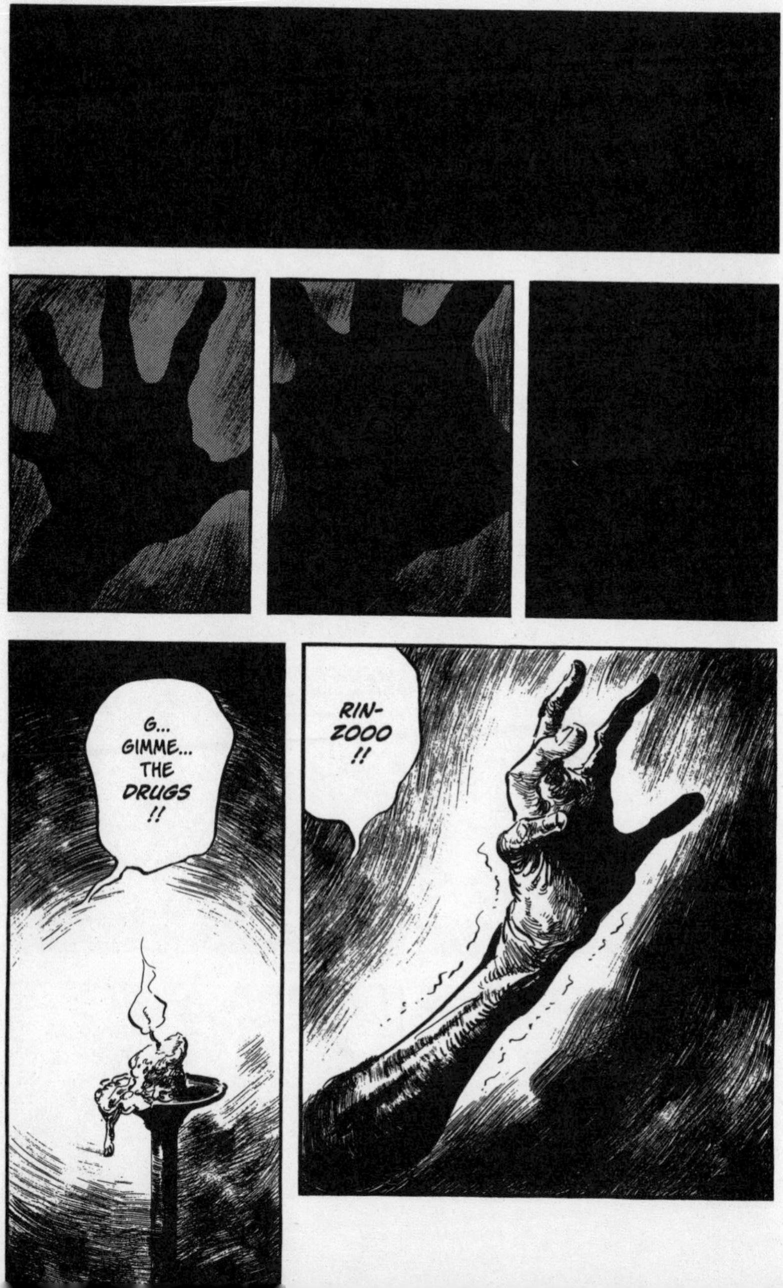
RIN-ZOOO !!
G... GIMME... THE DRUGS !!

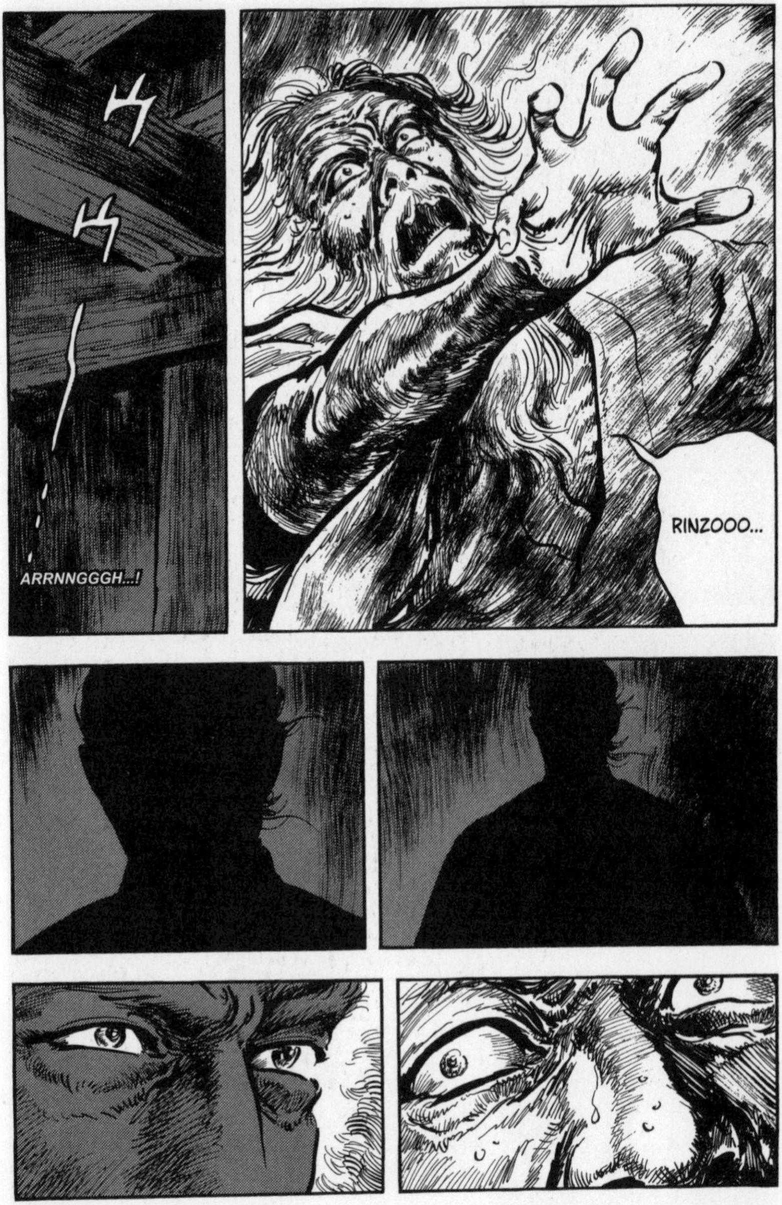
RINZOOO...
ムムー
ARRNNGGGH...!

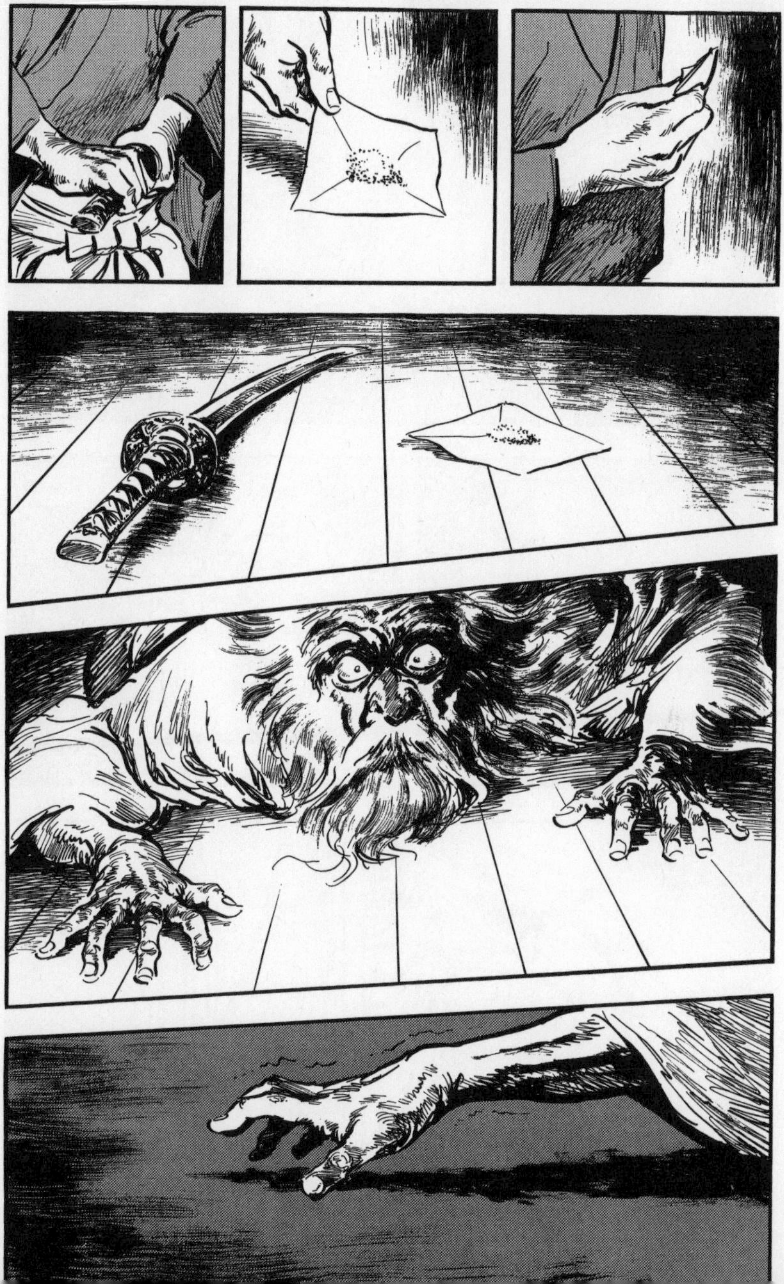

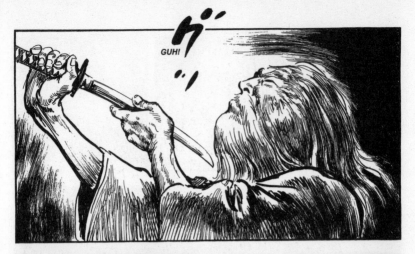

GUH!

SNATCH

NUOHHH!!

KCHAKK

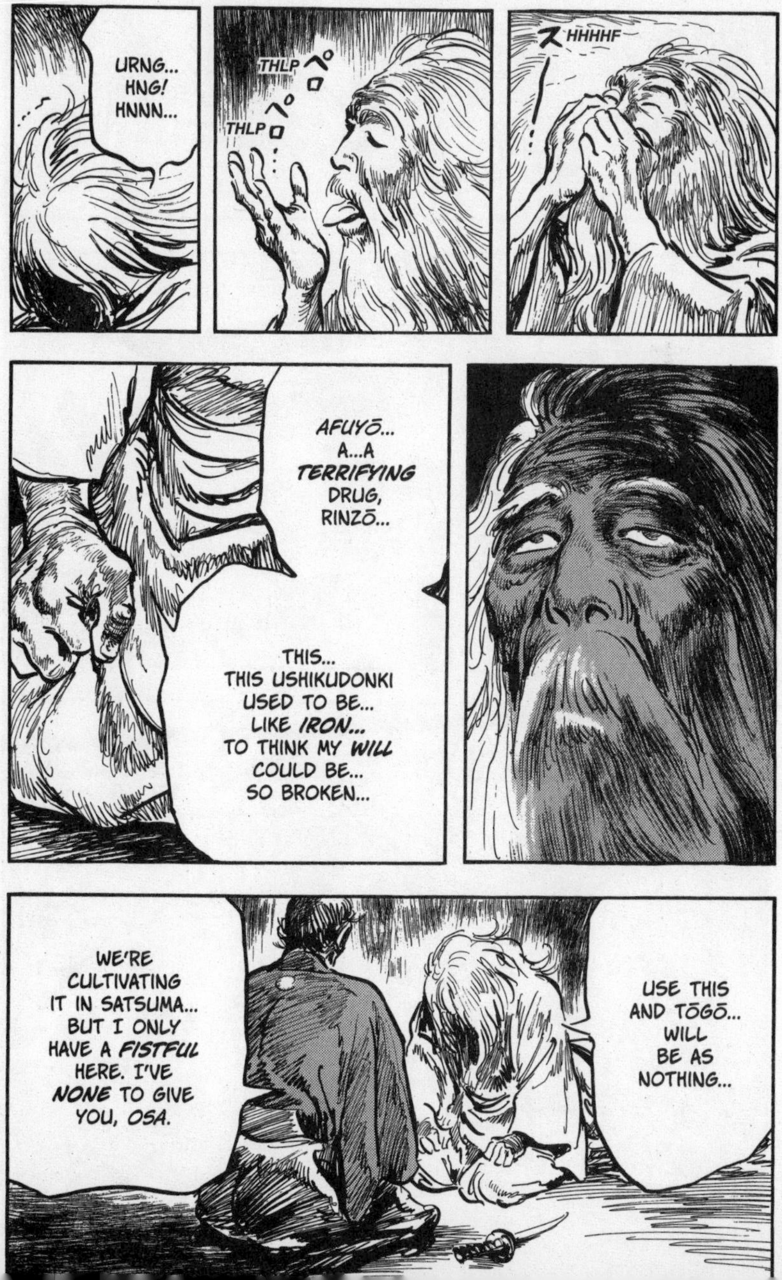

ス HHHHF
THLP ペロ
THLP ペロ
URNG... HNG! HNNN...
AFUYŌ... A...A TERRIFYING DRUG, RINZŌ...
THIS... THIS USHIKUDONKI USED TO BE... LIKE IRON... TO THINK MY WILL COULD BE... SO BROKEN...
USE THIS AND TŌGŌ... WILL BE AS NOTHING...
WE'RE CULTIVATING IT IN SATSUMA... BUT I ONLY HAVE A FISTFUL HERE. I'VE NONE TO GIVE YOU, OSA.

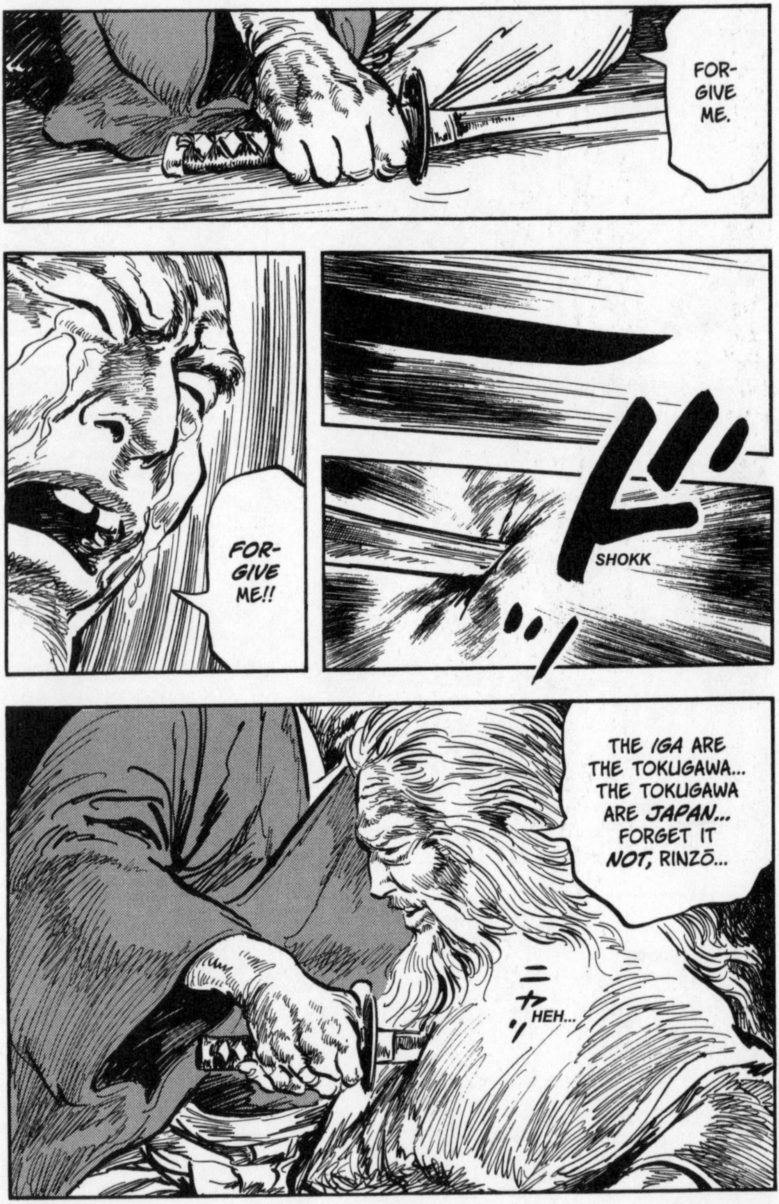
FOR-
GIVE
ME.
ドッ
SHOKK
FOR-
GIVE
ME!!
THE *IGA* ARE
THE TOKUGAWA...
THE TOKUGAWA
ARE *JAPAN*...
FORGET IT
NOT, RINZŌ...
ニヤッ
HEH...

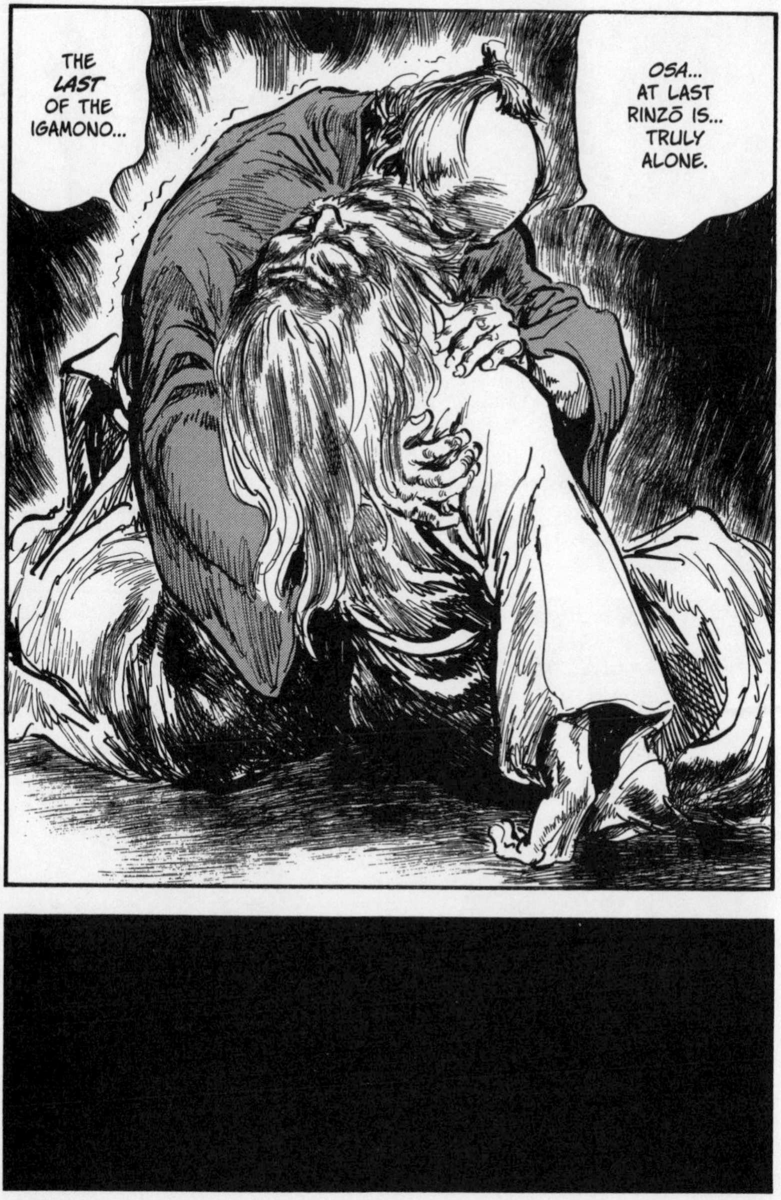
OSA... AT LAST RINZŌ IS... TRULY ALONE.
THE *LAST* OF THE IGAMONO...

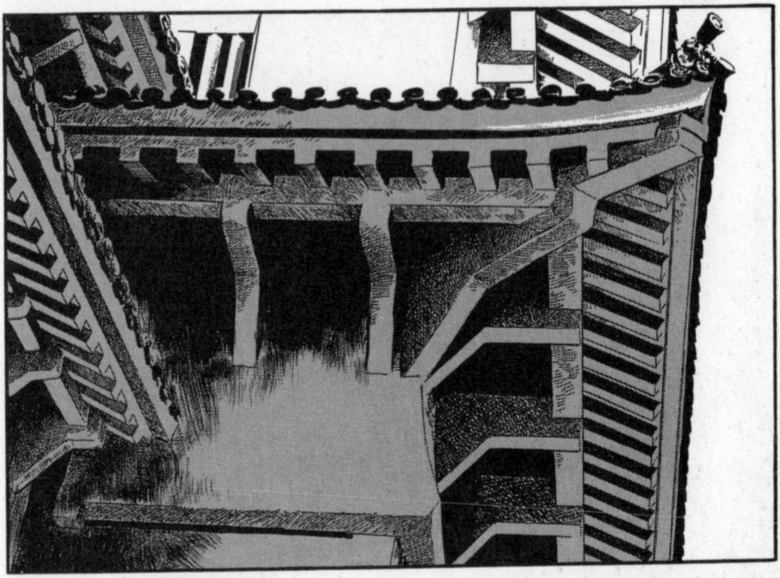
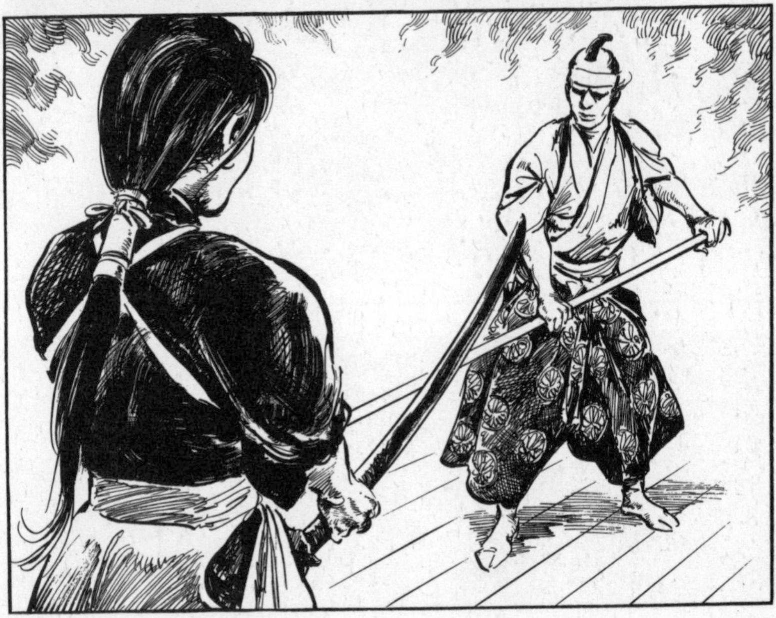

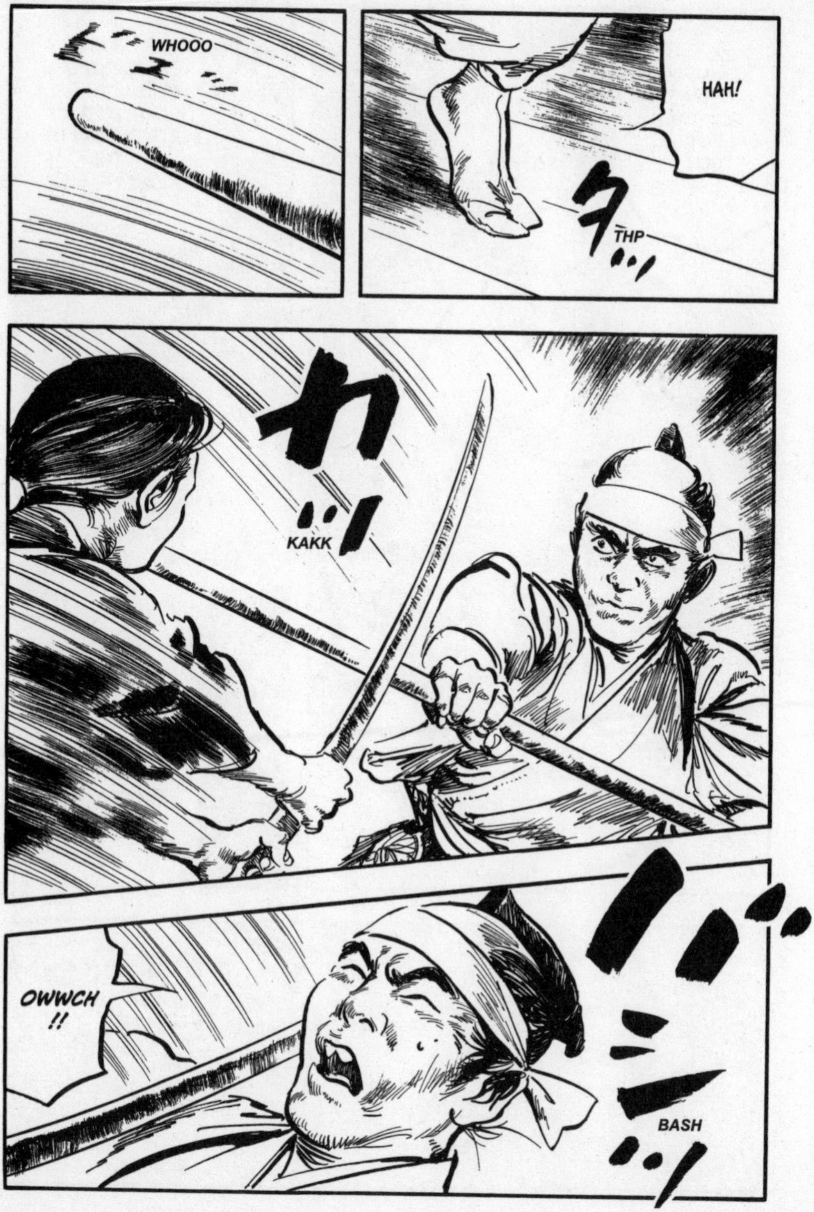
HAH!
THP
WHOOO
KAKK
BASH
OWWCH !!

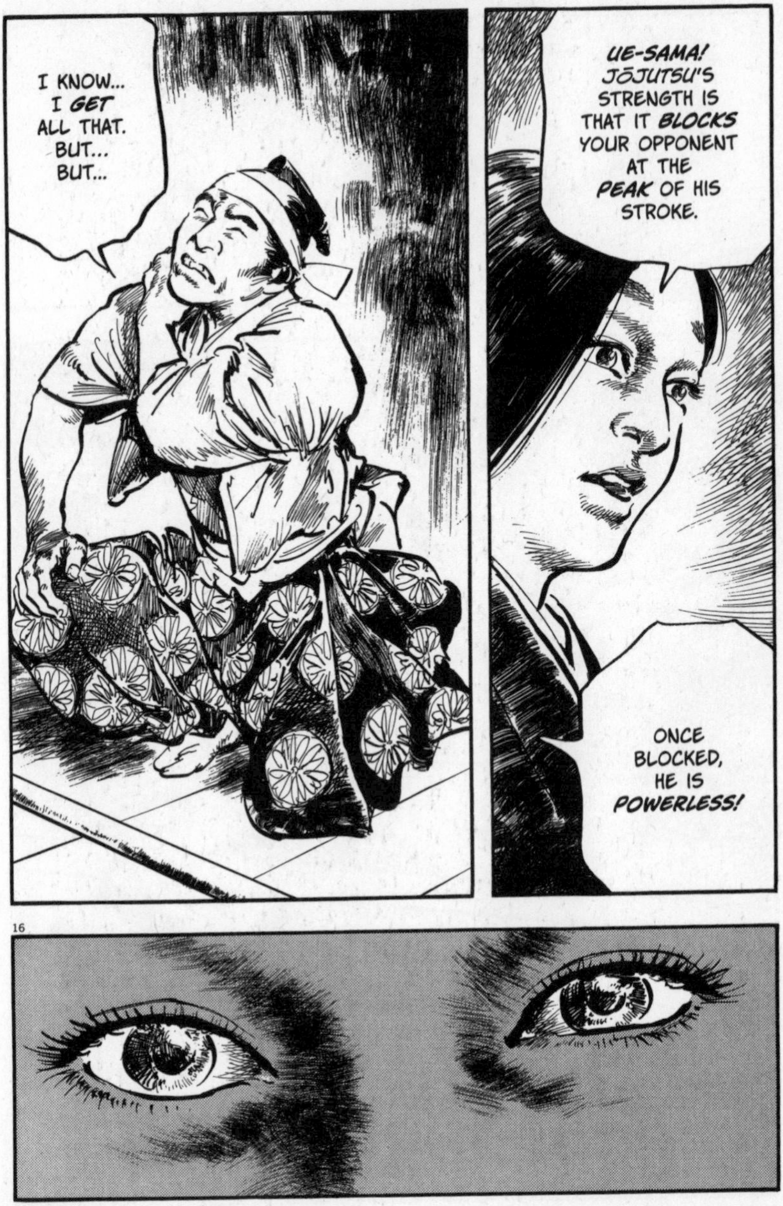
UE-SAMA! JŌJUTSU'S STRENGTH IS THAT IT BLOCKS YOUR OPPONENT AT THE PEAK OF HIS STROKE.
ONCE BLOCKED, HE IS POWERLESS!
I KNOW... I GET ALL THAT. BUT... BUT...
16

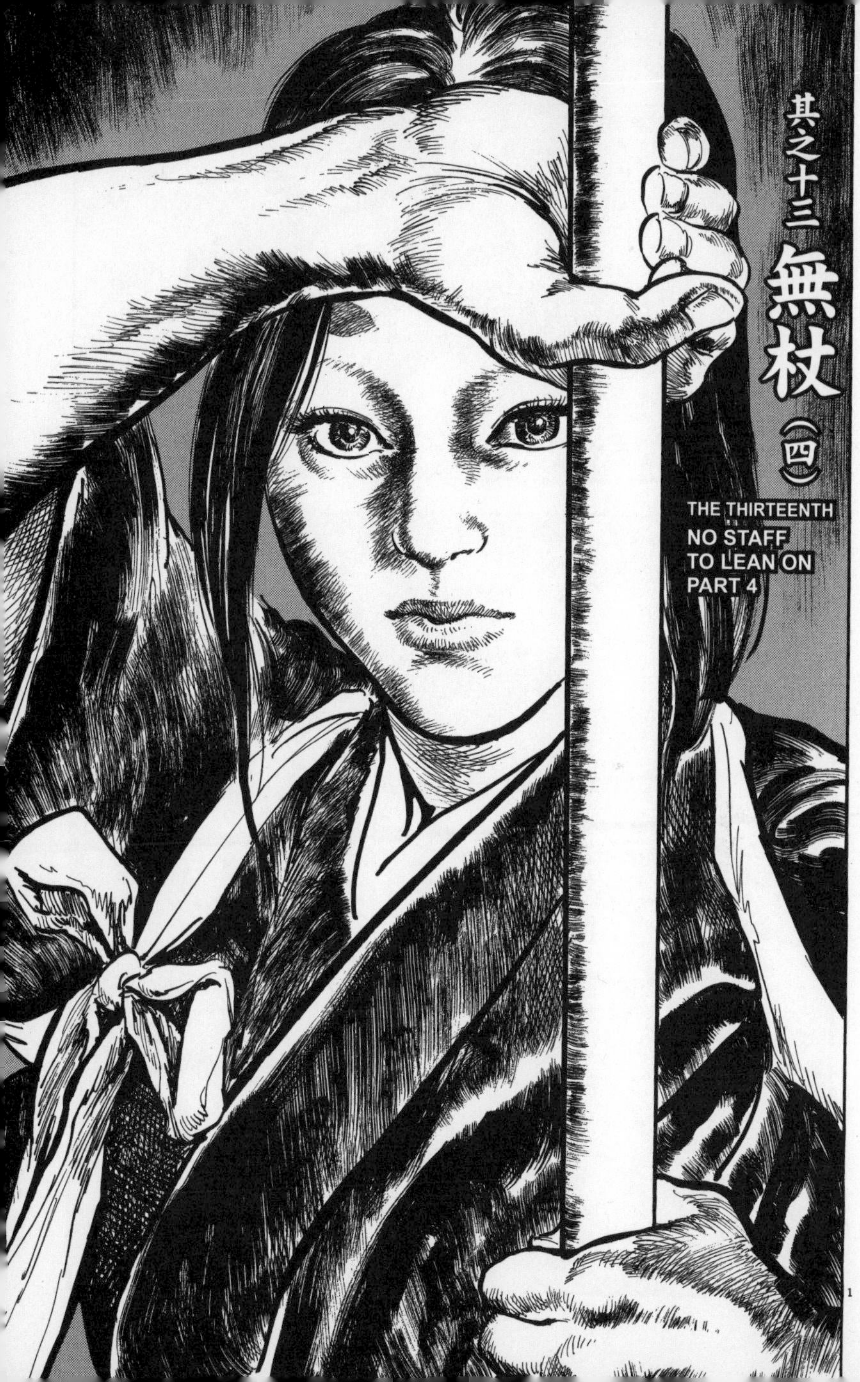
其之十三 無杖（四）
THE THIRTEENTH
NO STAFF
TO LEAN ON
PART 4

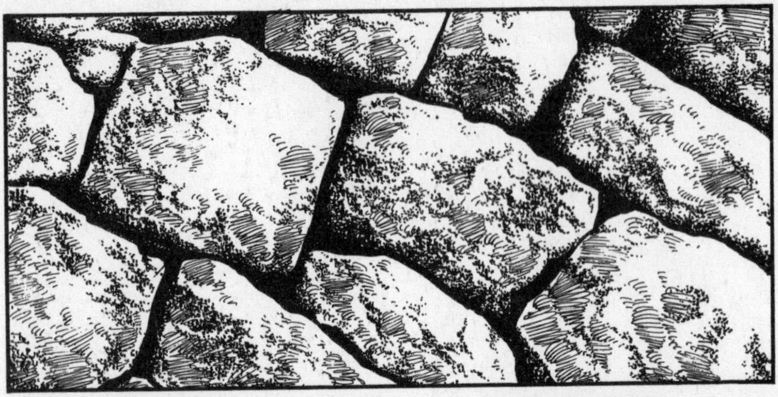

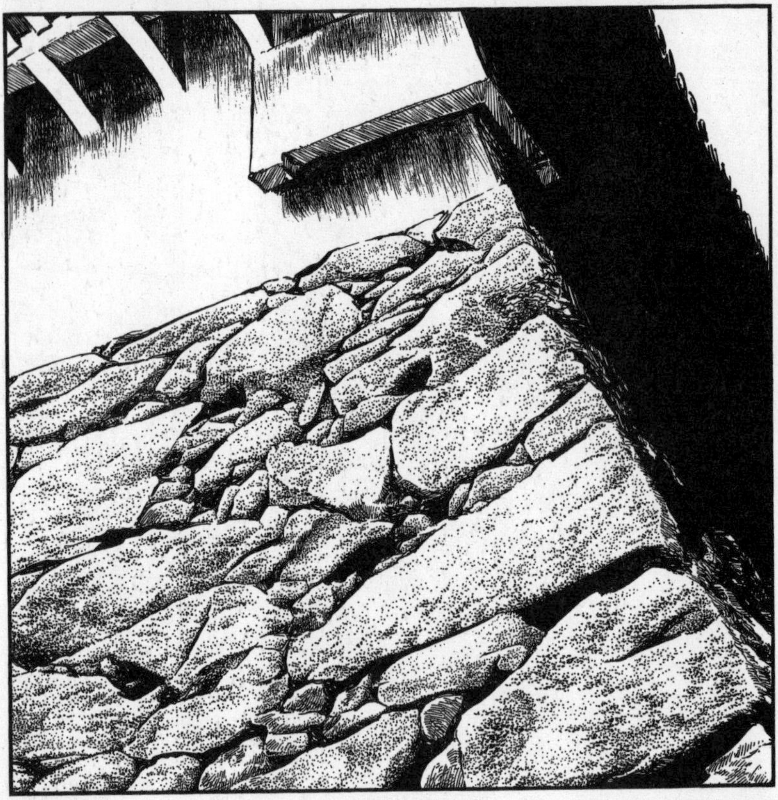

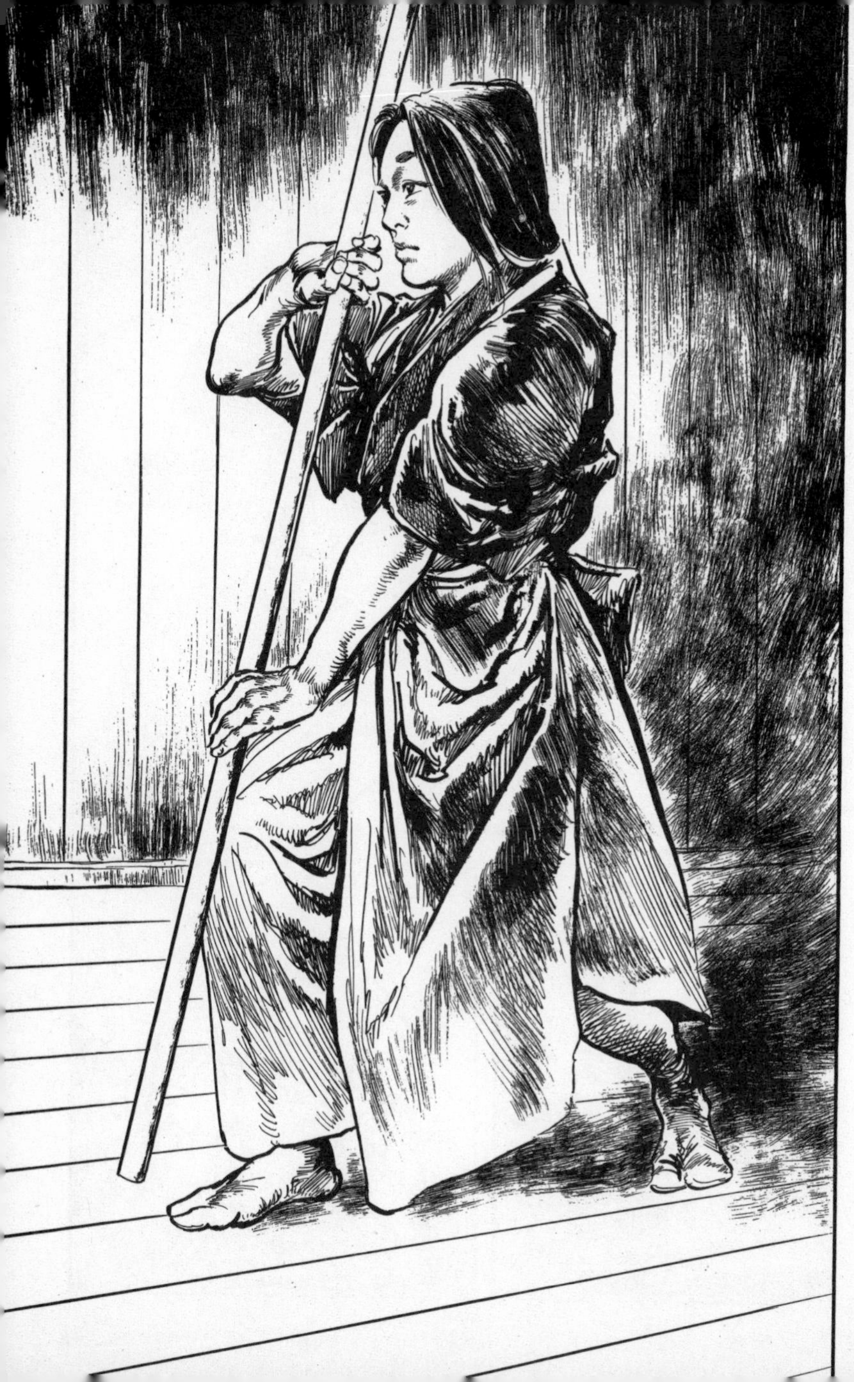

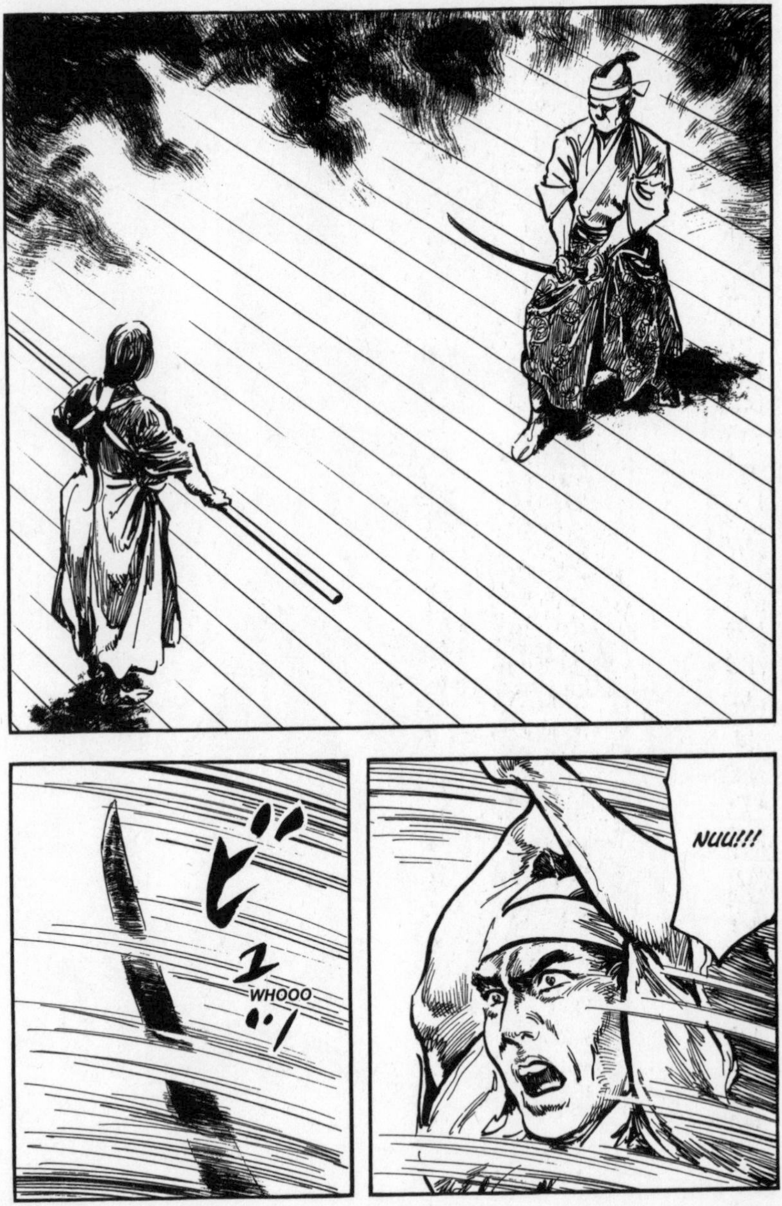
NUU!!!
WHOOO

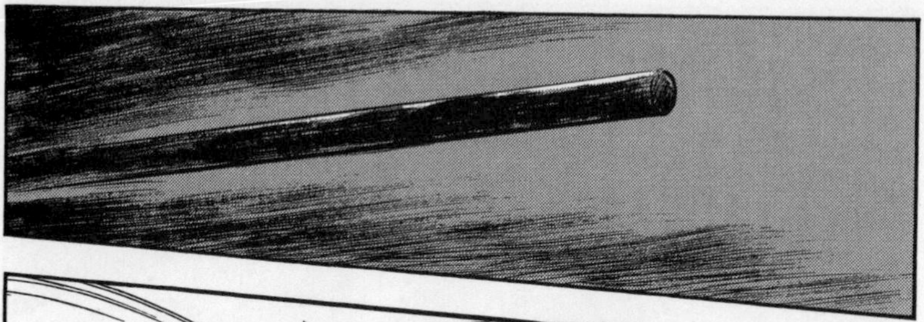

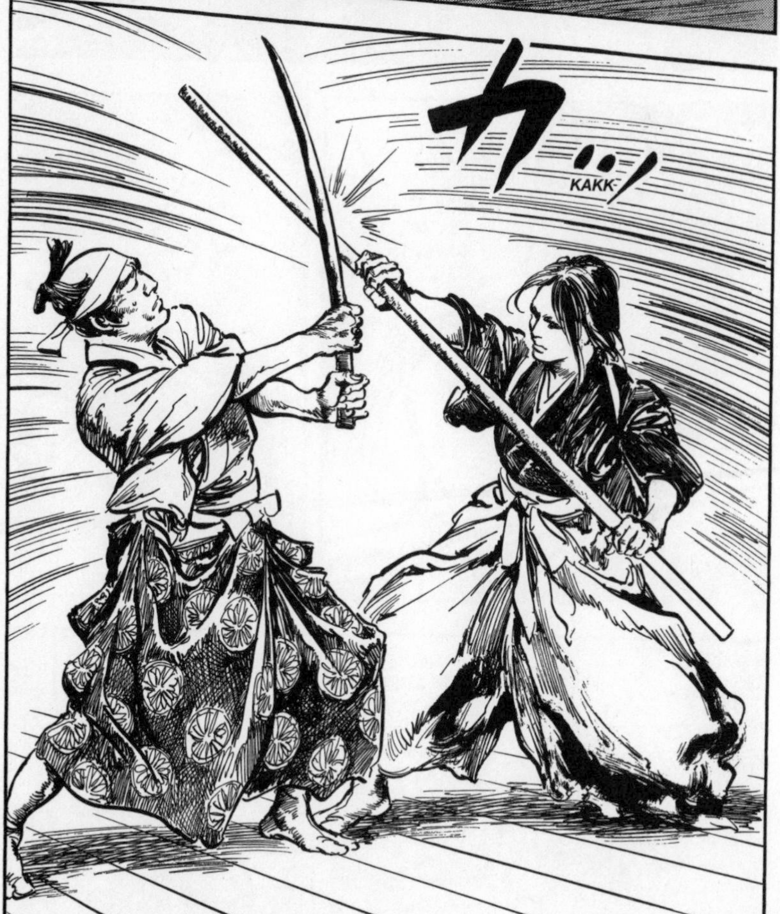
カッ!
KAKK-

IT'S BECAUSE YOU CAN BLOCK THAT HIGH THAT *JŌJUTSU* DEFEATS *KENJUTSU*.

GRGGK...

MY LORD! GO-RŌJŪ ŌKUBO KAGA-NO KAMI-SAMA!

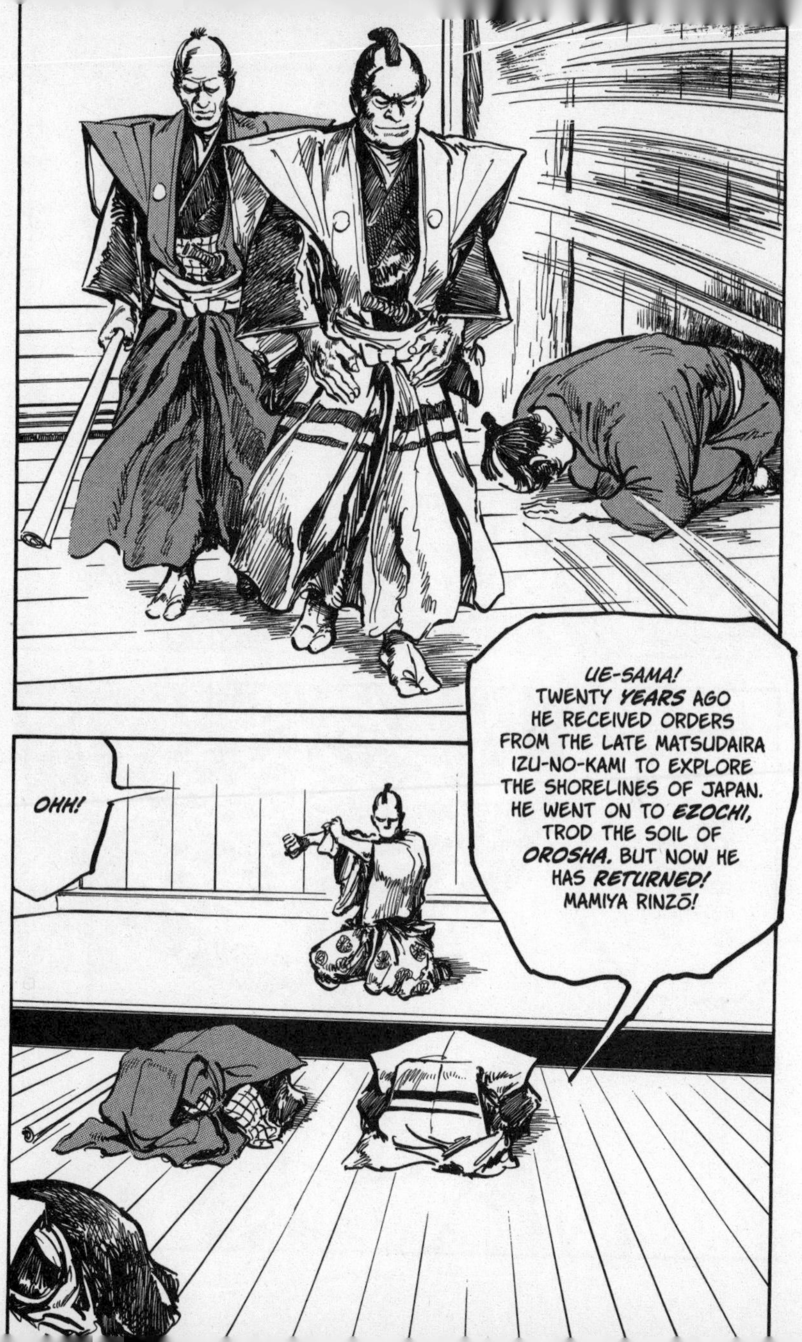
UE-SAMA!
TWENTY YEARS AGO HE RECEIVED ORDERS FROM THE LATE MATSUDAIRA IZU-NO-KAMI TO EXPLORE THE SHORELINES OF JAPAN. HE WENT ON TO EZOCHI, TROD THE SOIL OF OROSHA. BUT NOW HE HAS RETURNED! MAMIYA RINZŌ!
OHH!

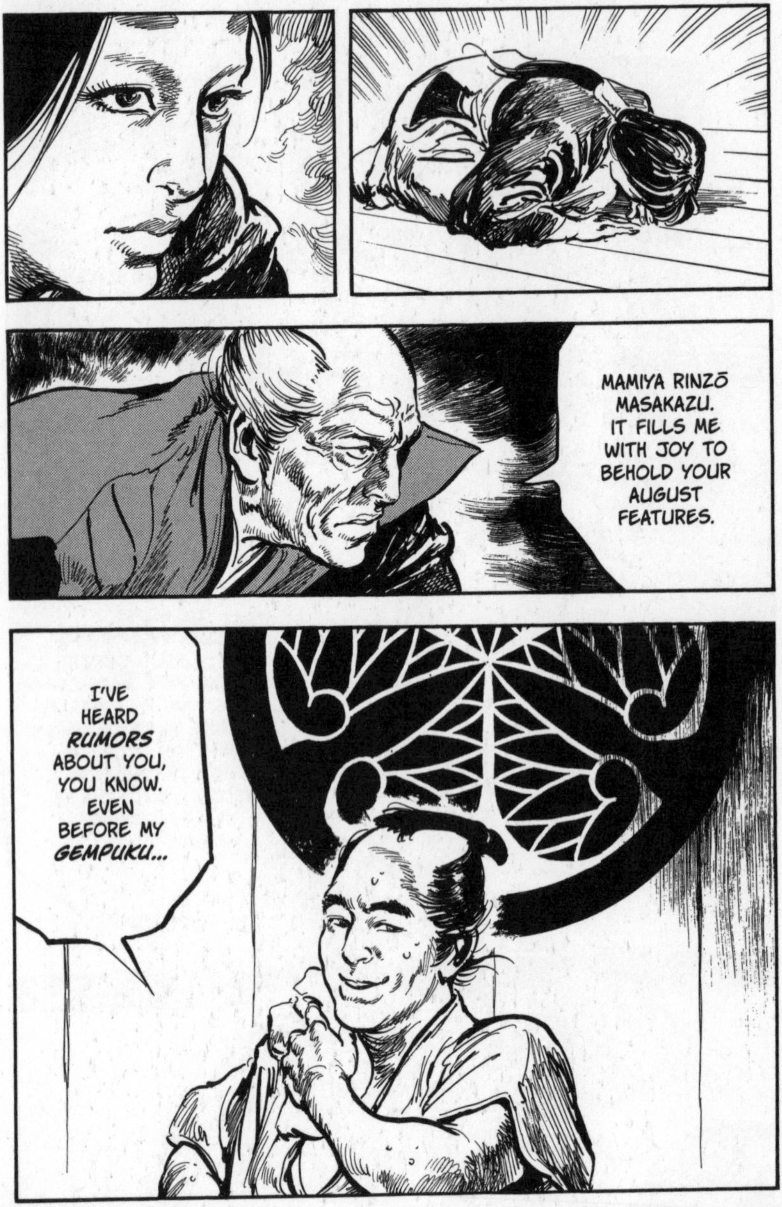
MAMIYA RINZŌ MASAKAZU. IT FILLS ME WITH JOY TO BEHOLD YOUR AUGUST FEATURES.
I'VE HEARD *RUMORS* ABOUT YOU, YOU KNOW. EVEN BEFORE MY *GEMPUKU*...

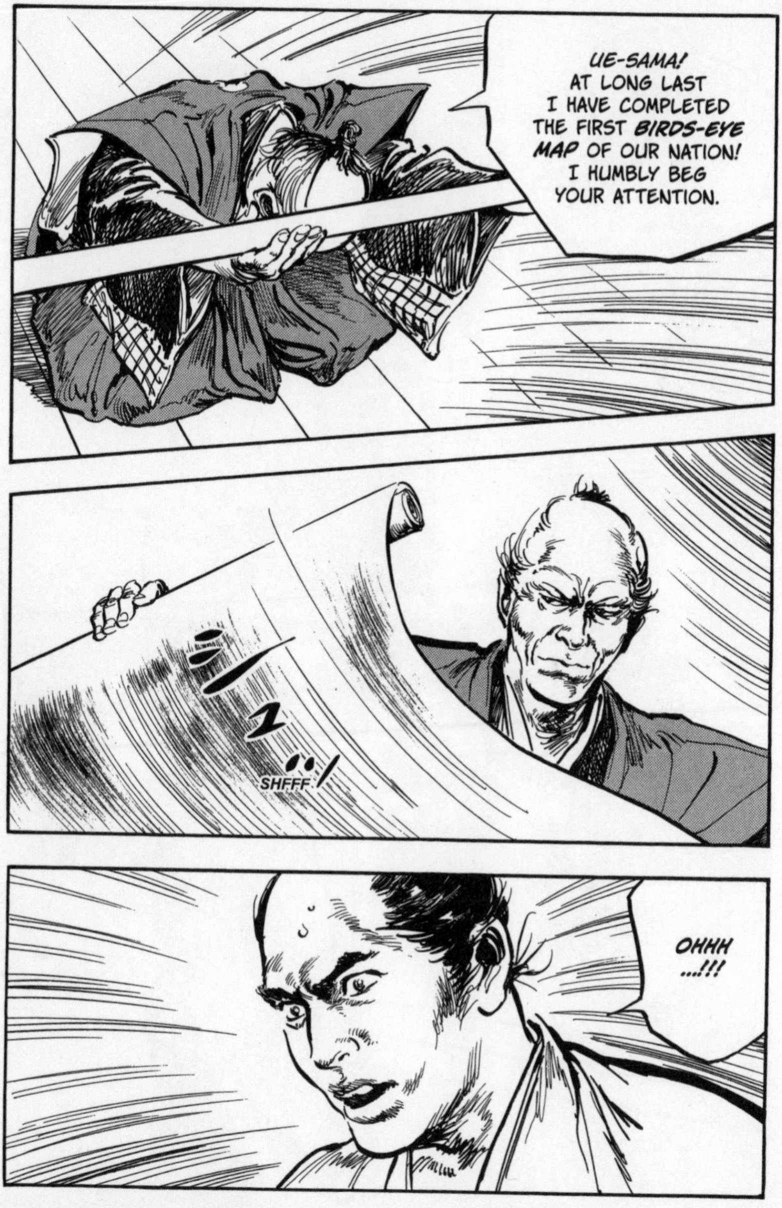
UE-SAMA! AT LONG LAST I HAVE COMPLETED THE FIRST BIRDS-EYE MAP OF OUR NATION! I HUMBLY BEG YOUR ATTENTION.
SHFFF
OHHH ...!!!

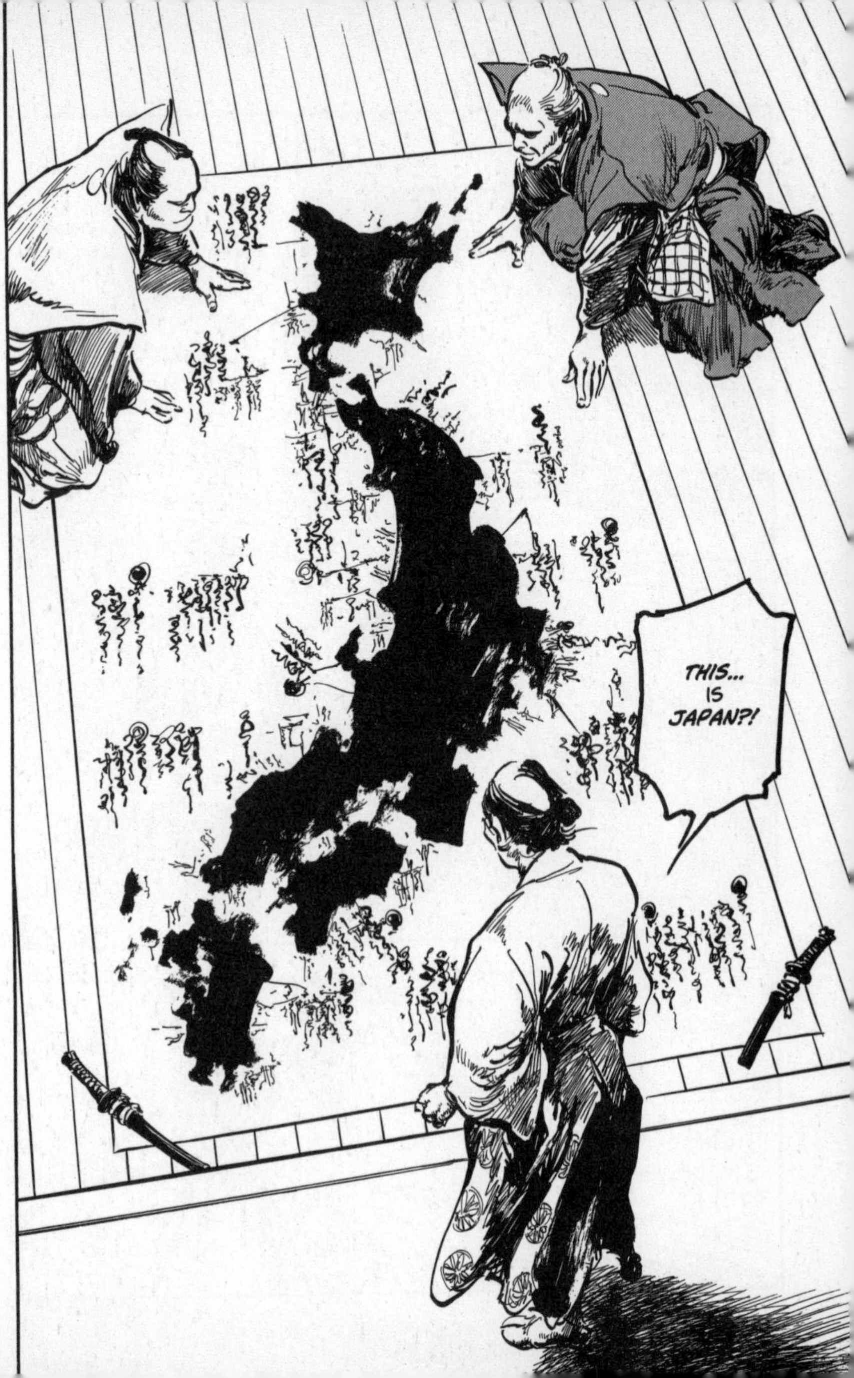
THIS... IS JAPAN?!

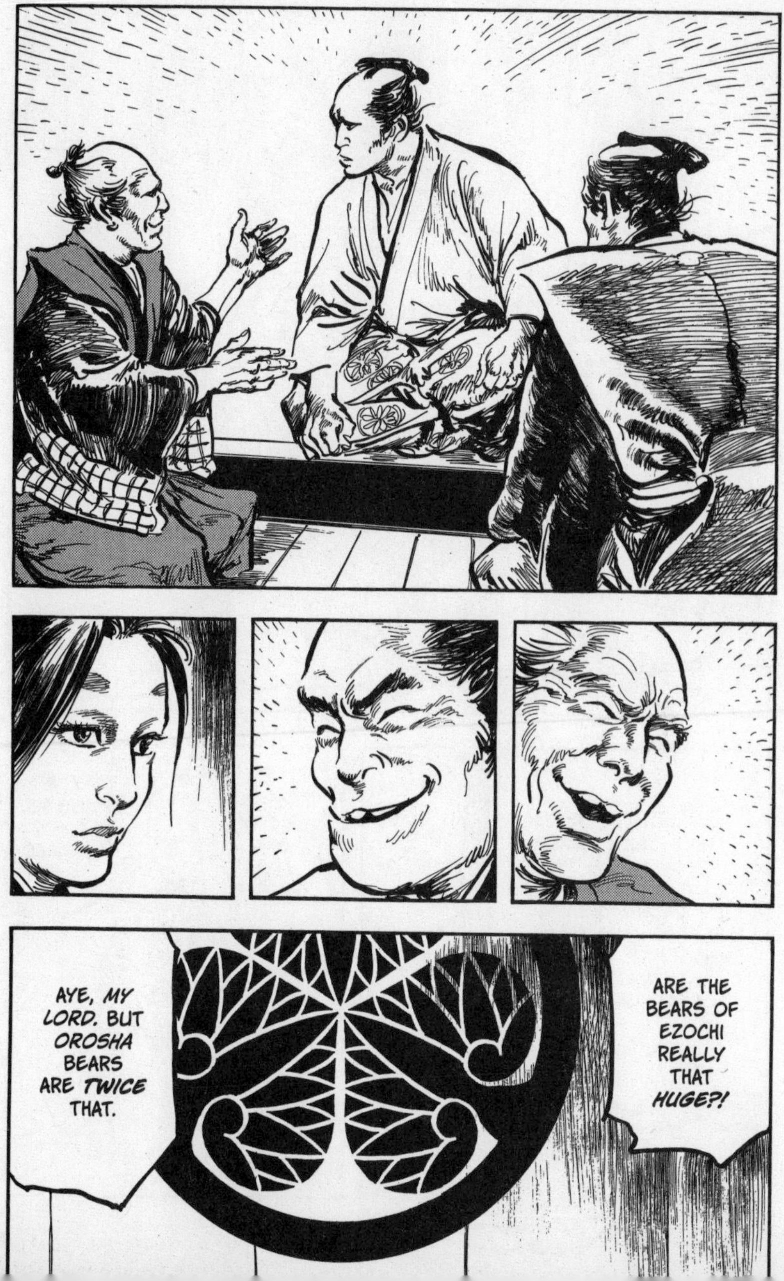
ARE THE BEARS OF EZOCHI REALLY THAT HUGE?!
AYE, MY LORD. BUT OROSHA BEARS ARE TWICE THAT.

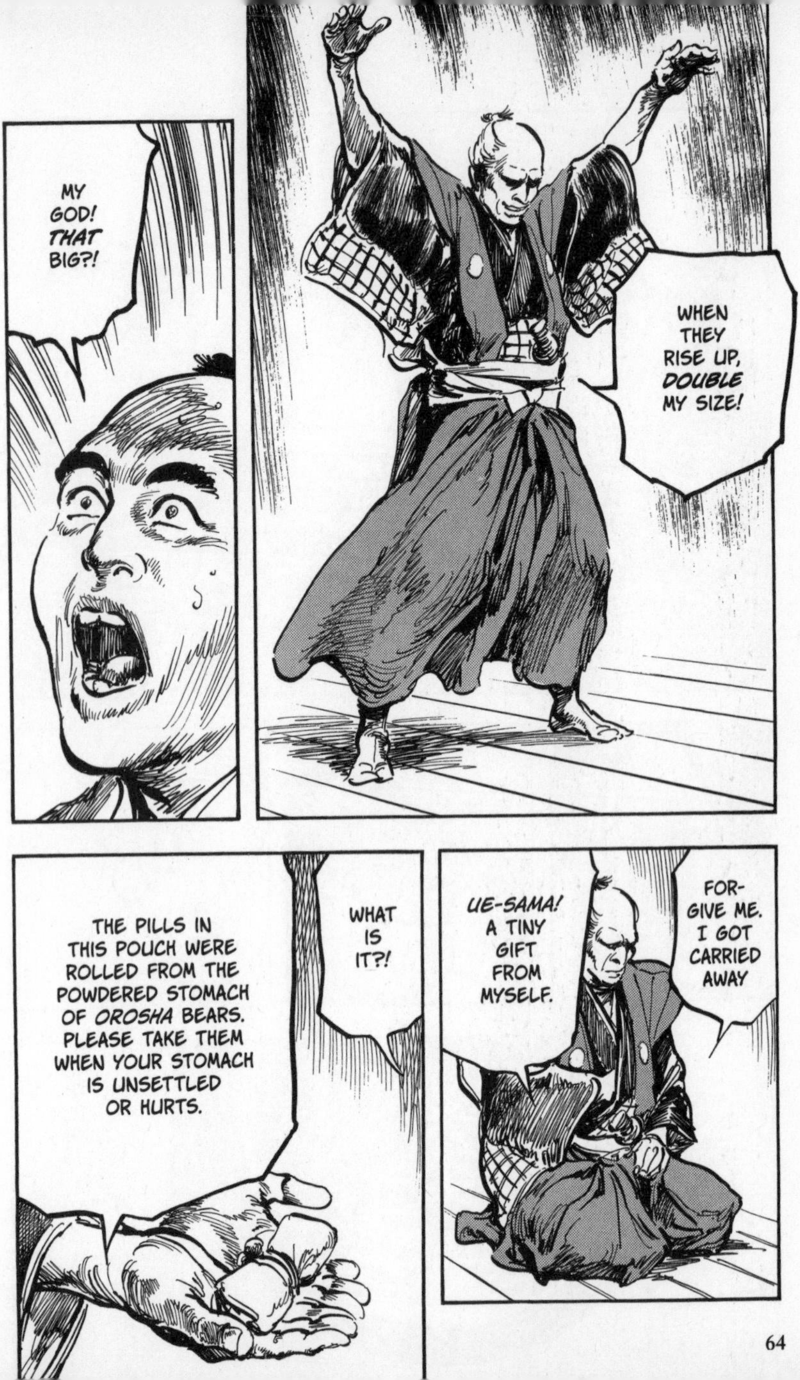
WHEN THEY RISE UP, *DOUBLE* MY SIZE!
MY GOD! *THAT* BIG?!
FOR-GIVE ME. I GOT CARRIED AWAY
UE-SAMA! A TINY GIFT FROM MYSELF.
WHAT IS IT?!
THE PILLS IN THIS POUCH WERE ROLLED FROM THE POWDERED STOMACH OF *OROSHA* BEARS. PLEASE TAKE THEM WHEN YOUR STOMACH IS UNSETTLED OR HURTS.

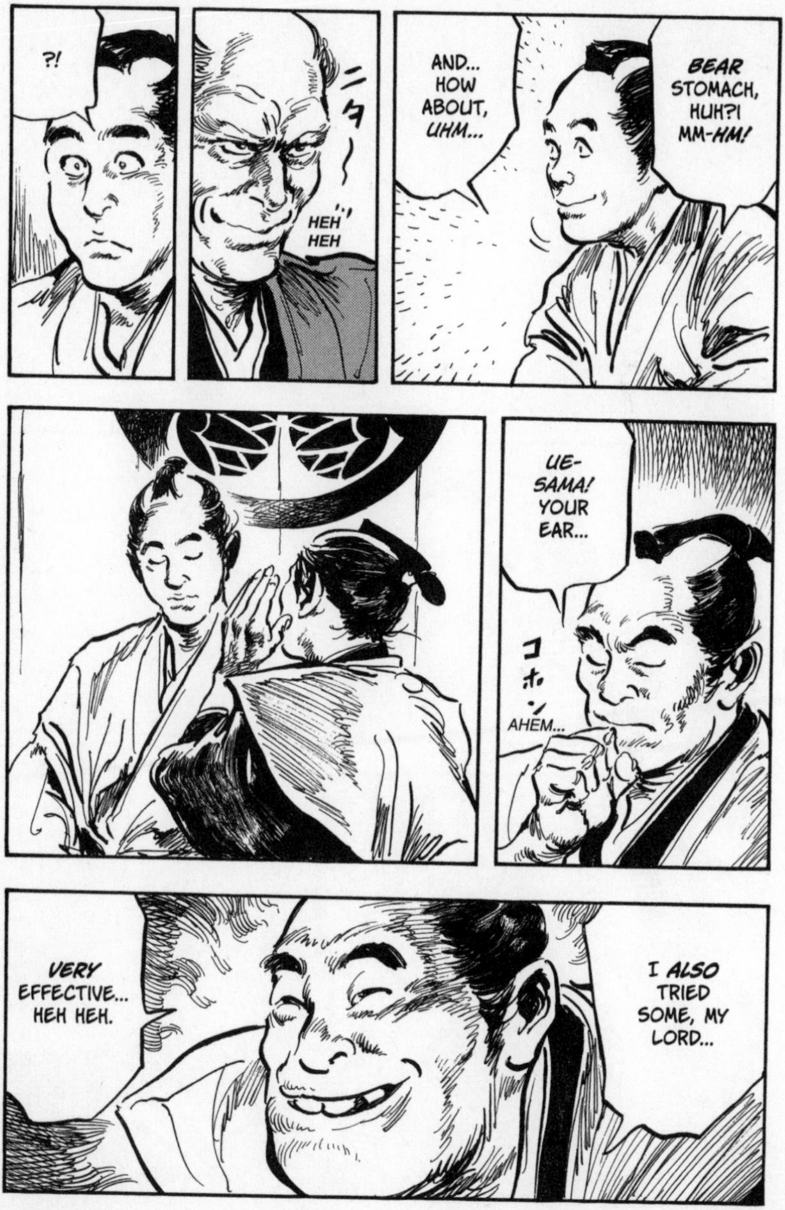
BEAR STOMACH, HUH?! MM-HM!
AND... HOW ABOUT, UHM...
ニタ
HEH HEH
?!
UE-SAMA! YOUR EAR...
コホン
AHEM...
I ALSO TRIED SOME, MY LORD...
VERY EFFECTIVE... HEH HEH.

TWO AT A TIME.

HOW *MANY*?!

ゴ″ク″″! GULLP

ガ″バ″″! FWMP

UE-SAMA!

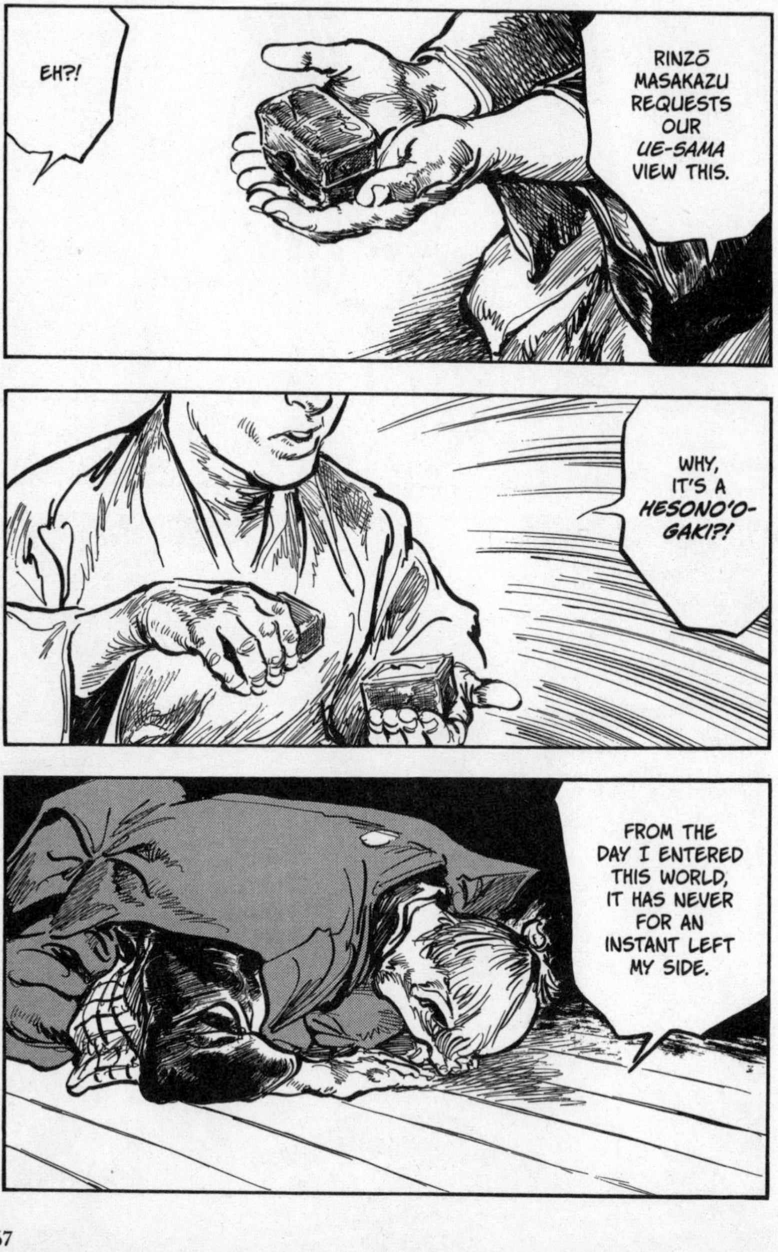
RINZŌ MASAKAZU REQUESTS OUR *UE-SAMA* VIEW THIS.
EH?!
WHY, IT'S A *HESONO'O-GAKI?!*
FROM THE DAY I ENTERED THIS WORLD, IT HAS NEVER FOR AN INSTANT LEFT MY SIDE.

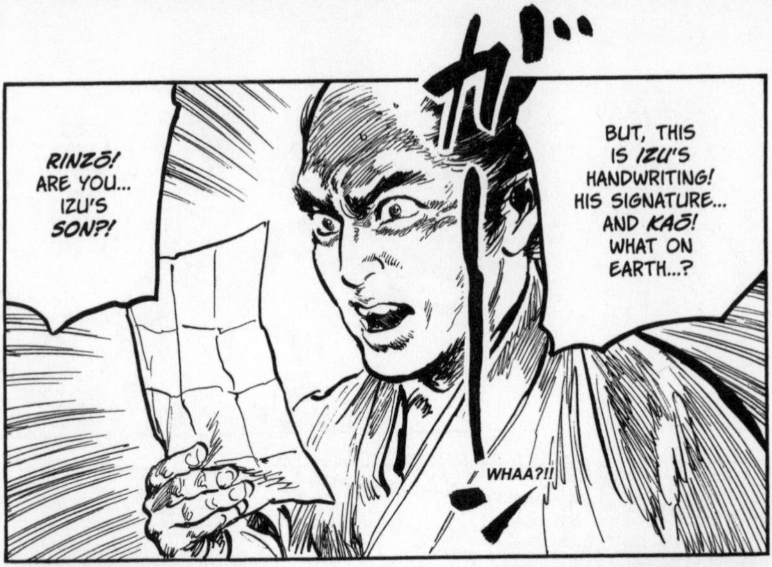
BUT, THIS IS *IZU*'S HANDWRITING! HIS SIGNATURE... AND *KAŌ*! WHAT ON EARTH...?
RINZŌ! ARE YOU... IZU'S *SON?!*
WHAA?!!

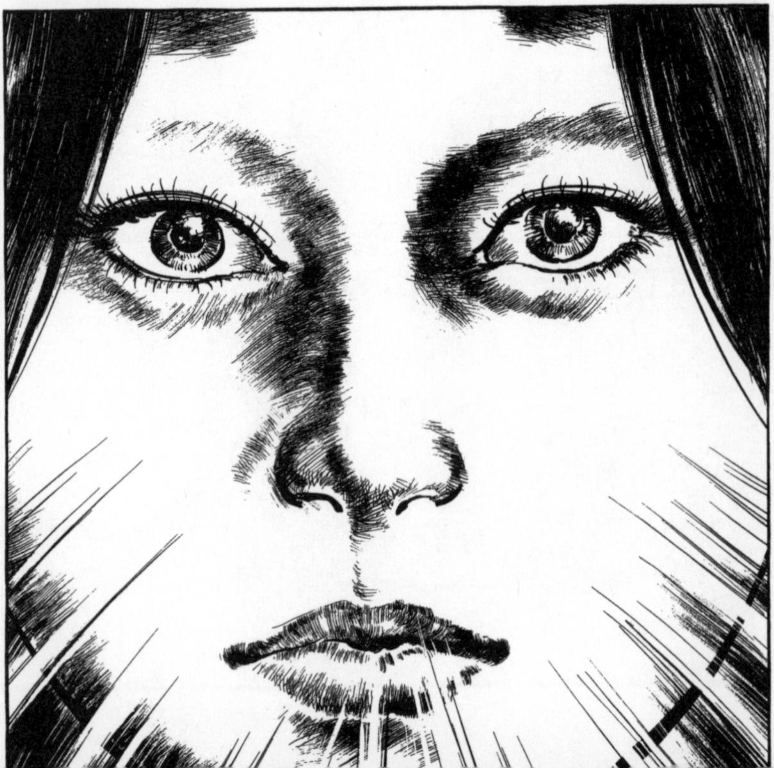

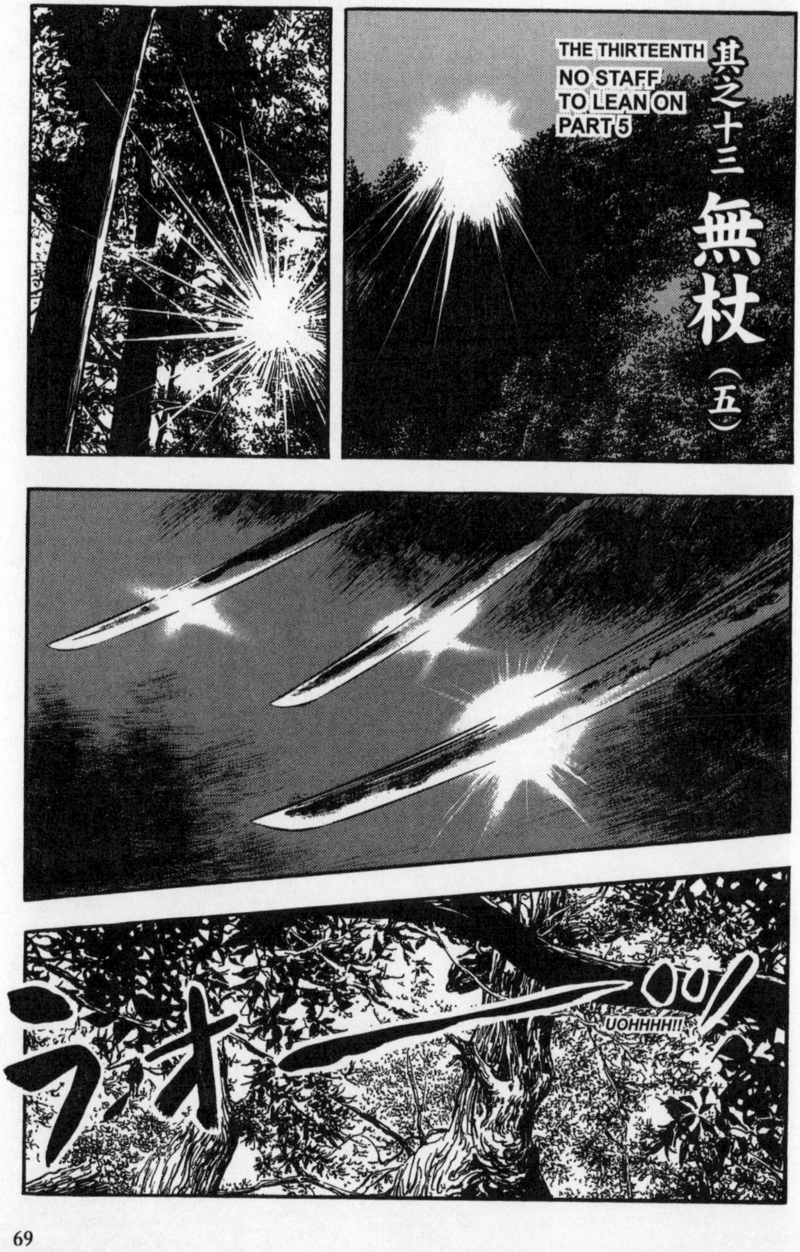
THE THIRTEENTH
NO STAFF TO LEAN ON PART 5
其之十三
無杖
（五）
ウオーーーッ!!
UOHHHH!!

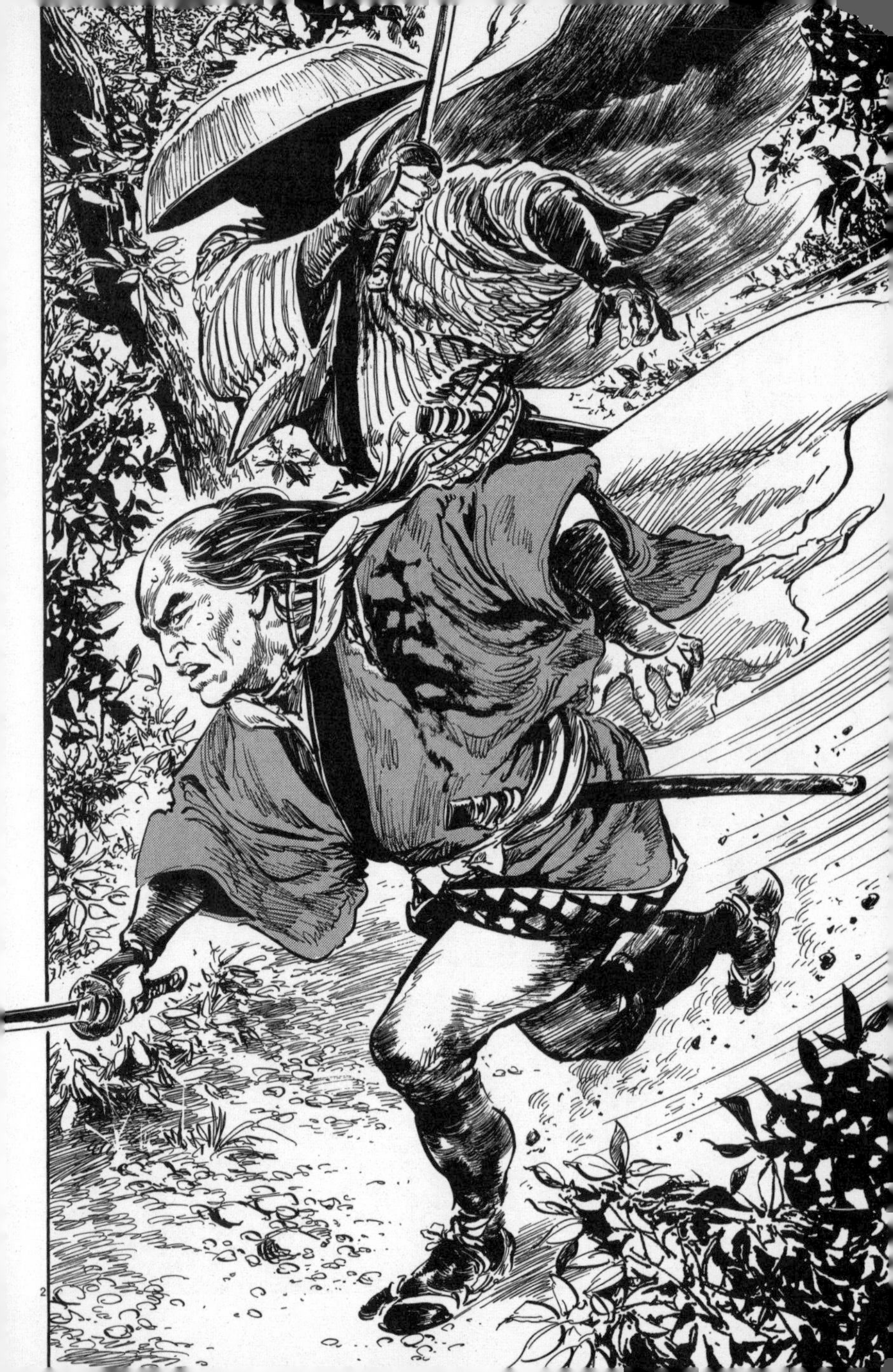

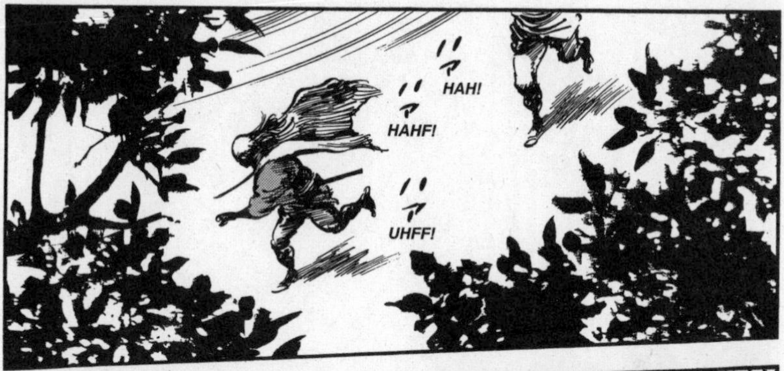
ハァ
HAH!
ハァ
HAHF!
ハァ
UHFF!

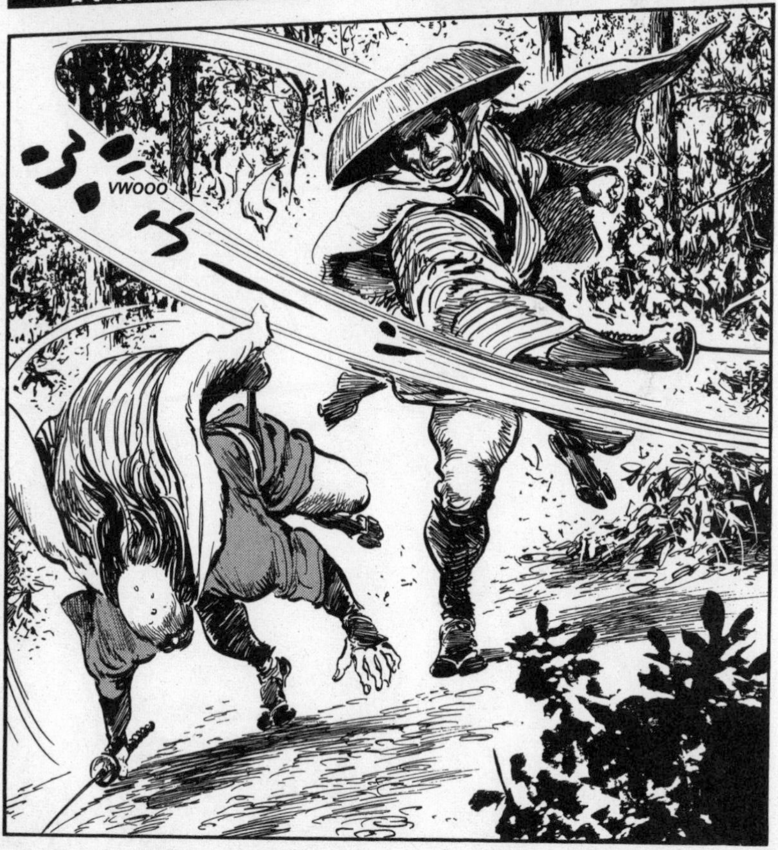
VWOOO

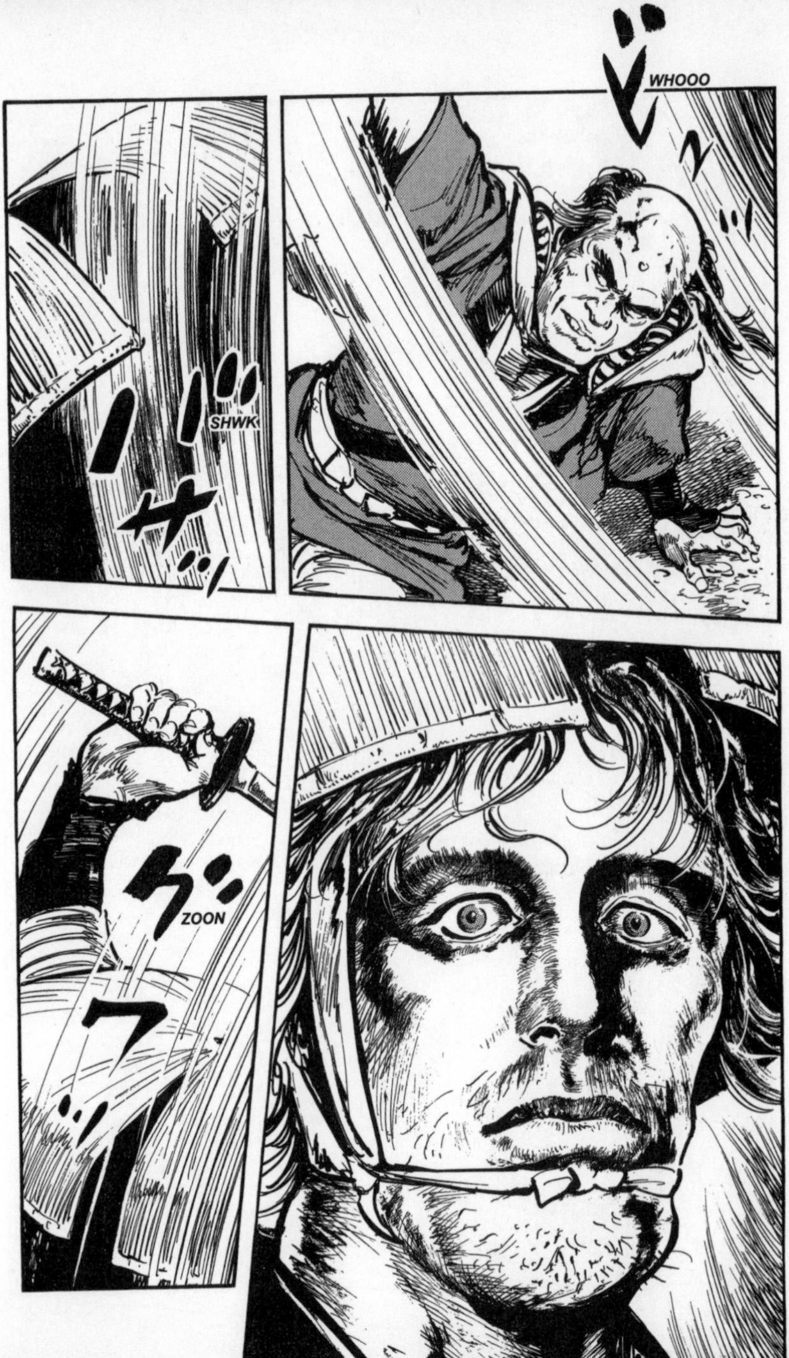
WHOOO
SHWK
ZOON

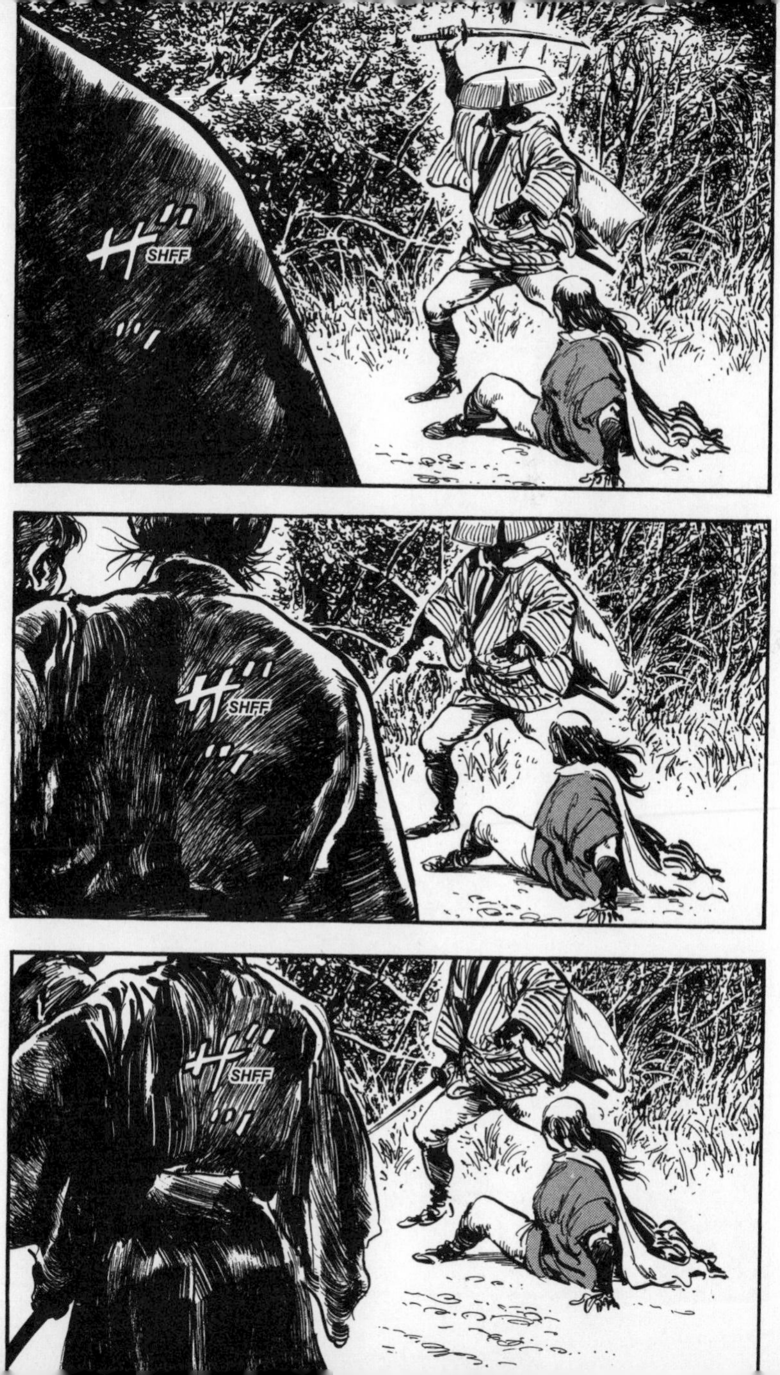
SHFF
SHFF
SHFF

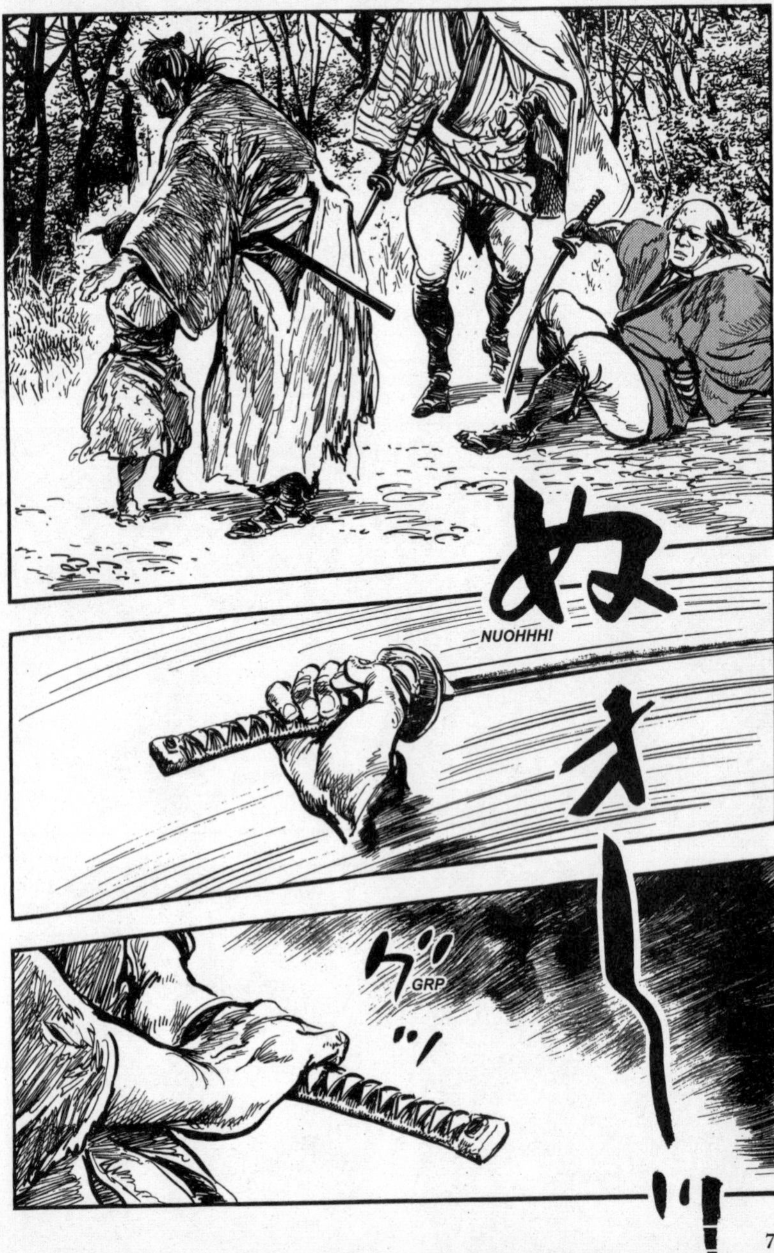

ぬオーーッ!
NUOHHH!
グッ
GRP

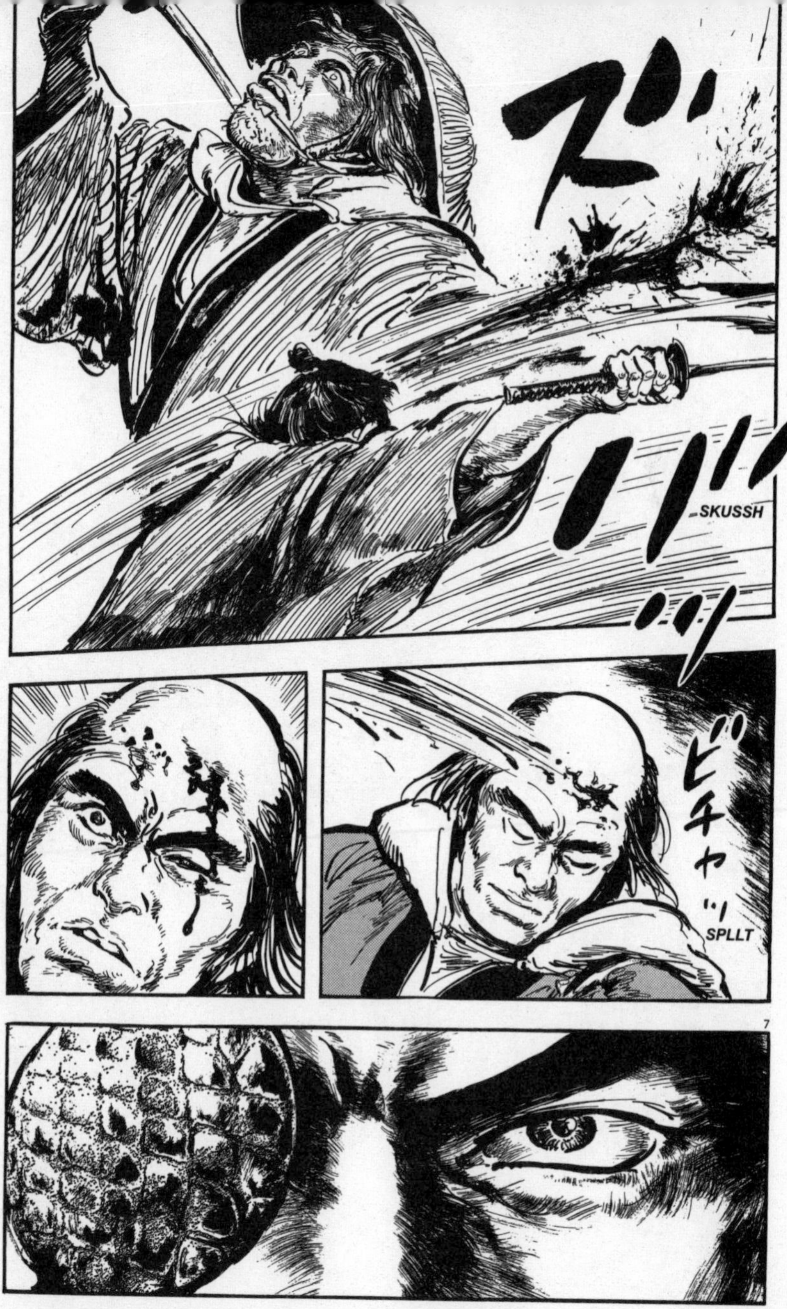
ズバッ
SKUSSH
ビチャッ
SPLLT

7

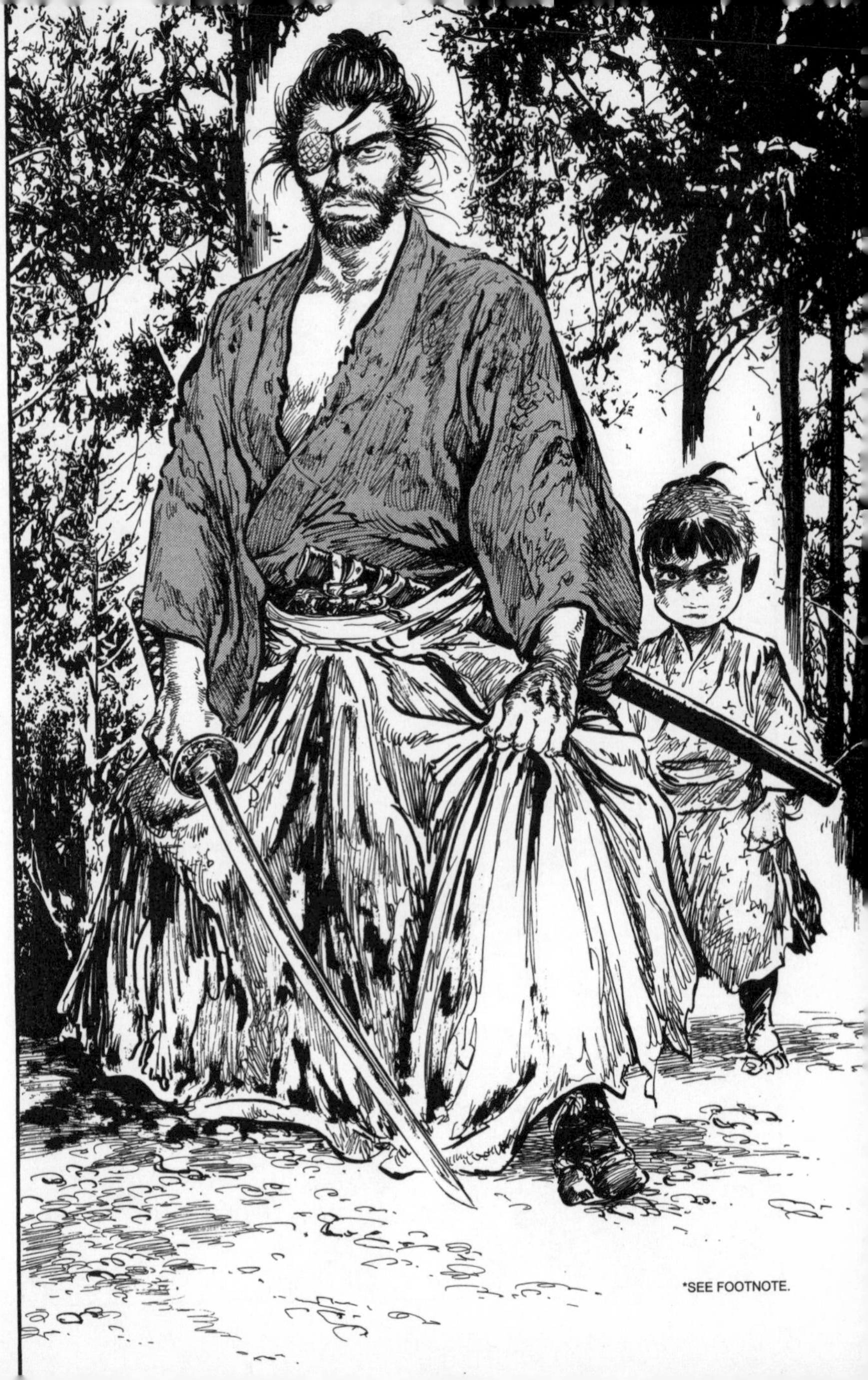

*SEE FOOTNOTE.

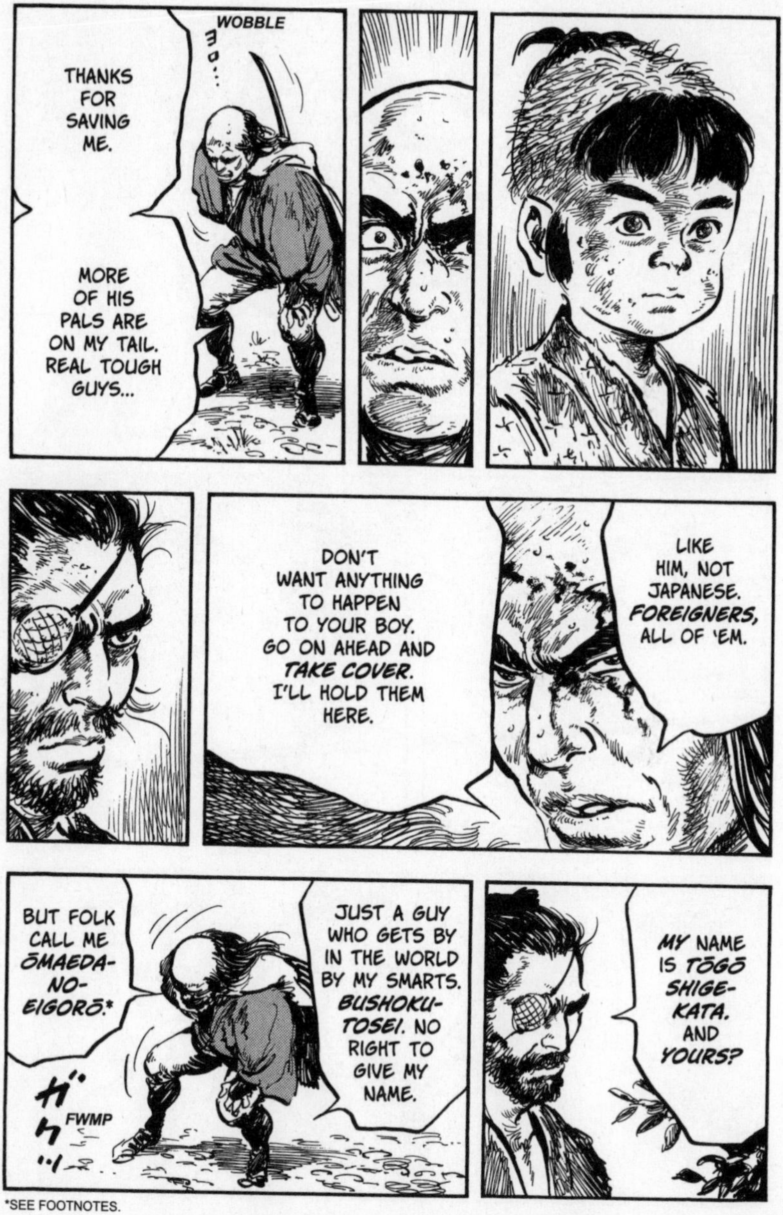
WOBBLE
ヨロ…
THANKS FOR SAVING ME.
MORE OF HIS PALS ARE ON MY TAIL. REAL TOUGH GUYS...
LIKE HIM, NOT JAPANESE. FOREIGNERS, ALL OF 'EM.
DON'T WANT ANYTHING TO HAPPEN TO YOUR BOY. GO ON AHEAD AND TAKE COVER. I'LL HOLD THEM HERE.
MY NAME IS TŌGŌ SHIGE-KATA. AND YOURS?
JUST A GUY WHO GETS BY IN THE WORLD BY MY SMARTS. BUSHOKU-TOSEI. NO RIGHT TO GIVE MY NAME.
BUT FOLK CALL ME ŌMAEDA-NO-EIGORŌ.*
ガクッ
FWMP

*SEE FOOTNOTES.

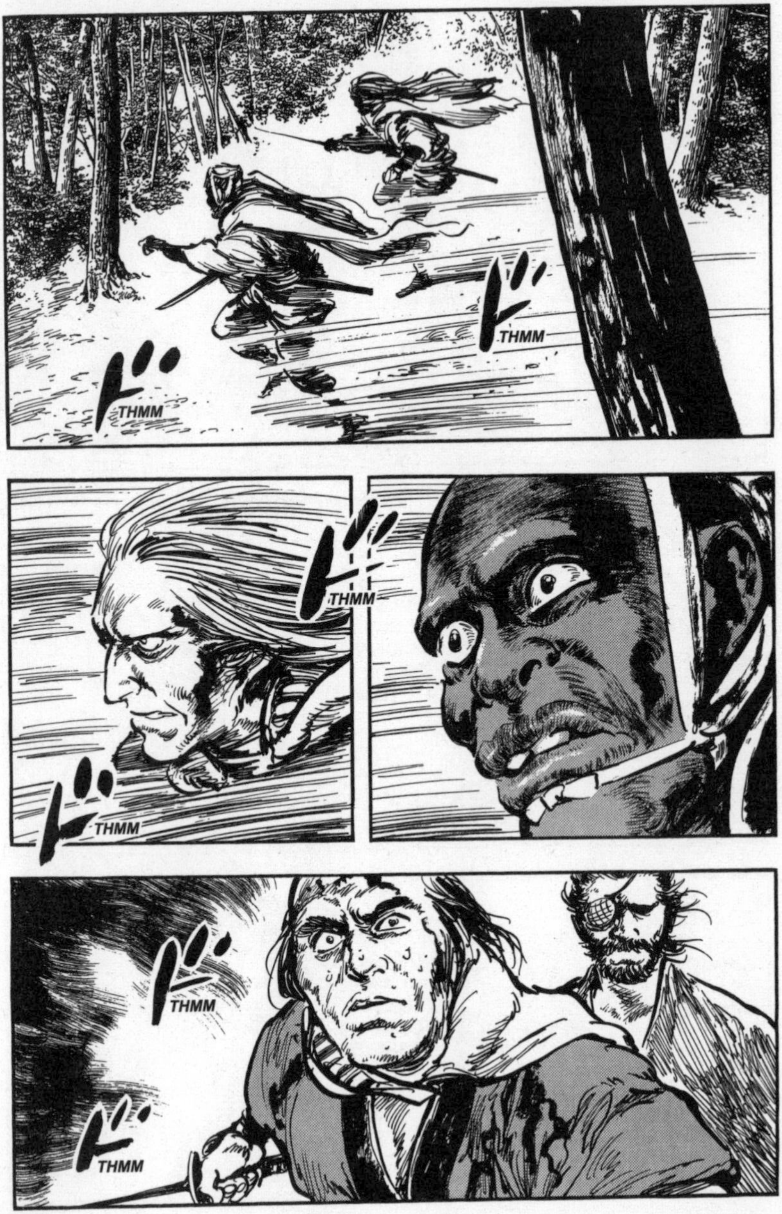
ド THMM
ド THMM
ド THMM
ド THMM
ド THMM
ド THMM

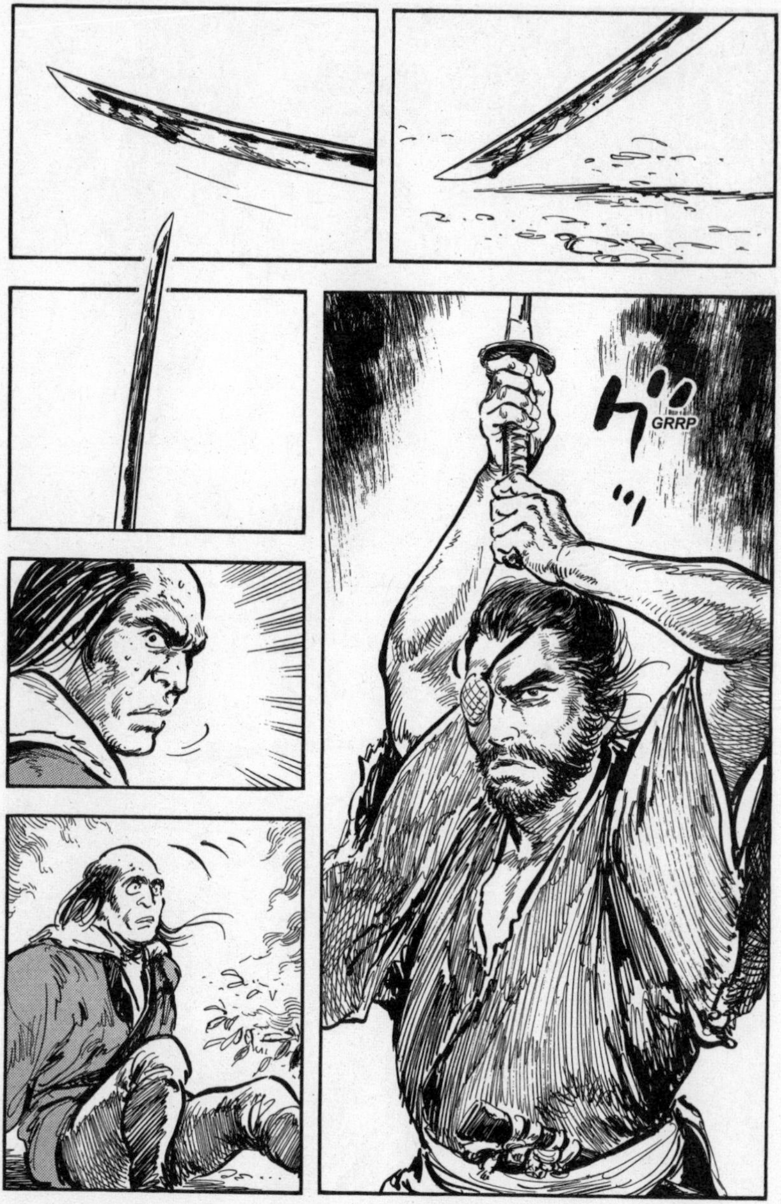
GRRP

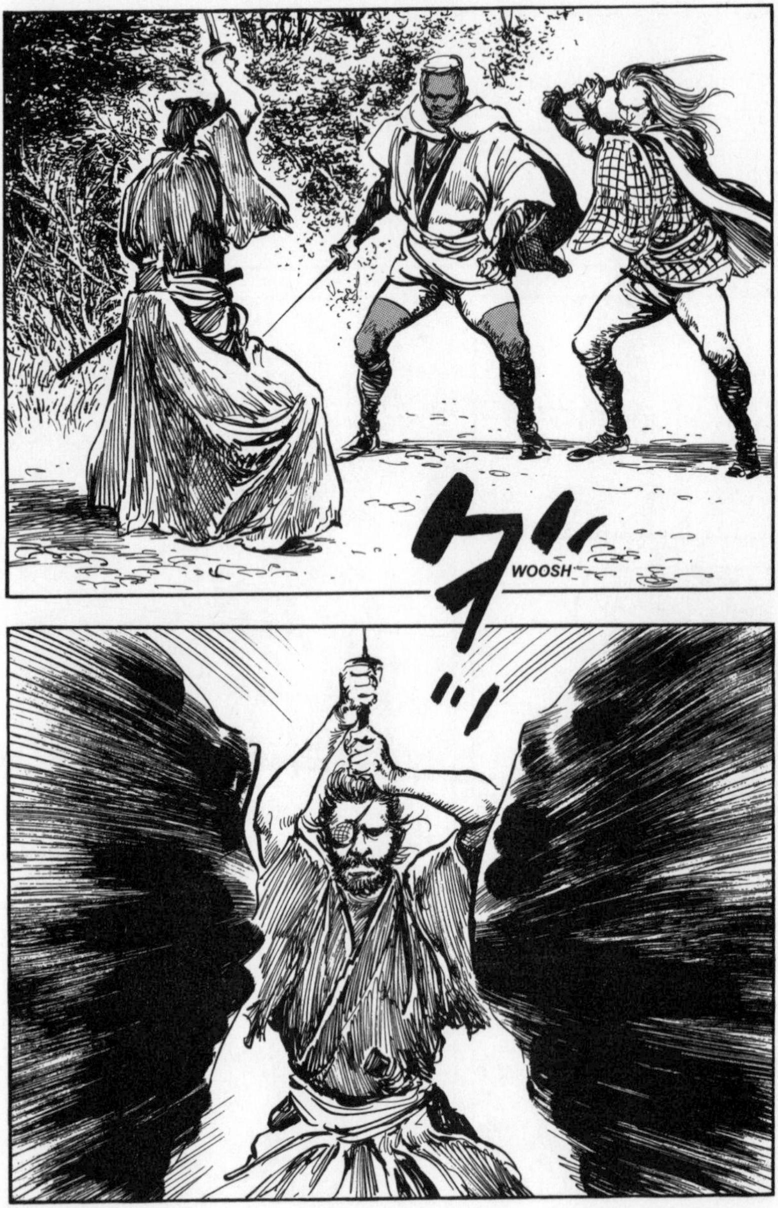
WOOSH

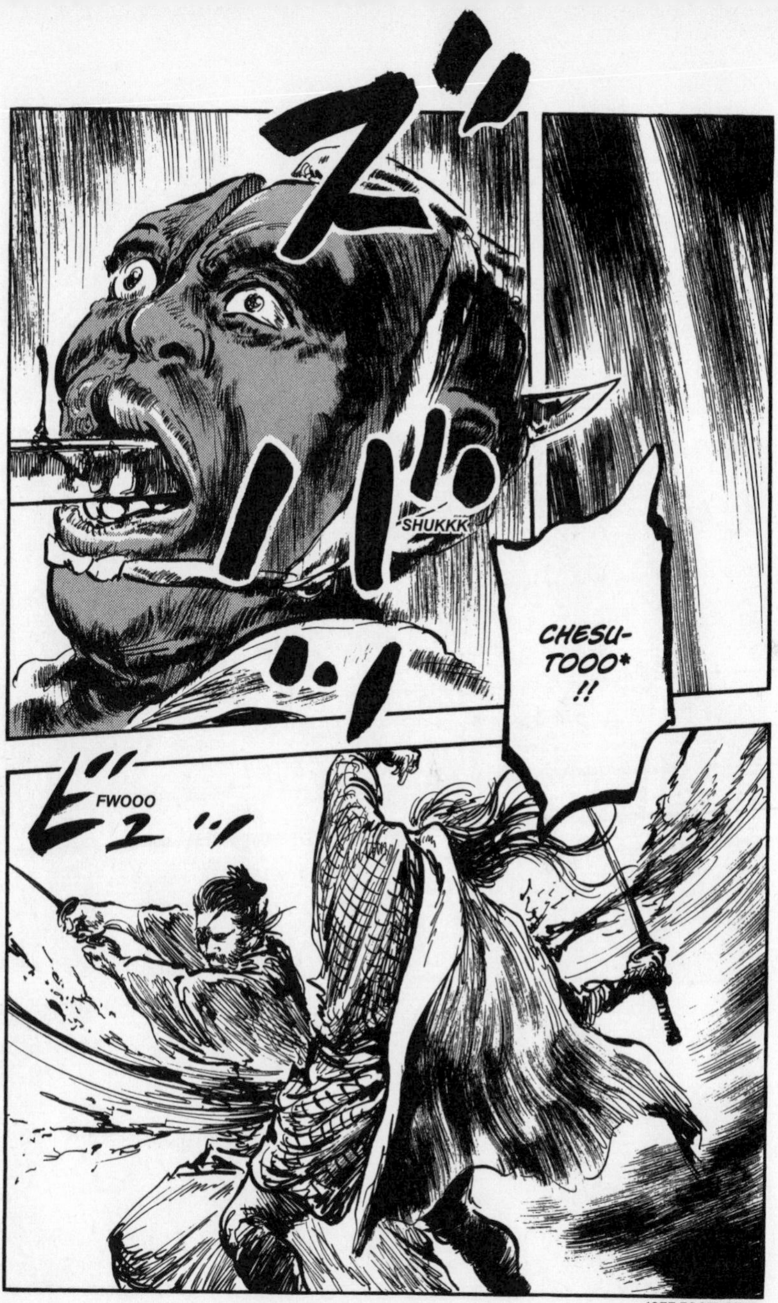

CHESU-TOOO* !!
SHUKKK
FWOOO

*SEE FOOTNOTES.

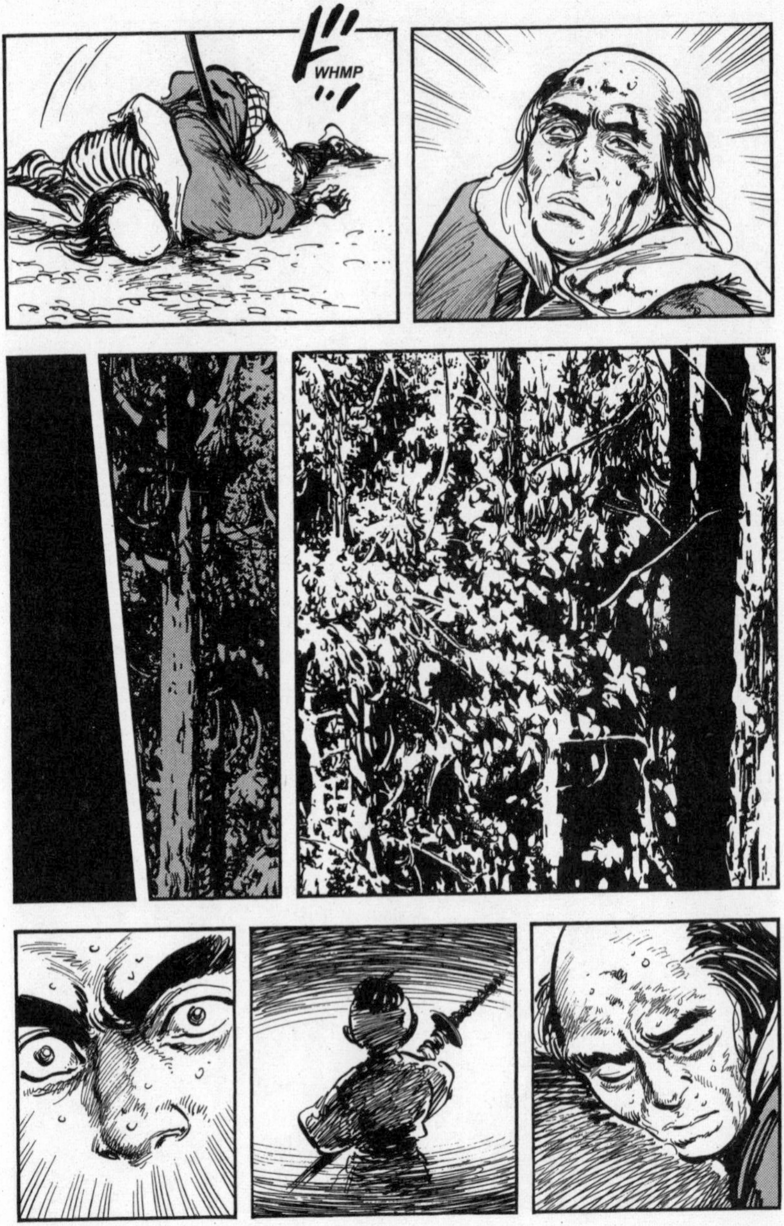
WHMP

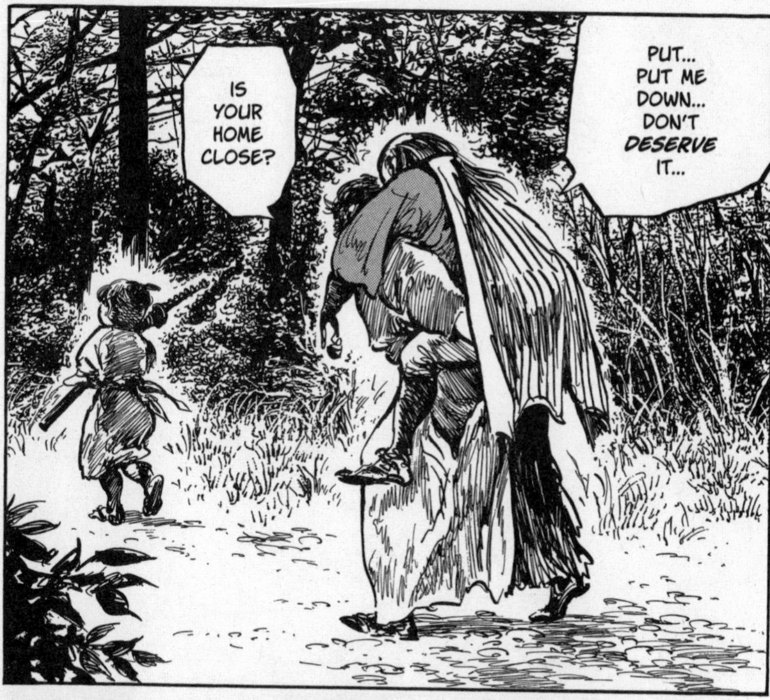
PUT... PUT ME DOWN... DON'T *DESERVE* IT...
IS YOUR HOME CLOSE?

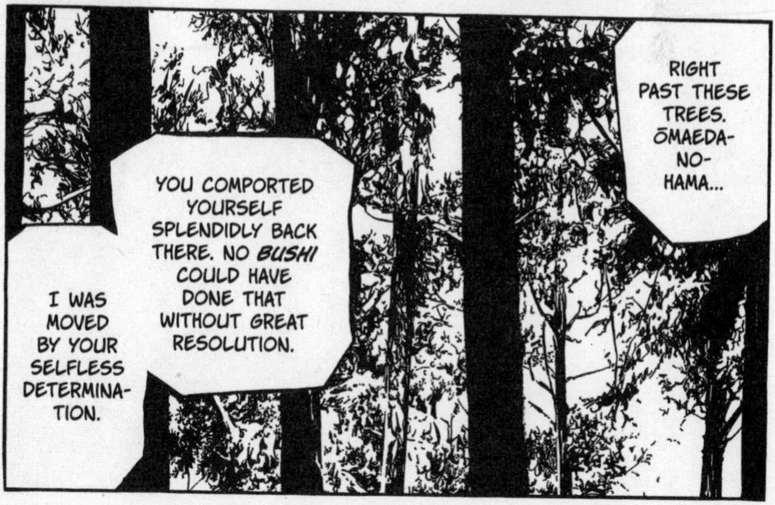
RIGHT PAST THESE TREES. ŌMAEDA-NO-HAMA...
YOU COMPORTED YOURSELF SPLENDIDLY BACK THERE. NO *BUSHI* COULD HAVE DONE THAT WITHOUT GREAT RESOLUTION.
I WAS MOVED BY YOUR SELFLESS DETERMINATION.

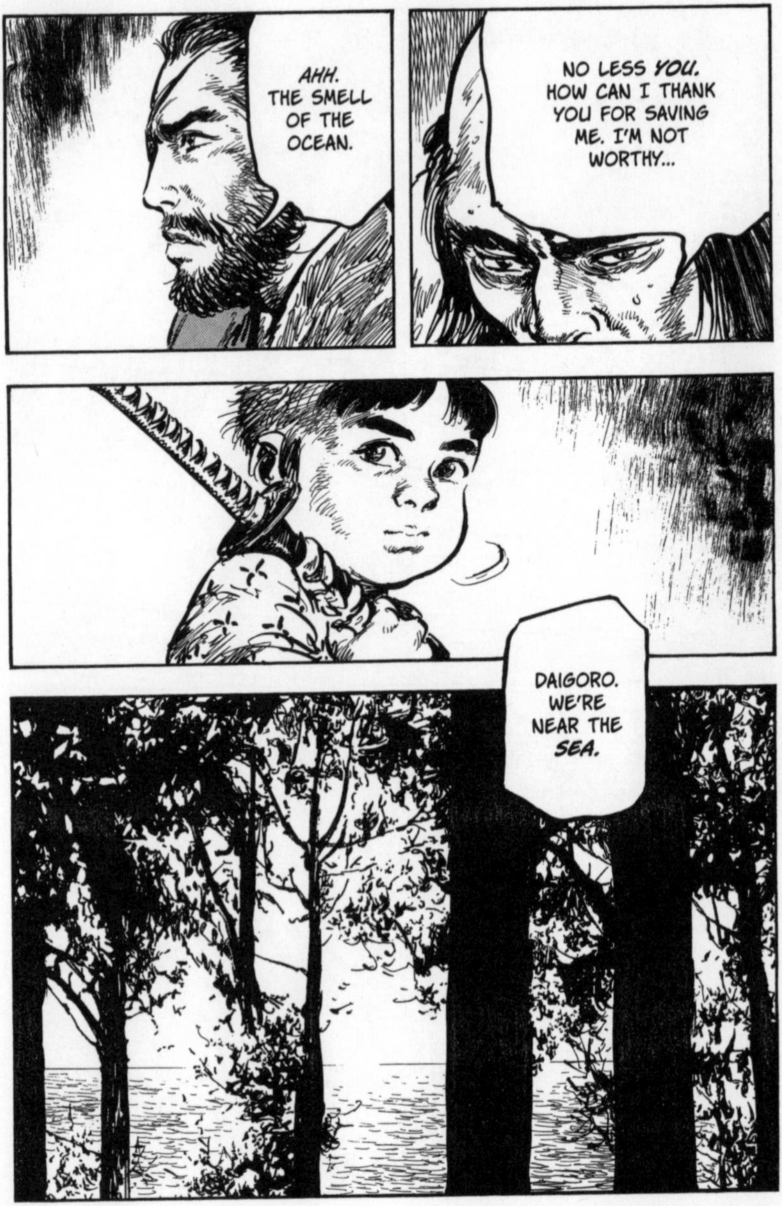
NO LESS YOU. HOW CAN I THANK YOU FOR SAVING ME. I'M NOT WORTHY...
AHH. THE SMELL OF THE OCEAN.
DAIGORO. WE'RE NEAR THE SEA.

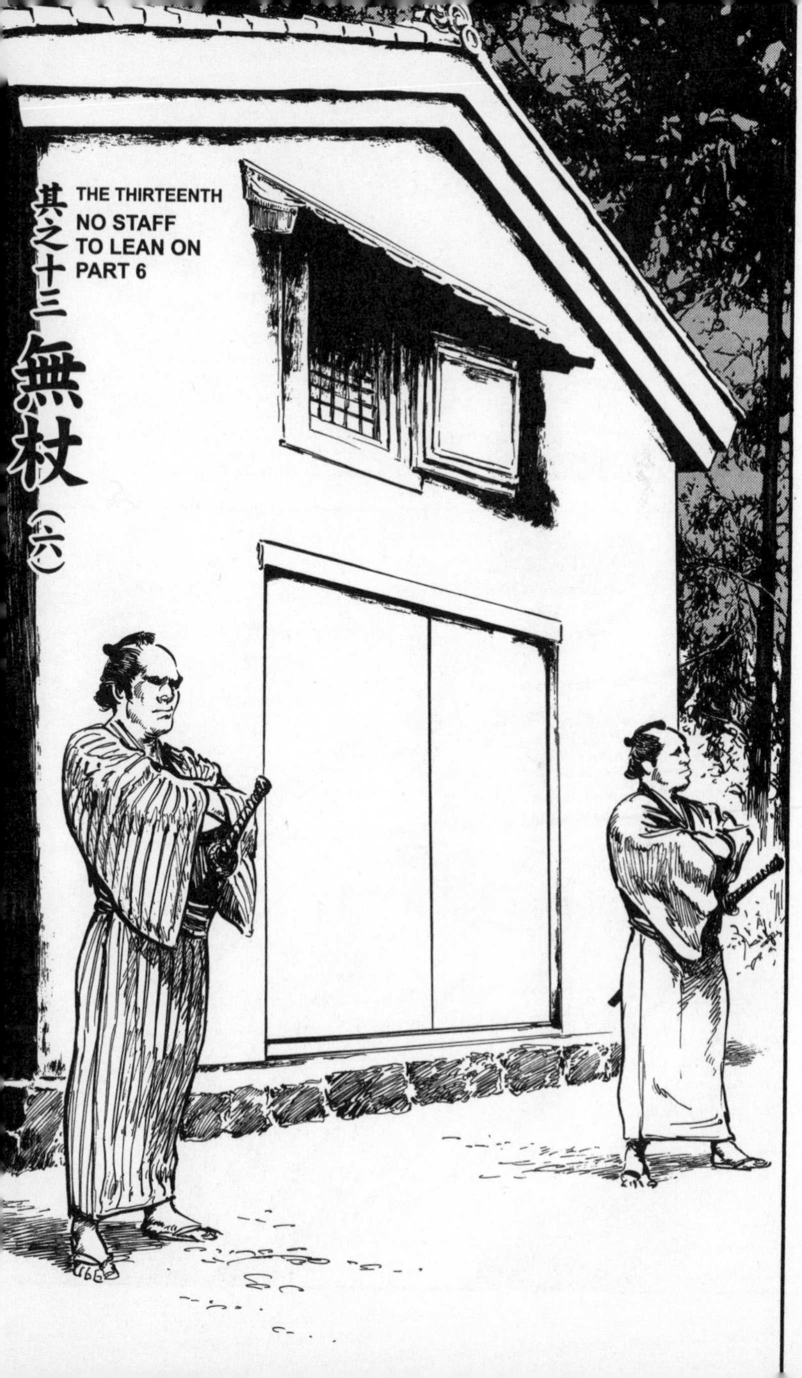
其之十三
THE THIRTEENTH
NO STAFF
TO LEAN ON
PART 6
無杖（六）

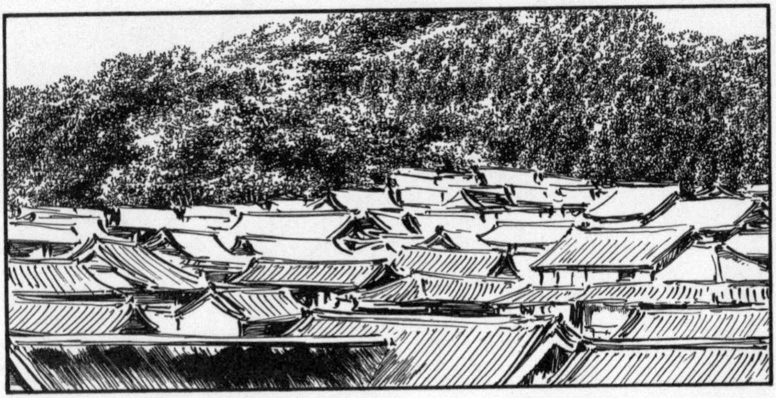

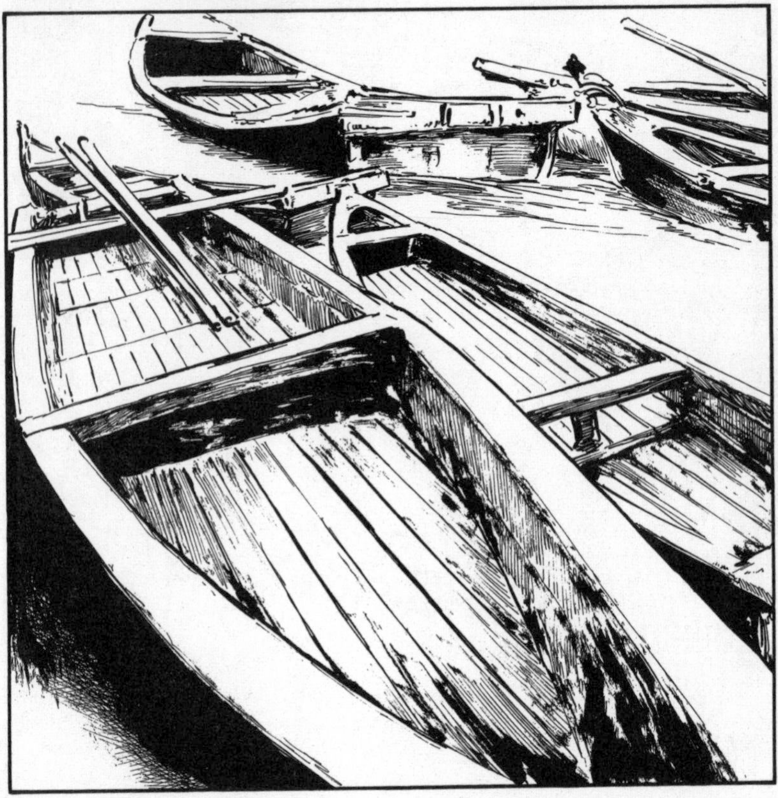

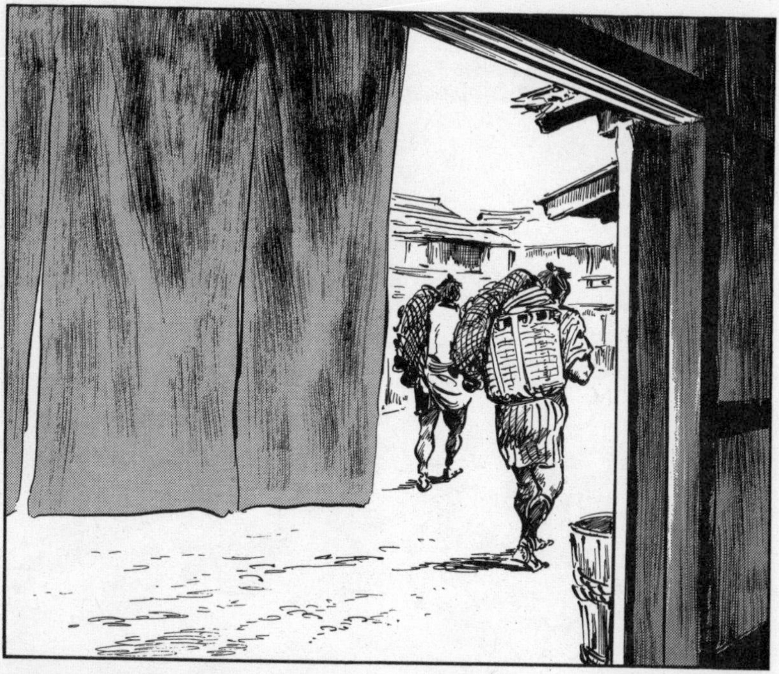

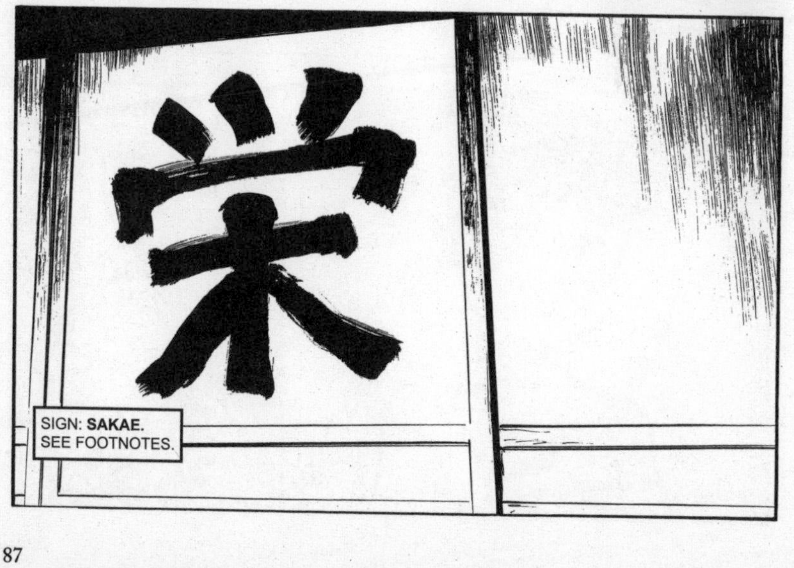
栄
SIGN: SAKAE.
SEE FOOTNOTES.

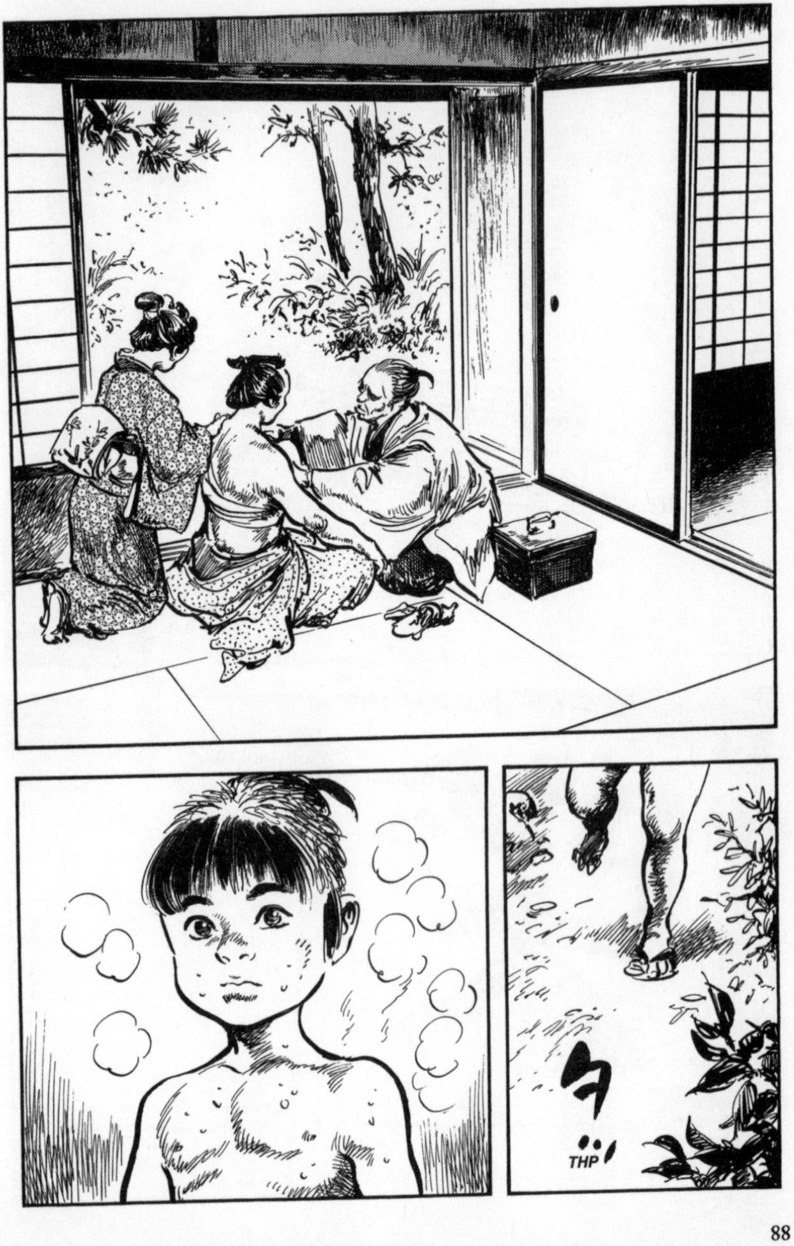
THP

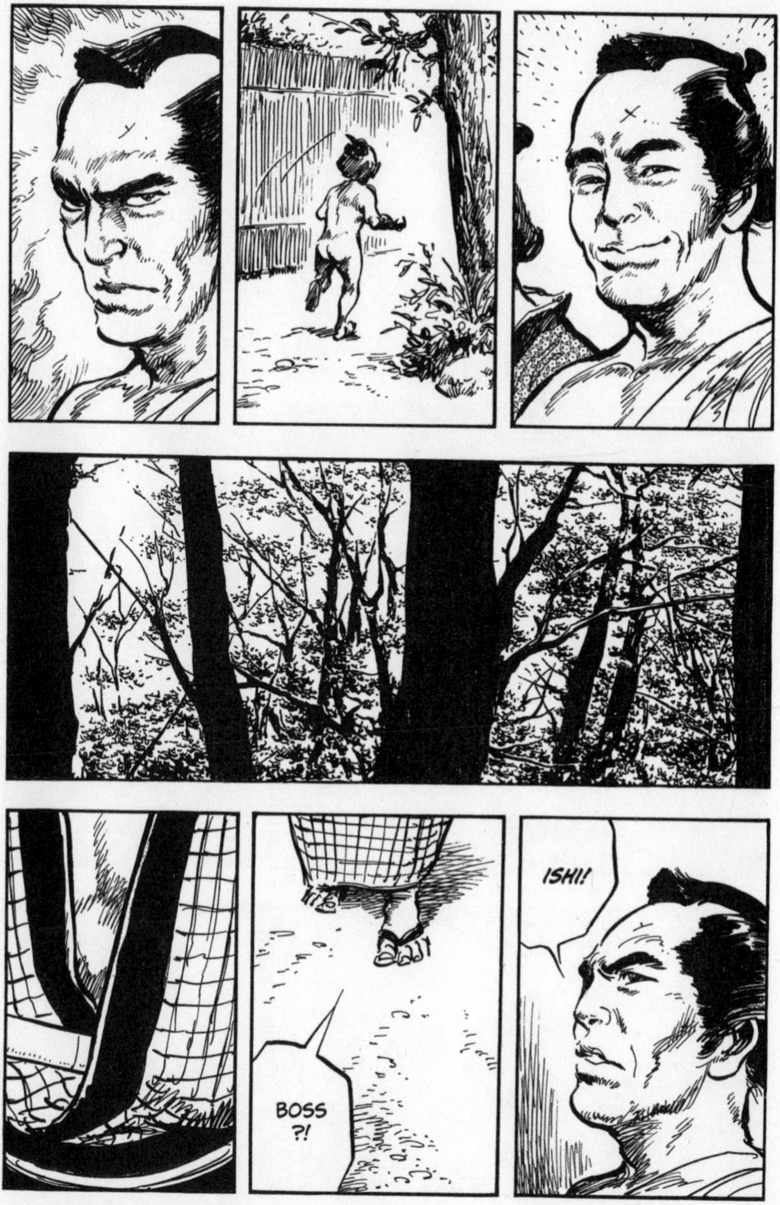
ISHI!
BOSS ?!

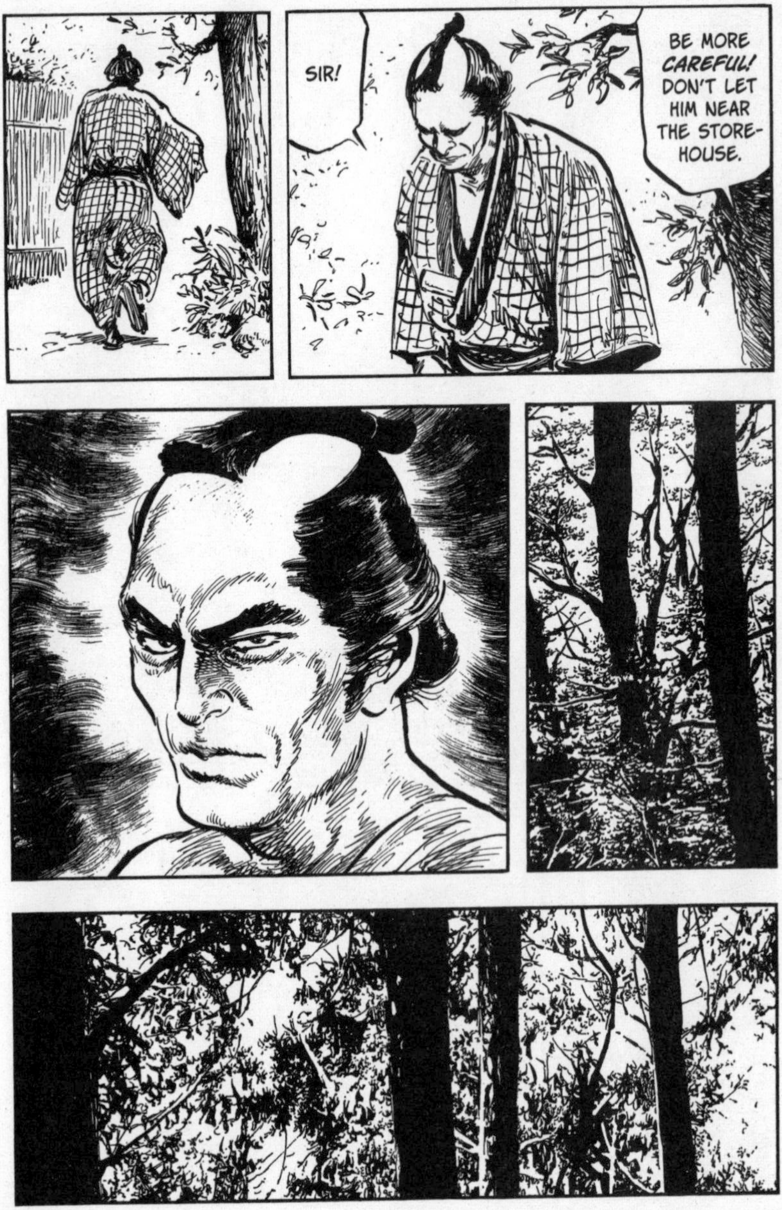
BE MORE *CAREFUL!* DON'T LET HIM NEAR THE STORE-HOUSE.
SIR!

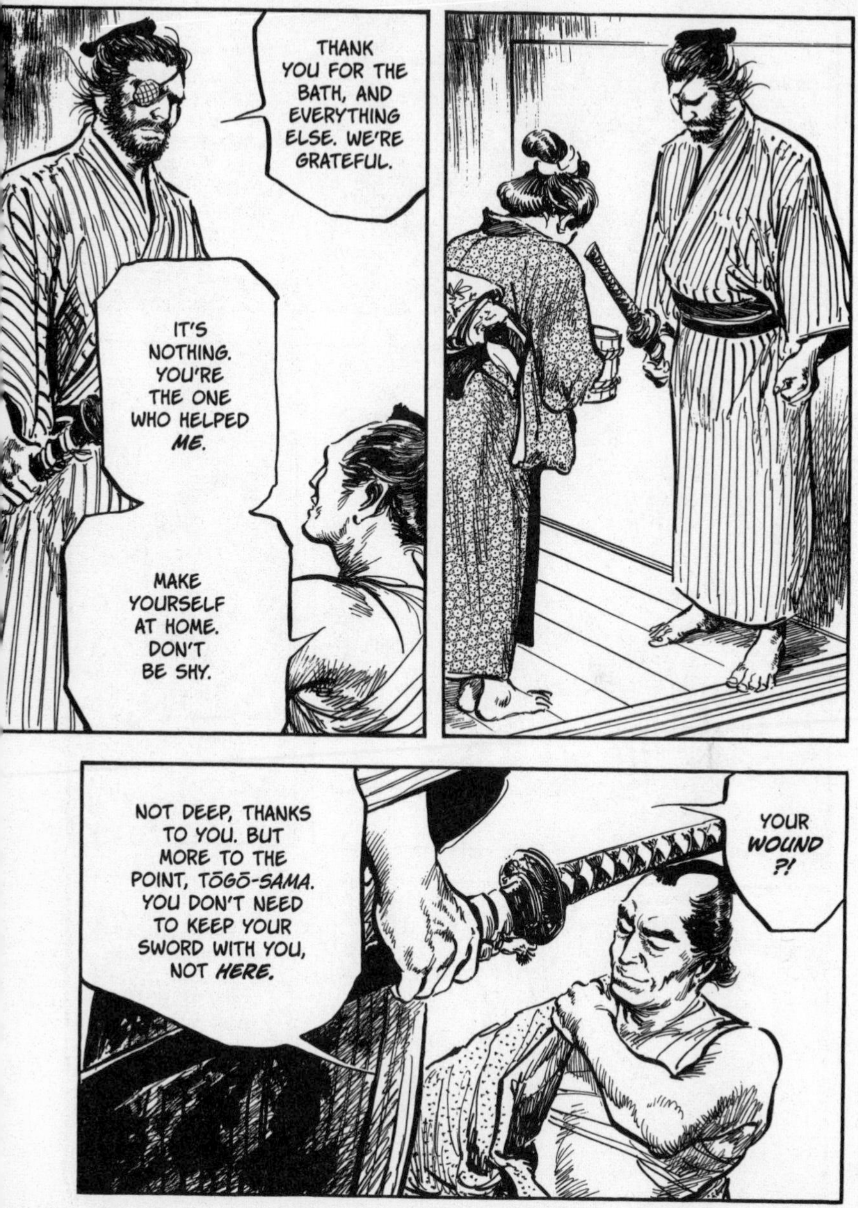
THANK YOU FOR THE BATH, AND EVERYTHING ELSE. WE'RE GRATEFUL.
IT'S NOTHING. YOU'RE THE ONE WHO HELPED *ME.*
MAKE YOURSELF AT HOME. DON'T BE SHY.
YOUR *WOUND* ?!
NOT DEEP, THANKS TO YOU. BUT MORE TO THE POINT, TŌGŌ-*SAMA.* YOU DON'T NEED TO KEEP YOUR SWORD WITH YOU, NOT *HERE.*

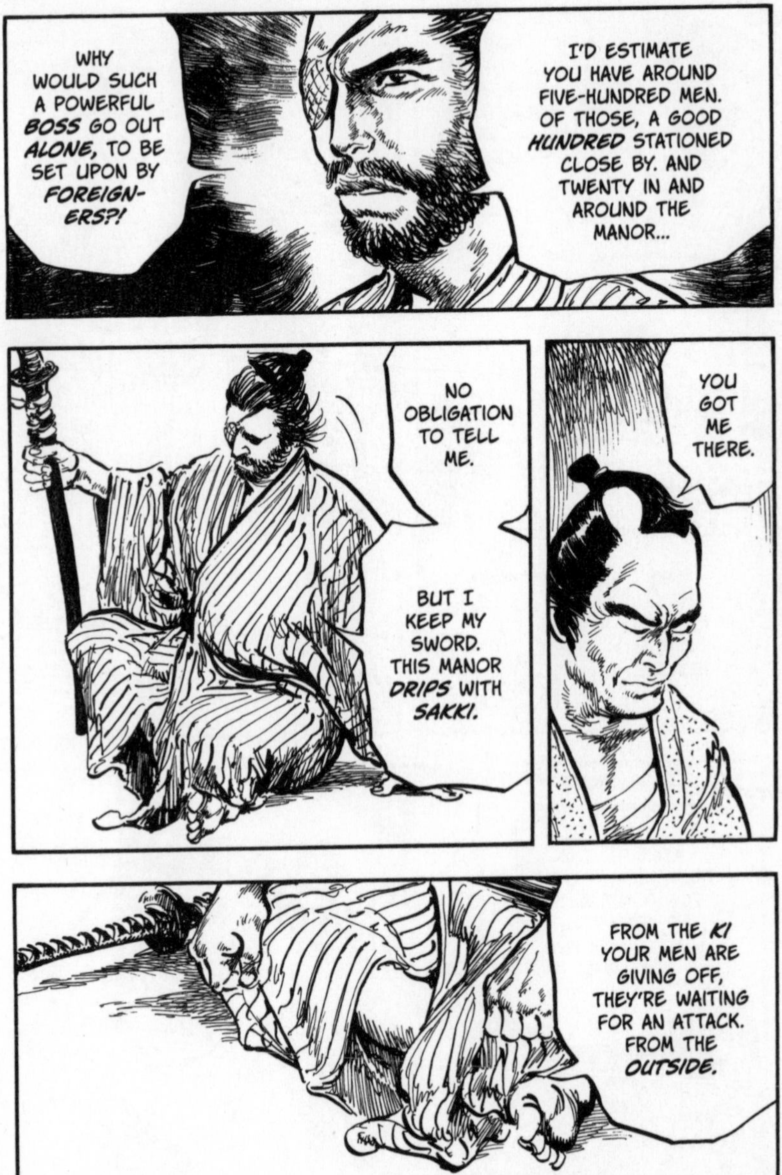
I'D ESTIMATE YOU HAVE AROUND FIVE-HUNDRED MEN. OF THOSE, A GOOD *HUNDRED* STATIONED CLOSE BY. AND TWENTY IN AND AROUND THE MANOR...
WHY WOULD SUCH A POWERFUL *BOSS* GO OUT *ALONE,* TO BE SET UPON BY *FOREIGNERS?!*
YOU GOT ME THERE.
NO OBLIGATION TO TELL ME.
BUT I KEEP MY SWORD. THIS MANOR *DRIPS* WITH *SAKKI.*
FROM THE *KI* YOUR MEN ARE GIVING OFF, THEY'RE WAITING FOR AN ATTACK. FROM THE *OUTSIDE.*

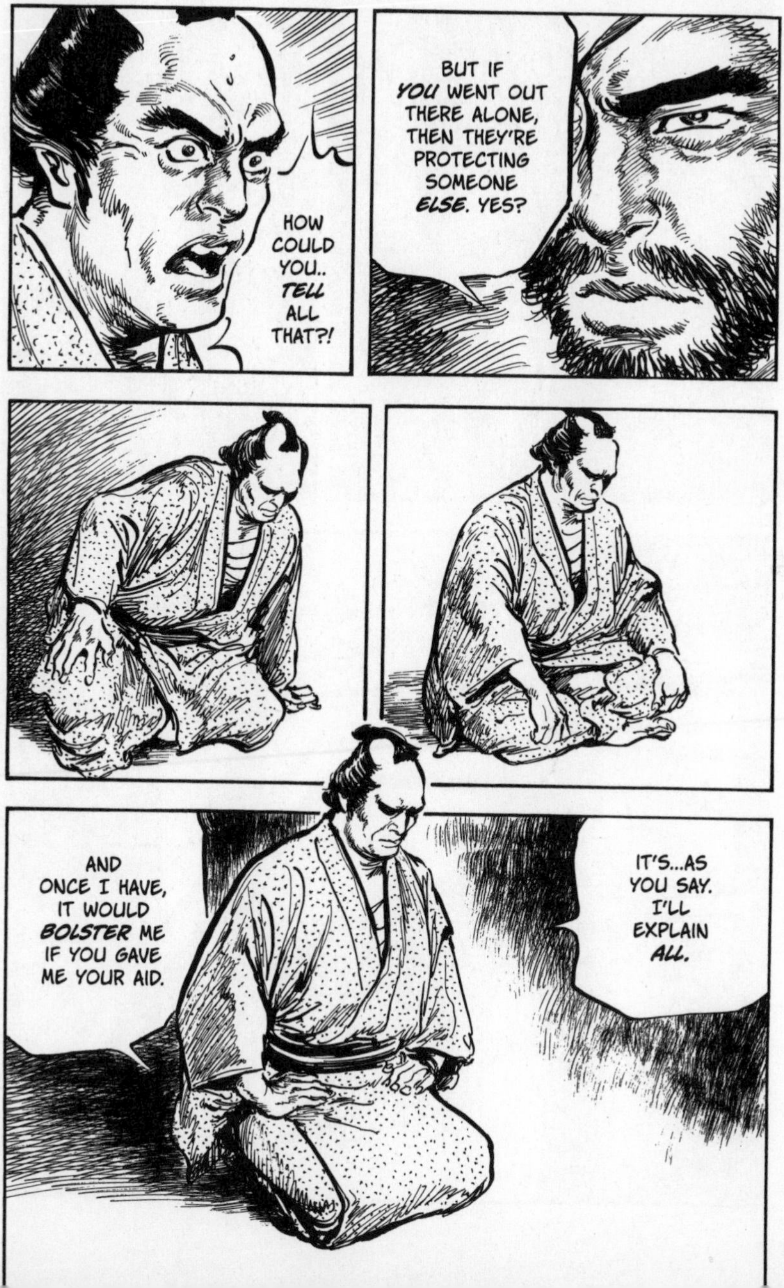
BUT IF YOU WENT OUT THERE ALONE, THEN THEY'RE PROTECTING SOMEONE ELSE. YES?
HOW COULD YOU.. TELL ALL THAT?!
IT'S...AS YOU SAY. I'LL EXPLAIN ALL.
AND ONCE I HAVE, IT WOULD BOLSTER ME IF YOU GAVE ME YOUR AID.

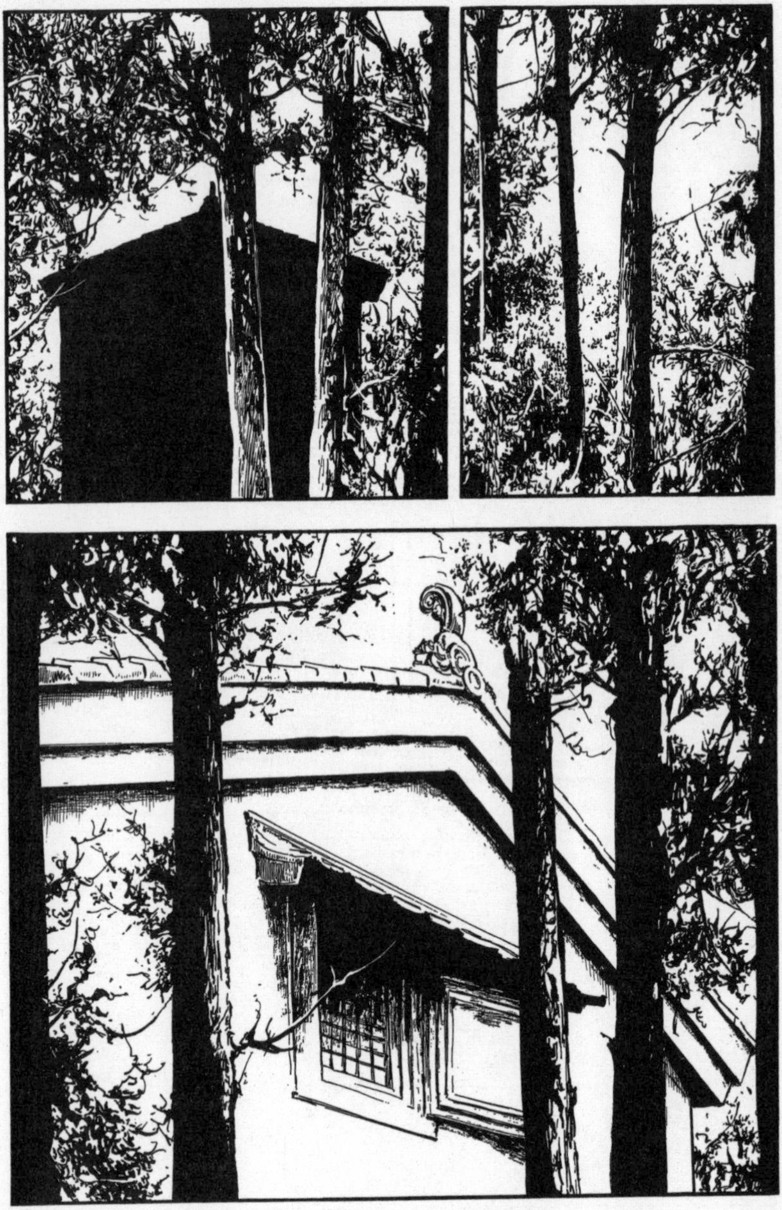

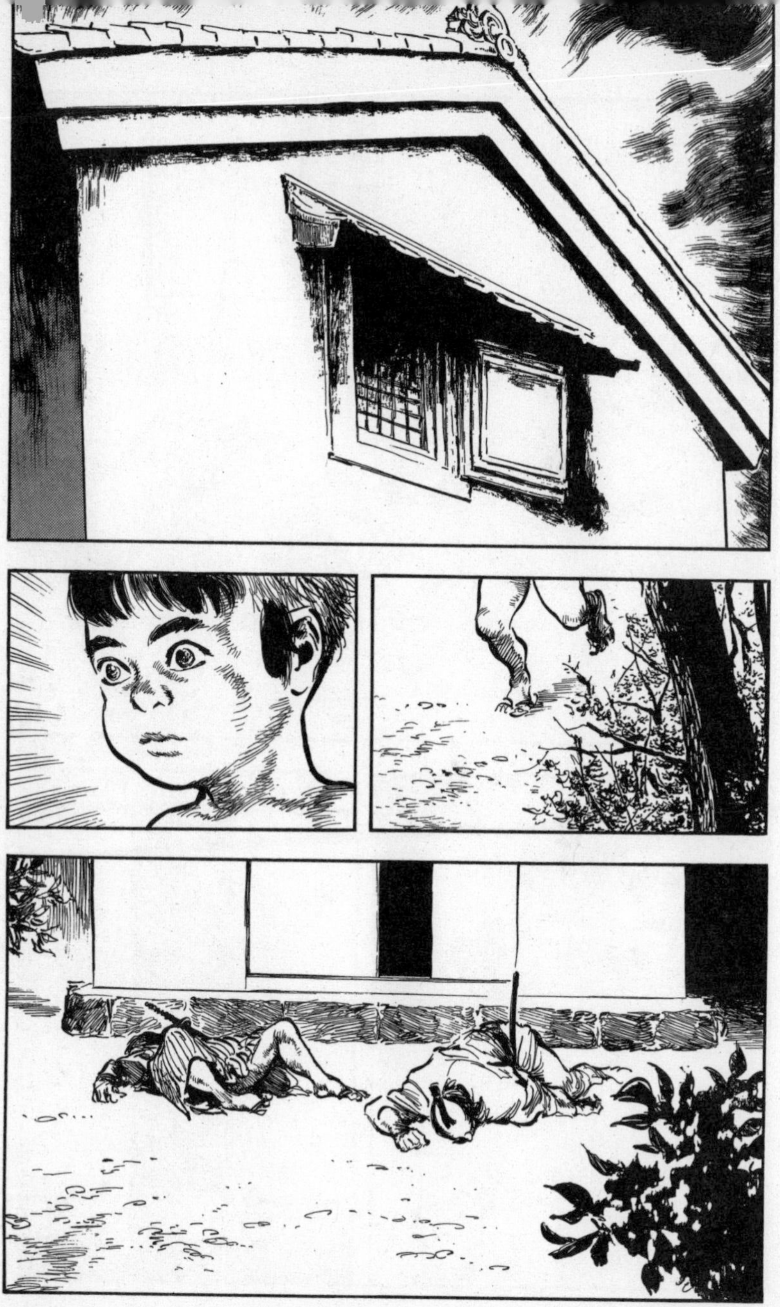

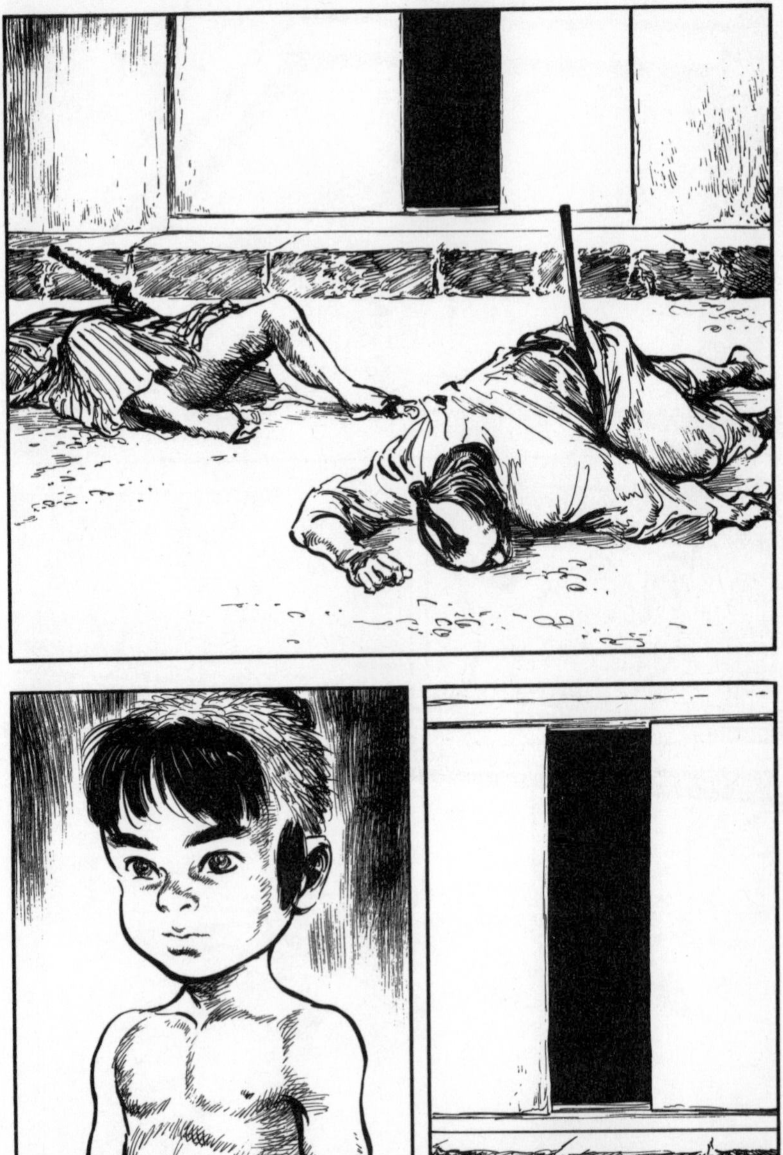

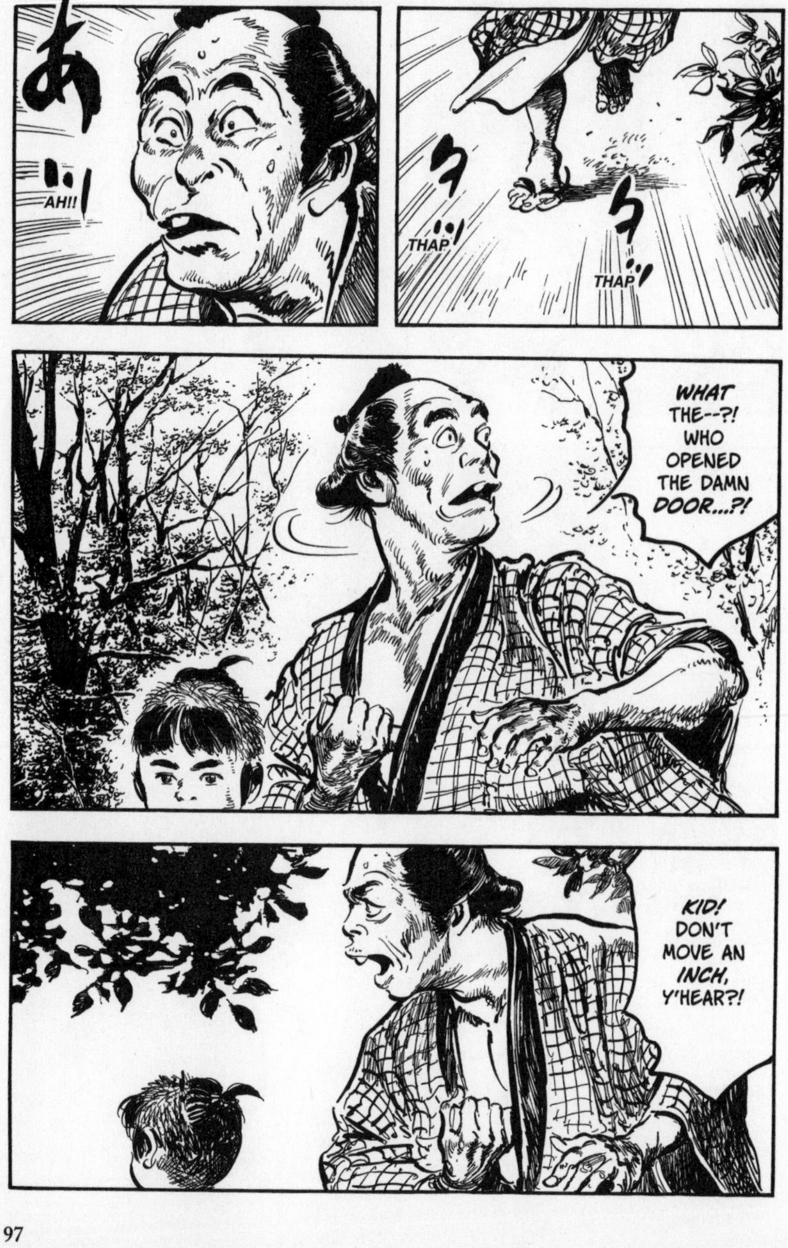
THAP
THAP
AH!!
WHAT THE--?! WHO OPENED THE DAMN DOOR...?!
KID! DON'T MOVE AN INCH, Y'HEAR?!

BOSS! BOSS !!
SHE FLEW THE COOP !!

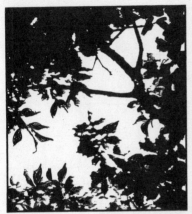

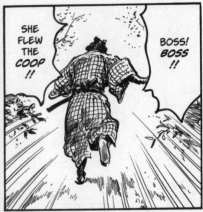

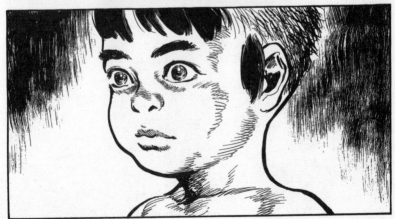

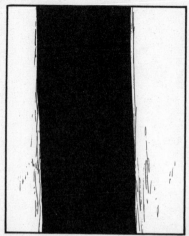

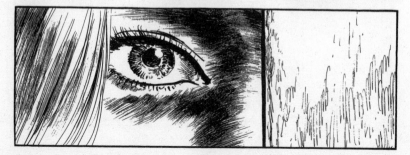

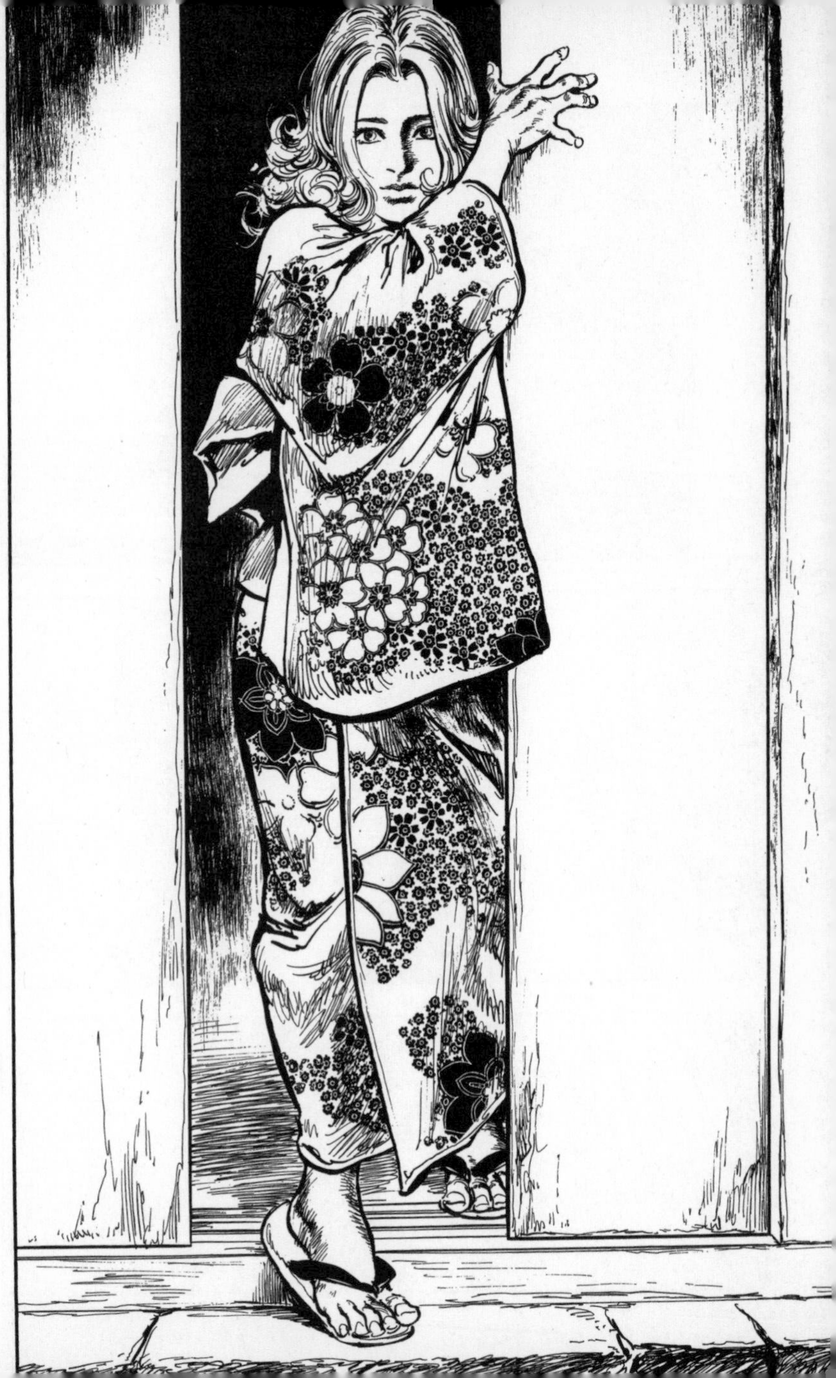

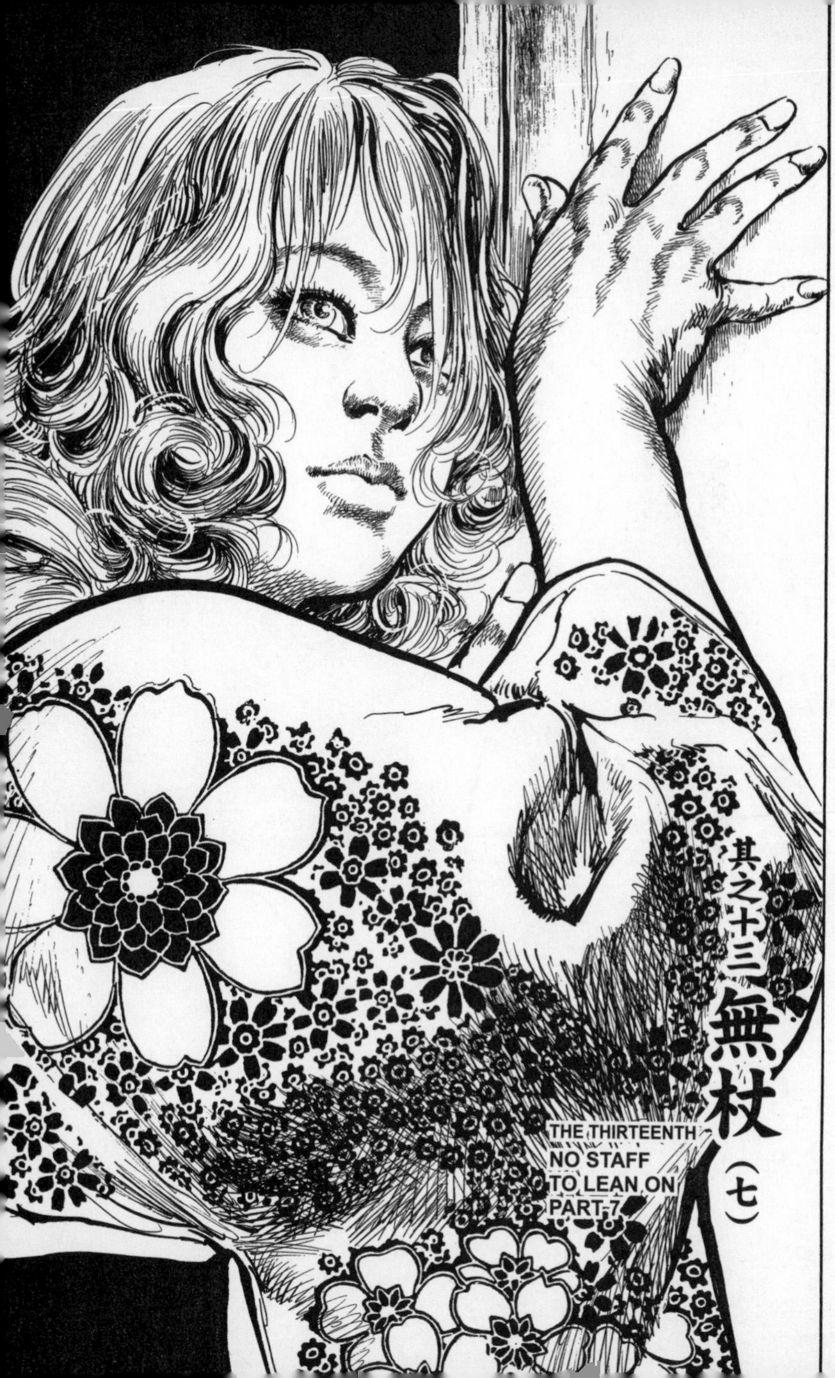
其之十三 無杖（七）
THE THIRTEENTH
NO STAFF
TO LEAN ON
PART 7

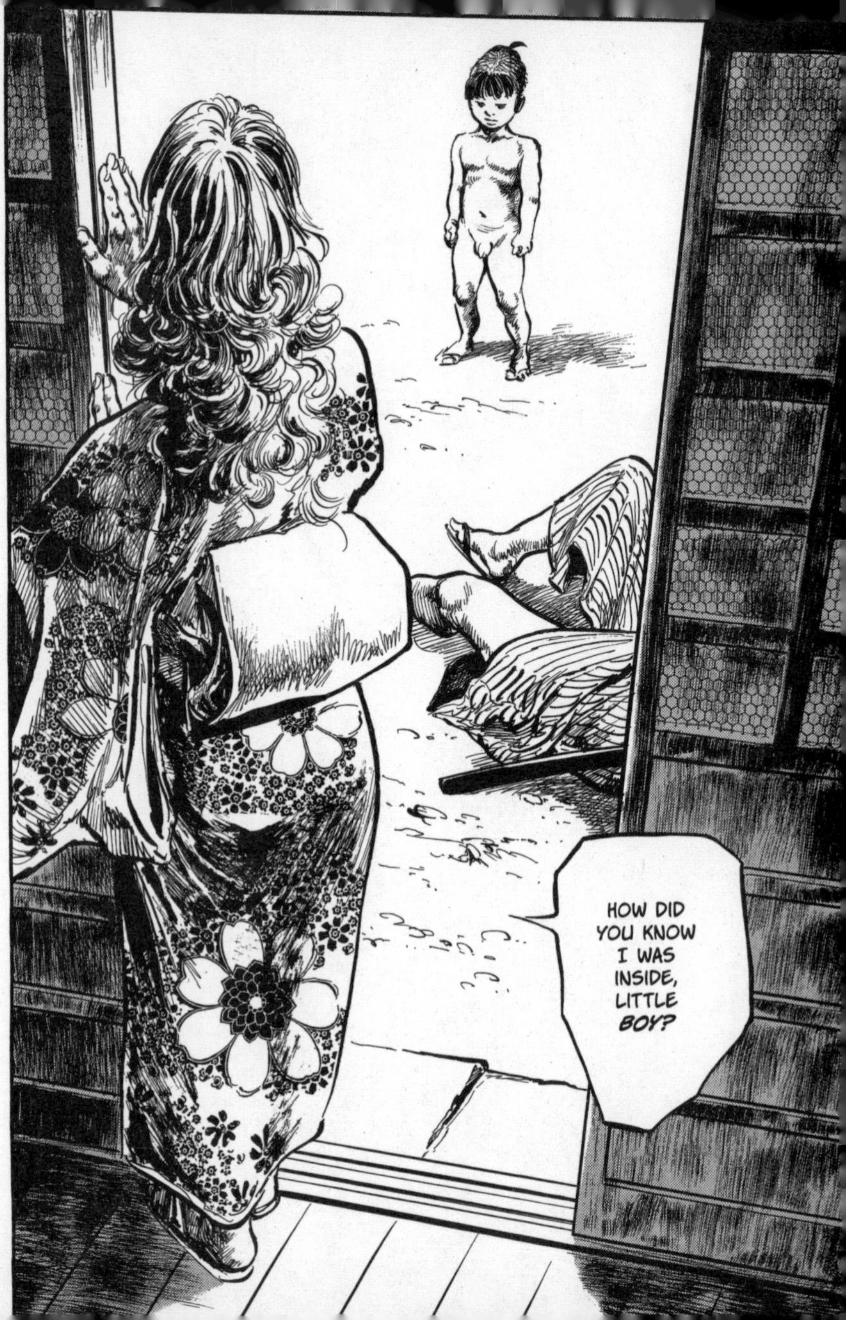
HOW DID YOU KNOW I WAS INSIDE, LITTLE *BOY?*

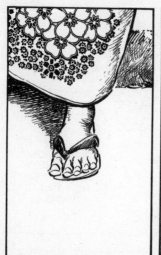

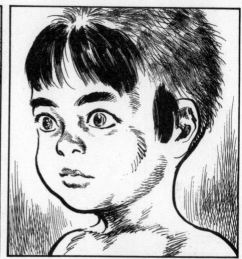

SHKK

103

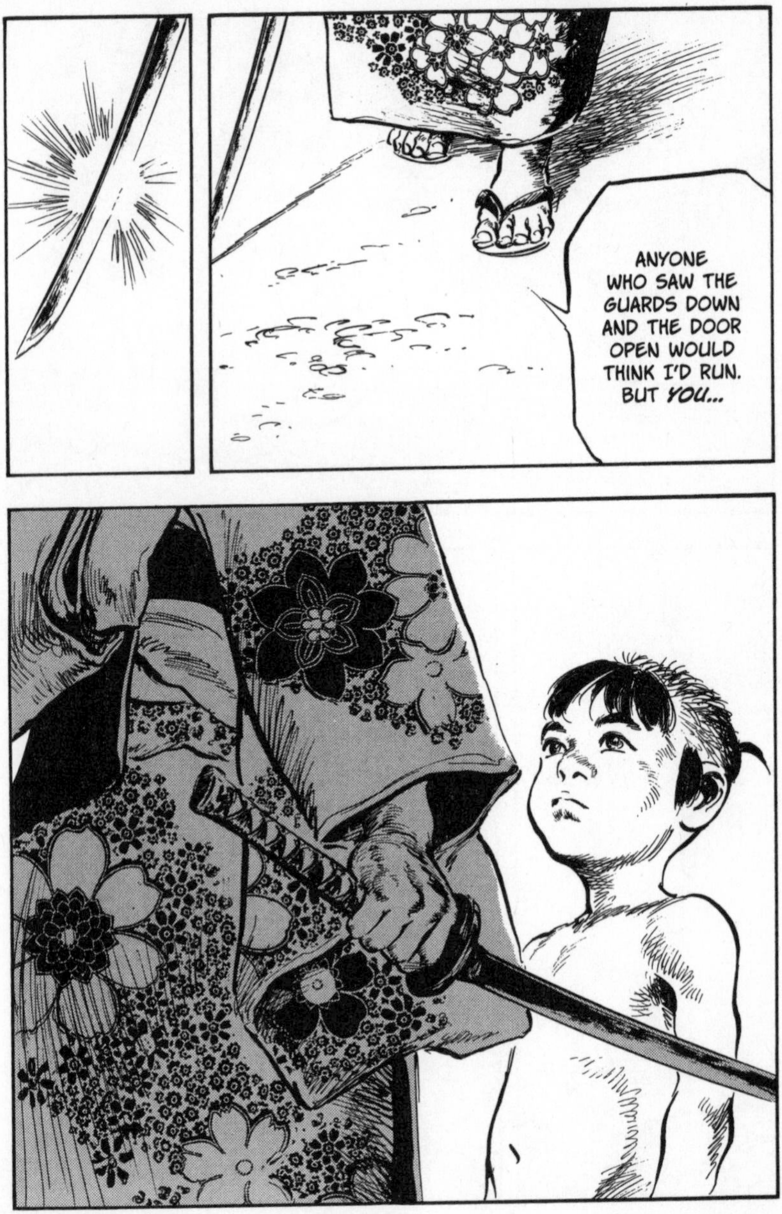
ANYONE WHO SAW THE GUARDS DOWN AND THE DOOR OPEN WOULD THINK I'D RUN. BUT *YOU*...

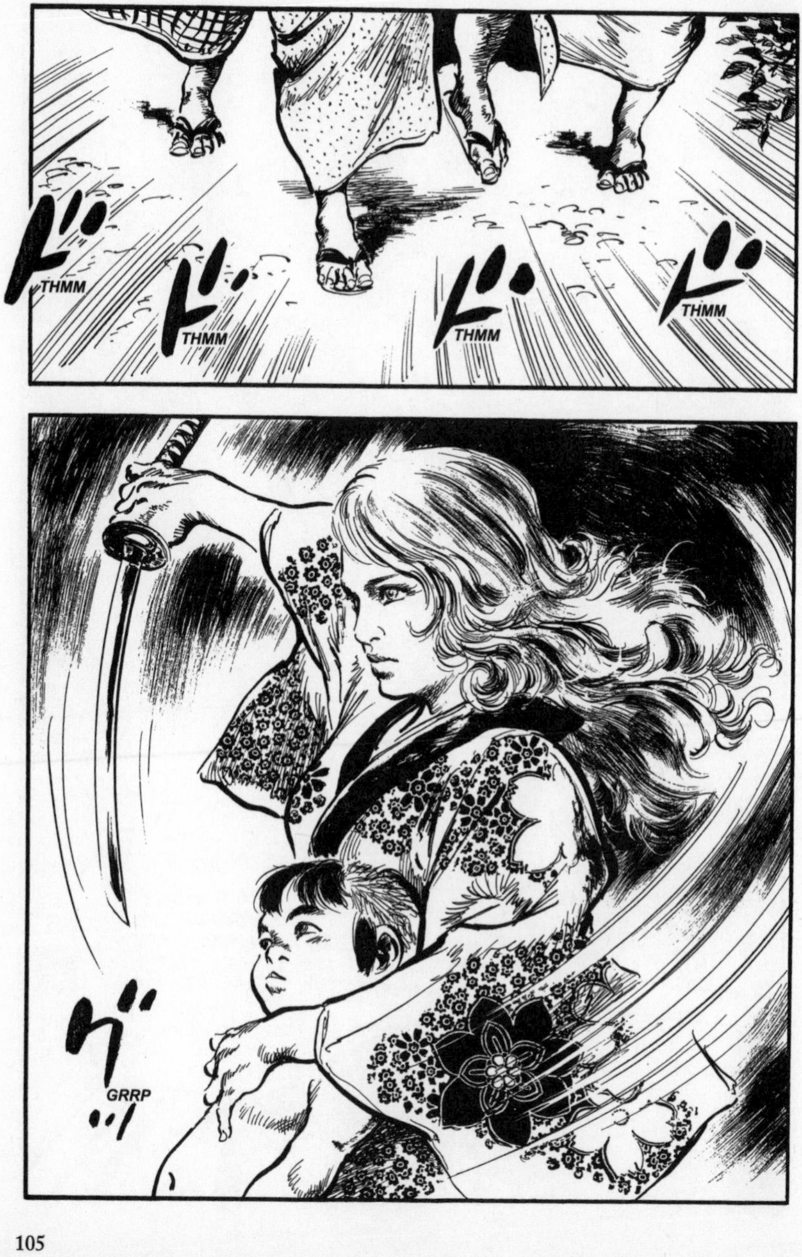
ド
THMM
ド
THMM
ド
THMM
ド
THMM
グッ
GRRP

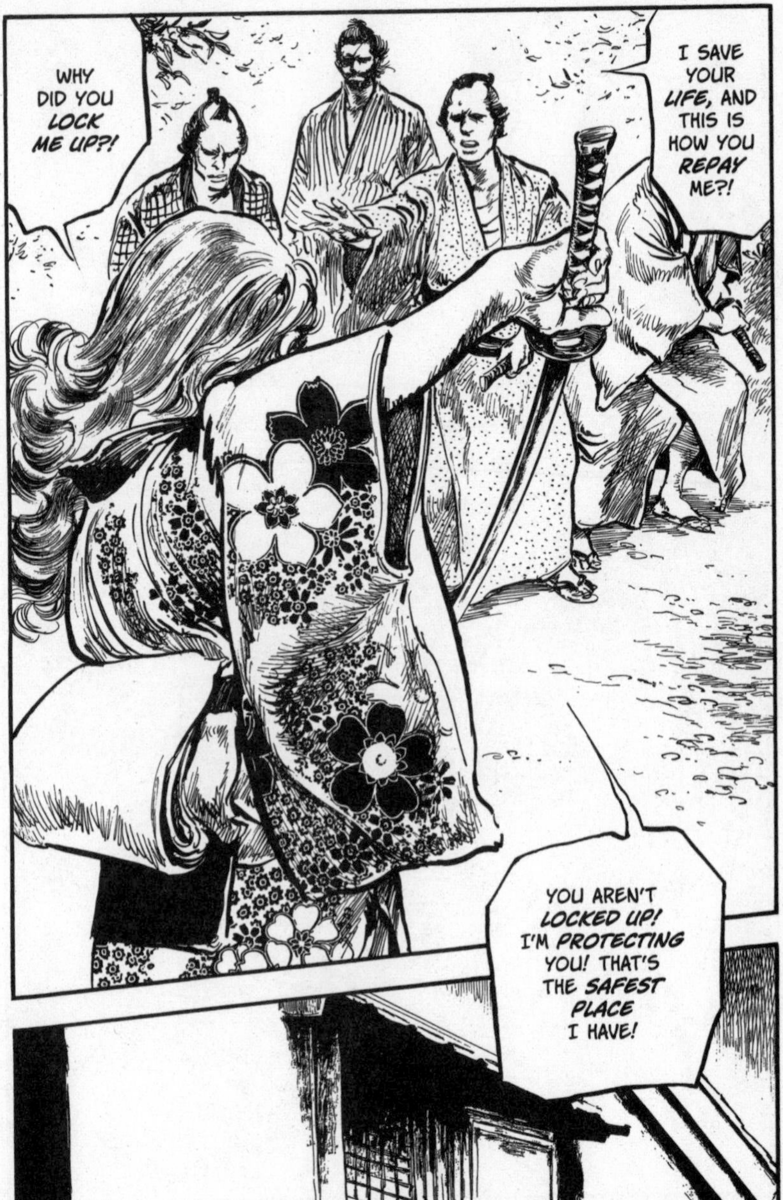
I SAVE YOUR LIFE, AND THIS IS HOW YOU REPAY ME?!
WHY DID YOU LOCK ME UP?!
YOU AREN'T LOCKED UP! I'M PROTECTING YOU! THAT'S THE SAFEST PLACE I HAVE!

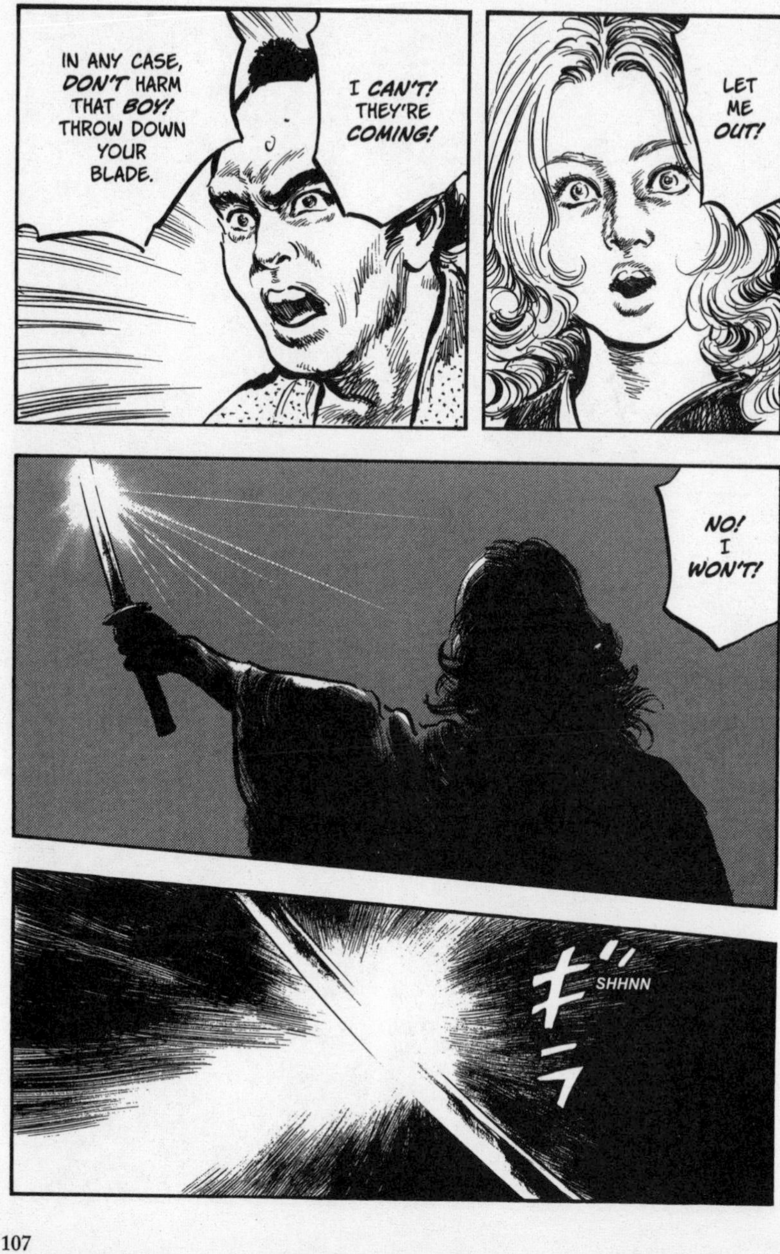
LET ME OUT!
I CAN'T! THEY'RE COMING!
IN ANY CASE, DON'T HARM THAT BOY! THROW DOWN YOUR BLADE.
NO! I WON'T!
SHHNN

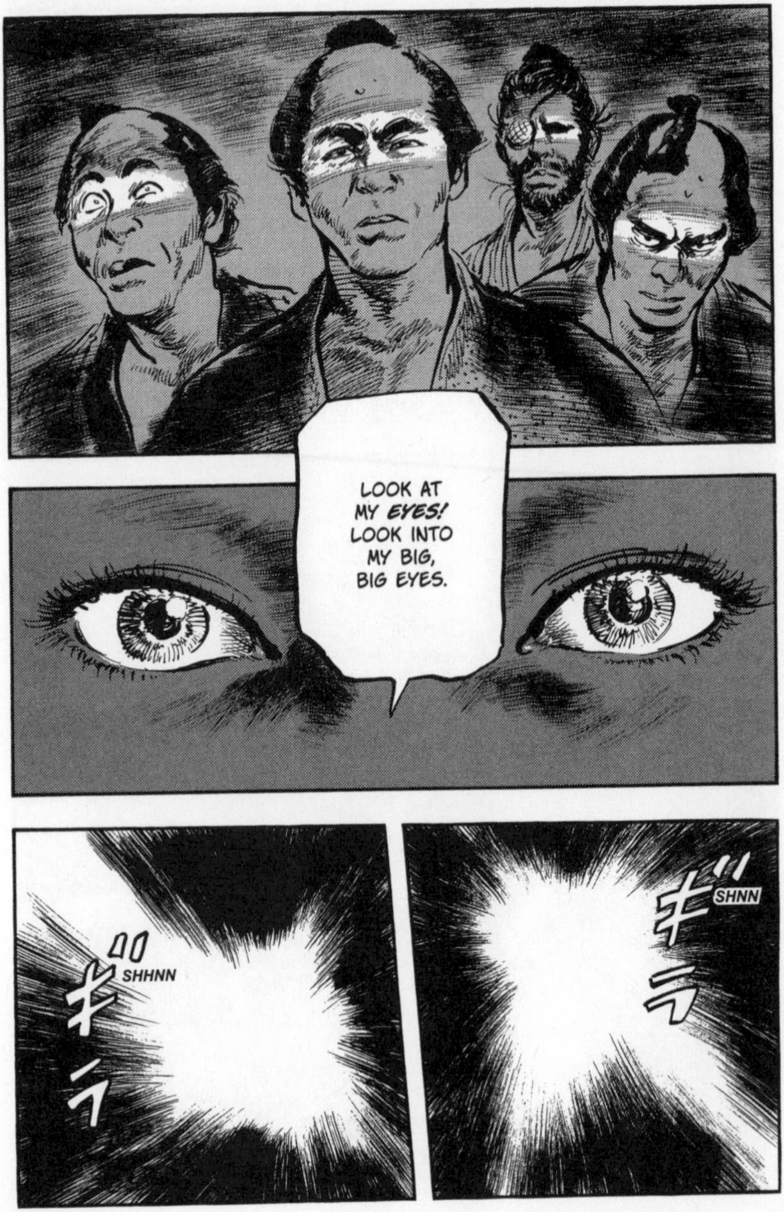
LOOK AT MY EYES! LOOK INTO MY BIG, BIG EYES.
ギラ
SHNN
ギラ
SHHNN

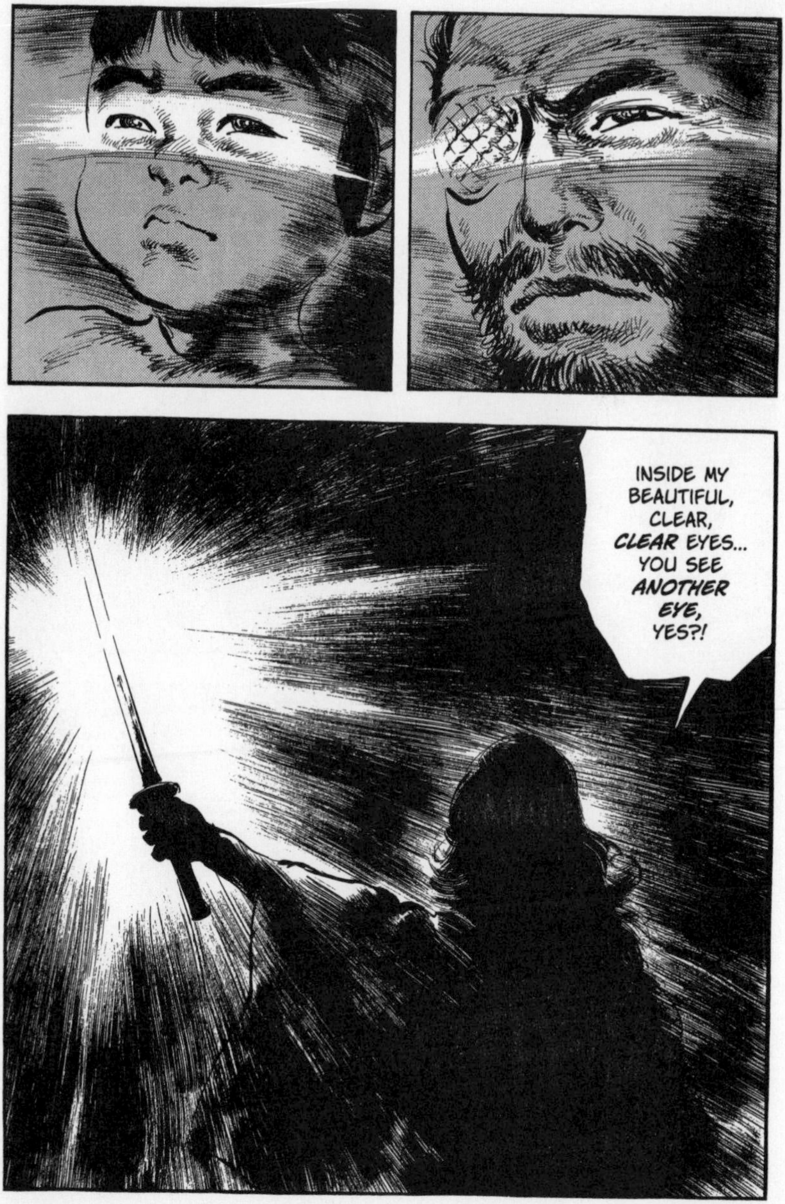
INSIDE MY BEAUTIFUL, CLEAR, *CLEAR* EYES... YOU SEE *ANOTHER EYE,* YES?!

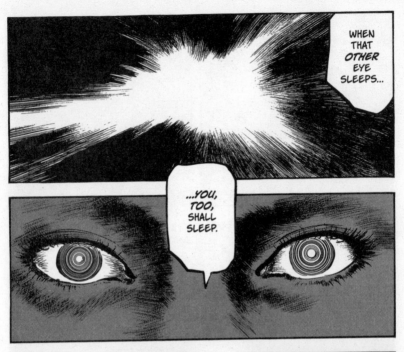

WHEN THAT *OTHER* EYE SLEEPS...

...*YOU,* *TOO,* SHALL SLEEP.

SLEEP...

SLEEP....

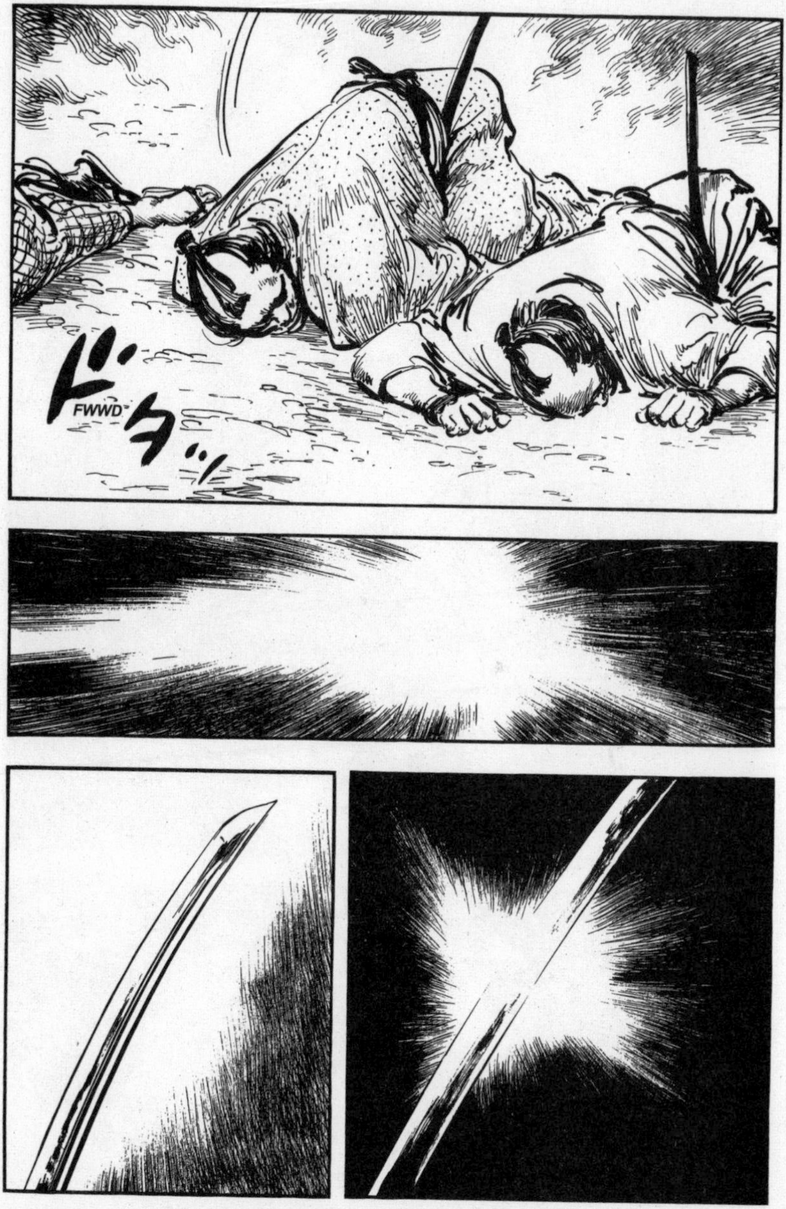
ドタッ
FWWD

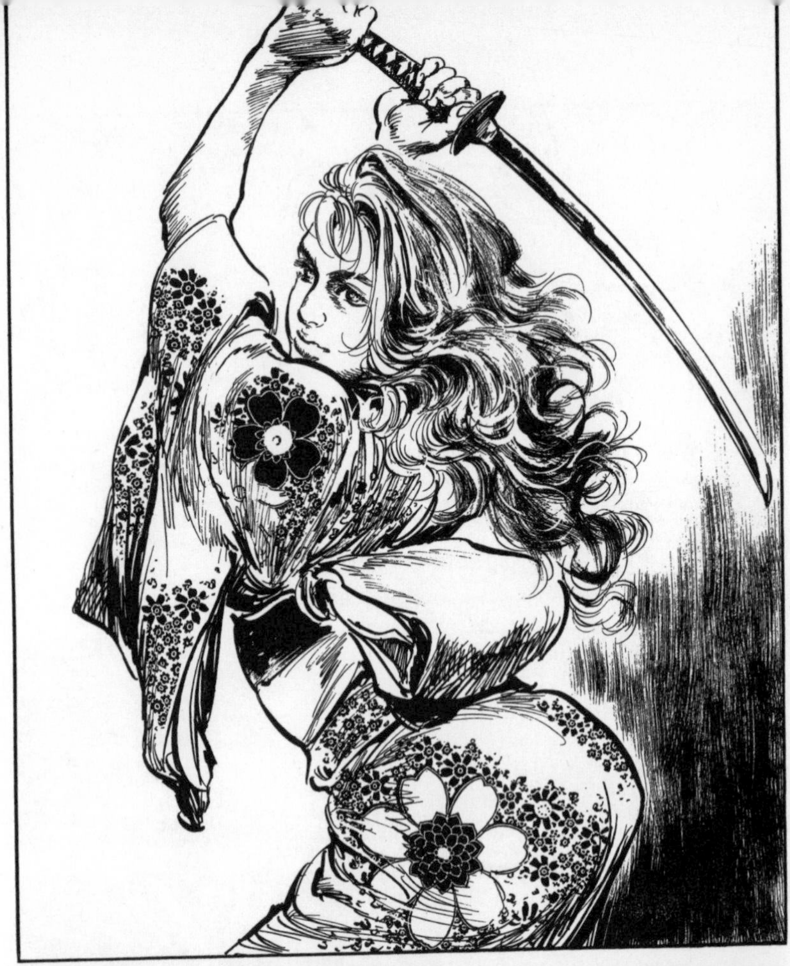

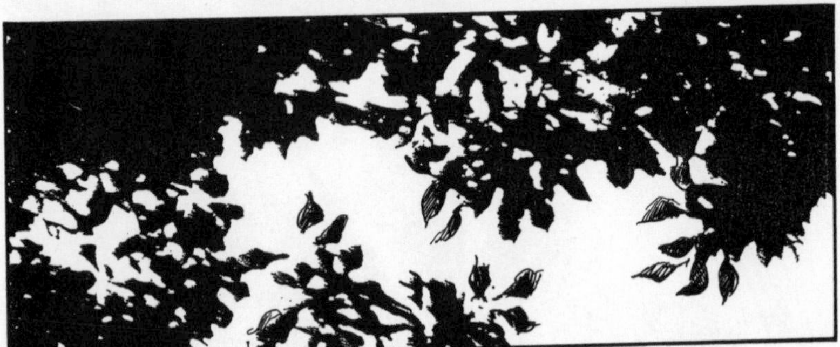

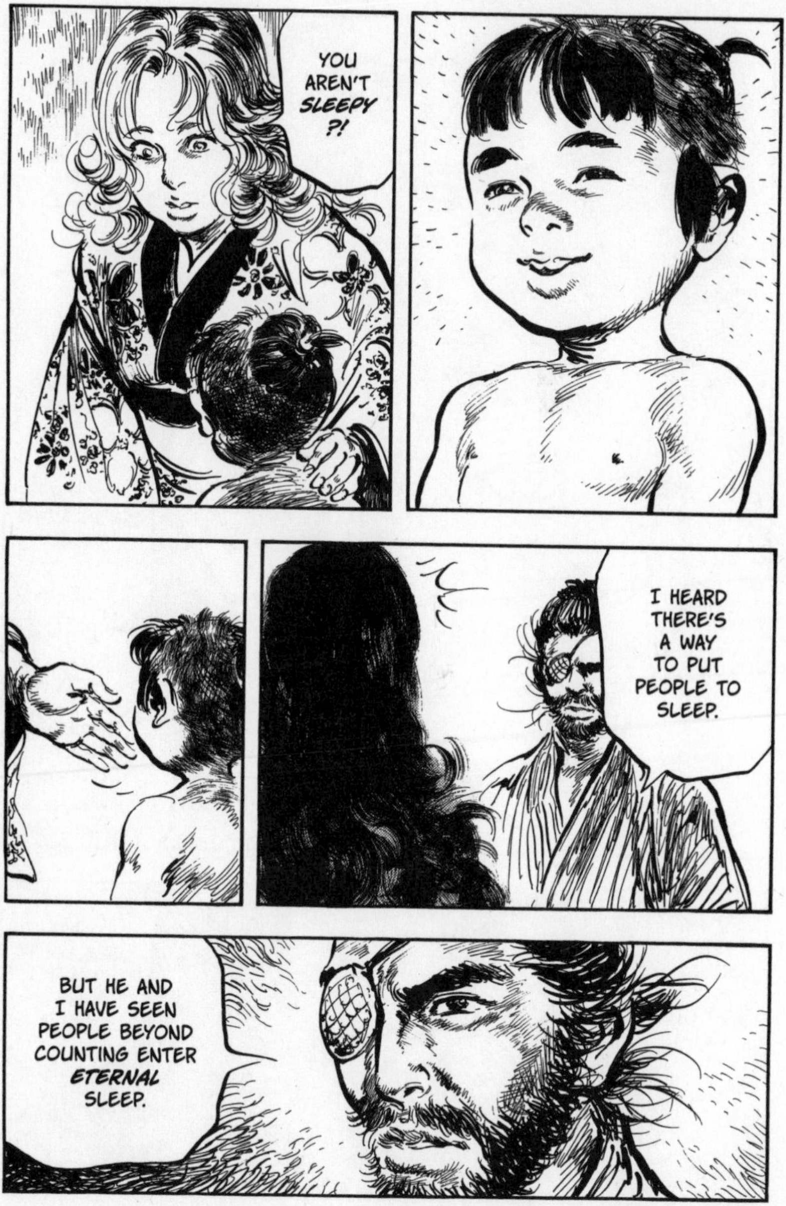
YOU AREN'T *SLEEPY* ?!
I HEARD THERE'S A WAY TO PUT PEOPLE TO SLEEP.
BUT HE AND I HAVE SEEN PEOPLE BEYOND COUNTING ENTER *ETERNAL* SLEEP.

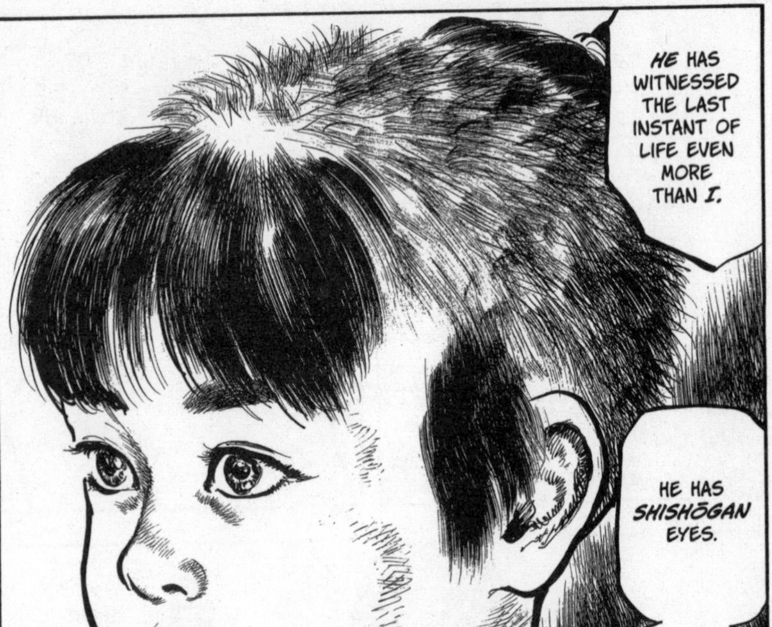
HE HAS WITNESSED THE LAST INSTANT OF LIFE EVEN MORE THAN *I*.
HE HAS *SHISHŌGAN* EYES.
KNOW THAT YOUR SKILLS CANNOT TOUCH US.

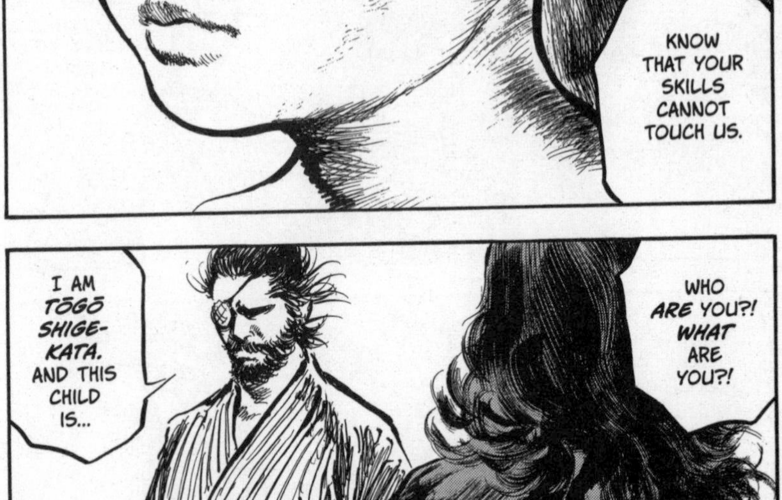
WHO *ARE* YOU?! *WHAT* ARE YOU?!
I AM *TŌGŌ SHIGE-KATA*. AND THIS CHILD IS...

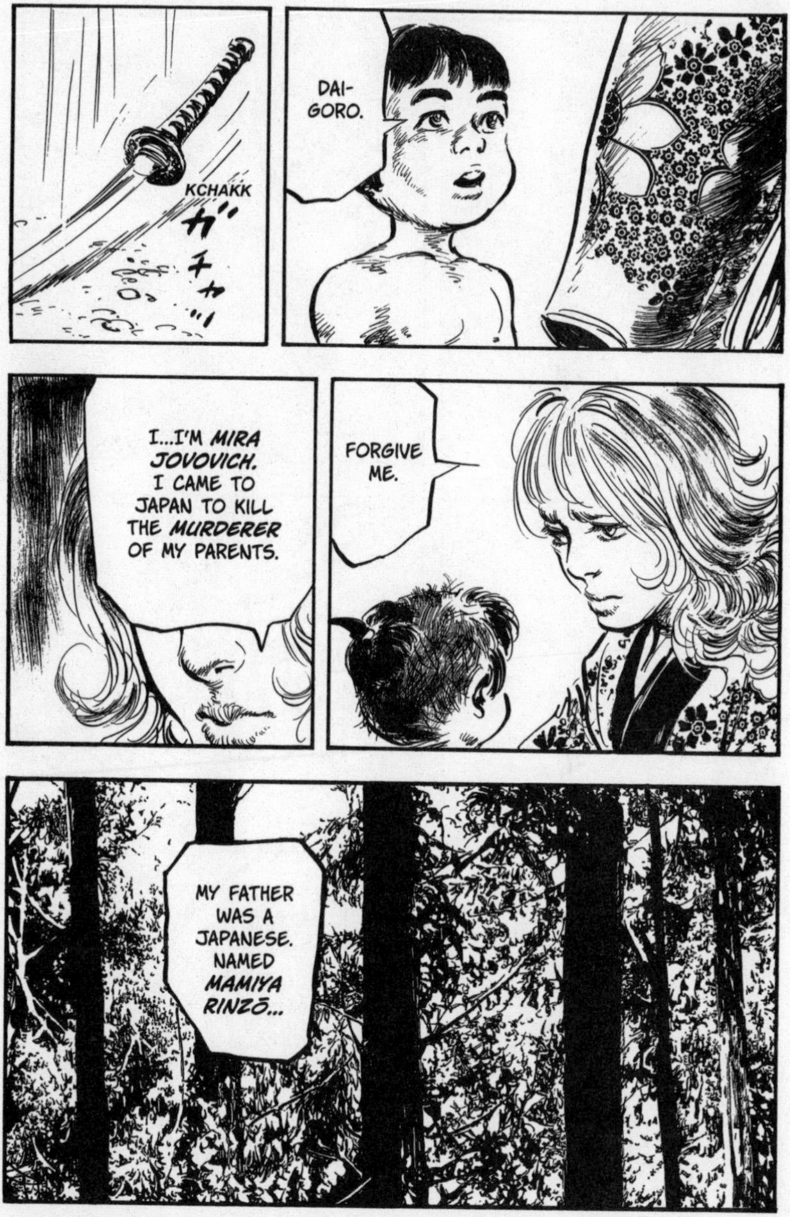
DAI-
GORO.
KCHAKK
ガチャッ
FORGIVE
ME.
I...I'M *MIRA JOVOVICH.* I CAME TO JAPAN TO KILL THE *MURDERER* OF MY PARENTS.
MY FATHER WAS A JAPANESE. NAMED *MAMIYA RINZŌ*...

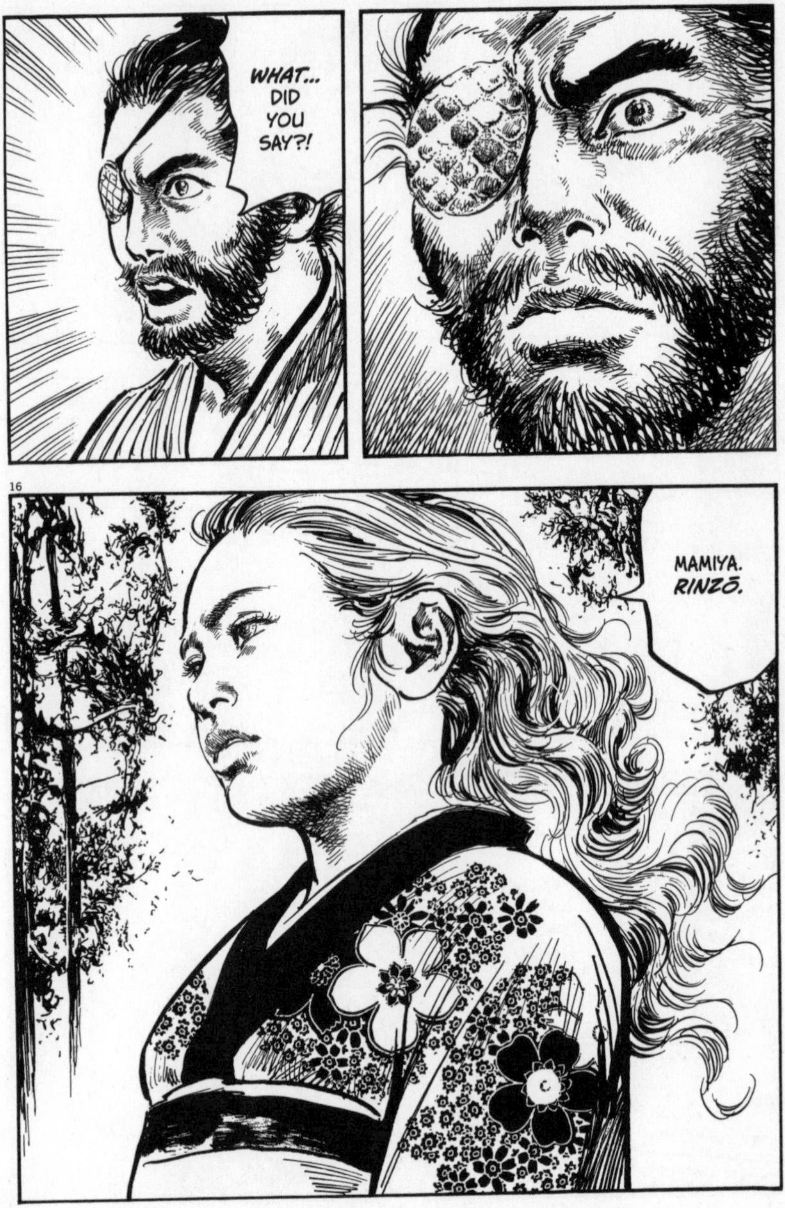
WHAT... DID YOU SAY?!
MAMIYA. RINZŌ.

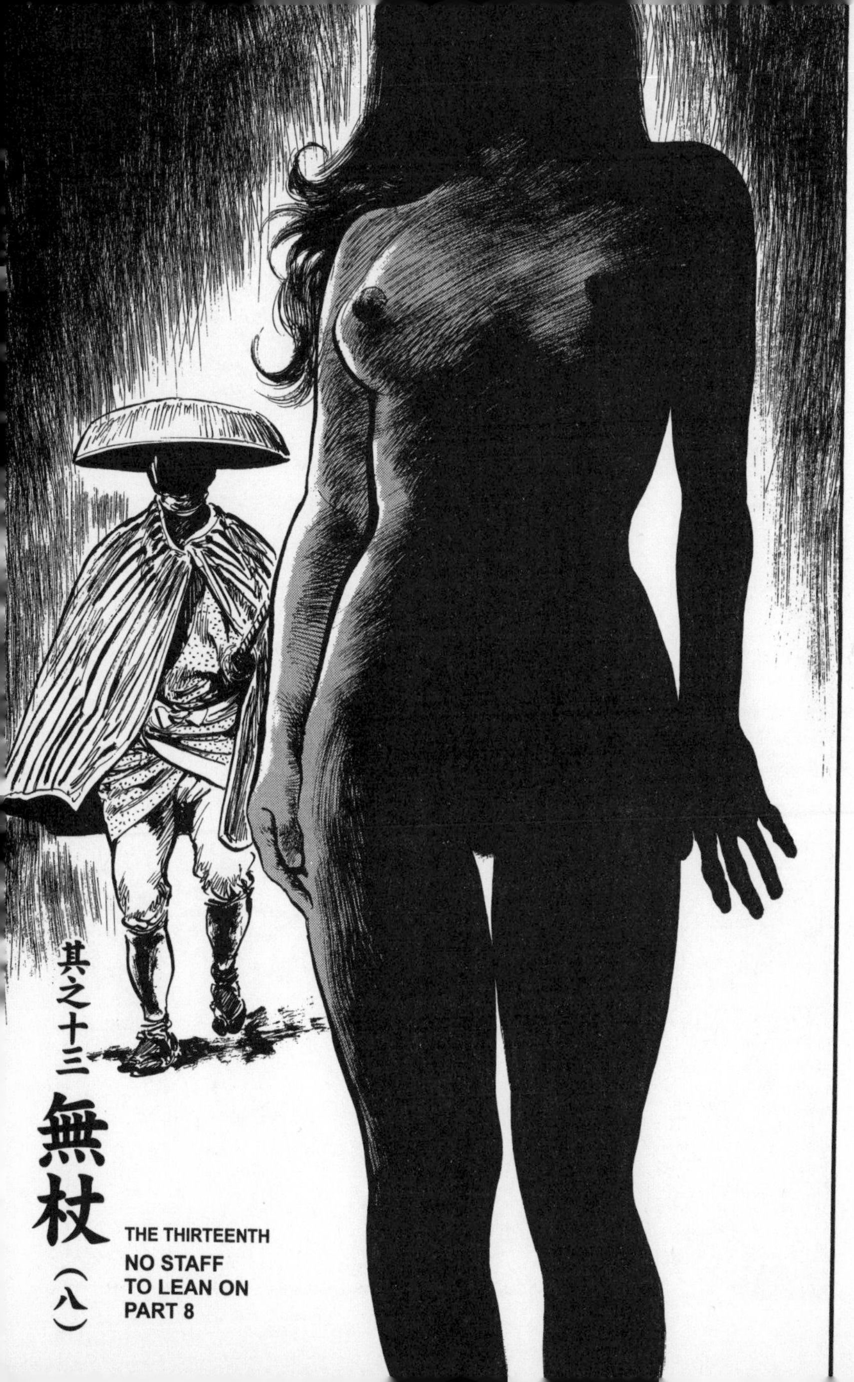
其之十三
無杖（八）
THE THIRTEENTH
NO STAFF
TO LEAN ON
PART 8

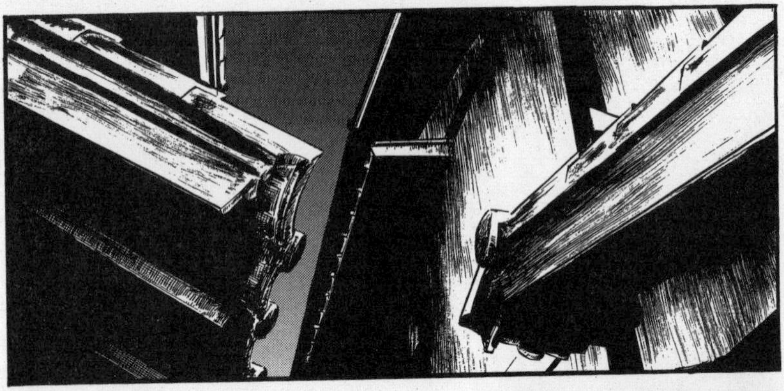
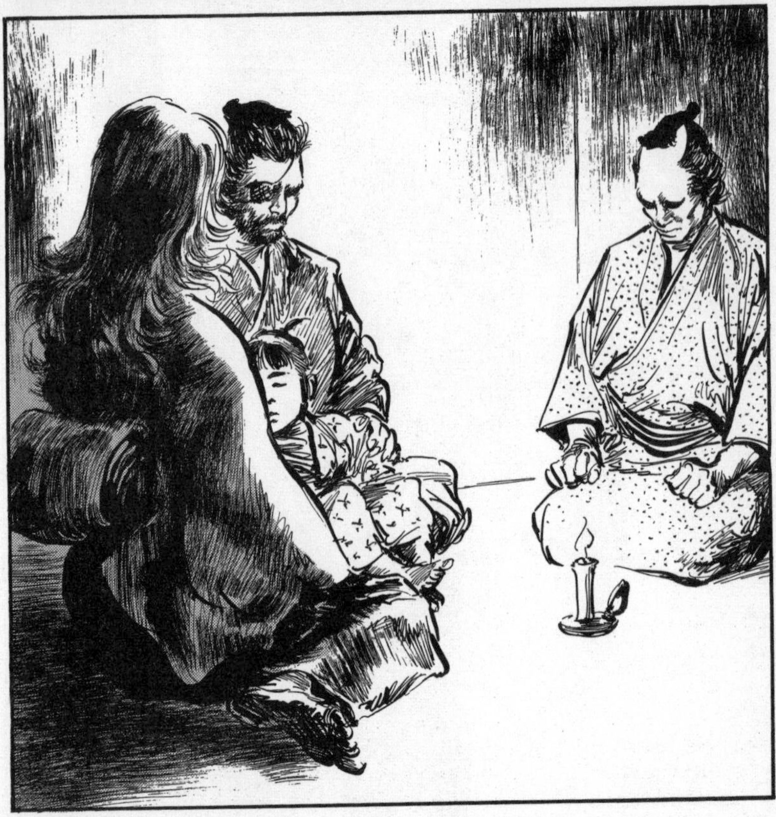

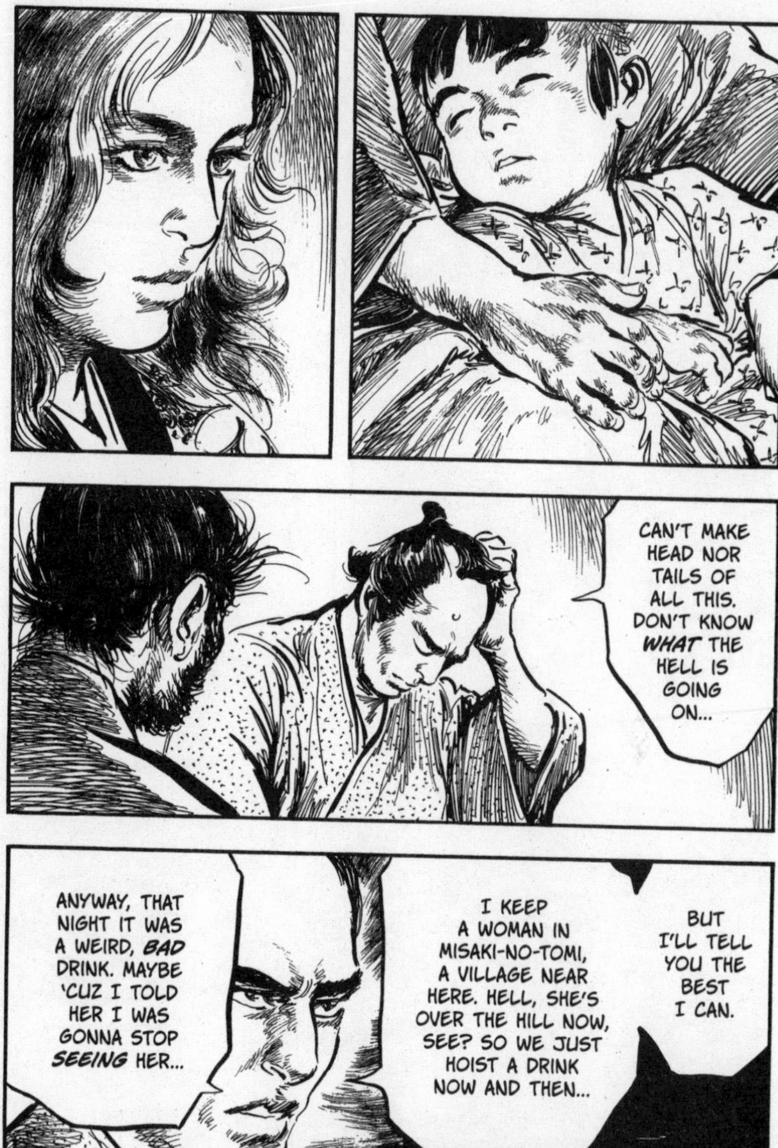
CAN'T MAKE HEAD NOR TAILS OF ALL THIS. DON'T KNOW WHAT THE HELL IS GOING ON...
BUT I'LL TELL YOU THE BEST I CAN.
I KEEP A WOMAN IN MISAKI-NO-TOMI, A VILLAGE NEAR HERE. HELL, SHE'S OVER THE HILL NOW, SEE? SO WE JUST HOIST A DRINK NOW AND THEN...
ANYWAY, THAT NIGHT IT WAS A WEIRD, BAD DRINK. MAYBE 'CUZ I TOLD HER I WAS GONNA STOP SEEING HER...

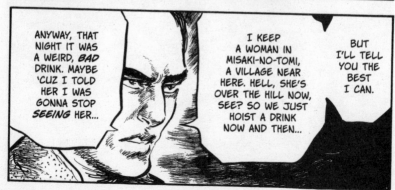

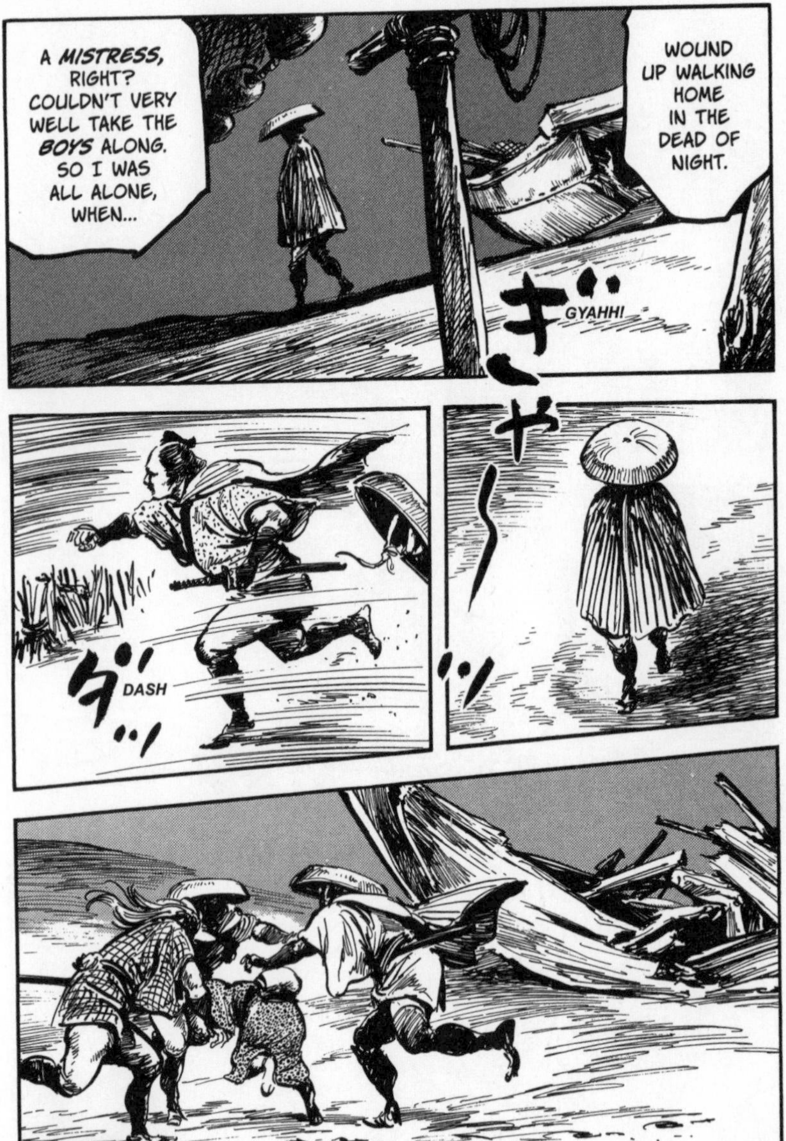
WOUND UP WALKING HOME IN THE DEAD OF NIGHT.
A *MISTRESS*, RIGHT? COULDN'T VERY WELL TAKE THE *BOYS* ALONG. SO I WAS ALL ALONE, WHEN...
GYAHH!
DASH

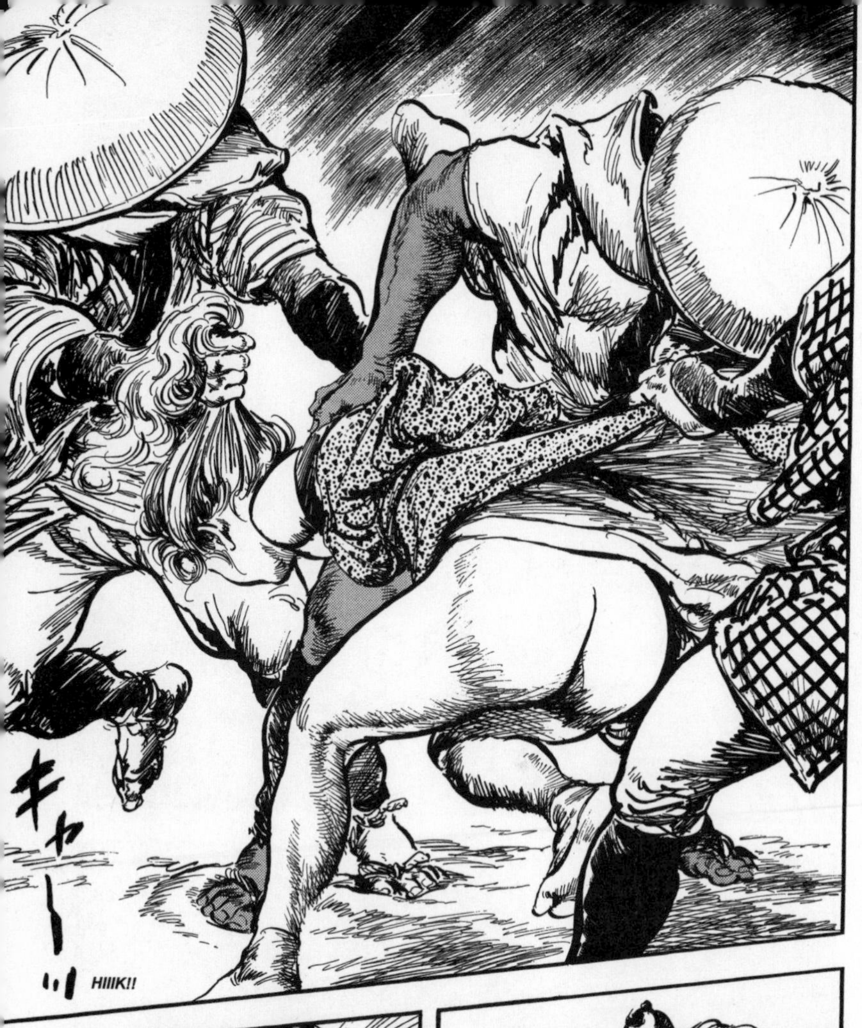
キャーッ
HIIIK!!

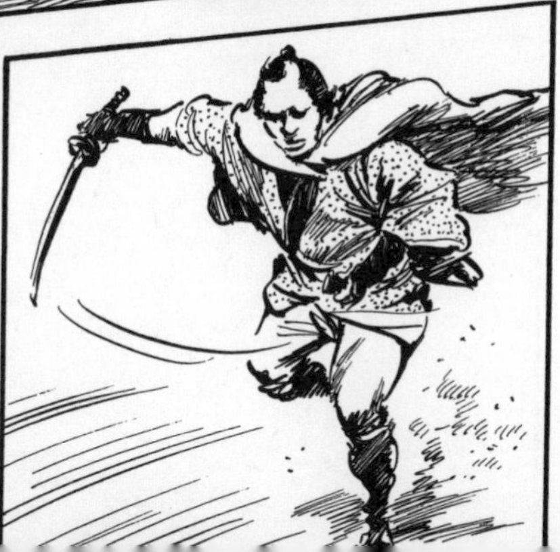

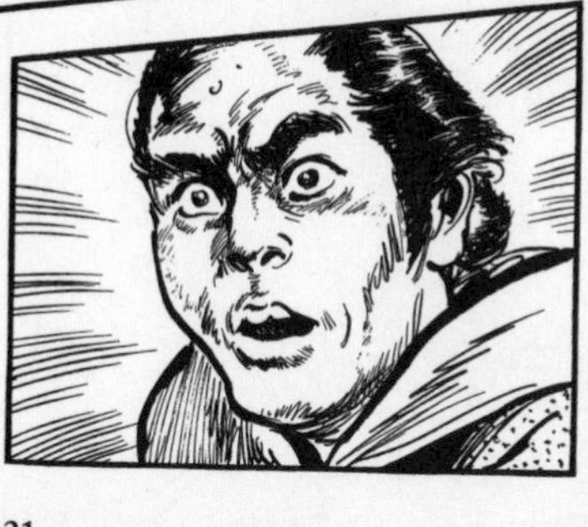

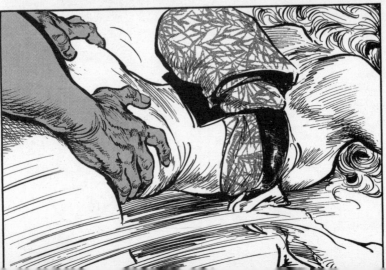

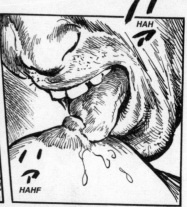

HAH

HAHF

それは脳天が
しびれるような
光景でございやした…

IT WAS A SIGHT THAT **FROZE** MY BRAIN...

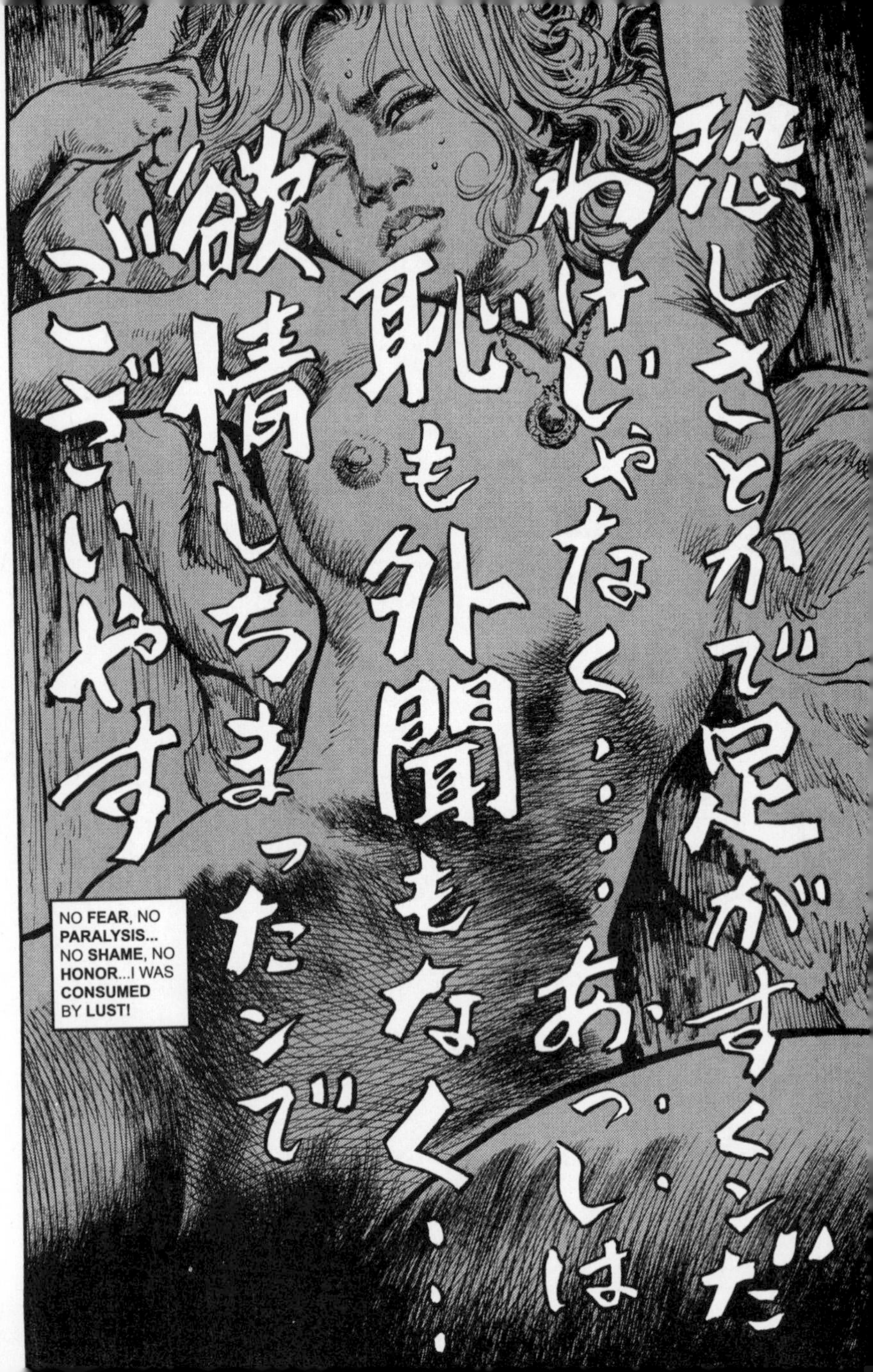
恐しさとかで足がすくんだ
わけじゃなく……あっしは
恥も外聞もなく……
欲情しちまったんで
……ございやす
NO **FEAR**, NO **PARALYSIS**... NO **SHAME**, NO **HONOR**...I WAS **CONSUMED** BY **LUST**!

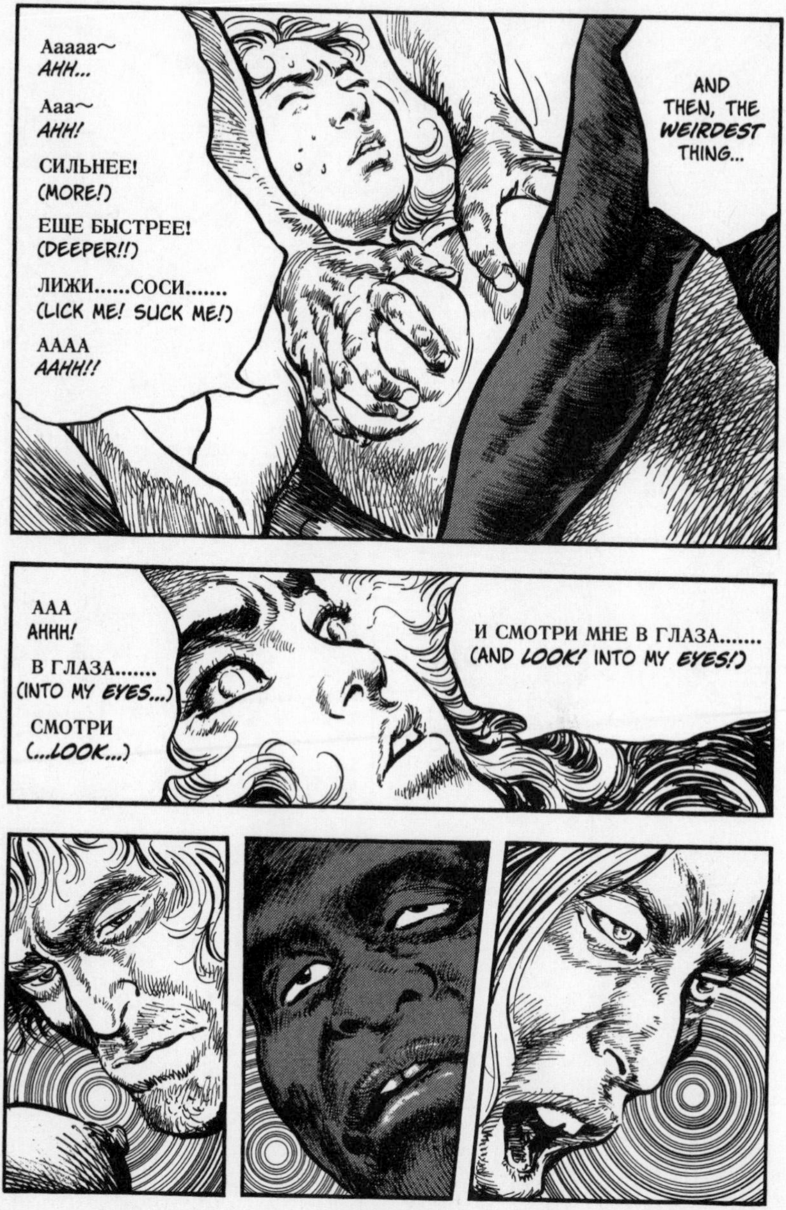
AND THEN, THE WEIRDEST THING...
Aaaaa~ AHH...
Aaa~ AHH!
СИЛЬНЕЕ! (MORE!)
ЕЩЕ БЫСТРЕЕ! (DEEPER!!)
ЛИЖИ......СОСИ....... (LICK ME! SUCK ME!)
АААА AAHH!!
И СМОТРИ МНЕ В ГЛАЗА....... (AND LOOK! INTO MY EYES!)
ААА AHHH!
В ГЛАЗА....... (INTO MY EYES...)
СМОТРИ (...LOOK...)

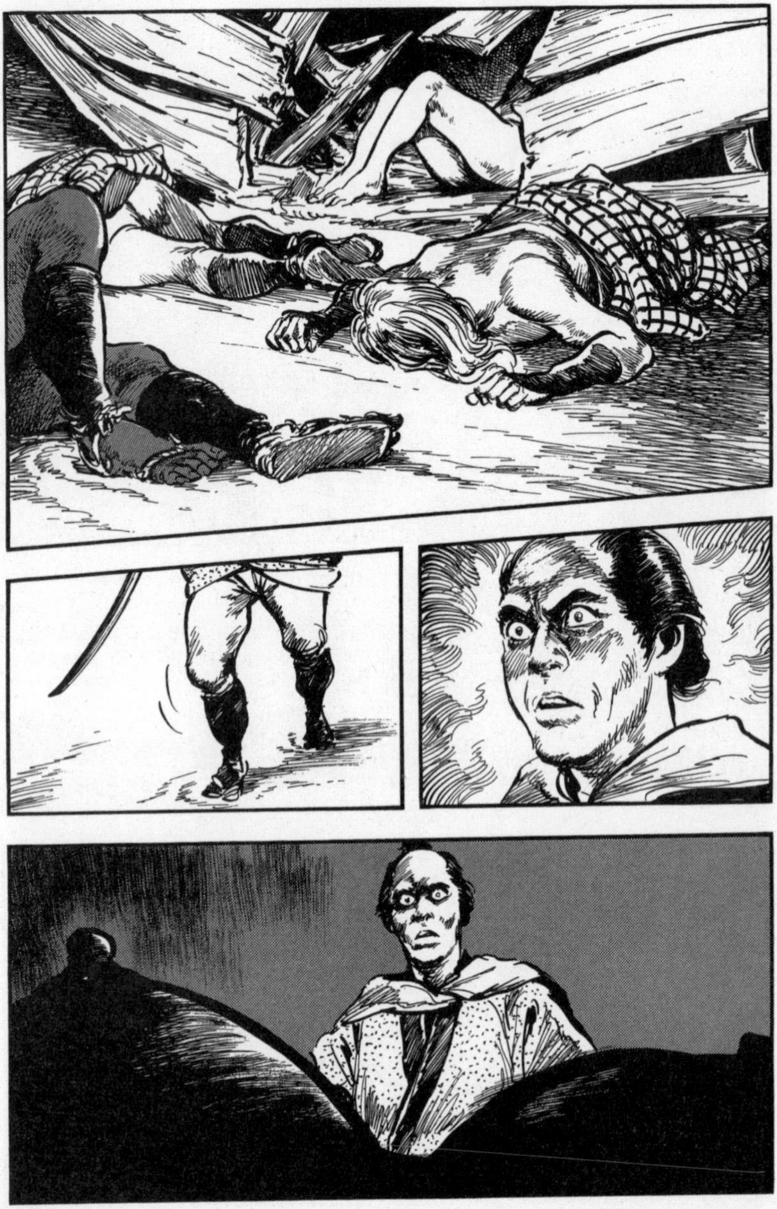

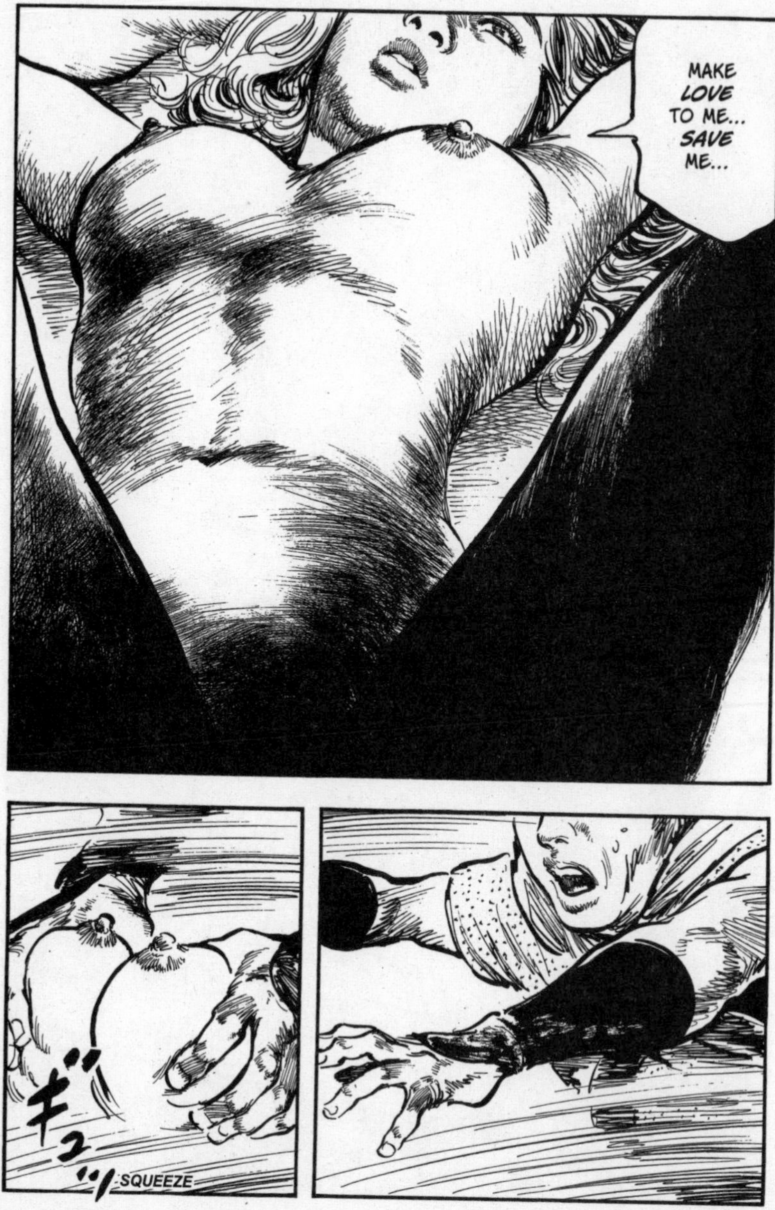
MAKE LOVE TO ME... SAVE ME...
ギュッ
SQUEEZE

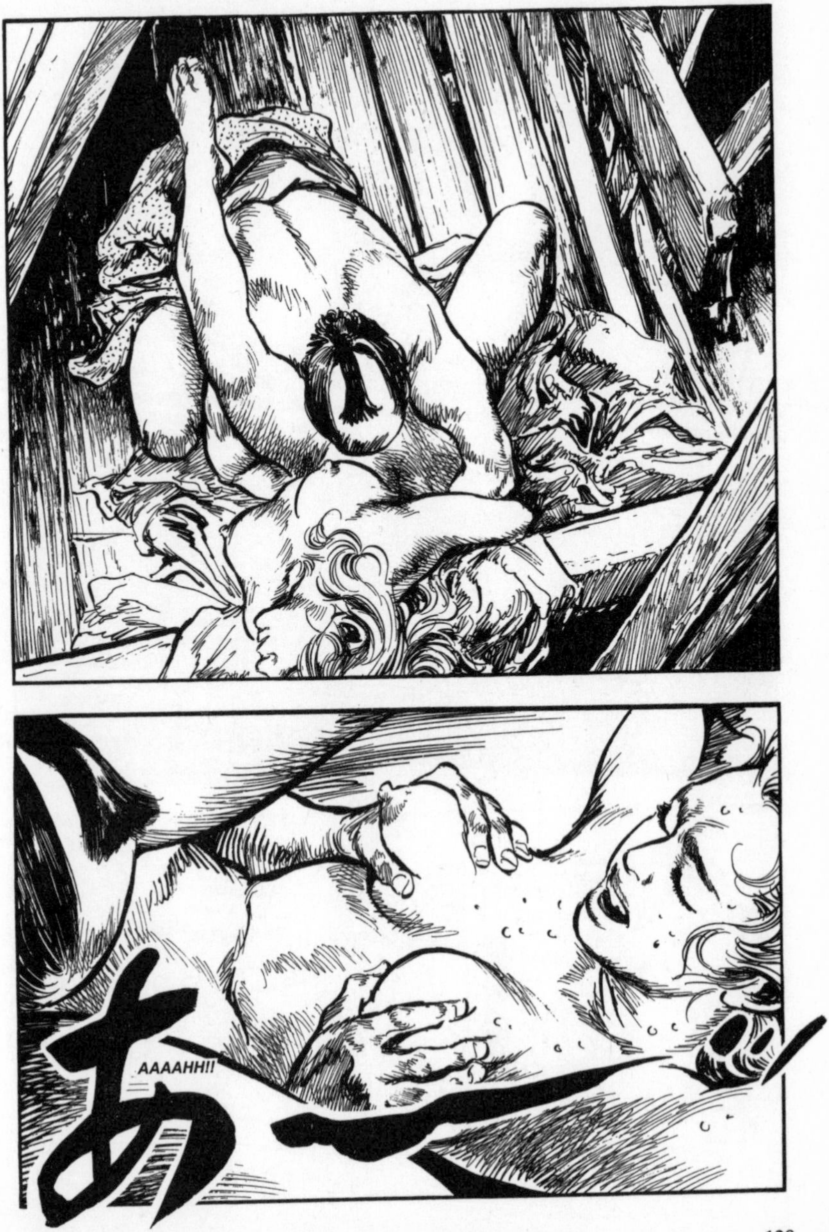
AAAAHH!!
あ

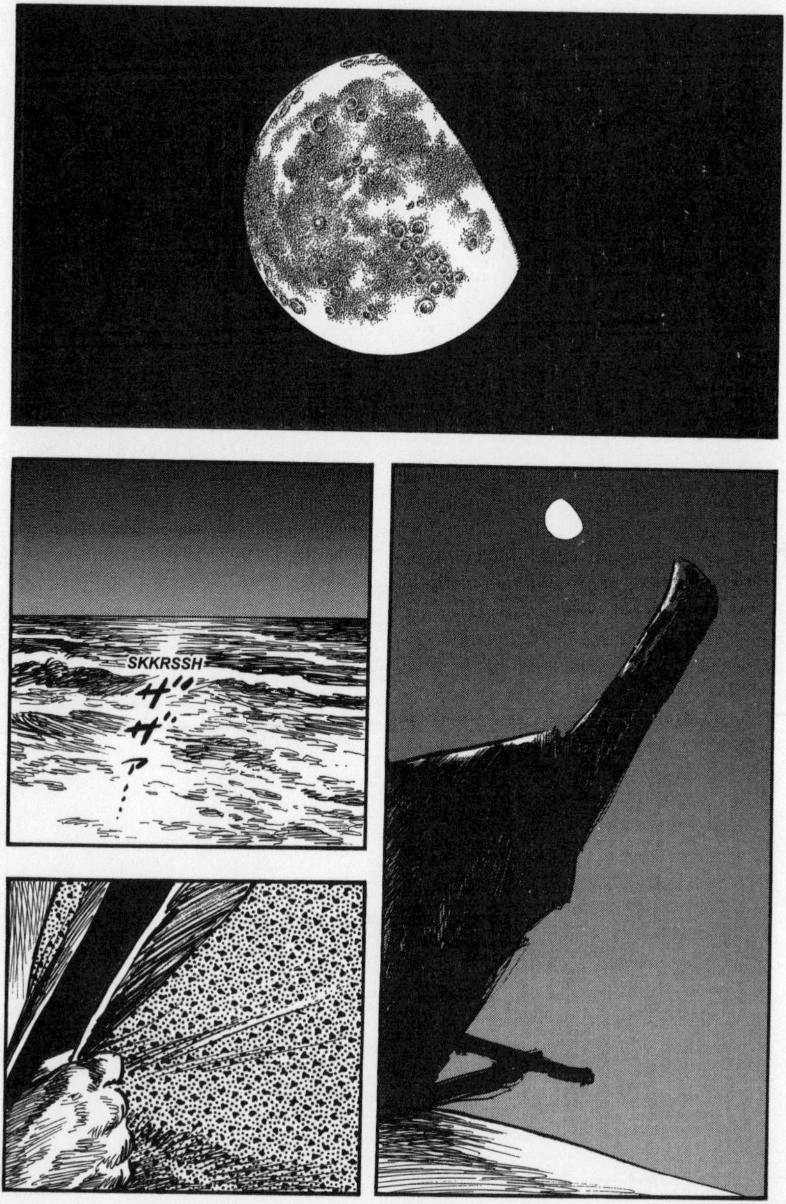
SKKRSSH
ザザァ

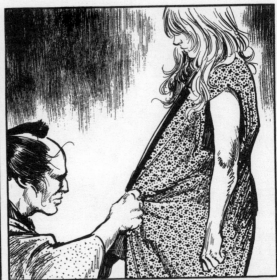

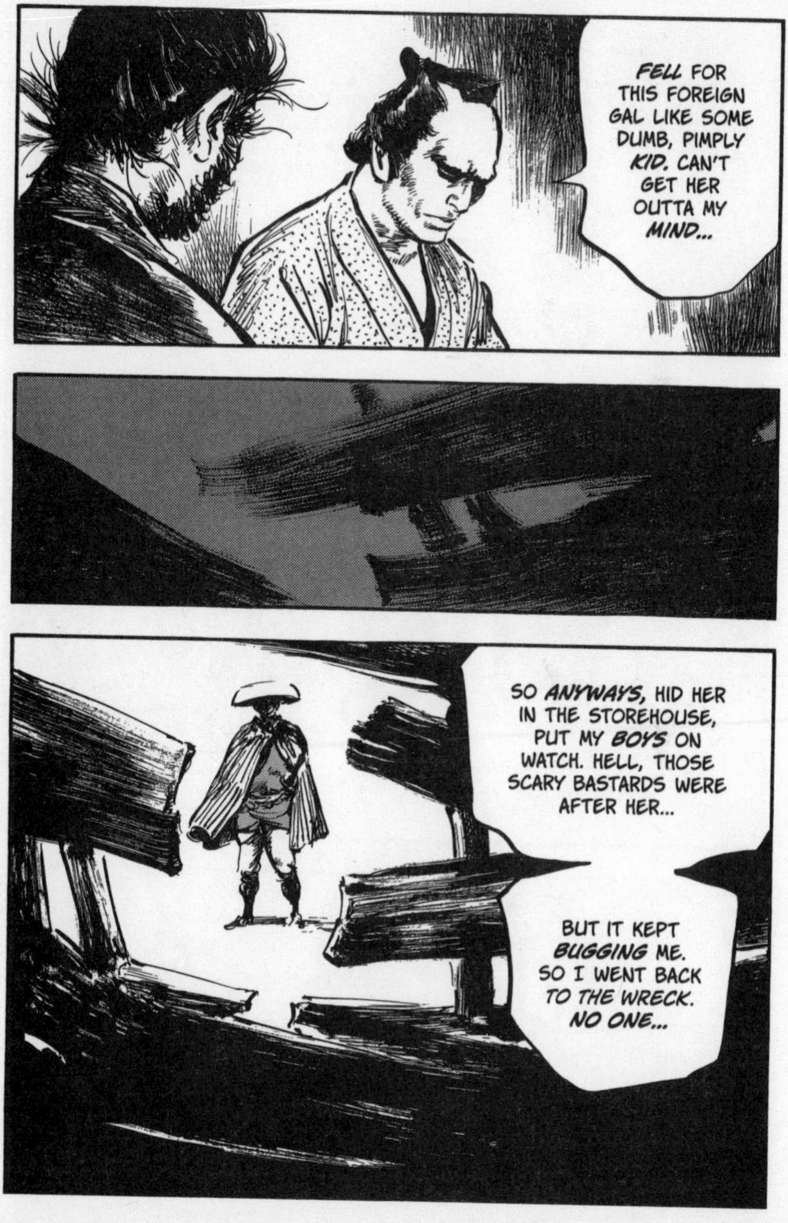
FELL FOR THIS FOREIGN GAL LIKE SOME DUMB, PIMPLY KID. CAN'T GET HER OUTTA MY MIND...
SO ANYWAYS, HID HER IN THE STOREHOUSE, PUT MY BOYS ON WATCH. HELL, THOSE SCARY BASTARDS WERE AFTER HER...
BUT IT KEPT BUGGING ME. SO I WENT BACK TO THE WRECK. NO ONE...

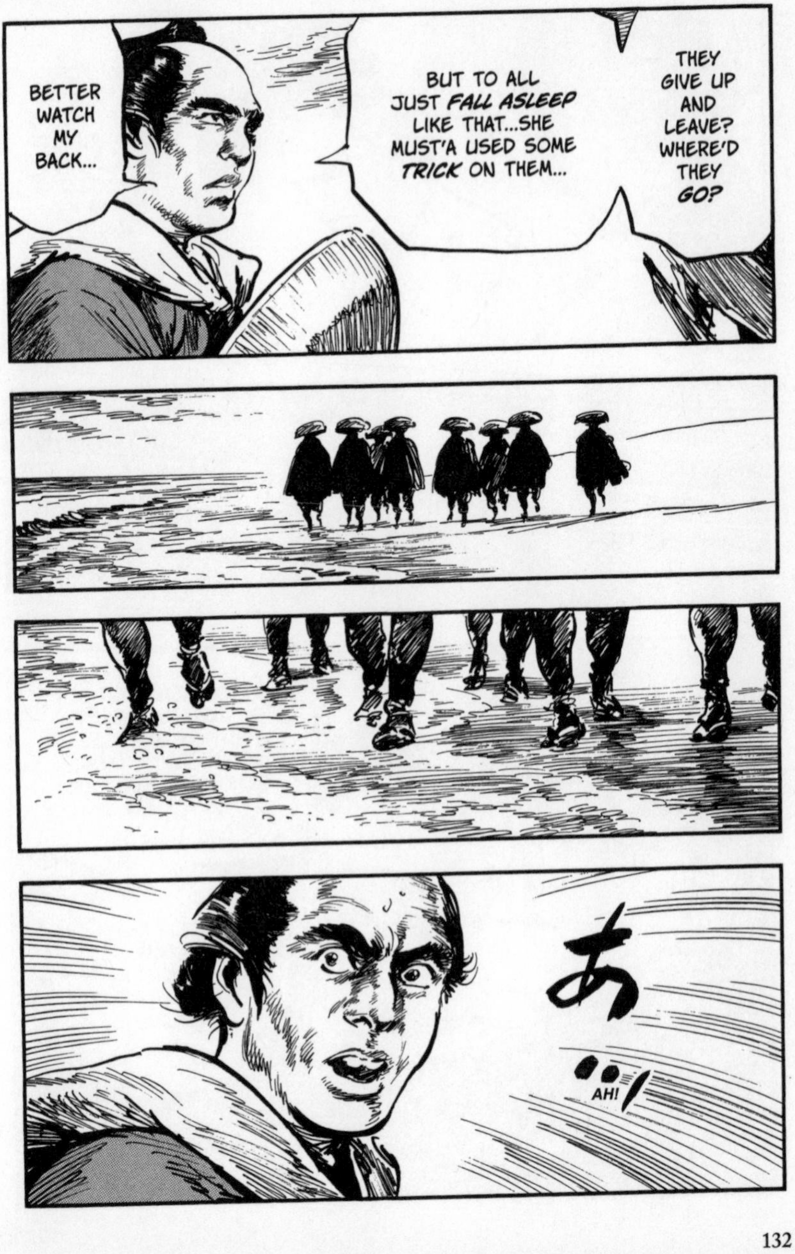
THEY GIVE UP AND LEAVE? WHERE'D THEY GO?
BUT TO ALL JUST FALL ASLEEP LIKE THAT...SHE MUST'A USED SOME TRICK ON THEM...
BETTER WATCH MY BACK...
あ..!
AH!

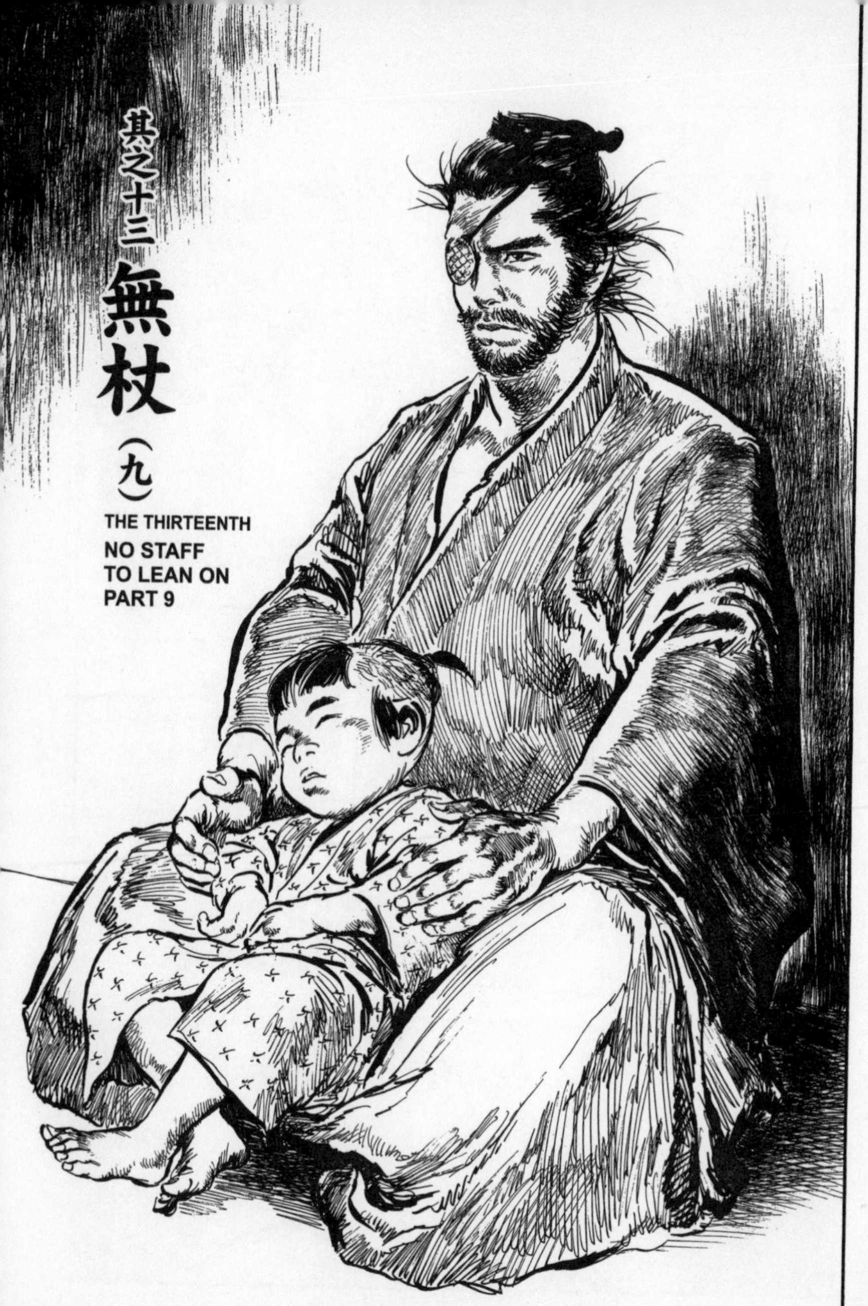
其之十三
無杖
（九）
THE THIRTEENTH
NO STAFF
TO LEAN ON
PART 9

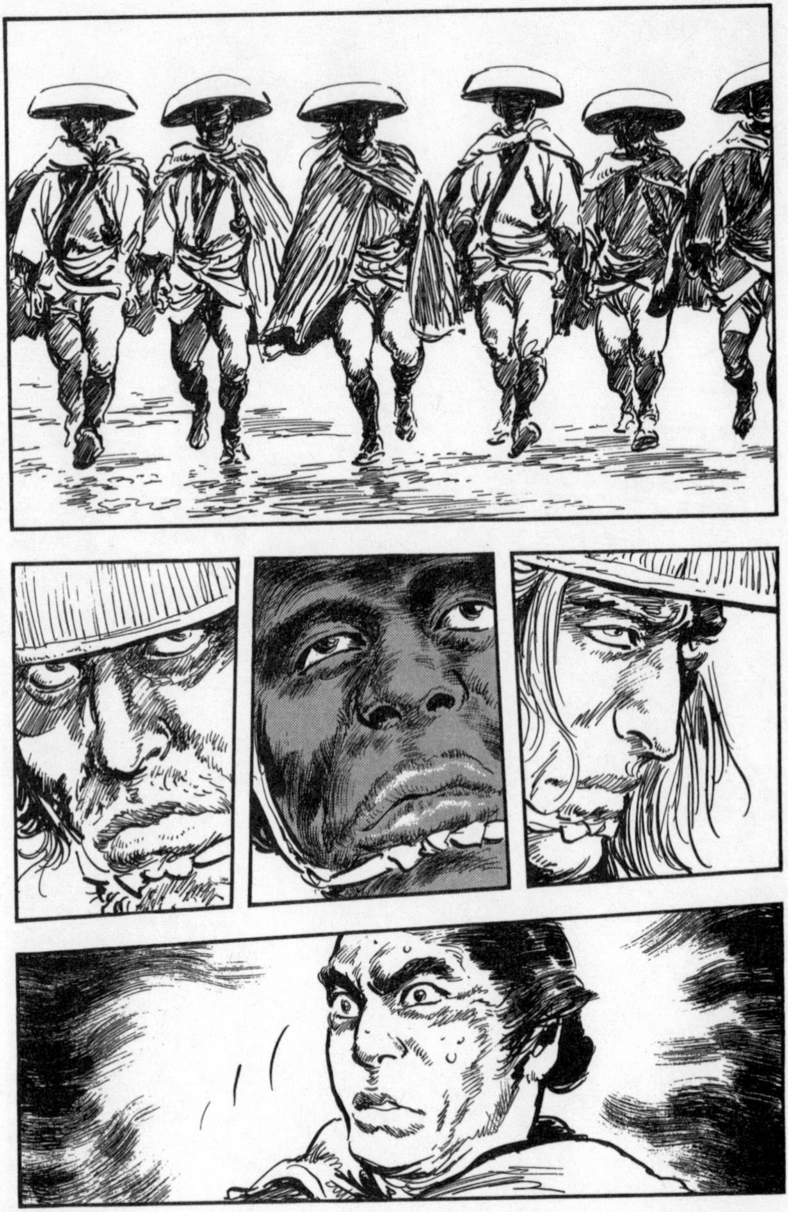

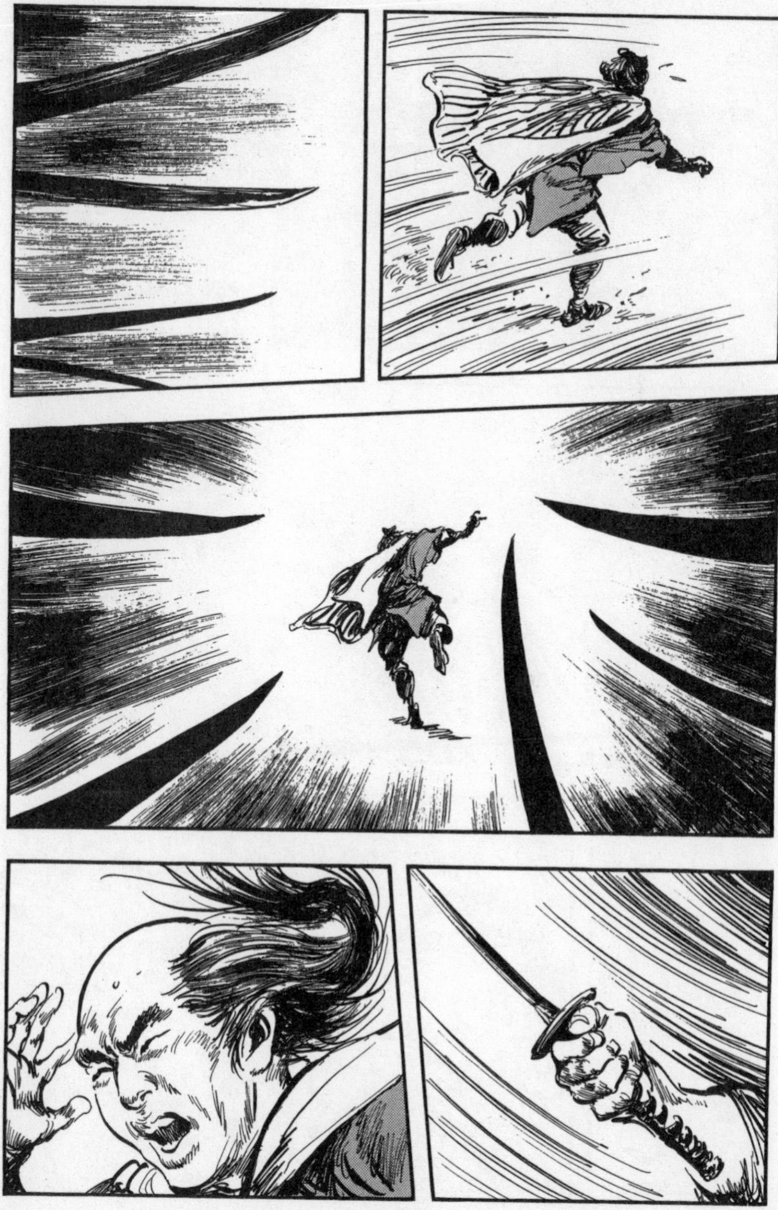

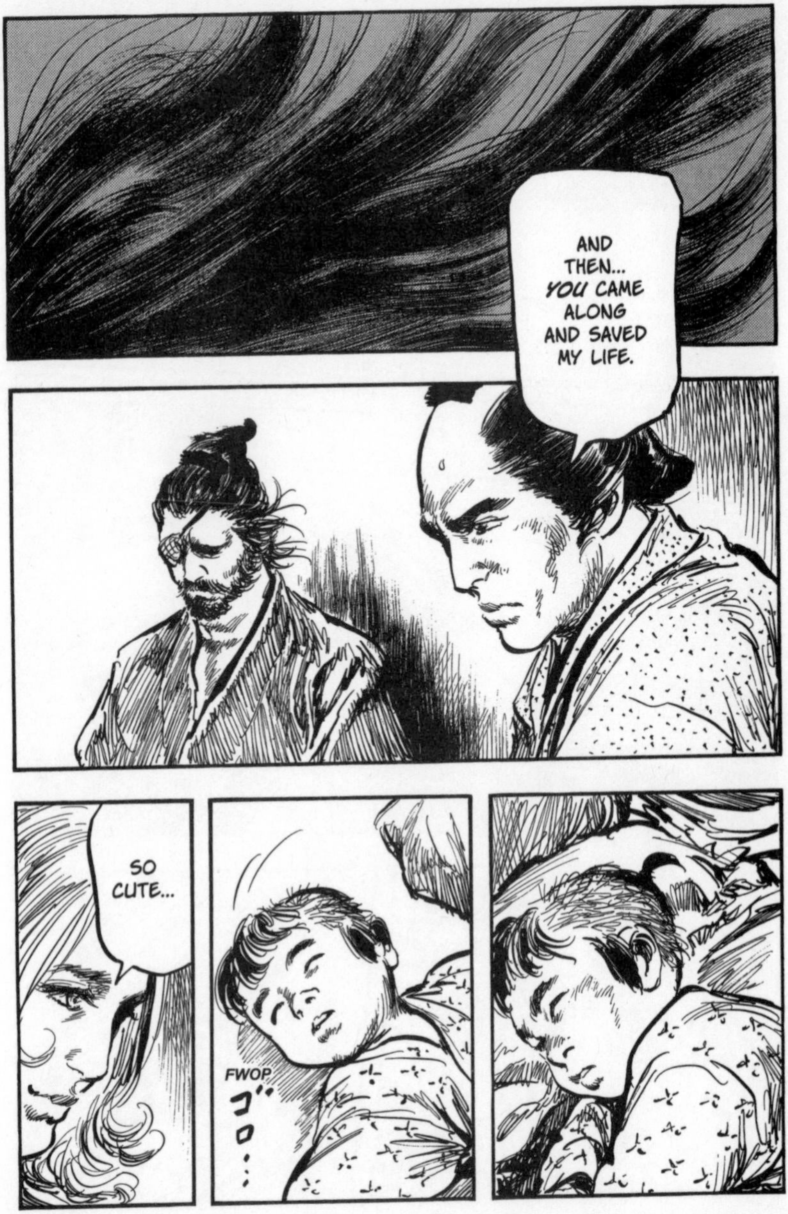
AND THEN... *YOU* CAME ALONG AND SAVED MY LIFE.
FWOP
ゴロ…
SO CUTE...

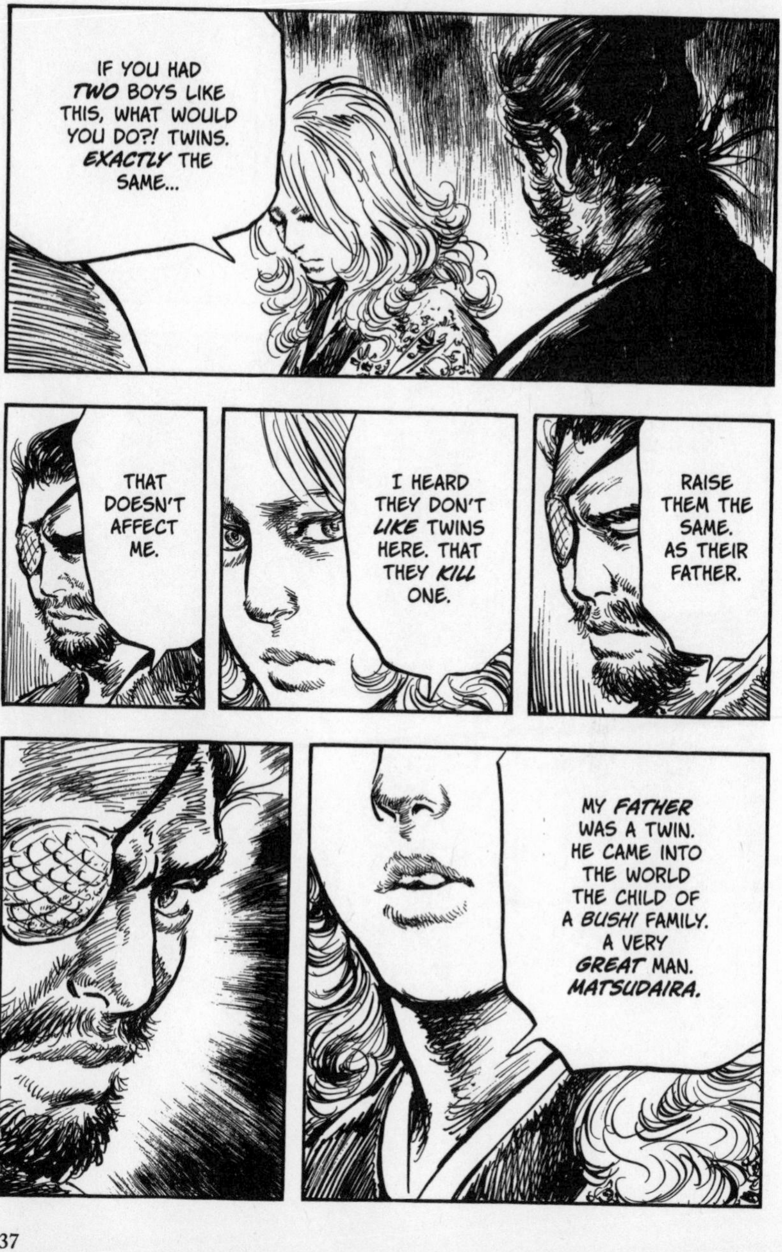
IF YOU HAD *TWO* BOYS LIKE THIS, WHAT WOULD YOU DO?! TWINS. *EXACTLY* THE SAME...
RAISE THEM THE SAME. AS THEIR FATHER.
I HEARD THEY DON'T *LIKE* TWINS HERE. THAT THEY *KILL* ONE.
THAT DOESN'T AFFECT ME.
MY *FATHER* WAS A TWIN. HE CAME INTO THE WORLD THE CHILD OF A *BUSHI* FAMILY. A VERY *GREAT* MAN. *MATSUDAIRA.*

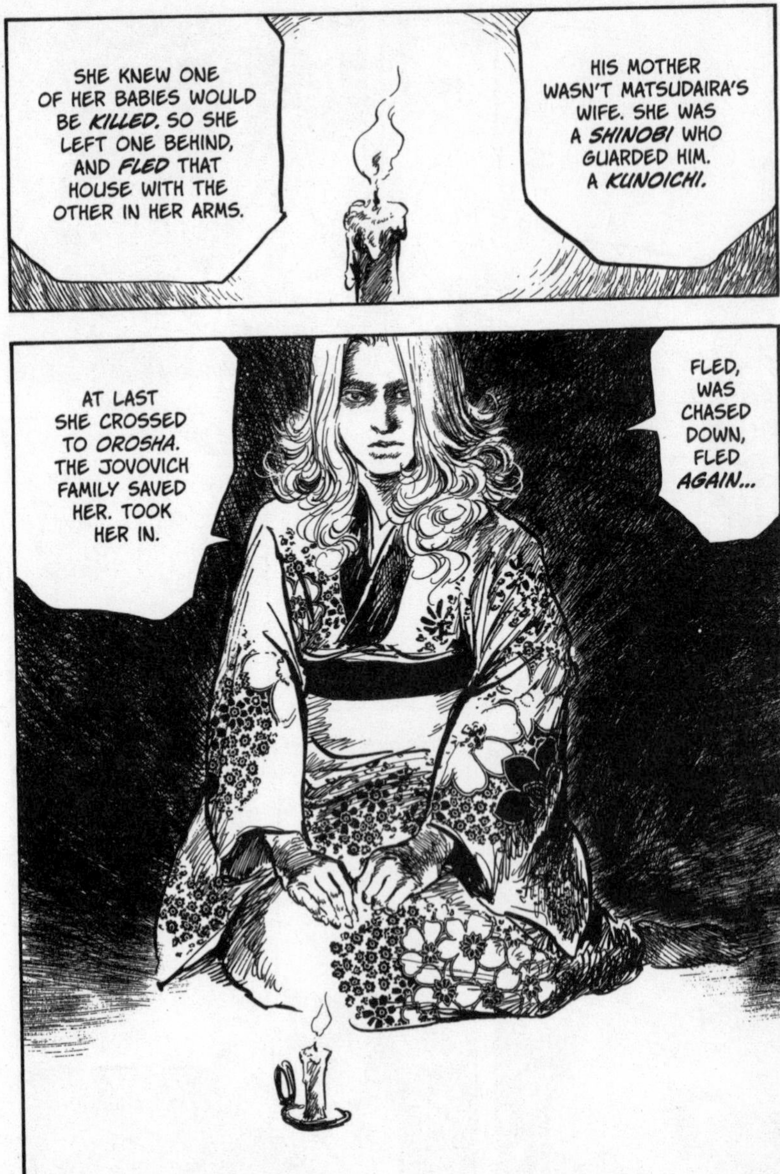
HIS MOTHER WASN'T MATSUDAIRA'S WIFE. SHE WAS A *SHINOBI* WHO GUARDED HIM. A *KUNOICHI.*
SHE KNEW ONE OF HER BABIES WOULD BE *KILLED.* SO SHE LEFT ONE BEHIND, AND *FLED* THAT HOUSE WITH THE OTHER IN HER ARMS.
FLED, WAS CHASED DOWN, FLED *AGAIN...*
AT LAST SHE CROSSED TO *OROSHA.* THE JOVOVICH FAMILY SAVED HER. TOOK HER IN.

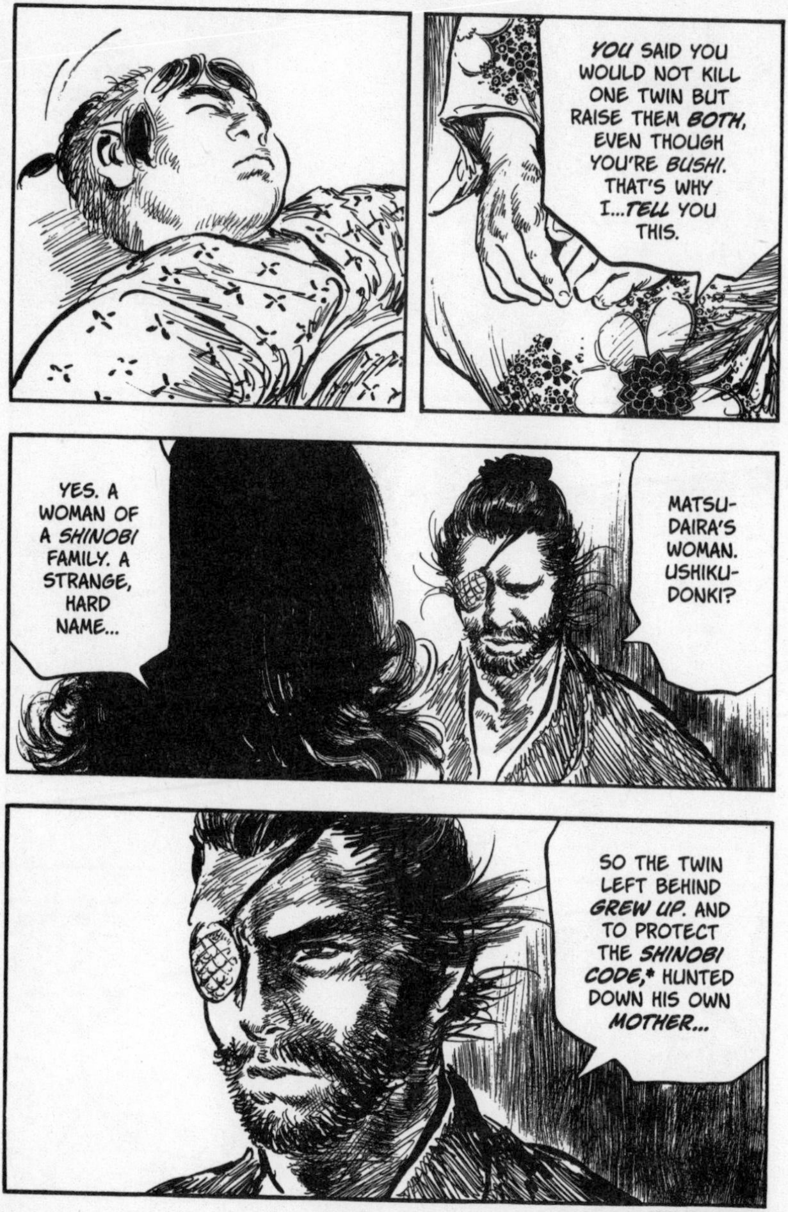
YOU SAID YOU WOULD NOT KILL ONE TWIN BUT RAISE THEM BOTH, EVEN THOUGH YOU'RE BUSHI. THAT'S WHY I...TELL YOU THIS.
MATSU-DAIRA'S WOMAN. USHIKU-DONKI?
YES. A WOMAN OF A SHINOBI FAMILY. A STRANGE, HARD NAME...
SO THE TWIN LEFT BEHIND GREW UP. AND TO PROTECT THE SHINOBI CODE,* HUNTED DOWN HIS OWN MOTHER...

*SEE FOOTNOTES.

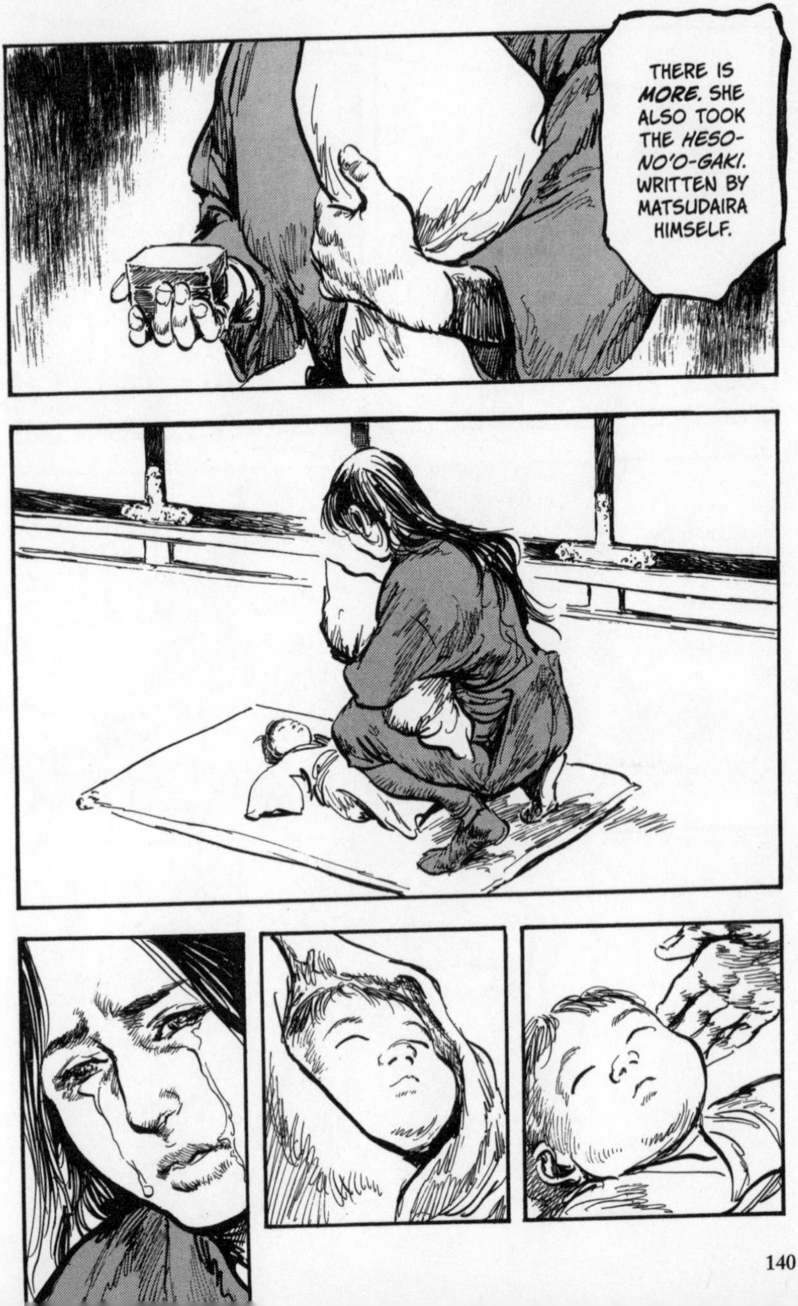
THERE IS *MORE.* SHE ALSO TOOK THE *HESO-NO'O-GAKI.* WRITTEN BY MATSUDAIRA HIMSELF.

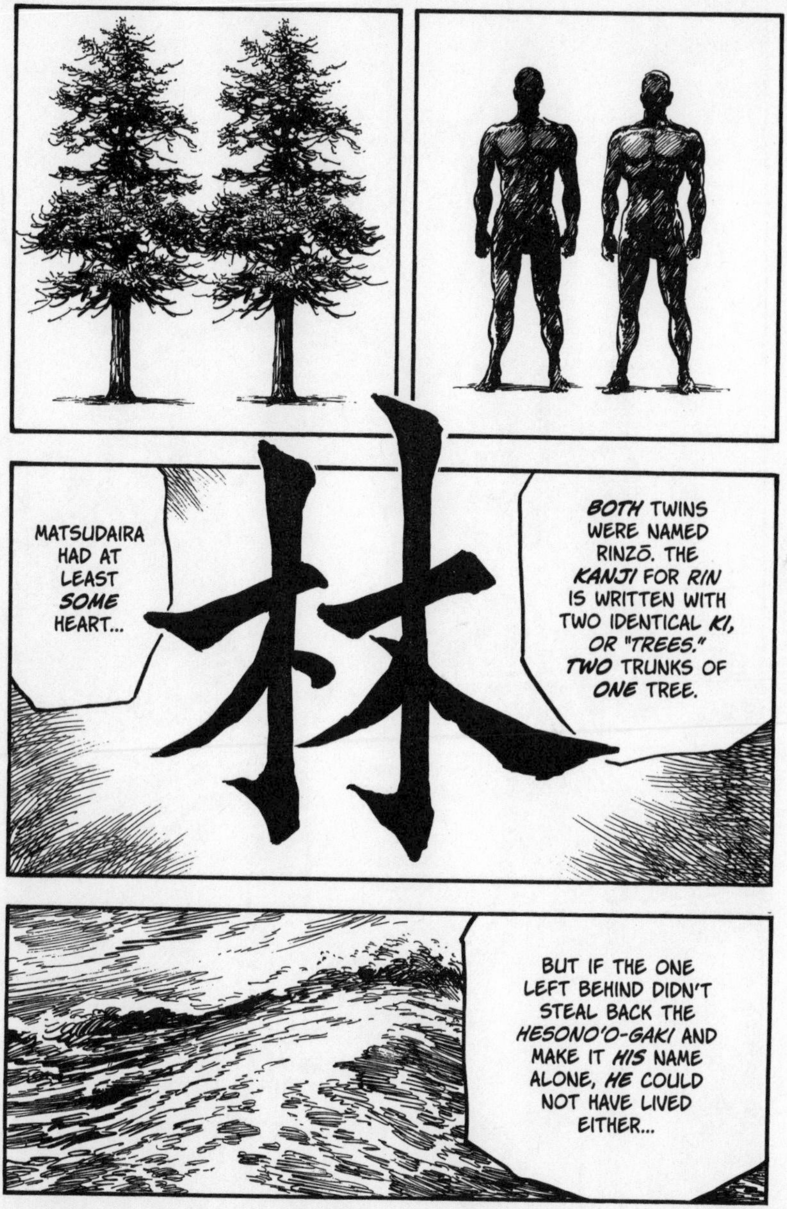
BOTH TWINS WERE NAMED RINZŌ. THE *KANJI* FOR *RIN* IS WRITTEN WITH TWO IDENTICAL *KI*, OR "*TREES.*" *TWO* TRUNKS OF *ONE* TREE.
林
MATSUDAIRA HAD AT LEAST *SOME* HEART...
BUT IF THE ONE LEFT BEHIND DIDN'T STEAL BACK THE *HESONO'O-GAKI* AND MAKE IT *HIS* NAME ALONE, *HE* COULD NOT HAVE LIVED EITHER...

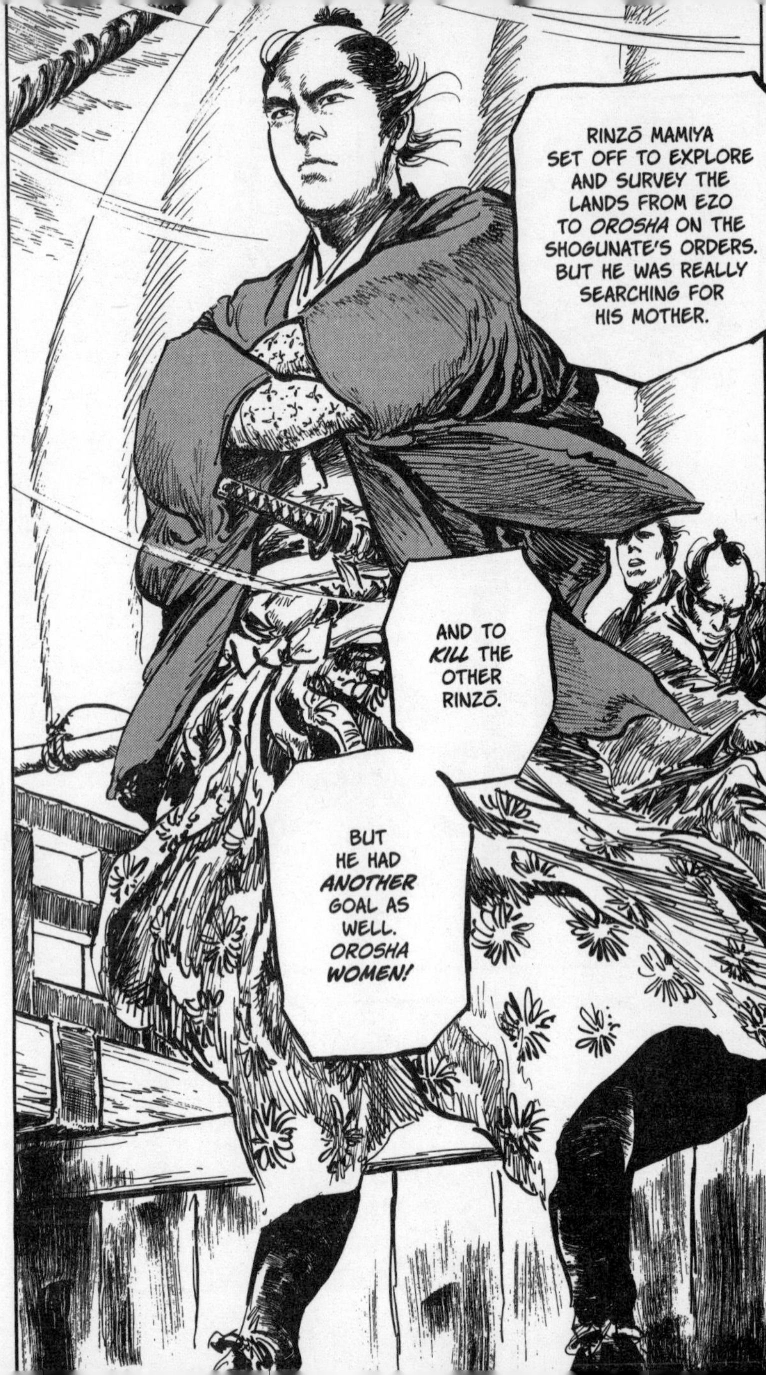
RINZŌ MAMIYA SET OFF TO EXPLORE AND SURVEY THE LANDS FROM EZO TO *OROSHA* ON THE SHOGUNATE'S ORDERS. BUT HE WAS REALLY SEARCHING FOR HIS MOTHER.
AND TO ***KILL*** THE OTHER RINZŌ.
BUT HE HAD ***ANOTHER*** GOAL AS WELL. ***OROSHA WOMEN!***

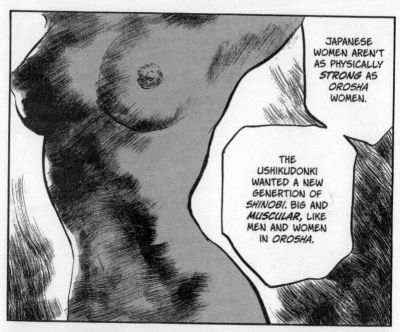

JAPANESE WOMEN AREN'T AS PHYSICALLY *STRONG* AS OROSHA WOMEN.

THE USHIKUDONKI WANTED A NEW GENERTION OF *SHINOBI.* BIG AND *MUSCULAR,* LIKE MEN AND WOMEN IN *OROSHA.*

RINZŌ SENT WOMAN AFTER WOMAN FROM *OROSHA* TO JAPAN, AND HAD THE USHIKUDONKI HE BROUGHT WITH HIM COUPLE WITH *OROSHA* WOMEN WHILE THEY WERE THERE.

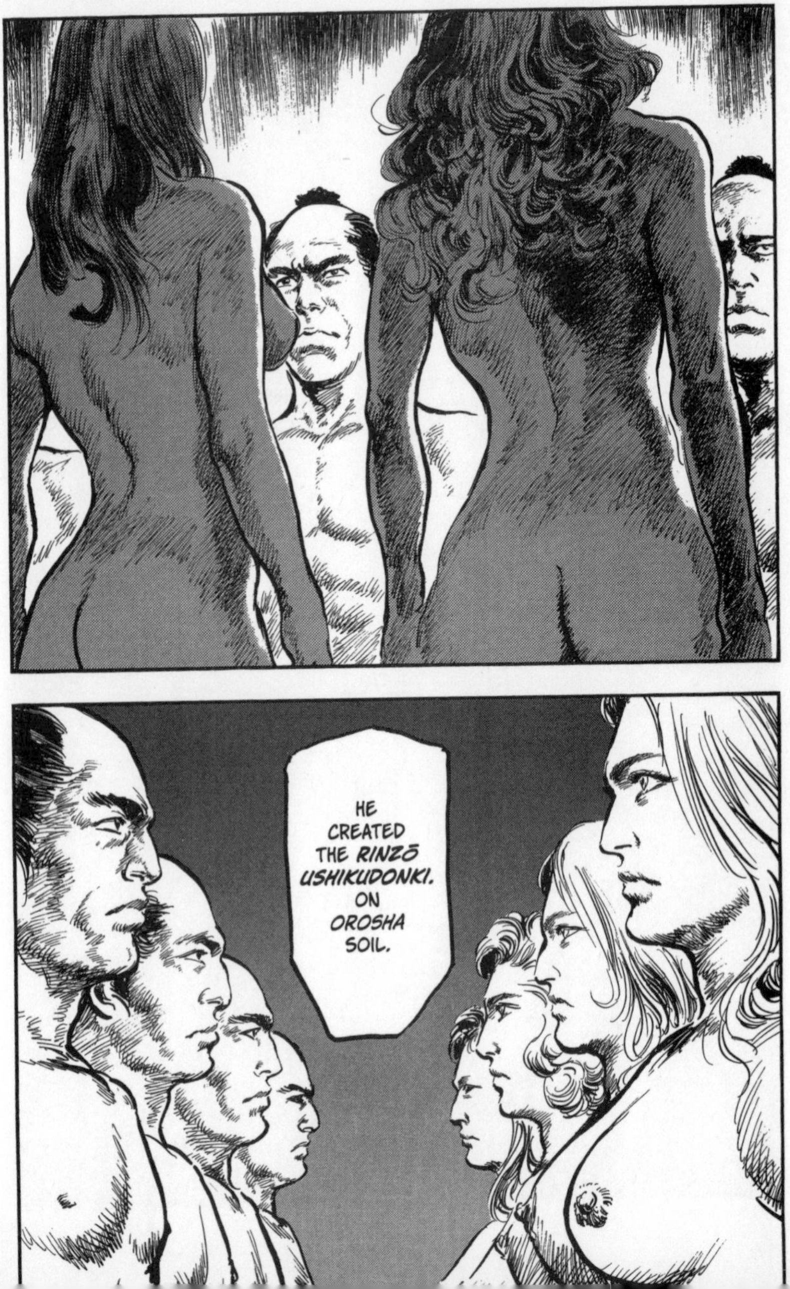
HE CREATED THE *RINZŌ USHIKUDONKI.* ON *OROSHA* SOIL.

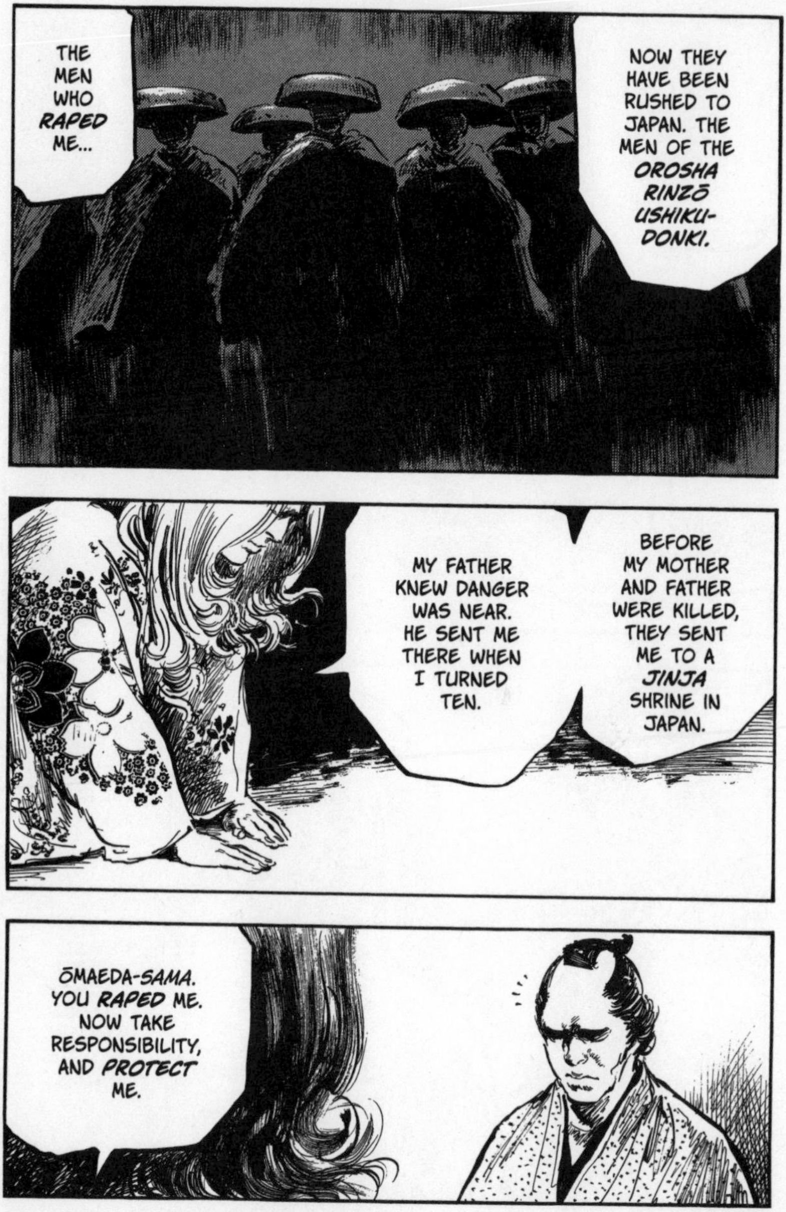
NOW THEY HAVE BEEN RUSHED TO JAPAN. THE MEN OF THE OROSHA RINZŌ USHIKU-DONKI.
THE MEN WHO RAPED ME...
BEFORE MY MOTHER AND FATHER WERE KILLED, THEY SENT ME TO A JINJA SHRINE IN JAPAN.
MY FATHER KNEW DANGER WAS NEAR. HE SENT ME THERE WHEN I TURNED TEN.
ŌMAEDA-SAMA. YOU RAPED ME. NOW TAKE RESPONSIBILITY, AND PROTECT ME.

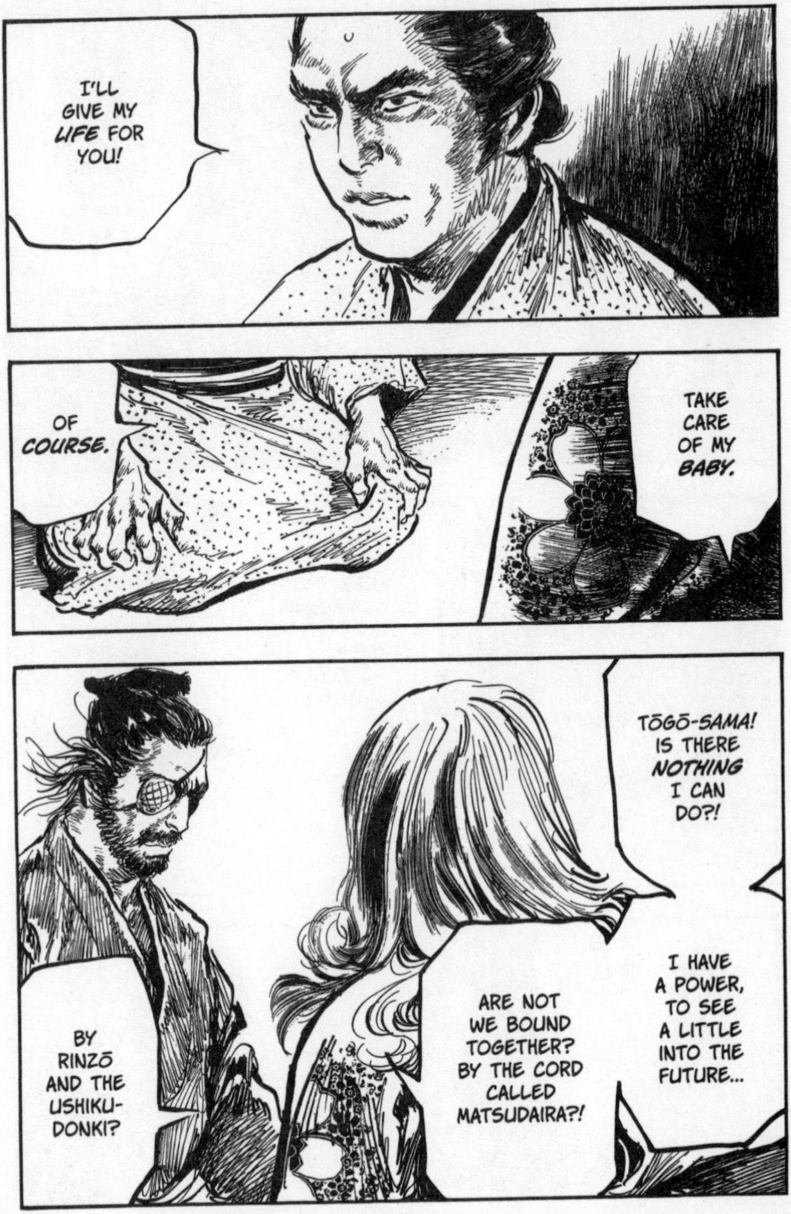
I'LL GIVE MY LIFE FOR YOU!
TAKE CARE OF MY BABY.
OF COURSE.
TŌGŌ-SAMA! IS THERE NOTHING I CAN DO?!
I HAVE A POWER, TO SEE A LITTLE INTO THE FUTURE...
ARE NOT WE BOUND TOGETHER? BY THE CORD CALLED MATSUDAIRA?!
BY RINZŌ AND THE USHIKU-DONKI?

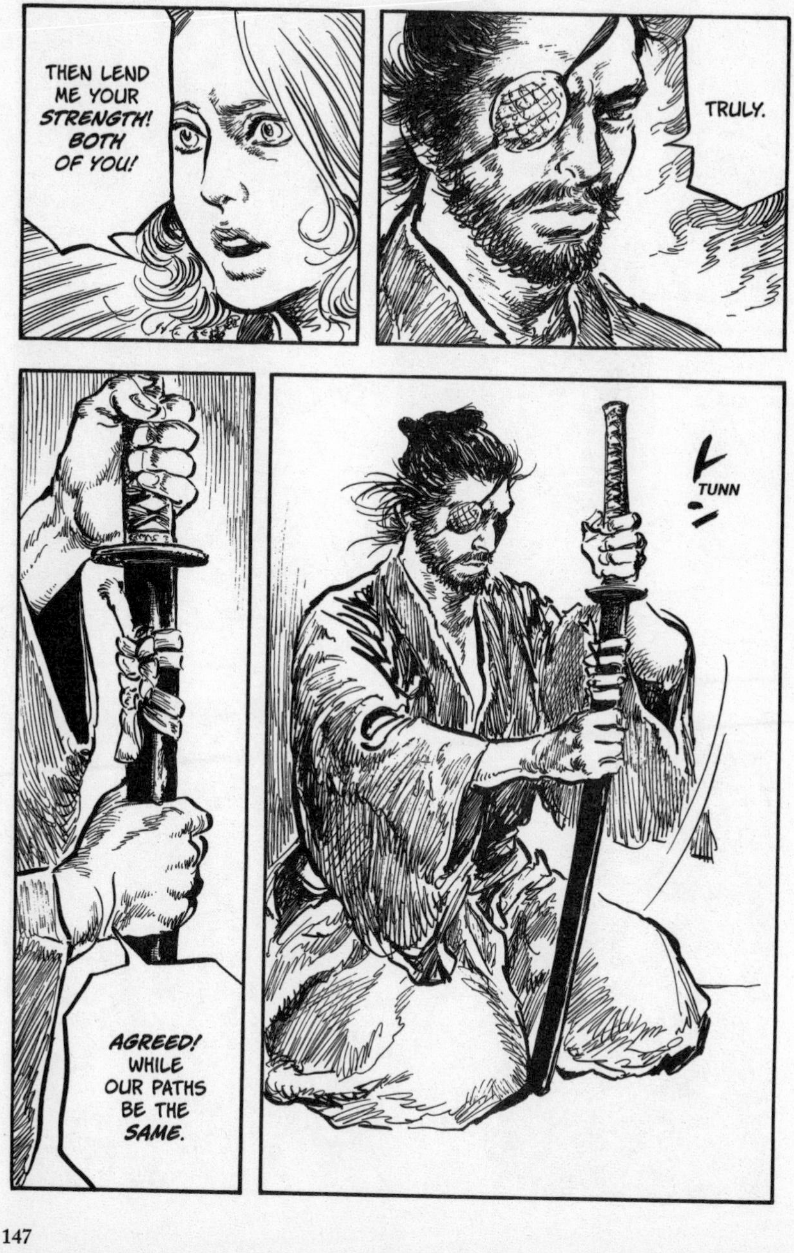
TRULY.
THEN LEND ME YOUR STRENGTH! BOTH OF YOU!
TUNN
AGREED! WHILE OUR PATHS BE THE SAME.

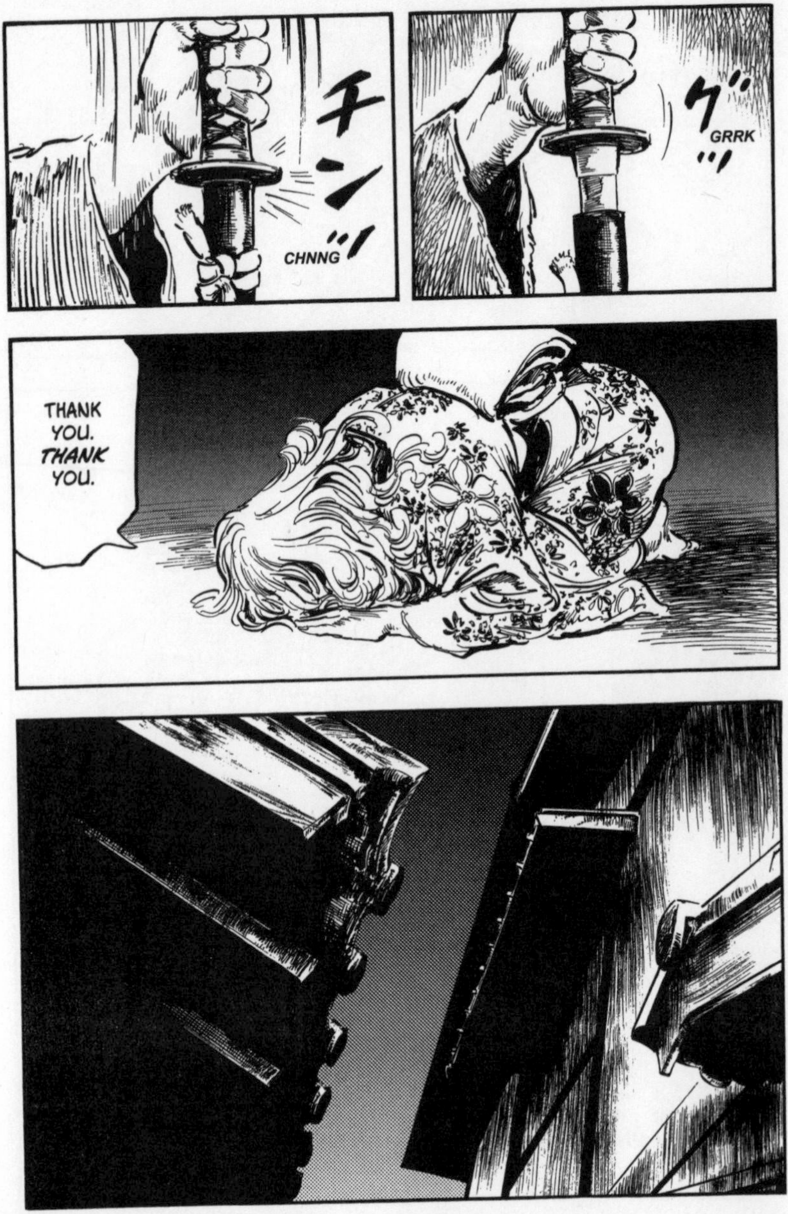
グッ
GRRK
チンッ
CHNNG
THANK YOU. *THANK* YOU.

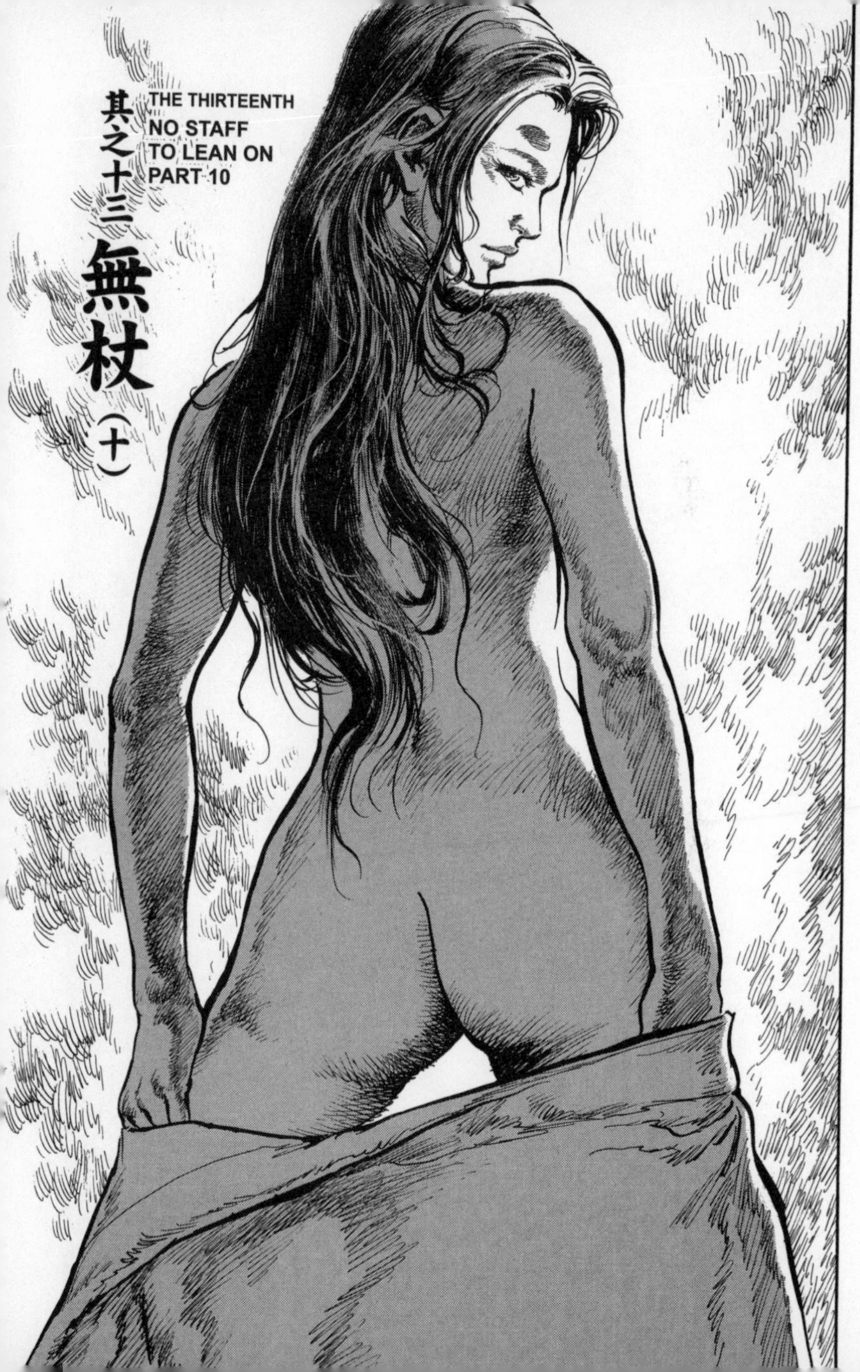
其之十三
THE THIRTEENTH
NO STAFF
TO LEAN ON
PART 10
無杖（十）

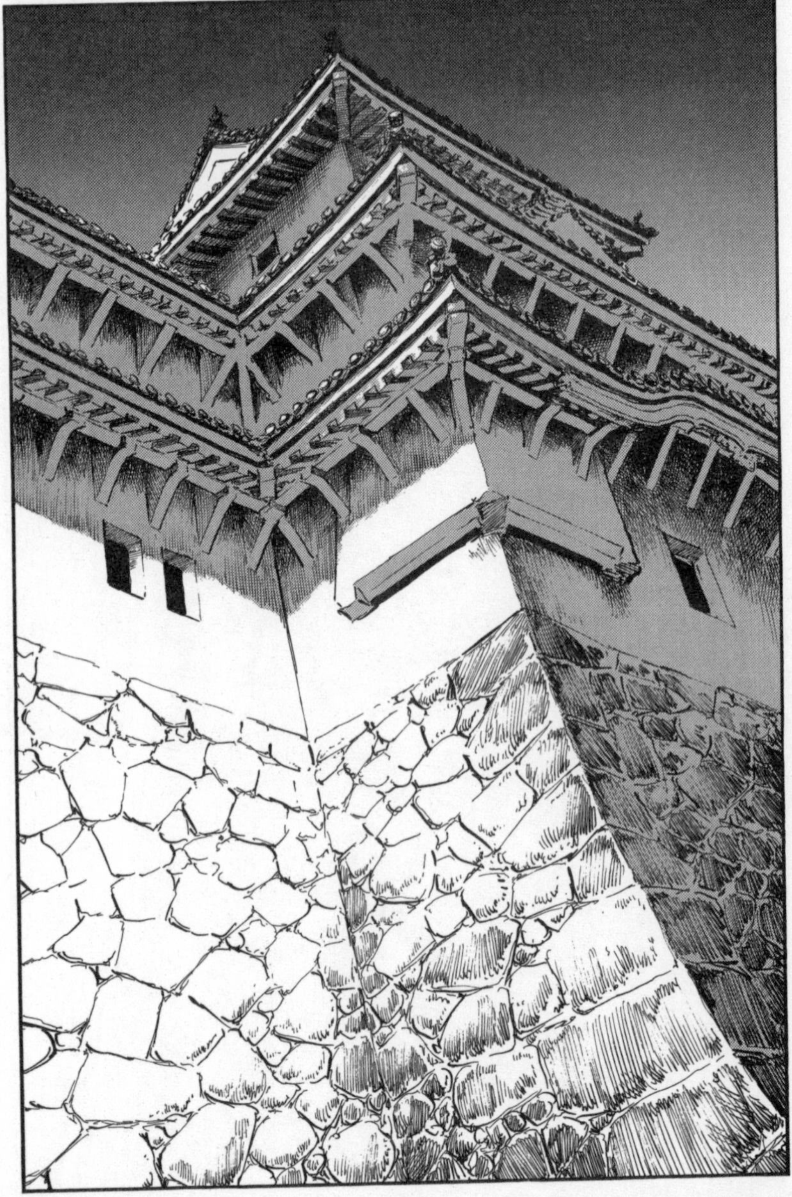

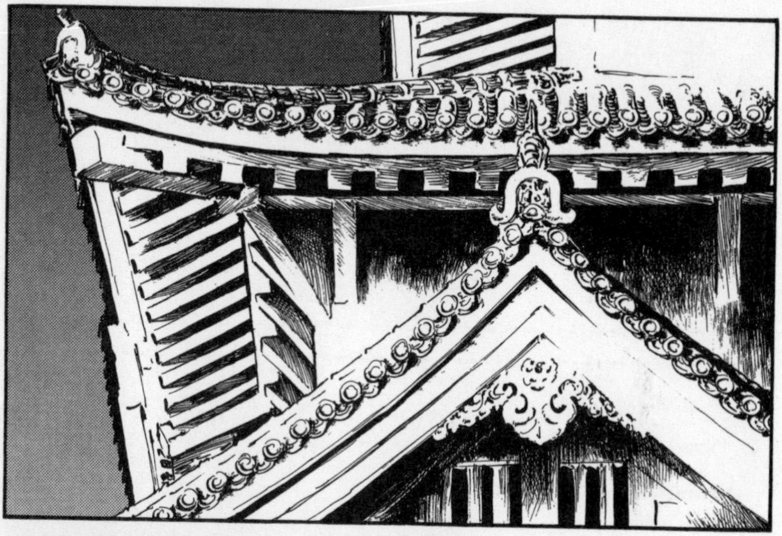
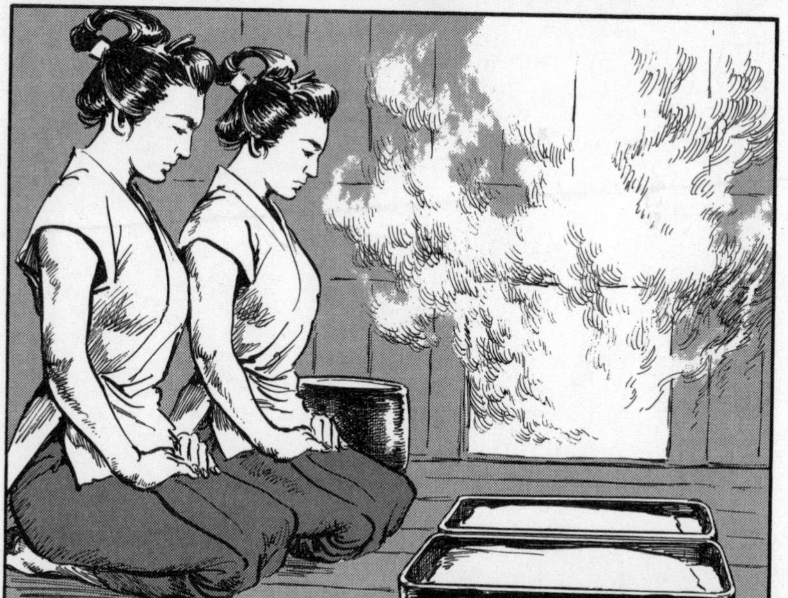

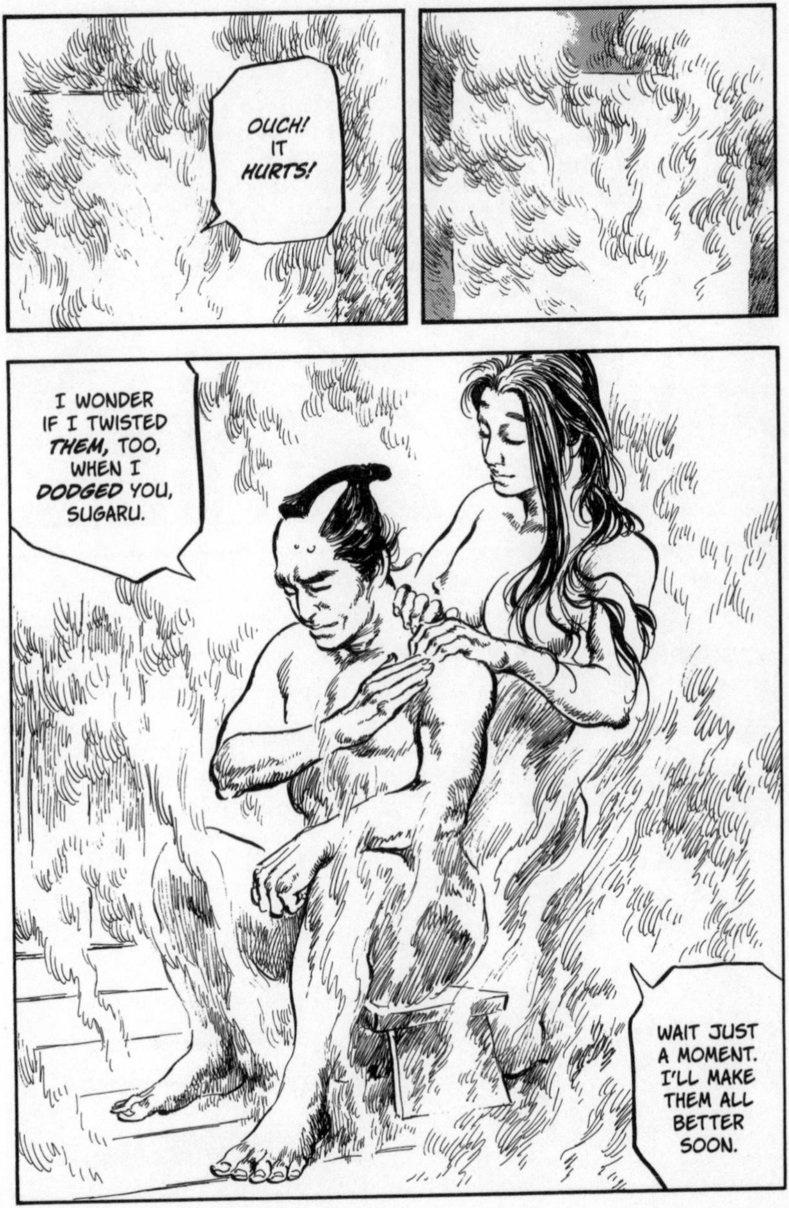
OUCH! IT HURTS!
I WONDER IF I TWISTED THEM, TOO, WHEN I DODGED YOU, SUGARU.
WAIT JUST A MOMENT. I'LL MAKE THEM ALL BETTER SOON.

ギ゛ッ
SQUEEZE
ギッ…!

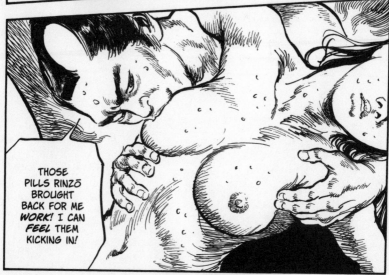

THOSE
PILLS RINZŌ
BROUGHT
BACK FOR ME
WORK! I CAN
FEEL THEM
KICKING IN!

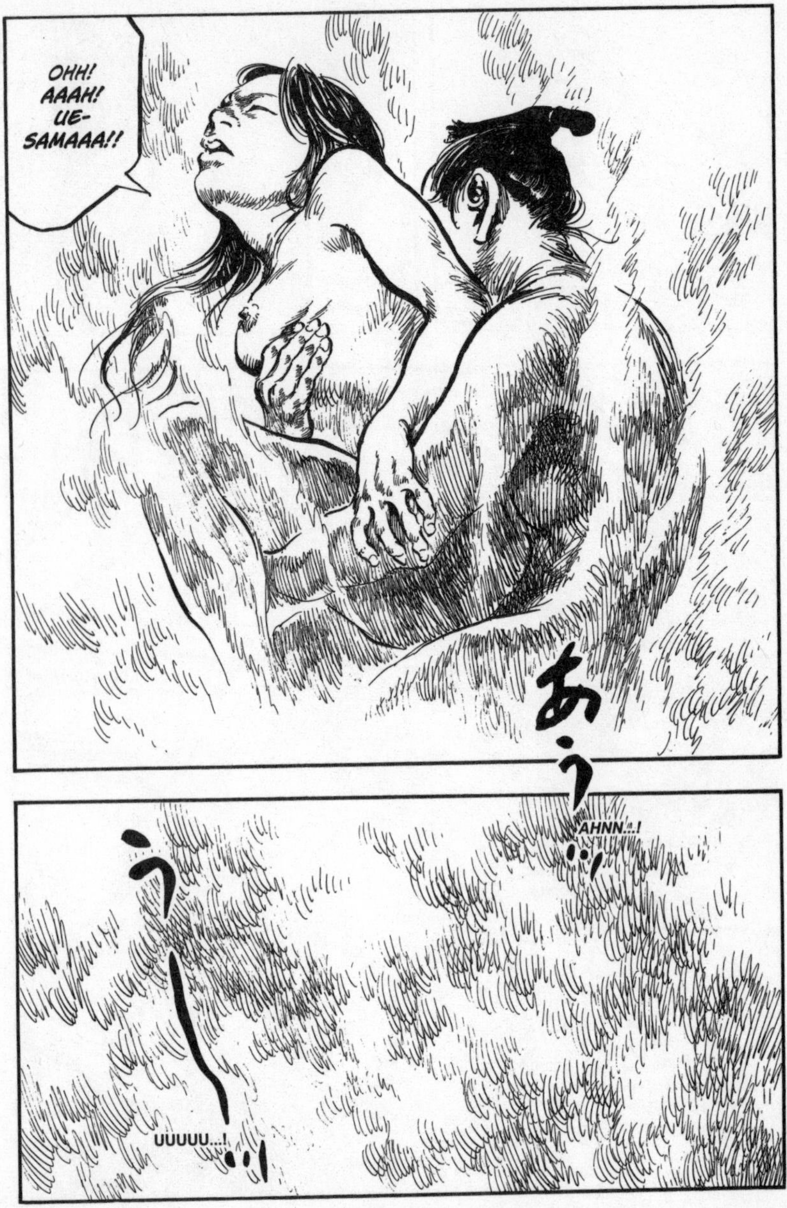
OHH! AAAH! UE-SAMAAA!!
あう…!
AHNN...!
う—…!
UUUUU...!

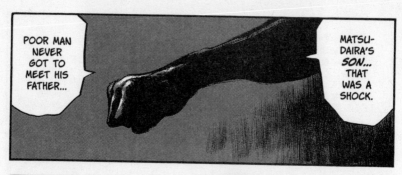

MATSU-DAIRA'S SON... THAT WAS A SHOCK.
POOR MAN NEVER GOT TO MEET HIS FATHER...
SO, SUGARU. HOW DO YOU THINK I SHOULD HANDLE HIM?
FORGVE MY INSOLENCE, BUT IS IT WISE TO CONCLUDE HE IS IZU-NO-KAMI-SAMA'S SON, JUST FROM A HESONO'O-GAKI.
IT'S NOT INCONCEIVABLE HE STOLE IT FROM ANOTHER.
HRMMM.

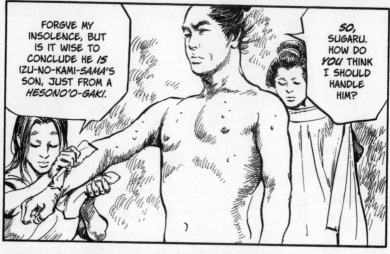

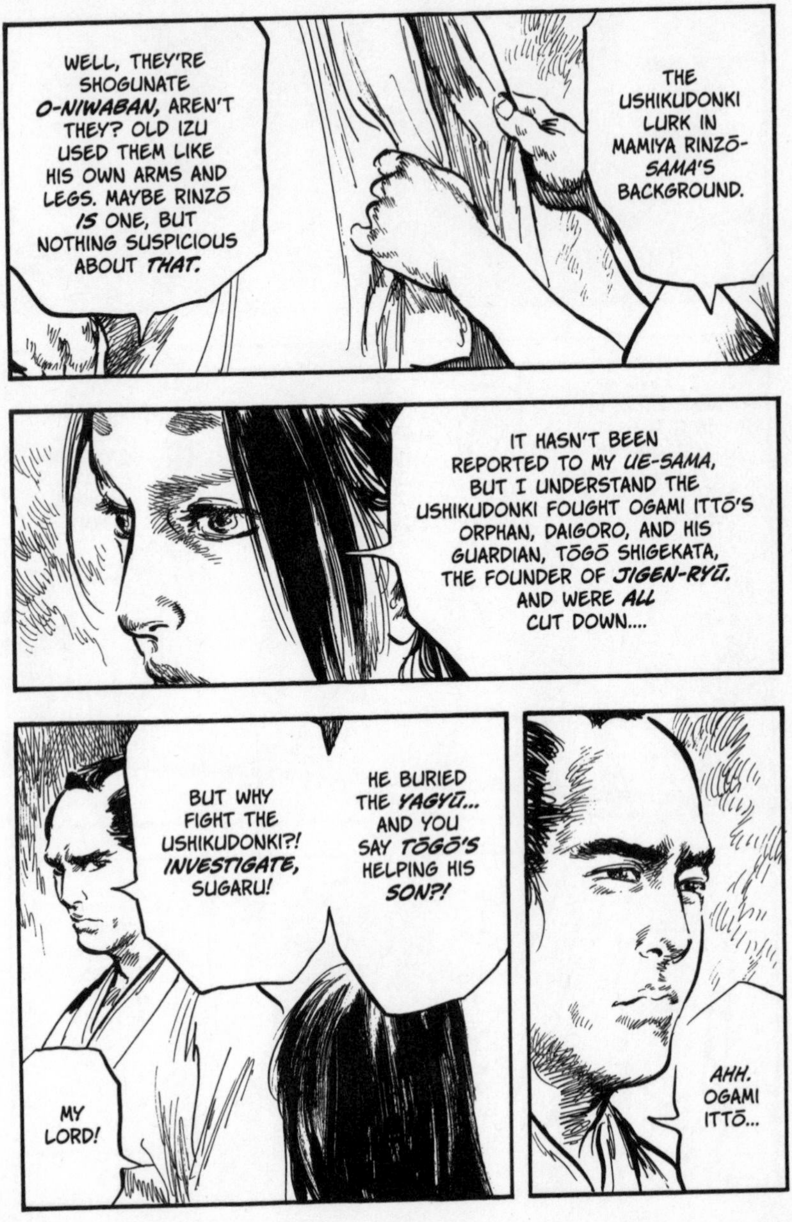
THE USHIKUDONKI LURK IN MAMIYA RINZŌ-SAMA'S BACKGROUND.
WELL, THEY'RE SHOGUNATE O-NIWABAN, AREN'T THEY? OLD IZU USED THEM LIKE HIS OWN ARMS AND LEGS. MAYBE RINZŌ IS ONE, BUT NOTHING SUSPICIOUS ABOUT THAT.
IT HASN'T BEEN REPORTED TO MY UE-SAMA, BUT I UNDERSTAND THE USHIKUDONKI FOUGHT OGAMI ITTŌ'S ORPHAN, DAIGORO, AND HIS GUARDIAN, TŌGŌ SHIGEKATA, THE FOUNDER OF JIGEN-RYŪ. AND WERE ALL CUT DOWN....
AHH. OGAMI ITTŌ...
HE BURIED THE YAGYŪ... AND YOU SAY TŌGŌ'S HELPING HIS SON?!
BUT WHY FIGHT THE USHIKUDONKI?! INVESTIGATE, SUGARU!
MY LORD!

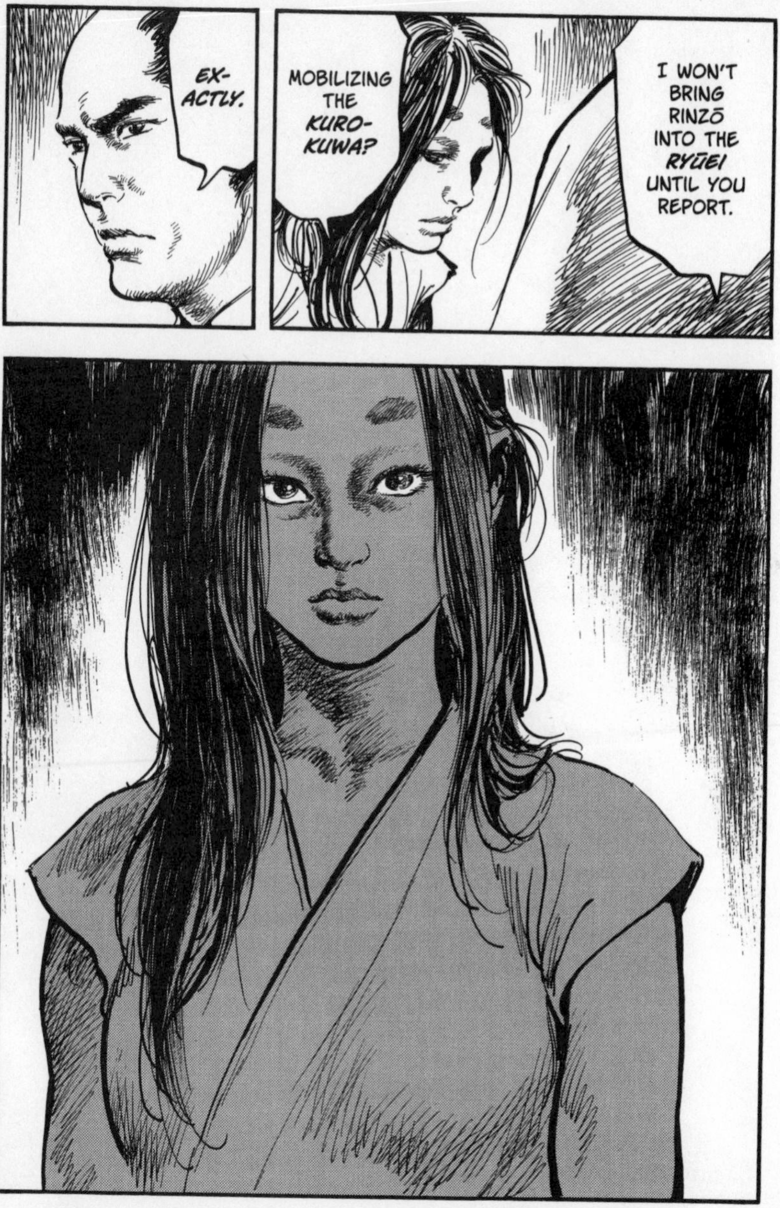
I WON'T BRING RINZŌ INTO THE *RYŪEI* UNTIL YOU REPORT.
MOBILIZING THE *KURO-KUWA?*
EX-ACTLY.

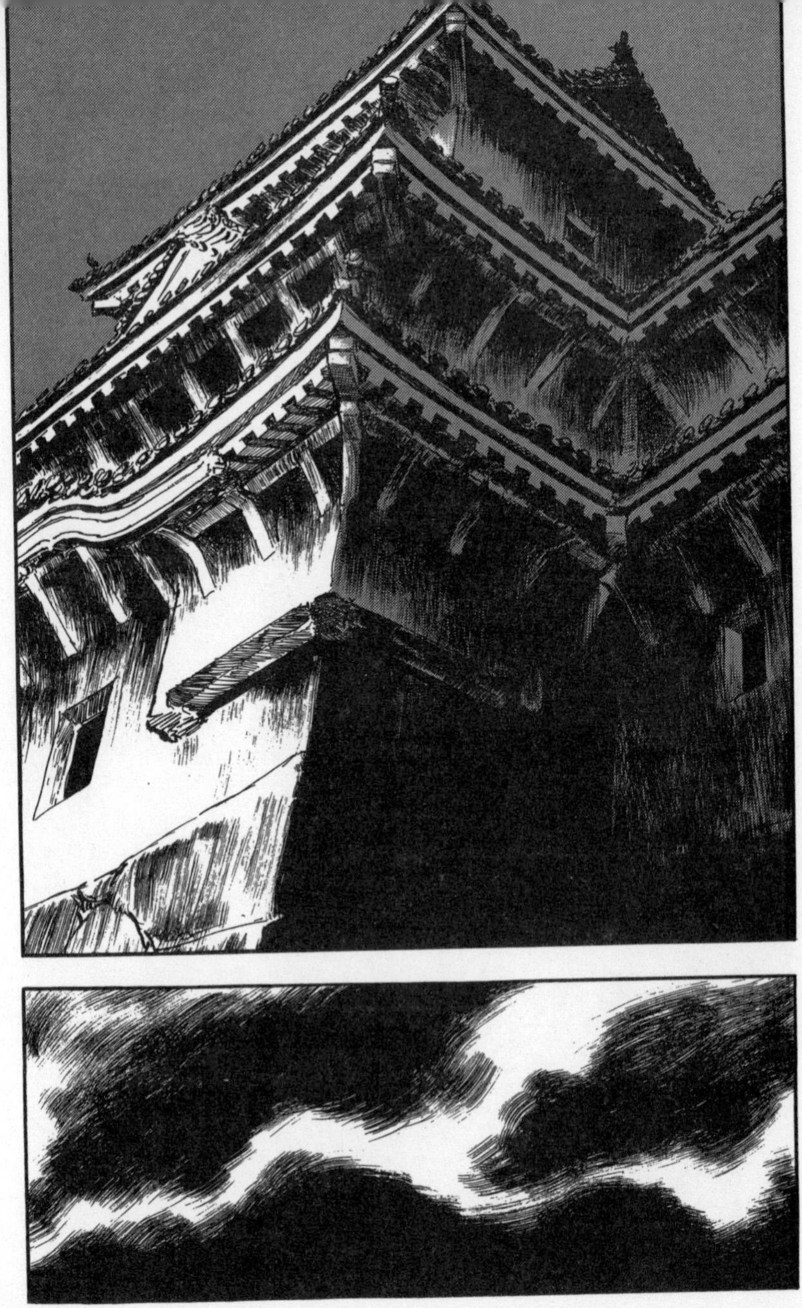

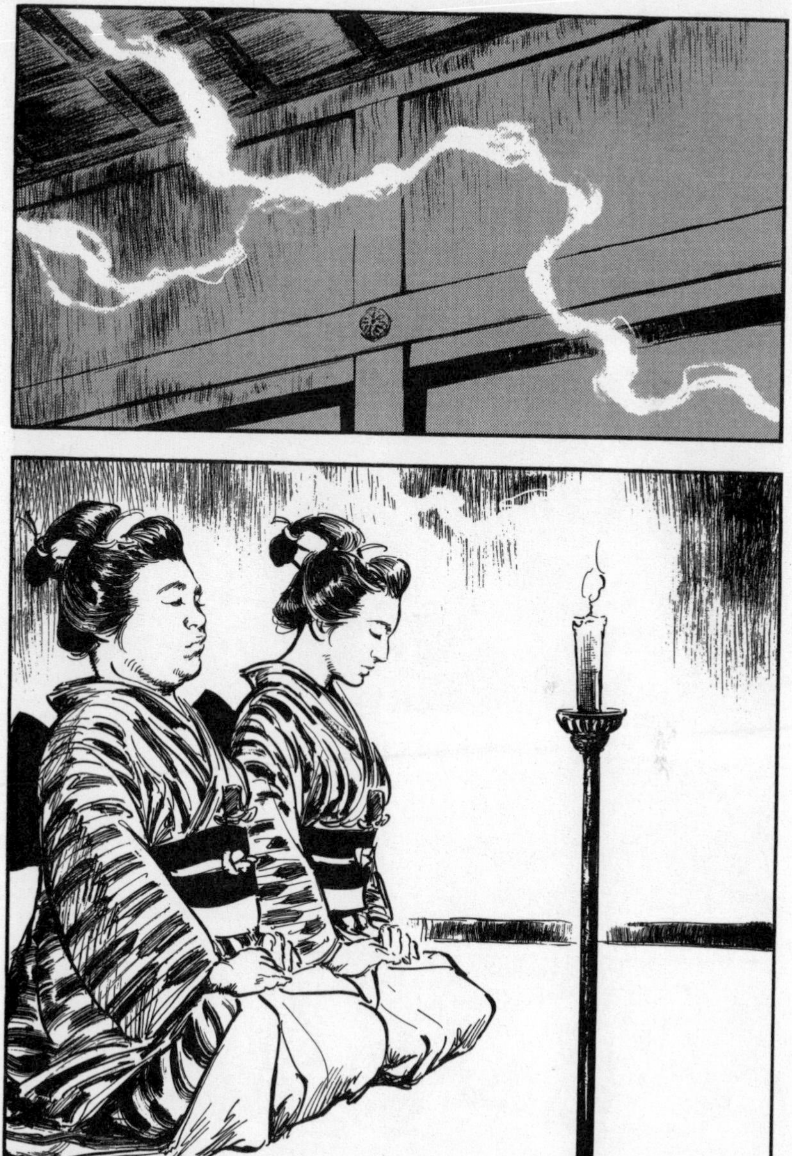

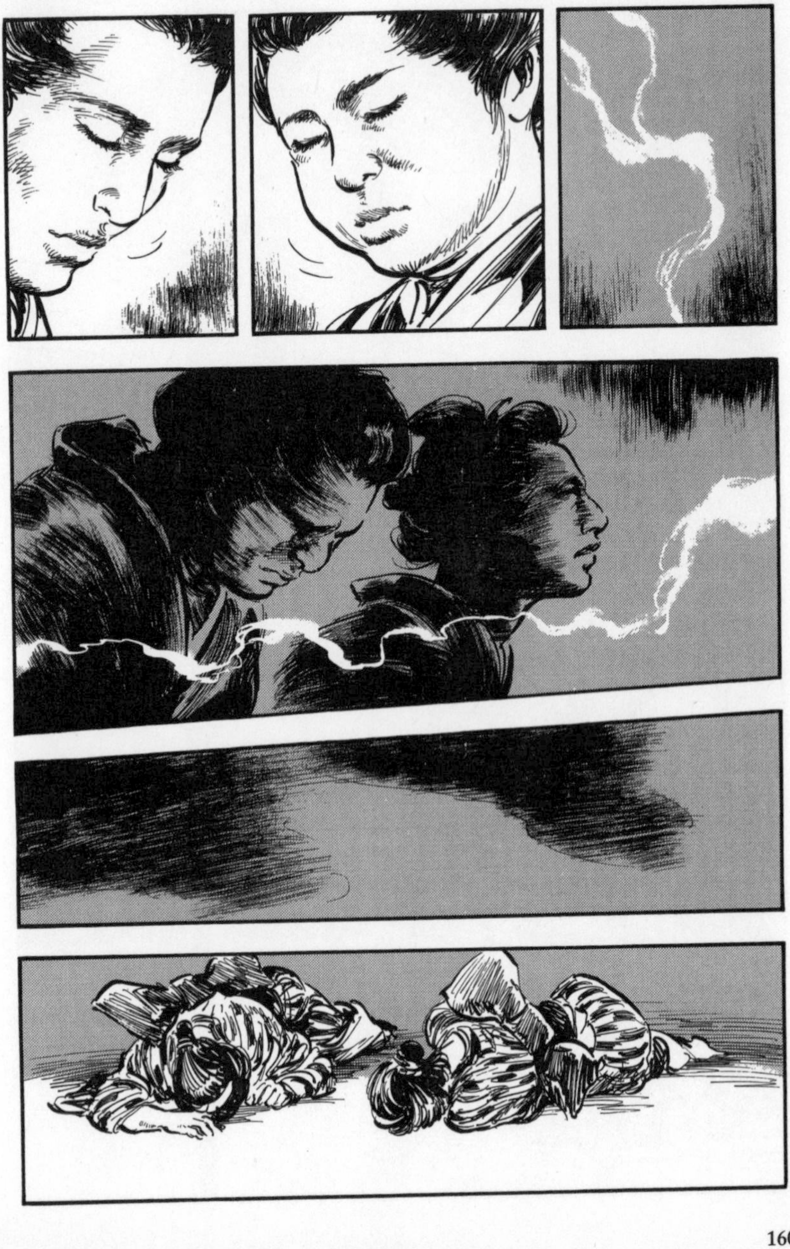

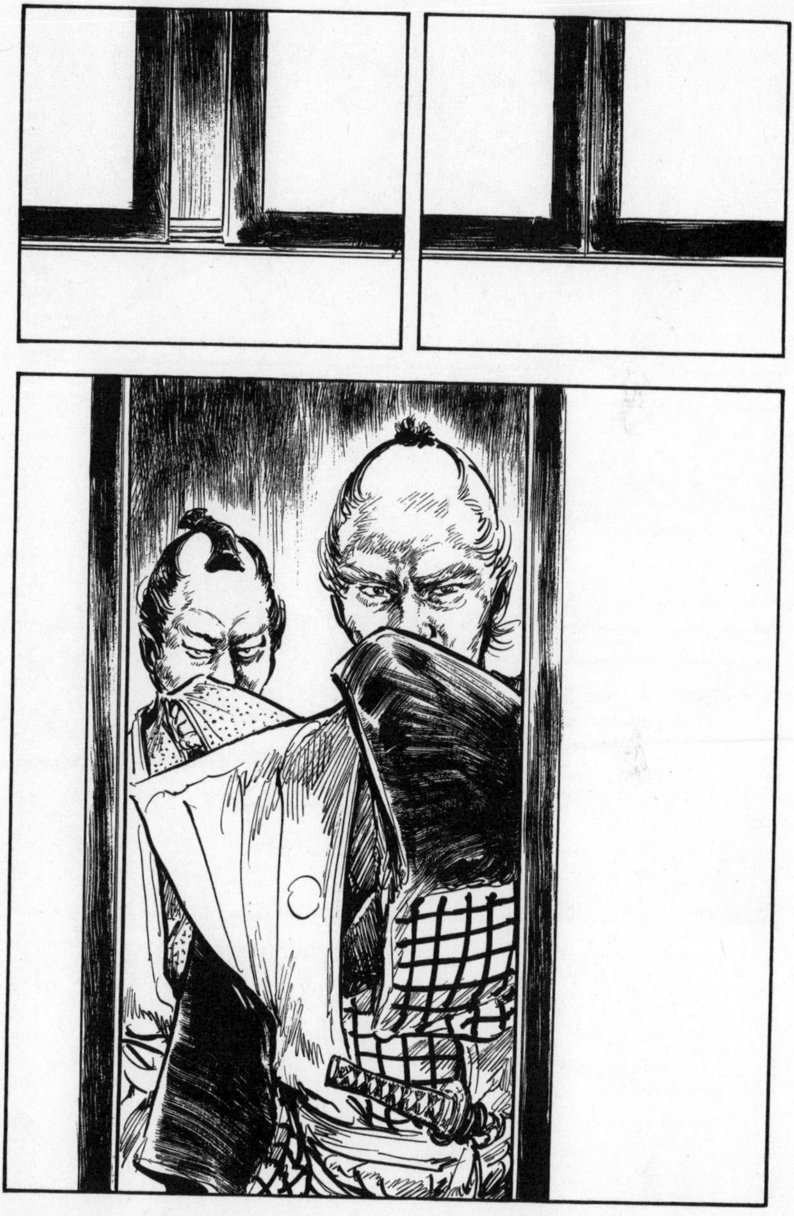

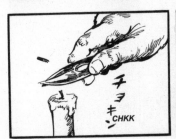

チョ
キン
CHKK

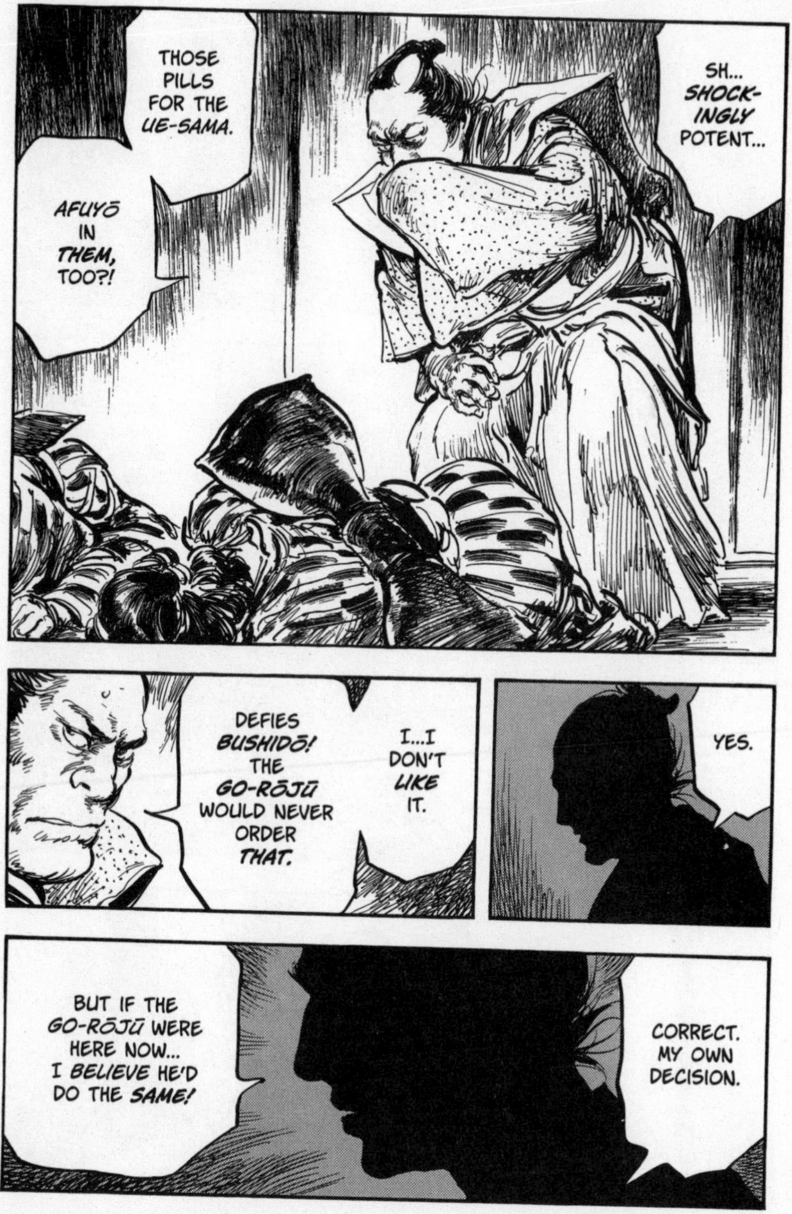
SH... SHOCKINGLY POTENT...
THOSE PILLS FOR THE UE-SAMA.
AFUYŌ IN THEM, TOO?!
YES.
I...I DON'T LIKE IT.
DEFIES BUSHIDŌ! THE GO-RŌJŪ WOULD NEVER ORDER THAT.
CORRECT. MY OWN DECISION.
BUT IF THE GO-RŌJŪ WERE HERE NOW... I BELIEVE HE'D DO THE SAME!

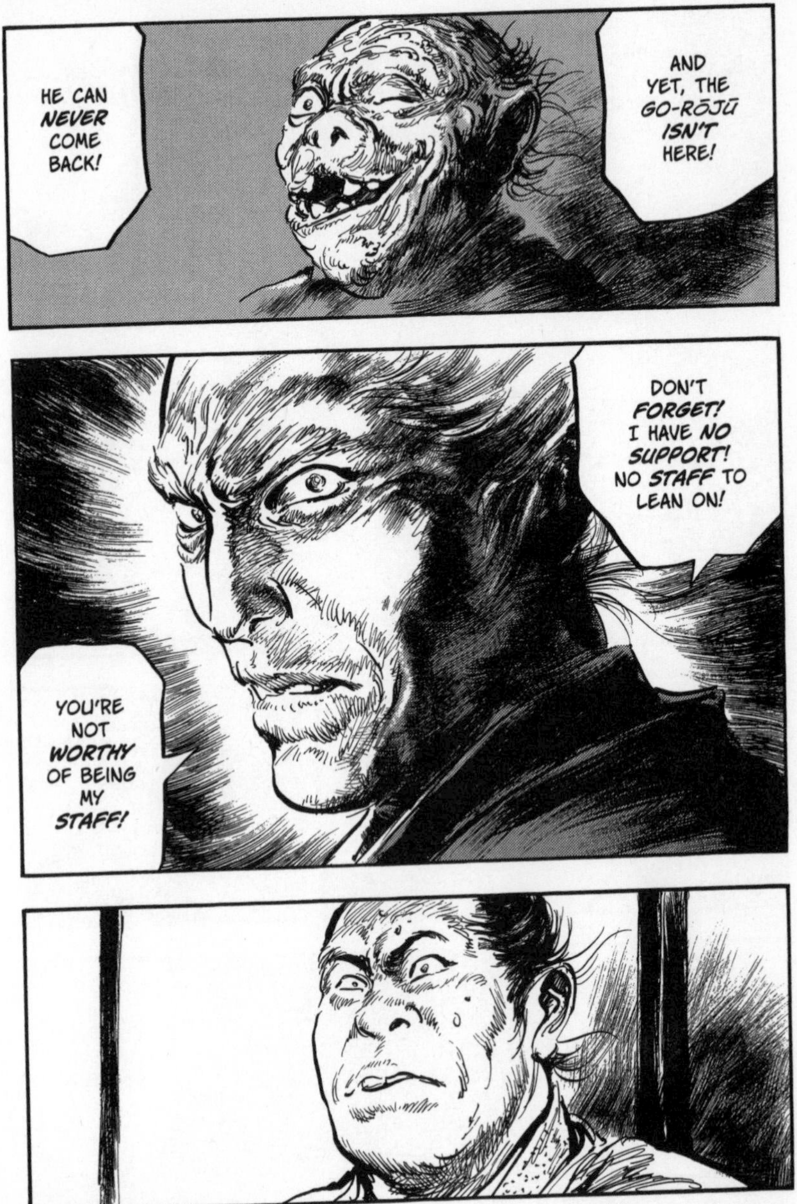
AND YET, THE GO-RŌJŪ ISN'T HERE!
HE CAN NEVER COME BACK!
DON'T FORGET! I HAVE NO SUPPORT! NO STAFF TO LEAN ON!
YOU'RE NOT WORTHY OF BEING MY STAFF!

其之十三 THE THIRTEENTH
NO STAFF TO LEAN ON PART 11
無杖（十一）

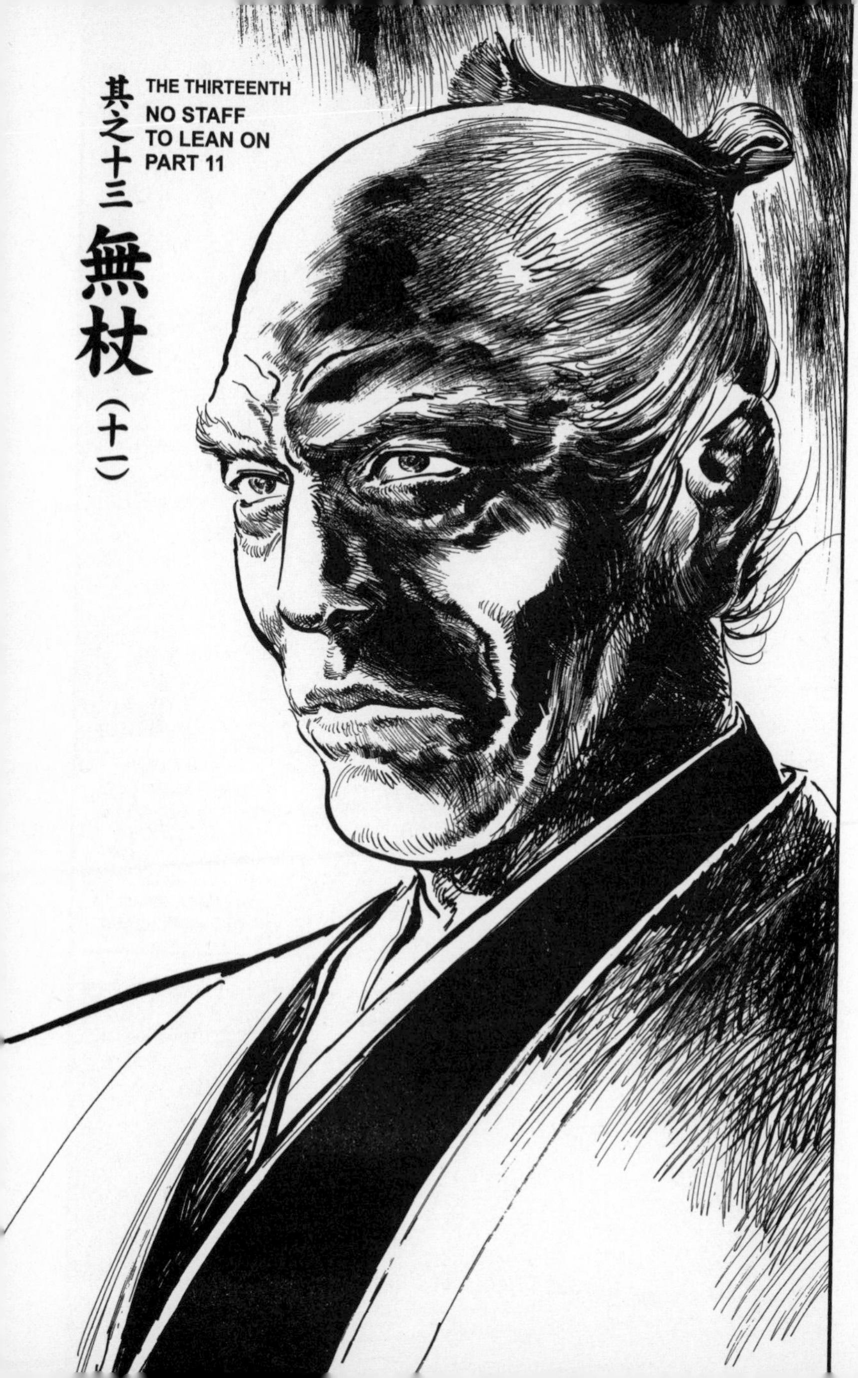

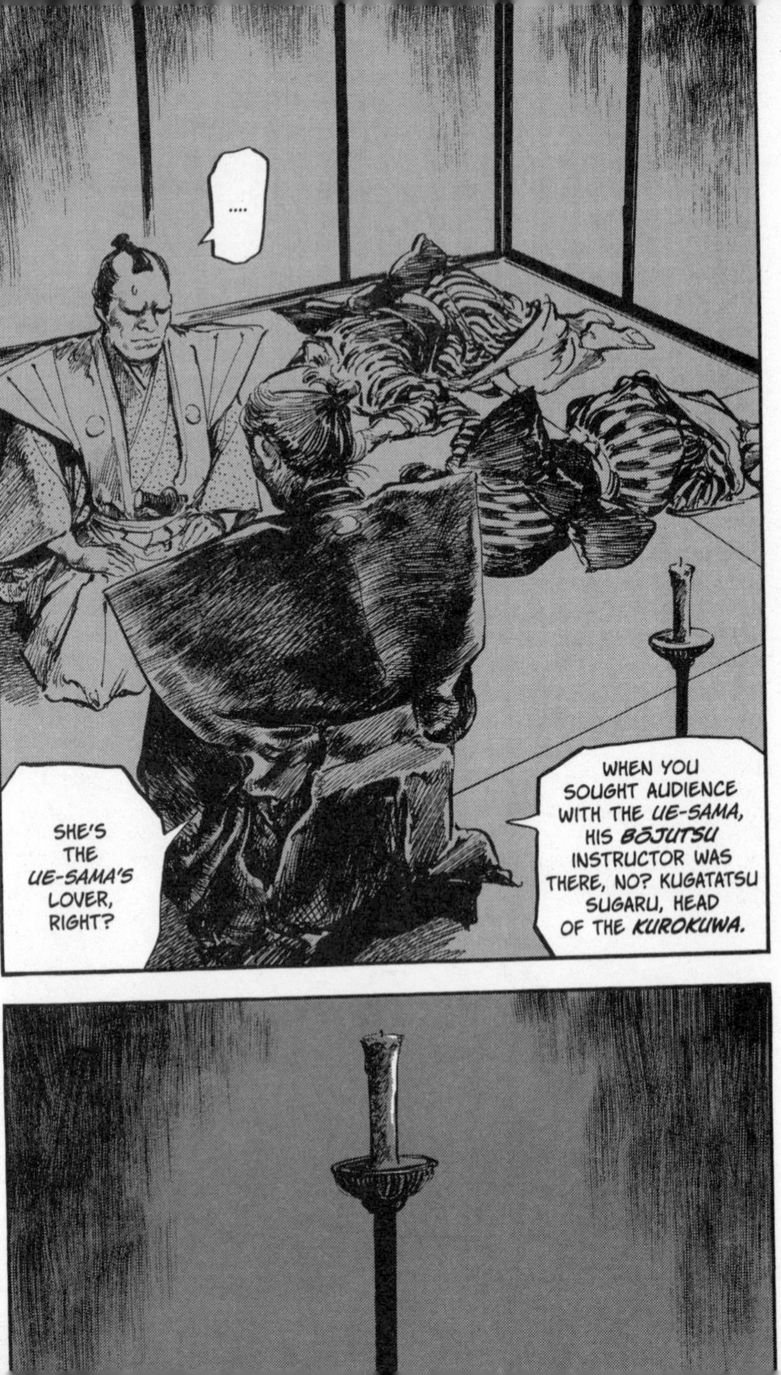
WHEN YOU SOUGHT AUDIENCE WITH THE *UE-SAMA*, HIS *BŌJUTSU* INSTRUCTOR WAS THERE, NO? KUGATATSU SUGARU, HEAD OF THE ***KUROKUWA.***
SHE'S THE *UE-SAMA'S* LOVER, RIGHT?
....

URM... YES. SHE IS.

RIGHT ?!

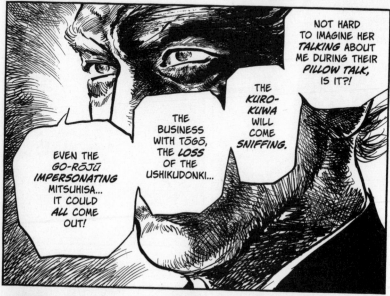

NOT HARD TO IMAGINE HER *TALKING* ABOUT ME DURING THEIR *PILLOW TALK*, IS IT?!

THE *KURO-KUWA* WILL COME *SNIFFING.*

THE BUSINESS WITH TŌGŌ, THE *LOSS* OF THE USHIKUDONKI...

EVEN THE *GO-RŌJŪ IMPERSONATING* MITSUHISA... IT COULD *ALL* COME OUT!

COULDN'T IT?!

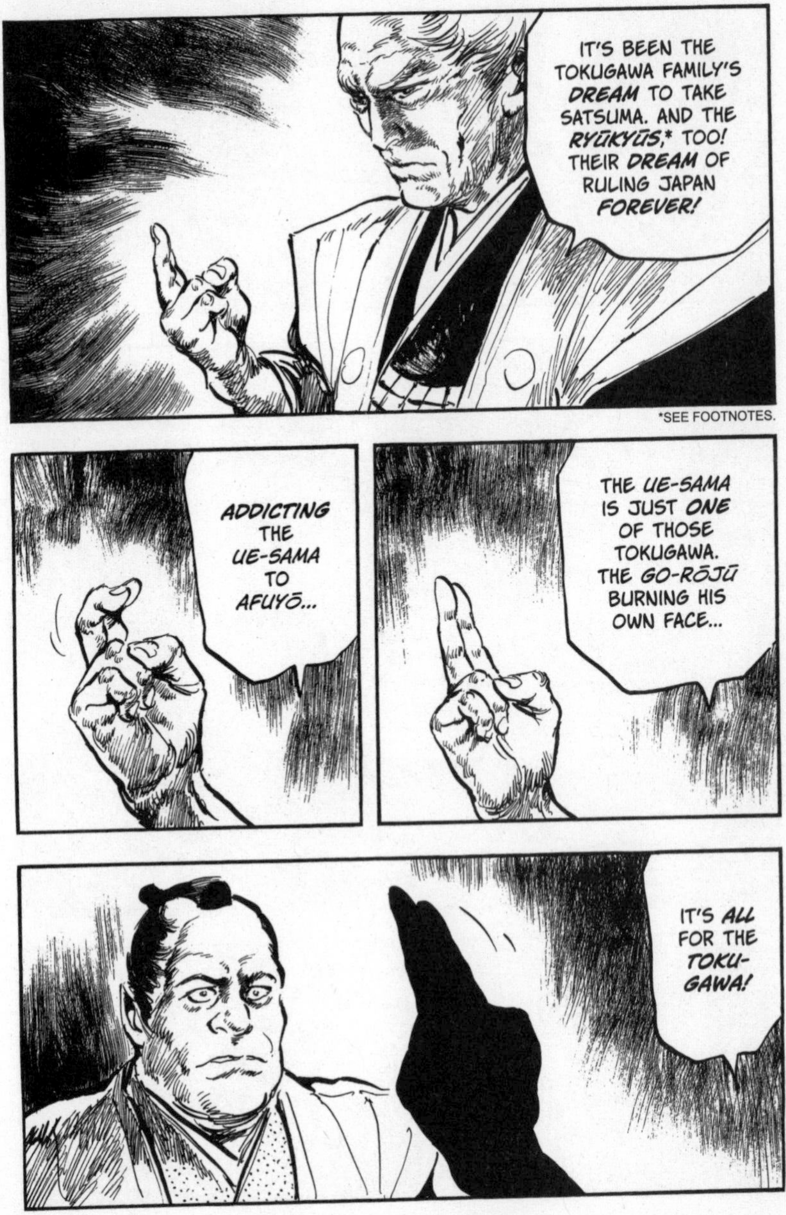
IT'S BEEN THE TOKUGAWA FAMILY'S *DREAM* TO TAKE SATSUMA. AND THE *RYŪKYŪS,** TOO! THEIR *DREAM* OF RULING JAPAN *FOREVER!*
THE *UE-SAMA* IS JUST *ONE* OF THOSE TOKUGAWA. THE *GO-RŌJŪ* BURNING HIS OWN FACE...
ADDICTING THE *UE-SAMA* TO *AFUYŌ*...
IT'S *ALL* FOR THE *TOKU-GAWA!*
*SEE FOOTNOTES.

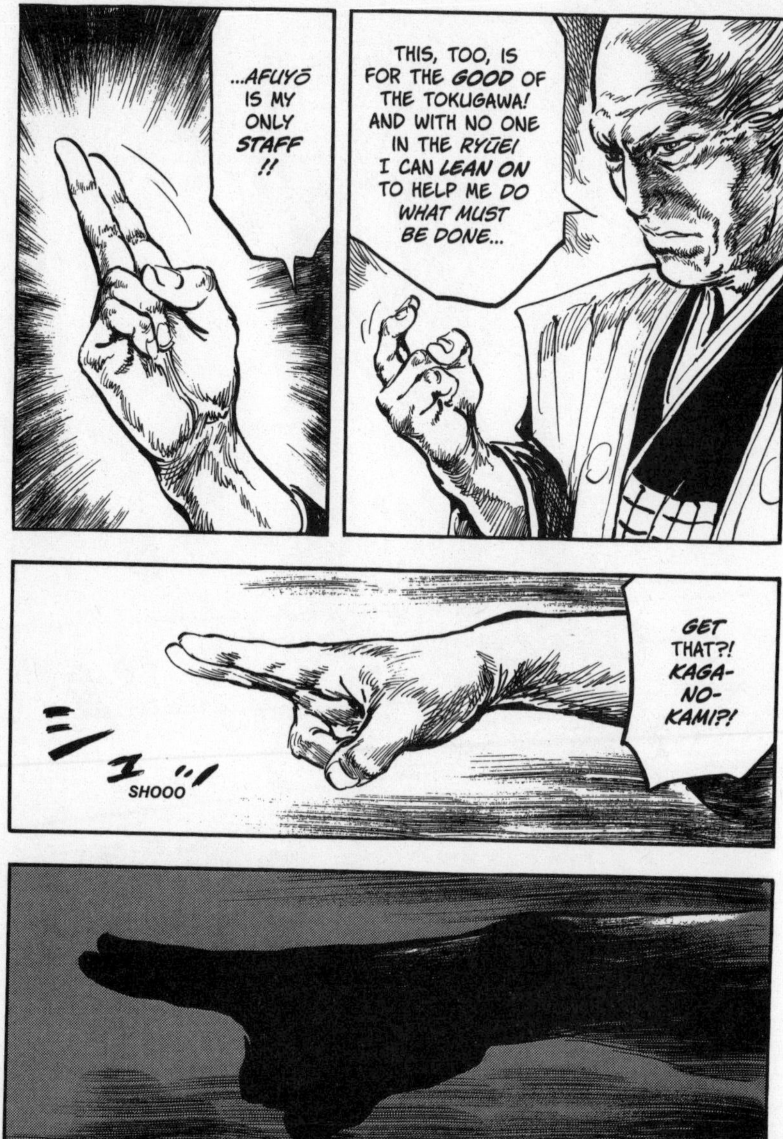
THIS, TOO, IS FOR THE GOOD OF THE TOKUGAWA! AND WITH NO ONE IN THE RYŪEI I CAN LEAN ON TO HELP ME DO WHAT MUST BE DONE...
...AFUYŌ IS MY ONLY STAFF !!
GET THAT?! KAGA-NO-KAMI?!
SHOOO

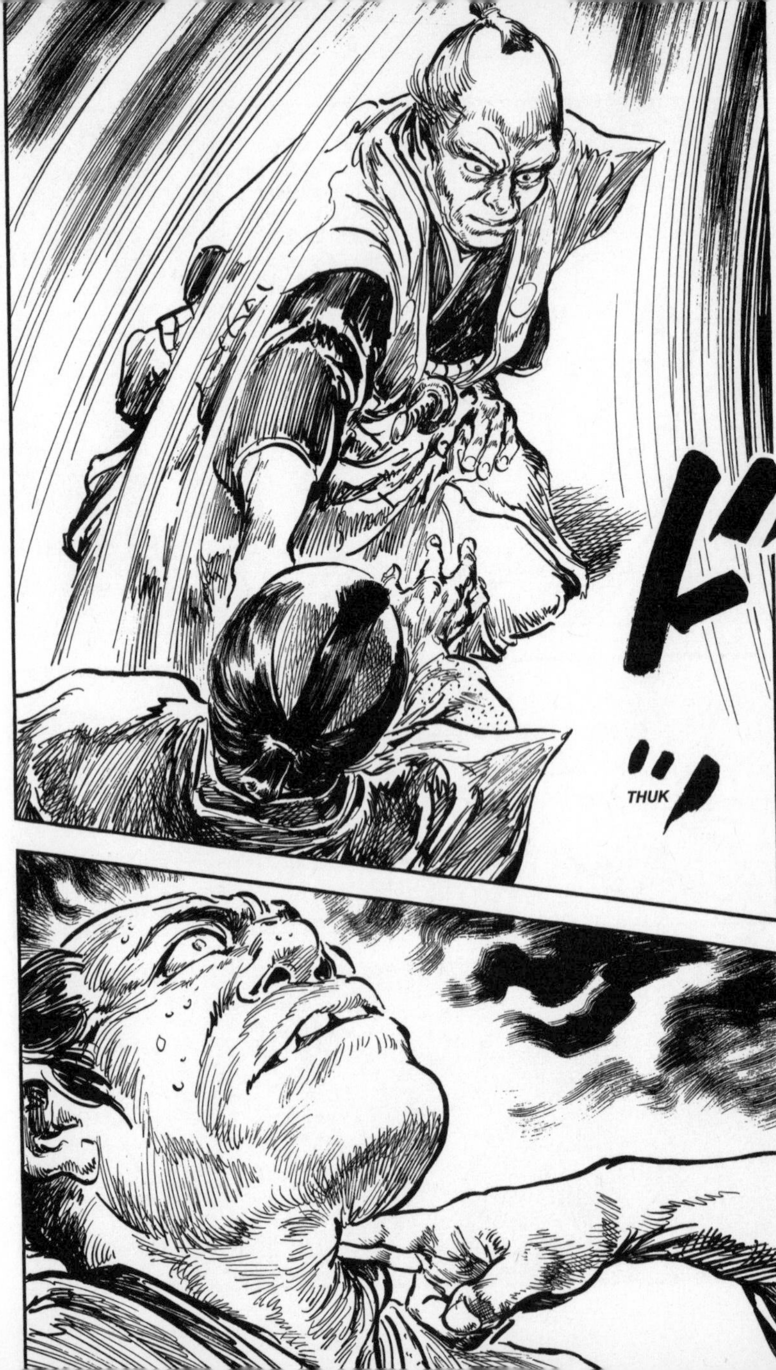
ドッ
THUK

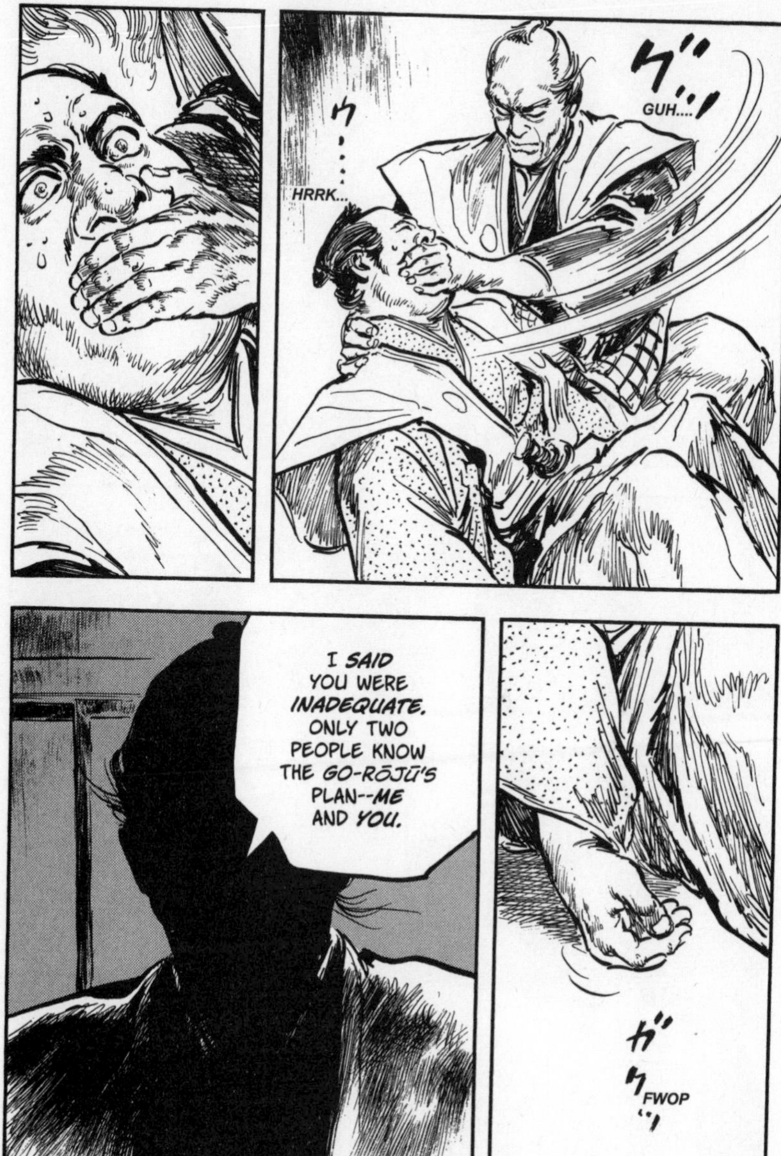
GUH....!
HRRK...
FWOP
I *SAID* YOU WERE *INADEQUATE.* ONLY TWO PEOPLE KNOW THE *GO-RŌJŪ'S* PLAN--*ME* AND *YOU.*

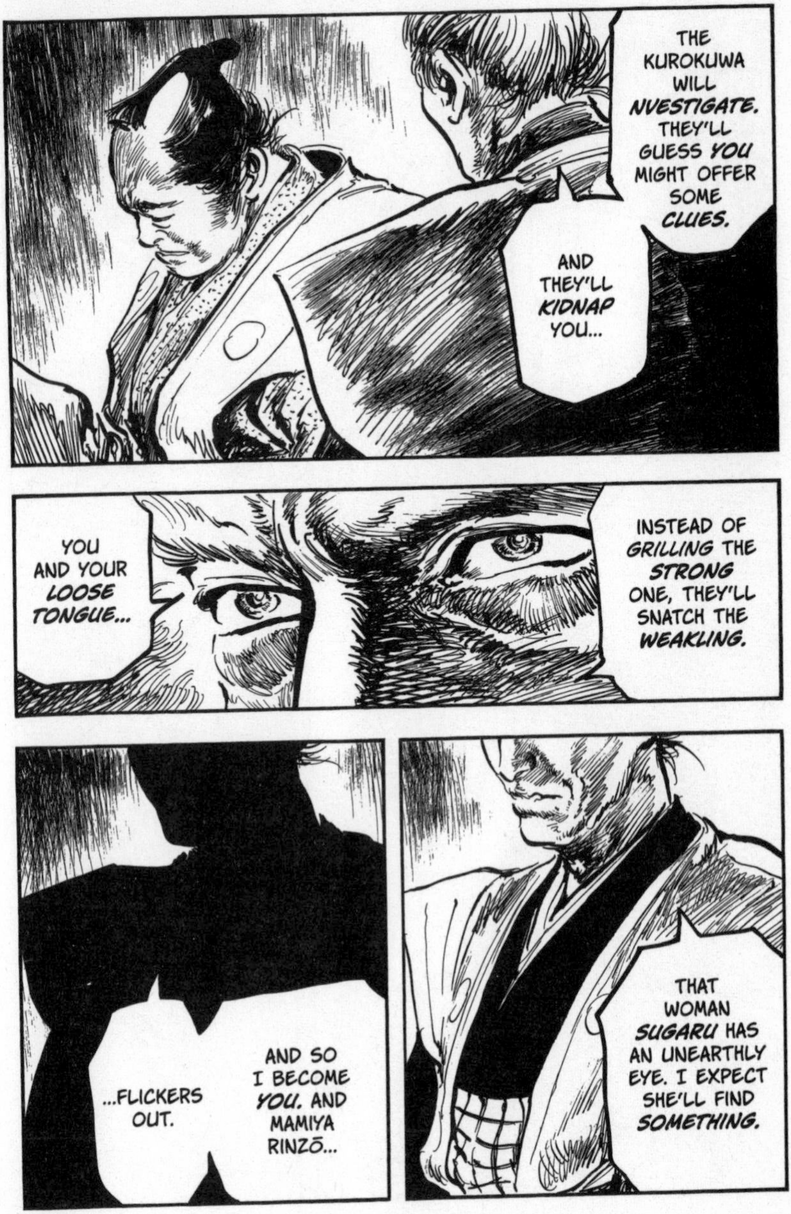
THE KUROKUWA WILL NVESTIGATE. THEY'LL GUESS YOU MIGHT OFFER SOME CLUES.
AND THEY'LL KIDNAP YOU...
INSTEAD OF GRILLING THE STRONG ONE, THEY'LL SNATCH THE WEAKLING.
YOU AND YOUR LOOSE TONGUE...
THAT WOMAN SUGARU HAS AN UNEARTHLY EYE. I EXPECT SHE'LL FIND SOMETHING.
AND SO I BECOME YOU. AND MAMIYA RINZŌ...
...FLICKERS OUT.

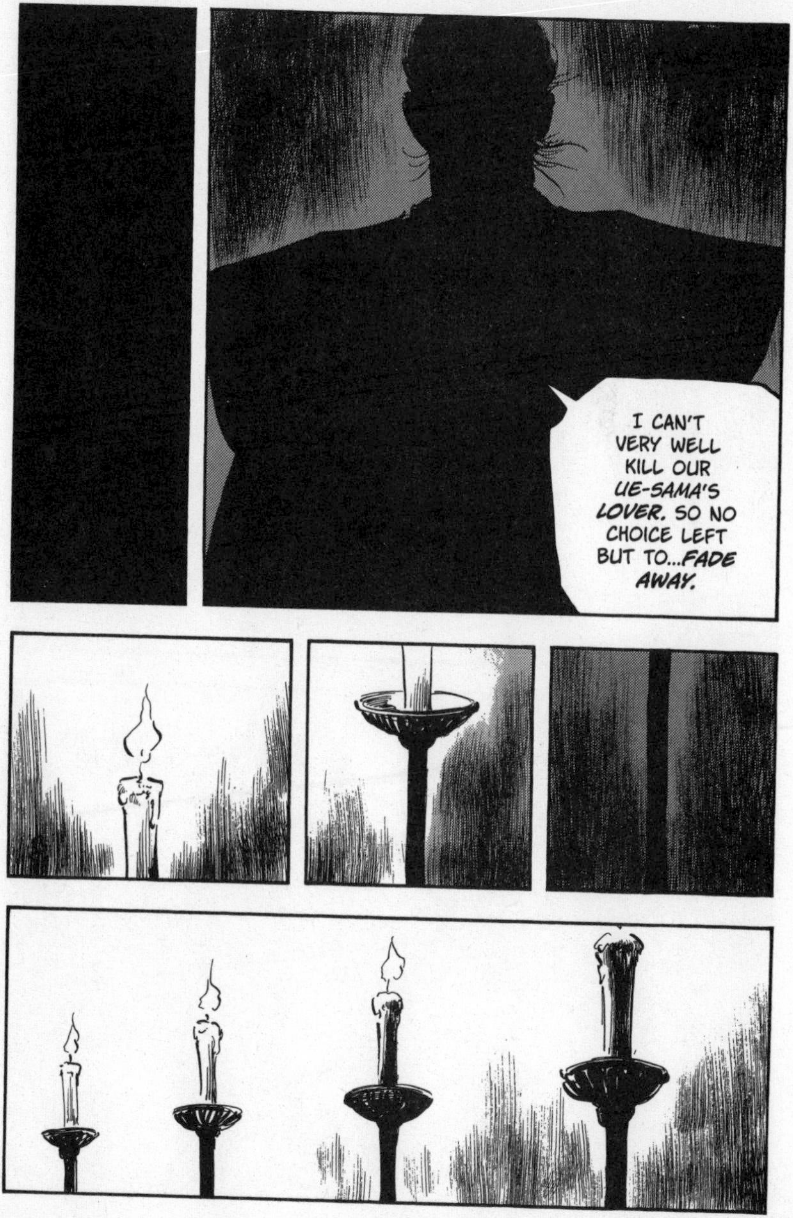
I CAN'T VERY WELL KILL OUR UE-SAMA'S LOVER. SO NO CHOICE LEFT BUT TO...FADE AWAY.

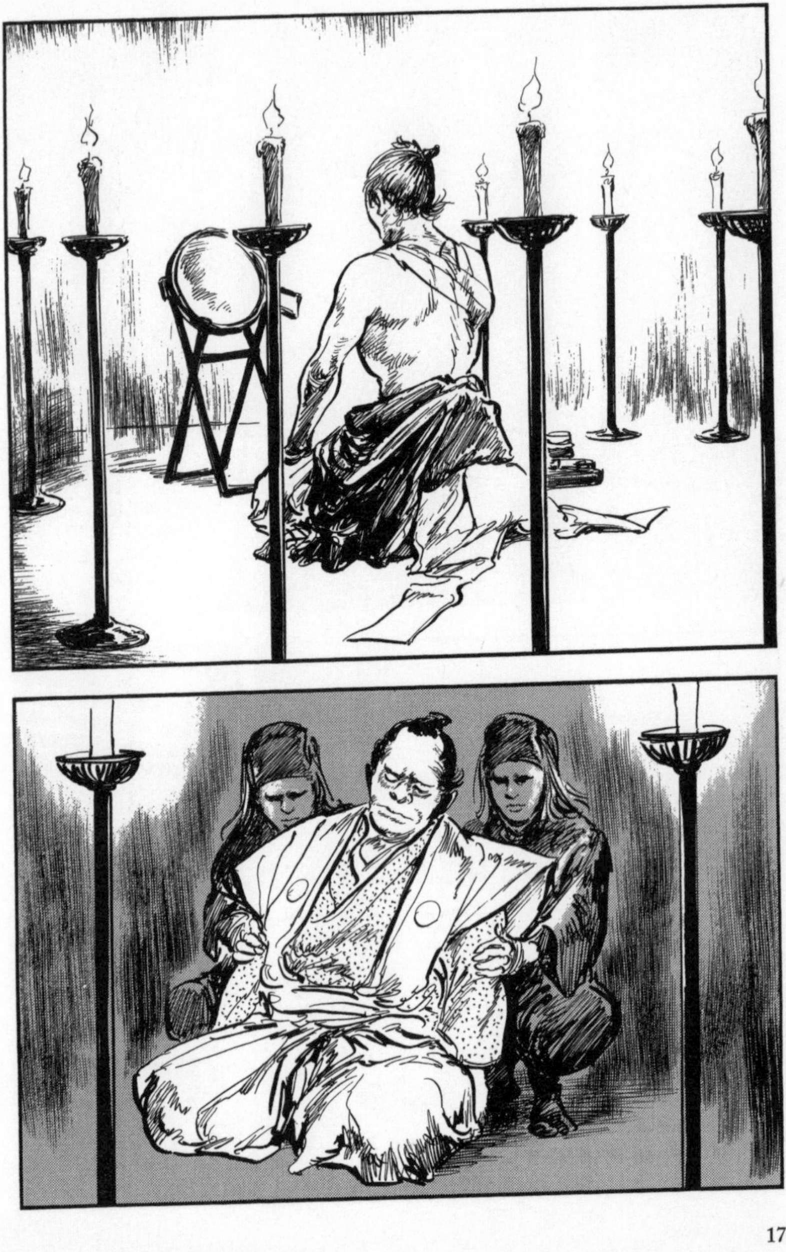

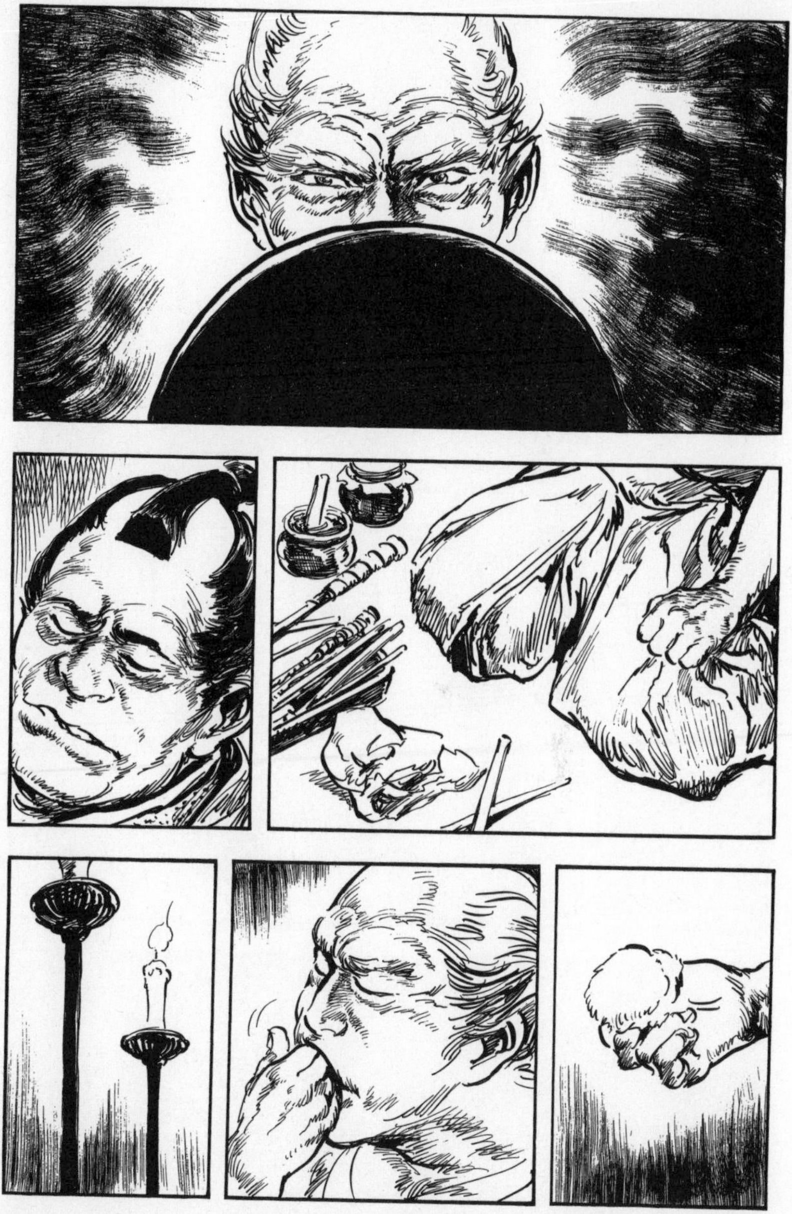

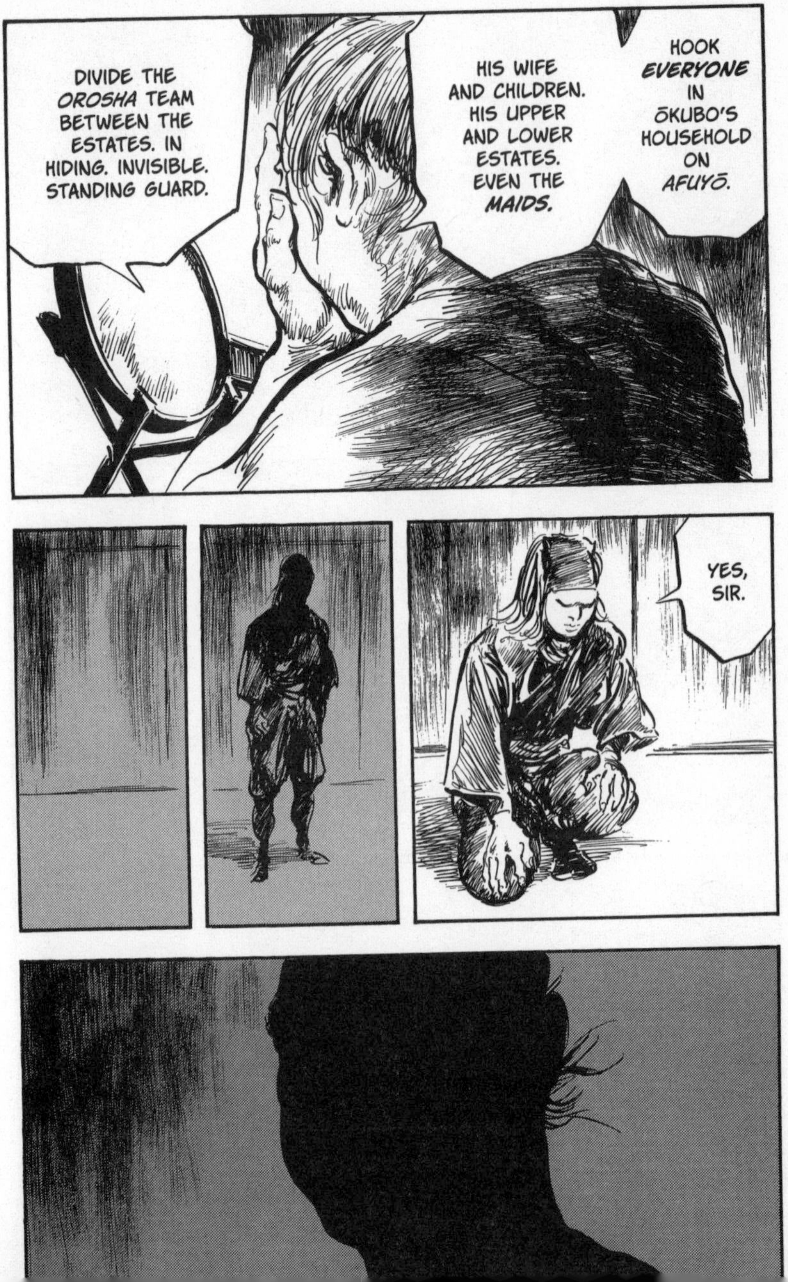
HOOK *EVERYONE* IN ŌKUBO'S HOUSEHOLD ON *AFUYŌ*.
HIS WIFE AND CHILDREN. HIS UPPER AND LOWER ESTATES. EVEN THE *MAIDS*.
DIVIDE THE *OROSHA* TEAM BETWEEN THE ESTATES. IN HIDING. INVISIBLE. STANDING GUARD.
YES, SIR.

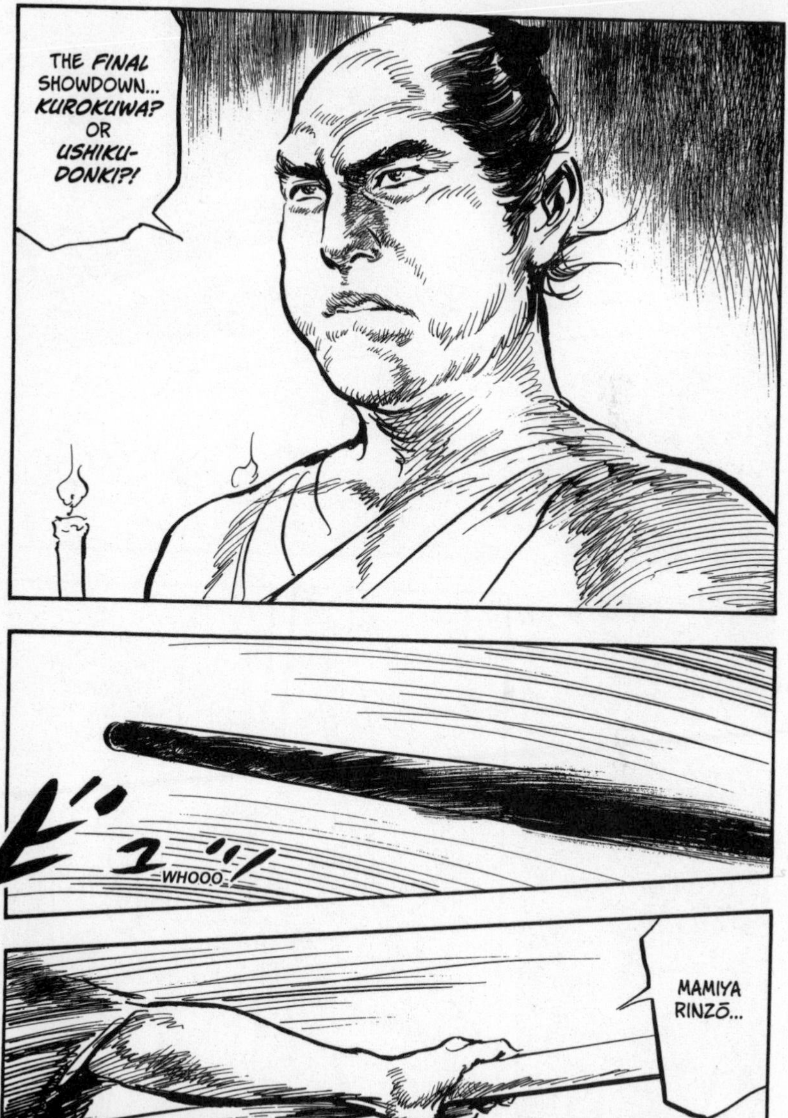

THE *FINAL* SHOWDOWN... *KUROKUWA?* OR *USHIKU-DONKI?!*
ビュッ!
WHOOO
MAMIYA RINZŌ...

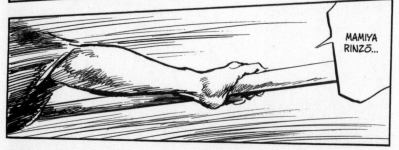

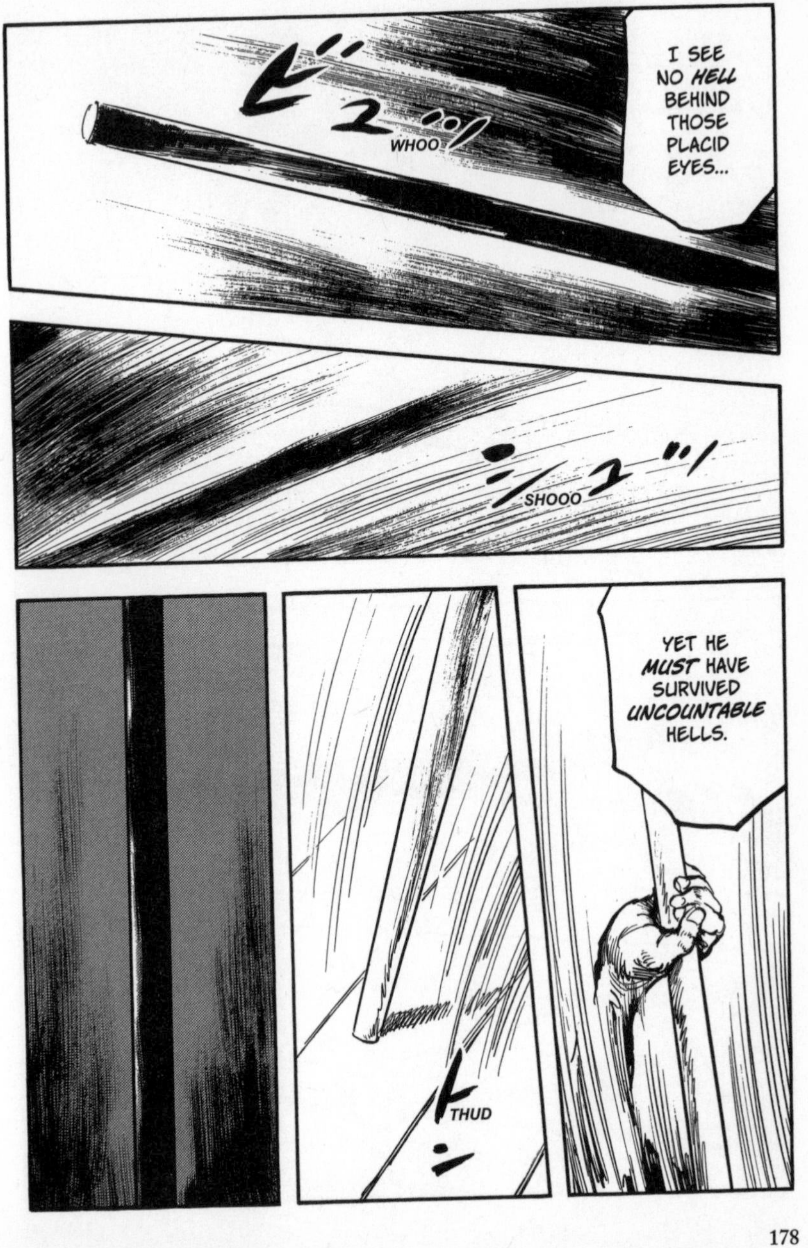
I SEE NO HELL BEHIND THOSE PLACID EYES...
ビュッ
WHOO
シュッ
SHOOO
YET HE MUST HAVE SURVIVED UNCOUNTABLE HELLS.
トッ
THUD

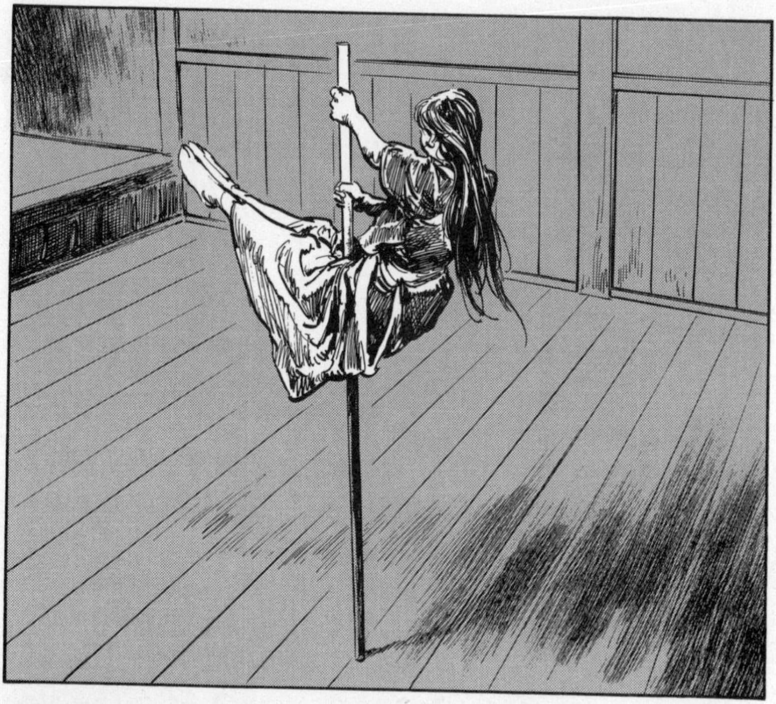

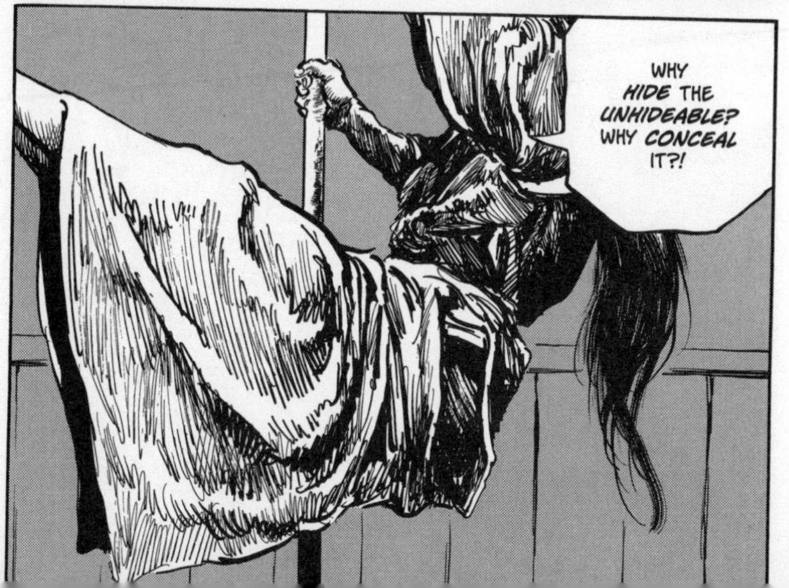
WHY *HIDE* THE *UNHIDEABLE?* WHY *CONCEAL* IT?!

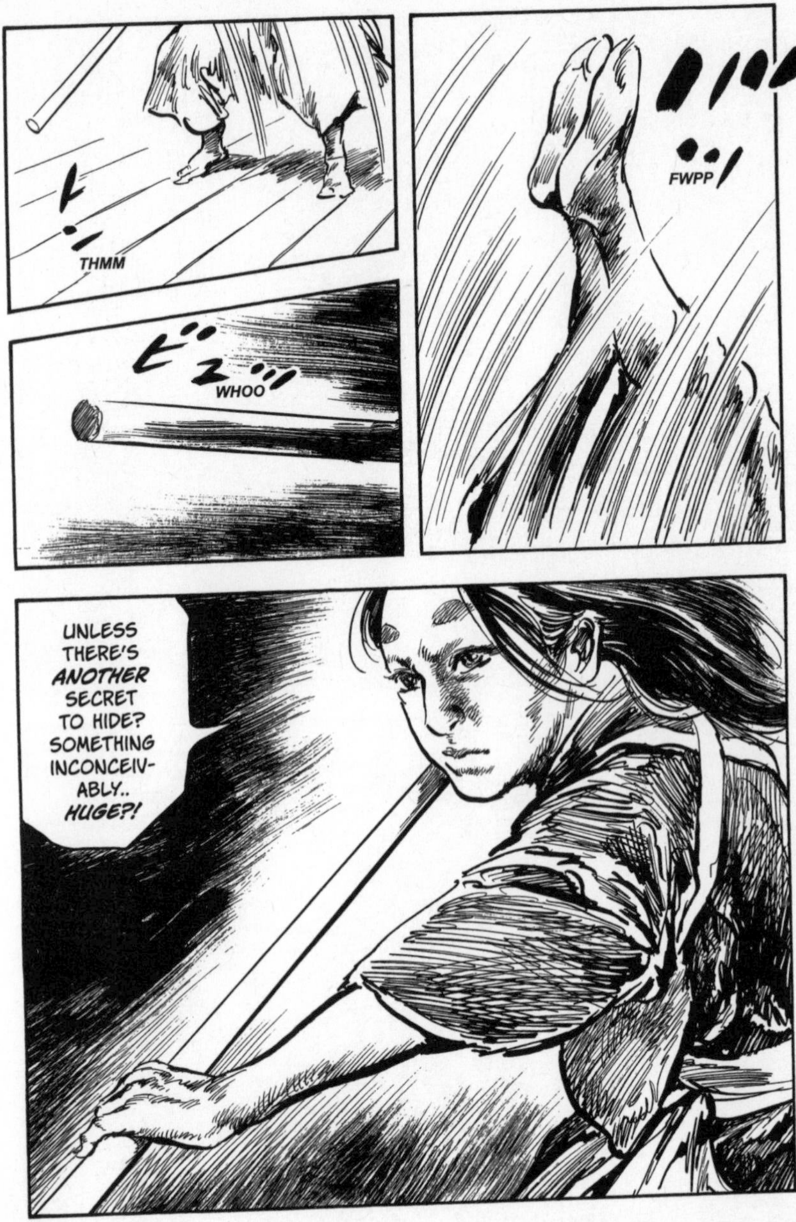
FWPP
THMM
WHOO
UNLESS THERE'S *ANOTHER* SECRET TO HIDE? SOMETHING INCONCEIV-ABLY.. *HUGE?!*

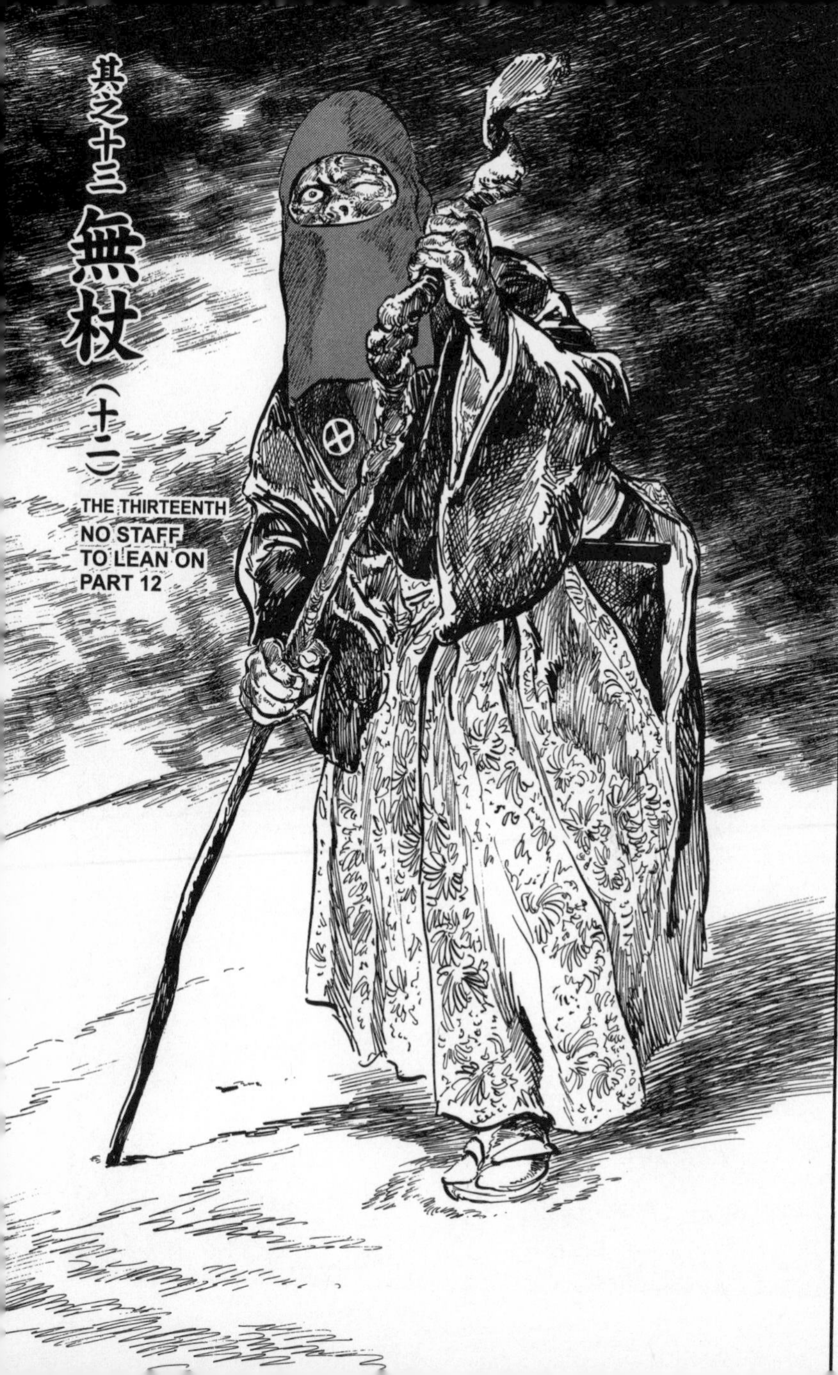
其之十三 無杖（十二）
THE THIRTEENTH
NO STAFF
TO LEAN ON
PART 12

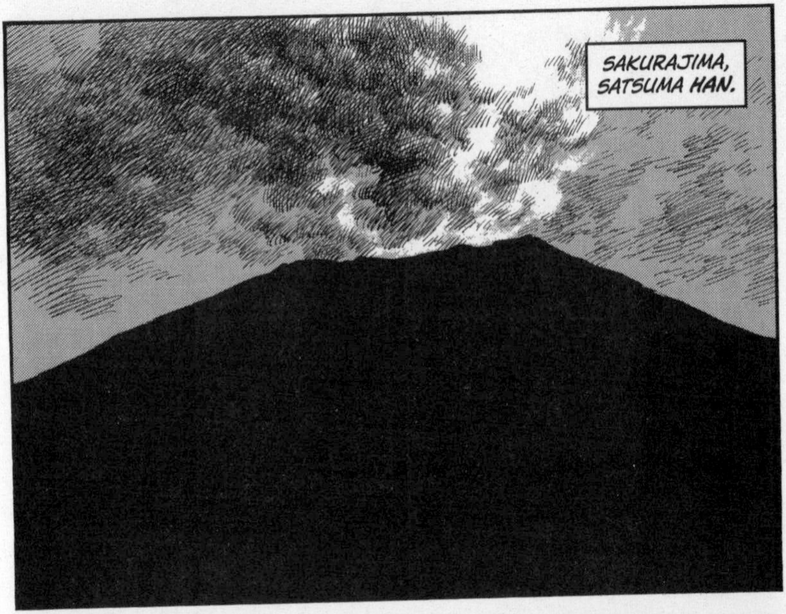
SAKURAJIMA,
SATSUMA HAN.

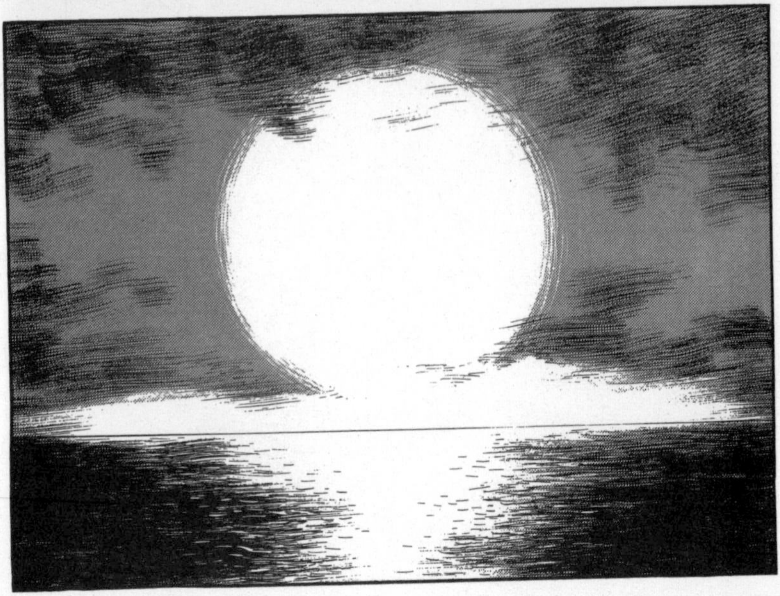

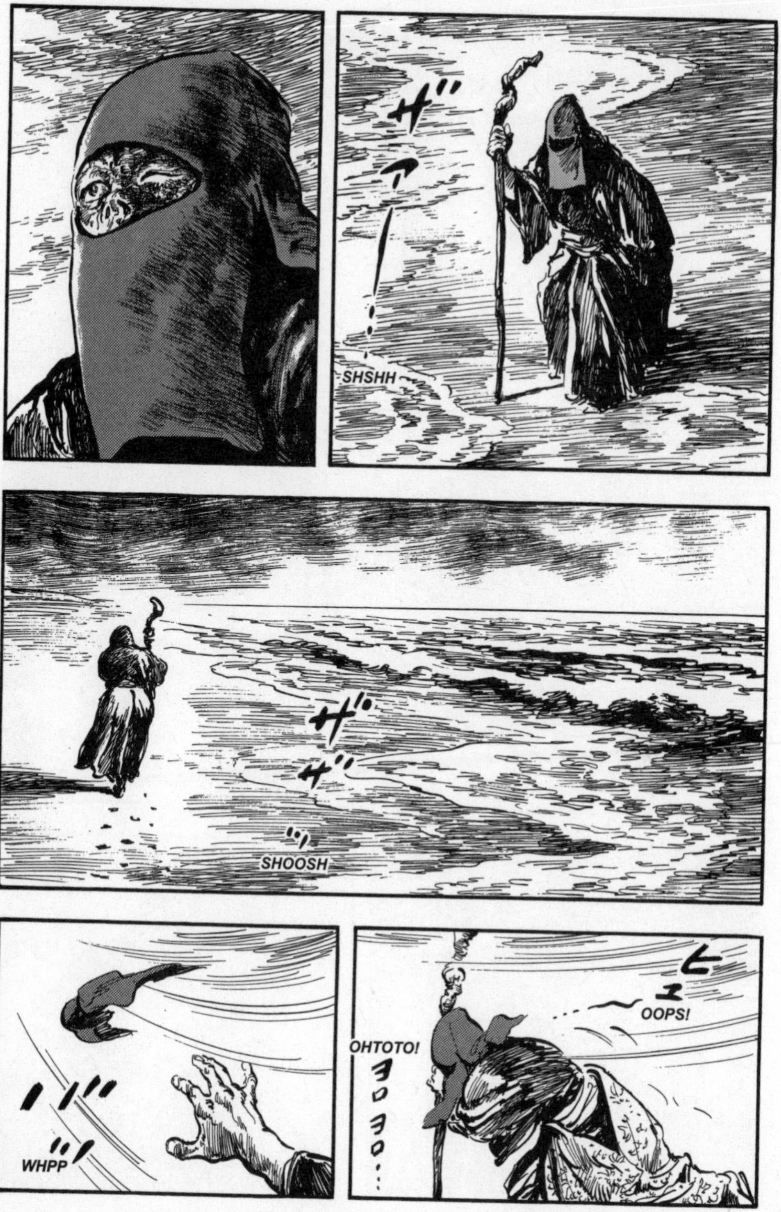
ザァー!…
SHSHH
ザザ
ッ
SHOOSH
ヒュ～…
OOPS!
OHTOTO!
ヨロヨロ…
バッ
WHPP

ROARR

WROOSH

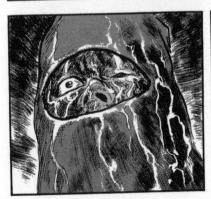

GRRK

184

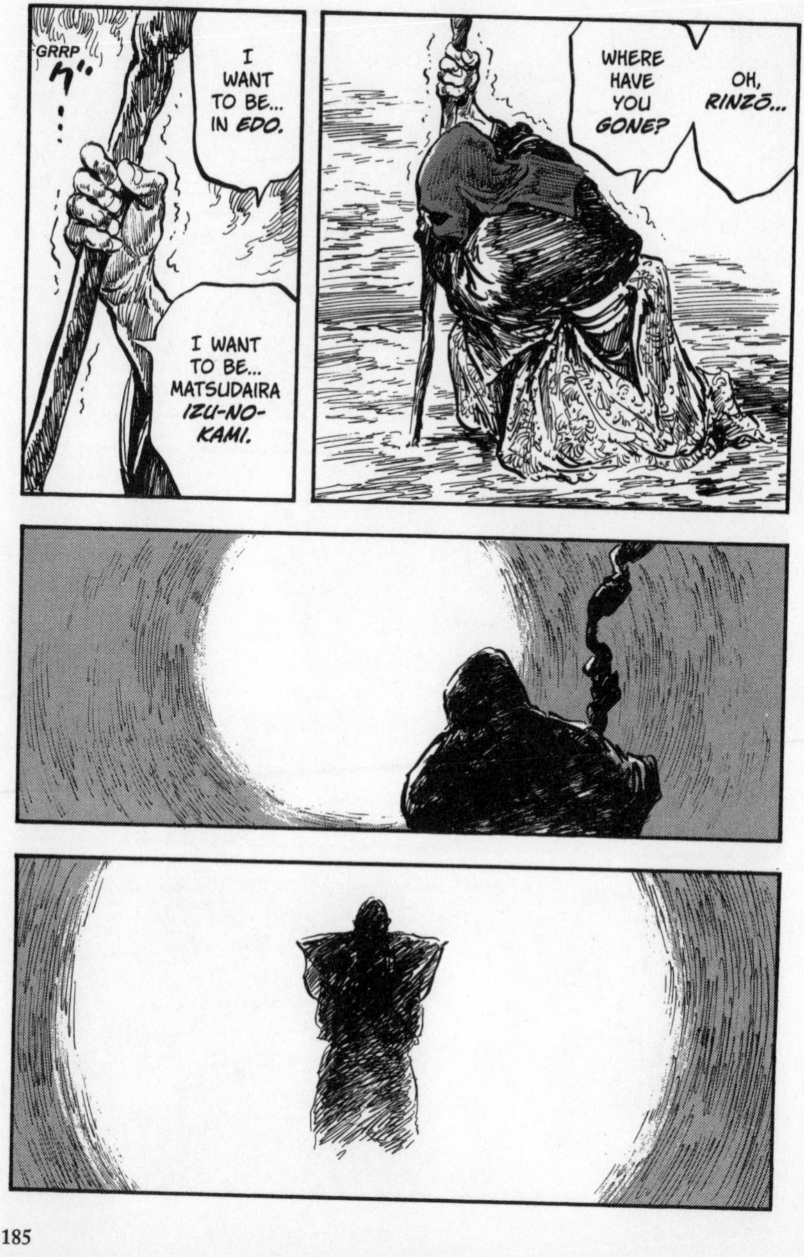
OH, RINZŌ...
WHERE HAVE YOU GONE?
GRRP
I WANT TO BE... IN EDO.
I WANT TO BE... MATSUDAIRA IZU-NO-KAMI.

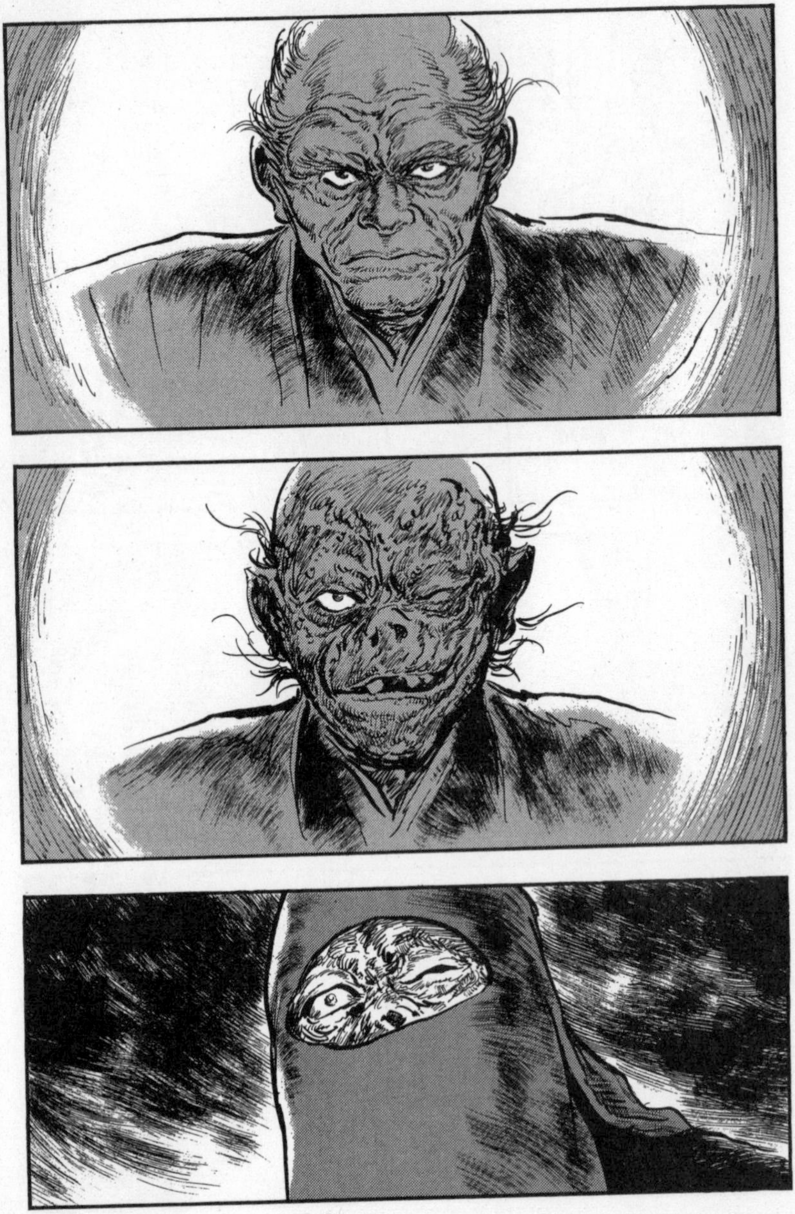

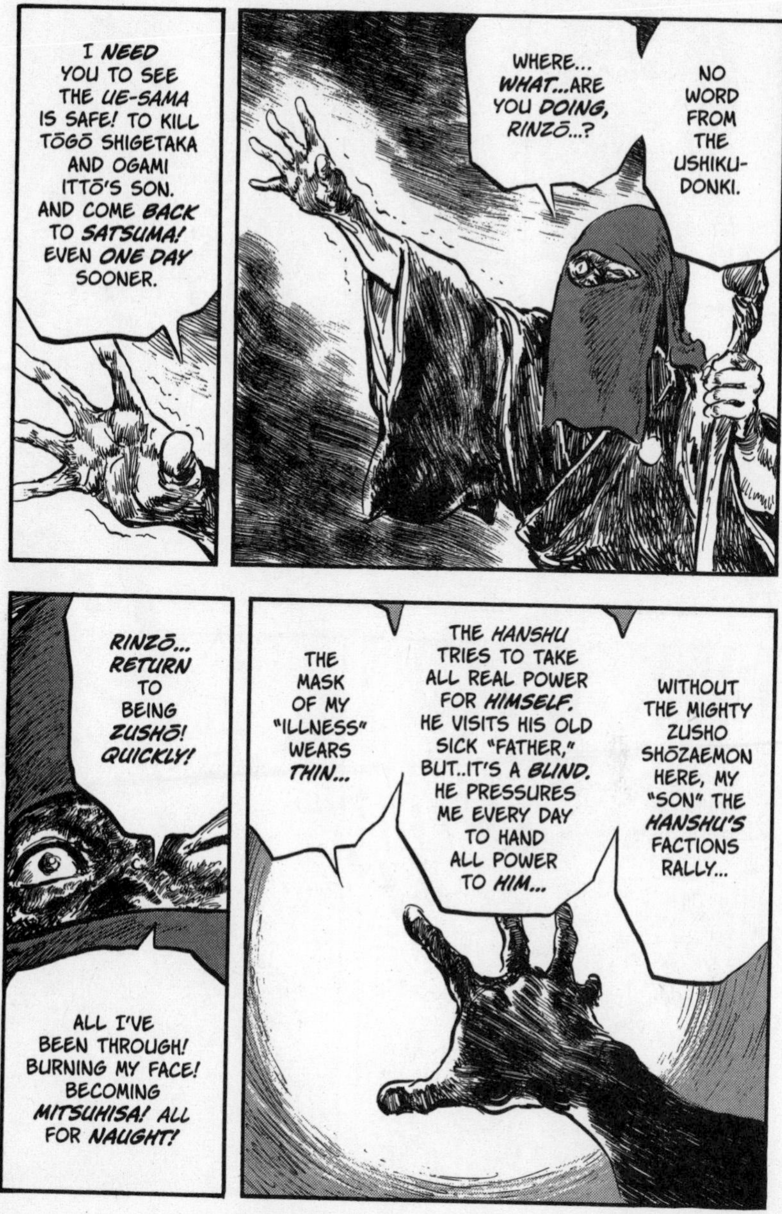
NO WORD FROM THE USHIKU-DONKI.
WHERE... WHAT...ARE YOU DOING, RINZŌ...?
I NEED YOU TO SEE THE UE-SAMA IS SAFE! TO KILL TŌGŌ SHIGETAKA AND OGAMI ITTŌ'S SON. AND COME BACK TO SATSUMA! EVEN ONE DAY SOONER.
WITHOUT THE MIGHTY ZUSHO SHŌZAEMON HERE, MY "SON" THE HANSHU'S FACTIONS RALLY...
THE HANSHU TRIES TO TAKE ALL REAL POWER FOR HIMSELF. HE VISITS HIS OLD SICK "FATHER," BUT..IT'S A BLIND. HE PRESSURES ME EVERY DAY TO HAND ALL POWER TO HIM...
THE MASK OF MY "ILLNESS" WEARS THIN...
RINZŌ... RETURN TO BEING ZUSHŌ! QUICKLY!
ALL I'VE BEEN THROUGH! BURNING MY FACE! BECOMING MITSUHISA! ALL FOR NAUGHT!

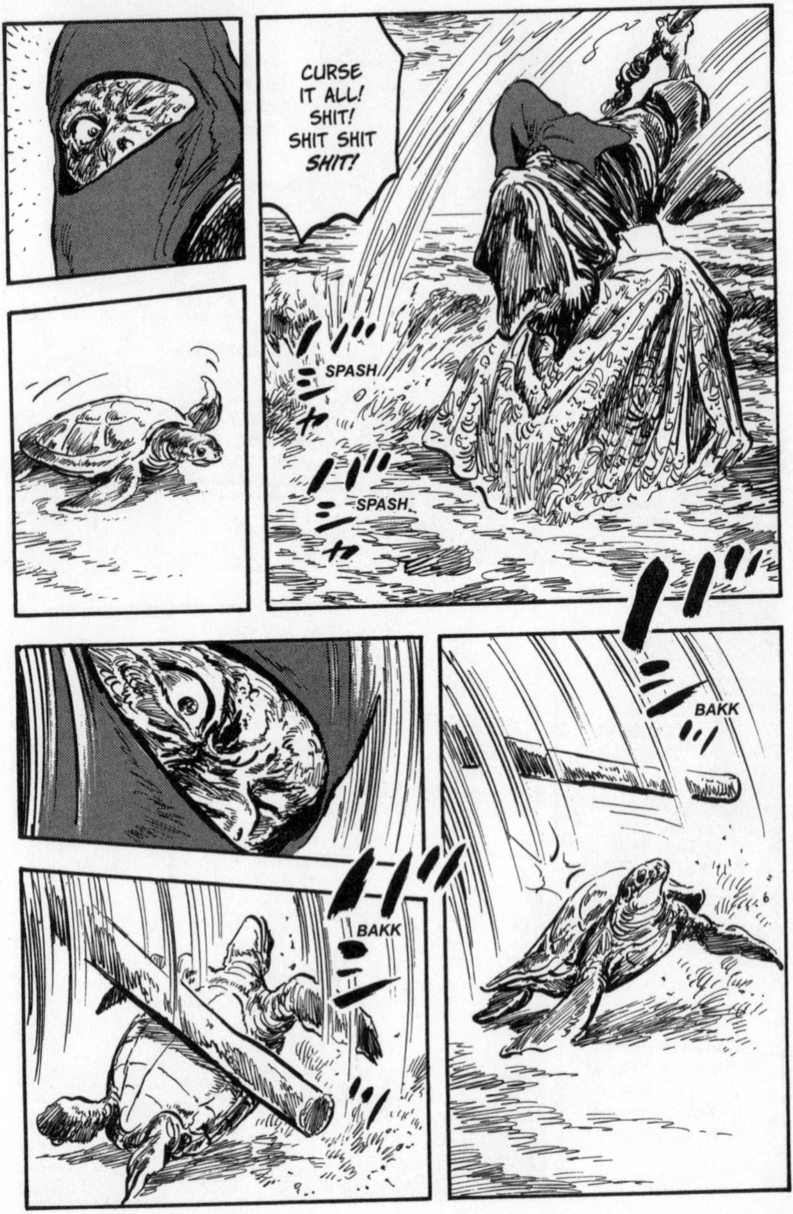
CURSE IT ALL! SHIT! SHIT SHIT SHIT!
SPASH
SPASH
BAKK
BAKK

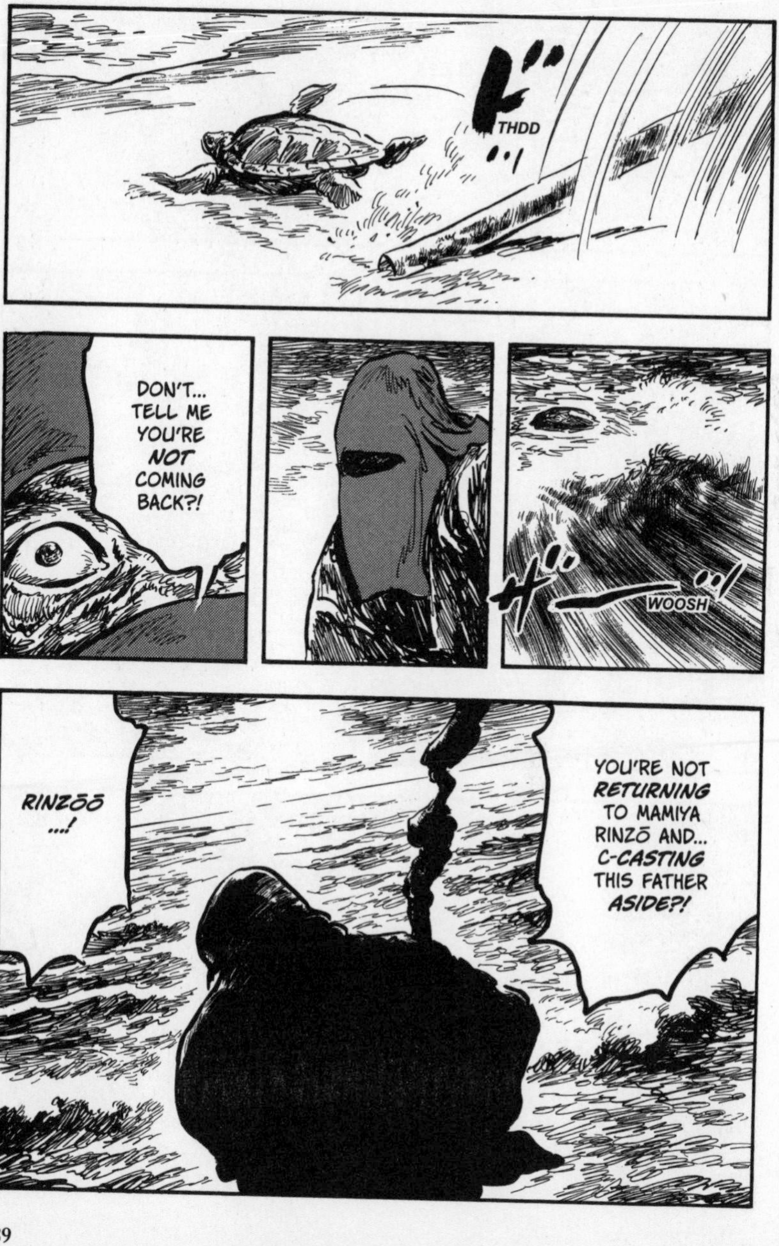
THDD
WOOSH
DON'T... TELL ME YOU'RE NOT COMING BACK?!
YOU'RE NOT RETURNING TO MAMIYA RINZŌ AND... C-CASTING THIS FATHER ASIDE?!
RINZŌŌ ...!

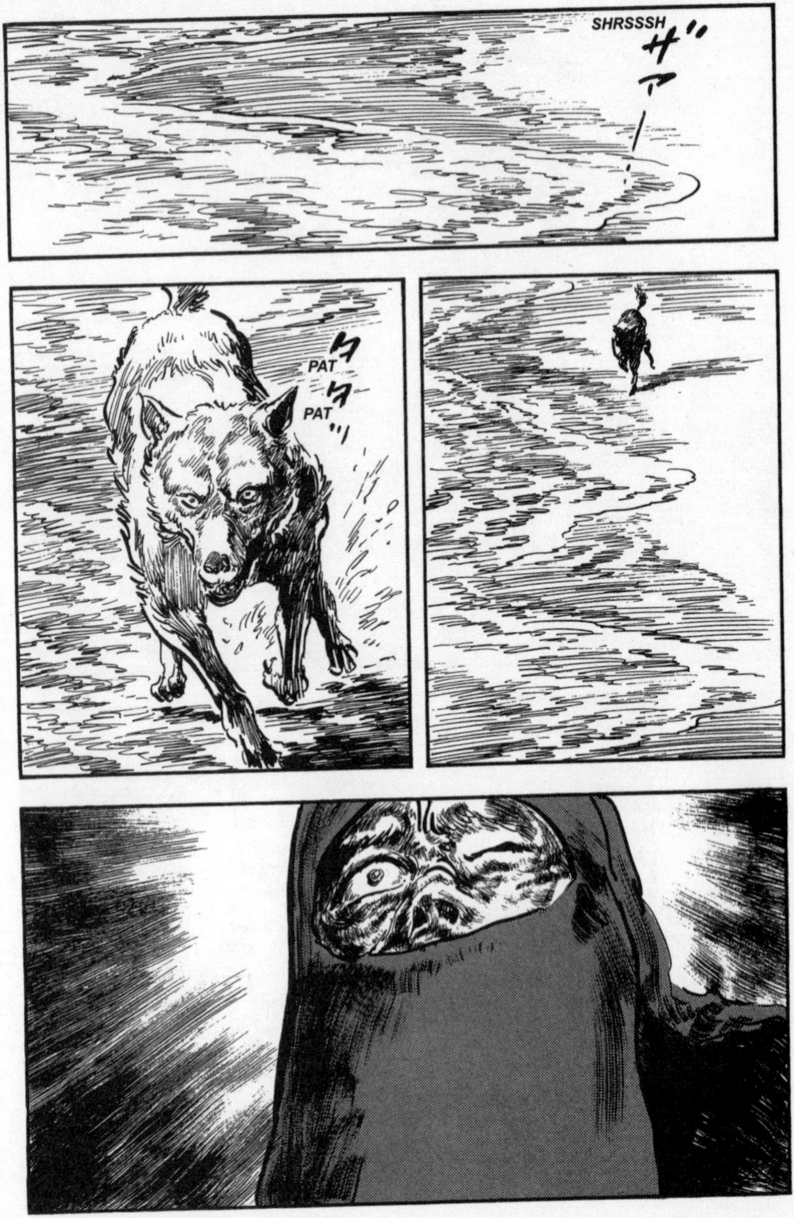
SHRSSSH
ザァー…
PAT
PAT
タタッ

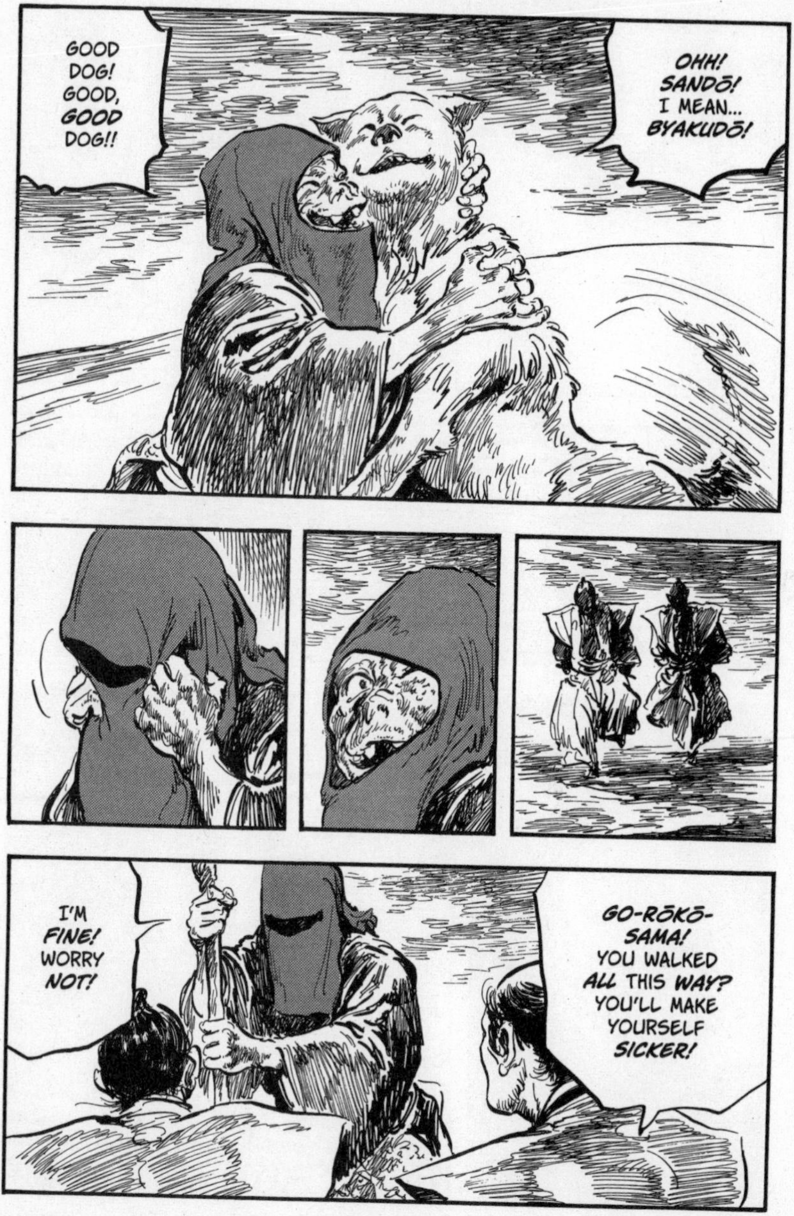
OHH! SANDŌ! I MEAN... BYAKUDŌ!
GOOD DOG! GOOD, GOOD DOG!!
GO-RŌKŌ-SAMA! YOU WALKED ALL THIS WAY? YOU'LL MAKE YOURSELF SICKER!
I'M FINE! WORRY NOT!

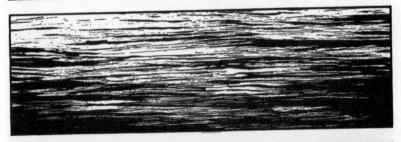

192

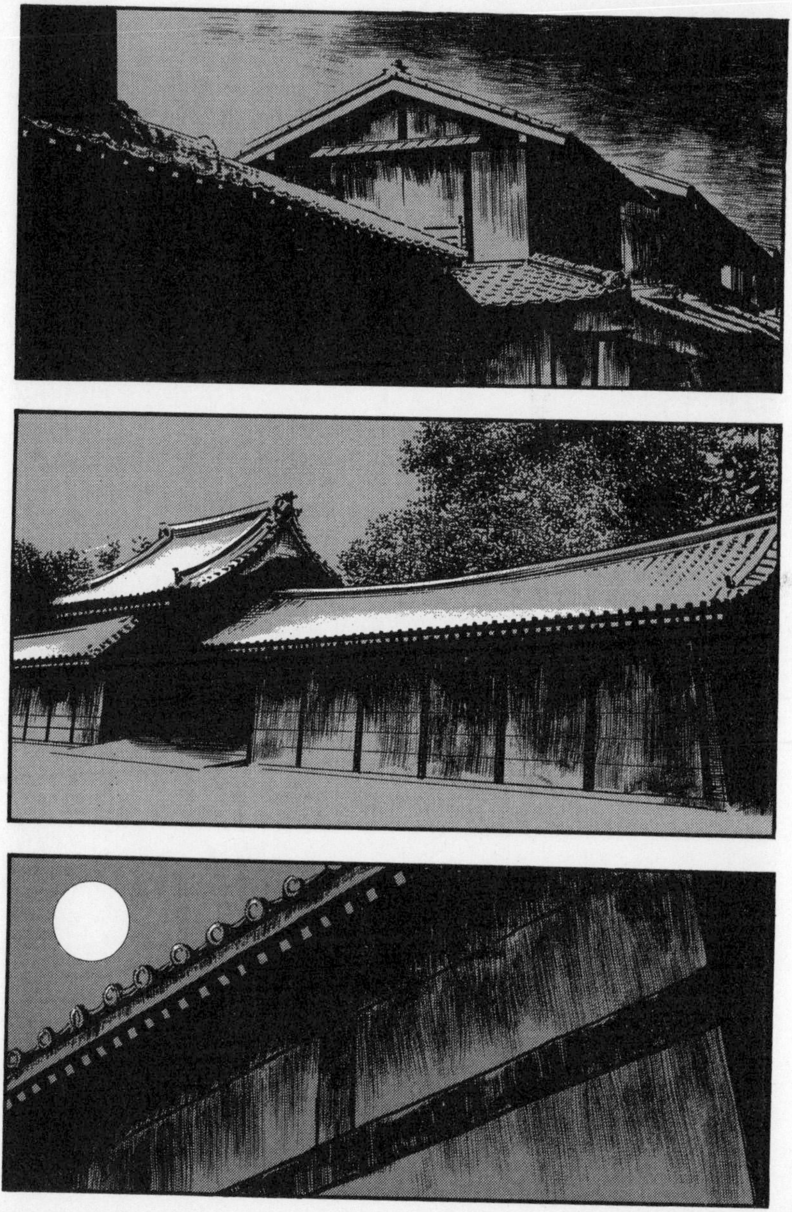

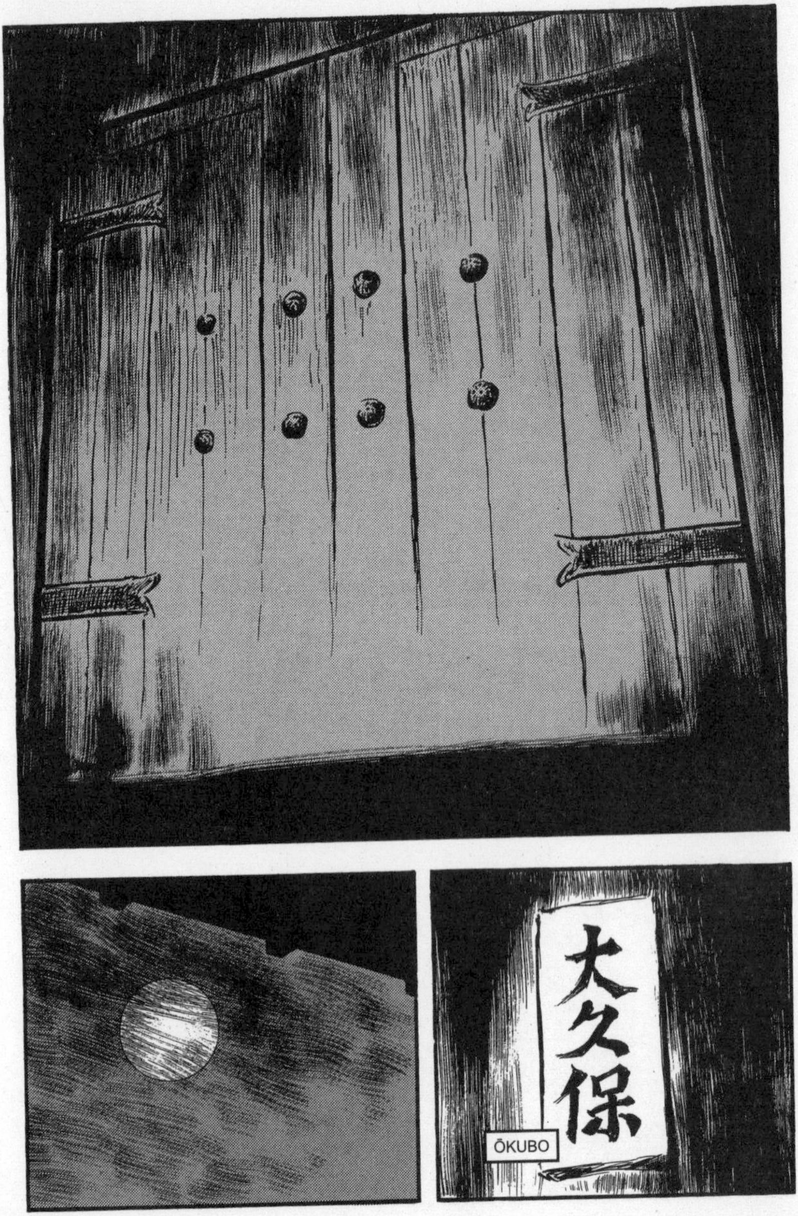
大久保
ŌKUBO

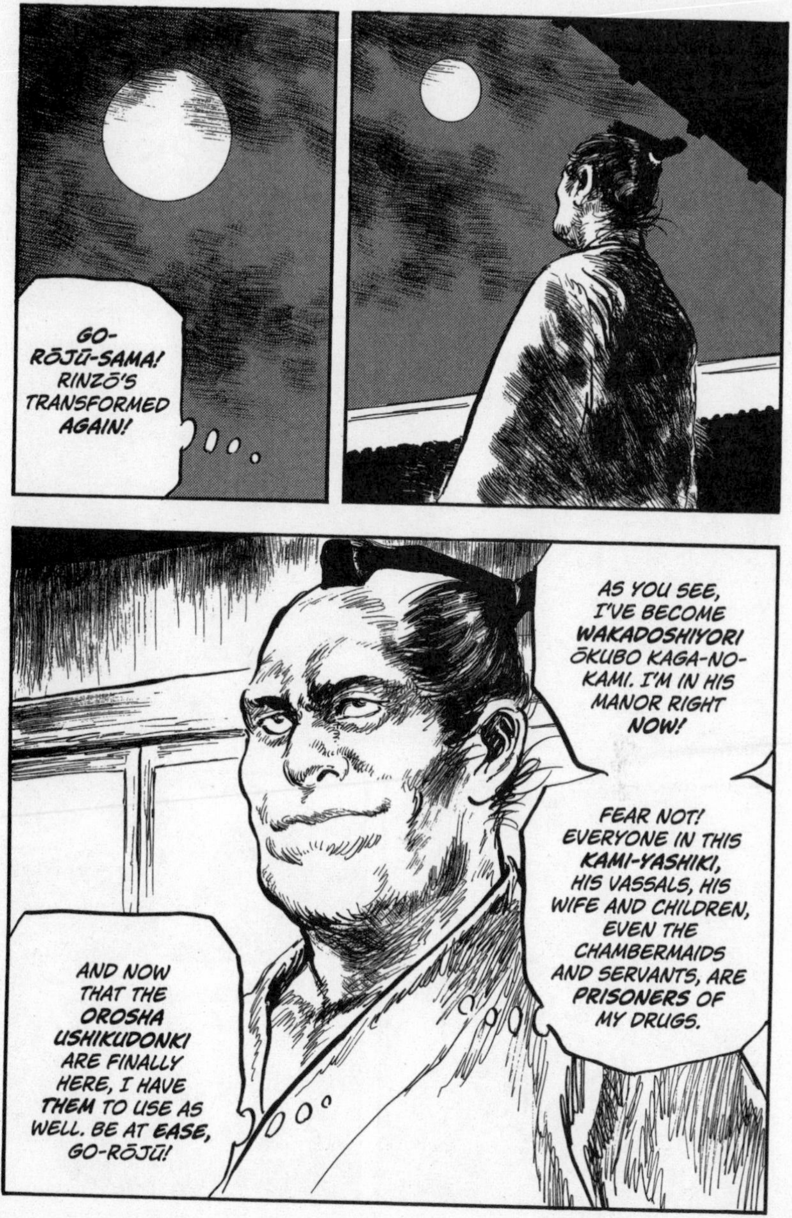
GO-RŌJŪ-SAMA! RINZŌ'S TRANSFORMED AGAIN!
AS YOU SEE, I'VE BECOME WAKADOSHIYORI ŌKUBO KAGA-NO-KAMI. I'M IN HIS MANOR RIGHT NOW!
FEAR NOT! EVERYONE IN THIS KAMI-YASHIKI, HIS VASSALS, HIS WIFE AND CHILDREN, EVEN THE CHAMBERMAIDS AND SERVANTS, ARE PRISONERS OF MY DRUGS.
AND NOW THAT THE OROSHA USHIKUDONKI ARE FINALLY HERE, I HAVE THEM TO USE AS WELL. BE AT EASE, GO-RŌJŪ!

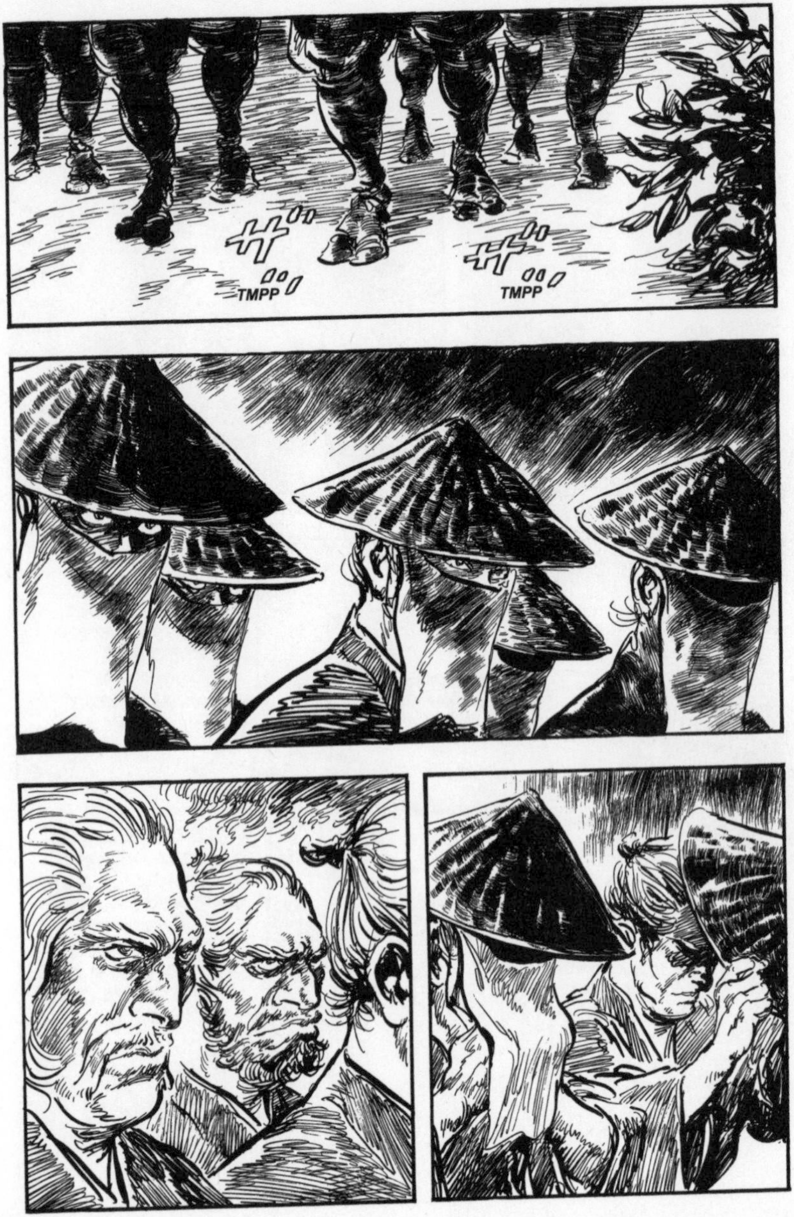
TMPP
TMPP

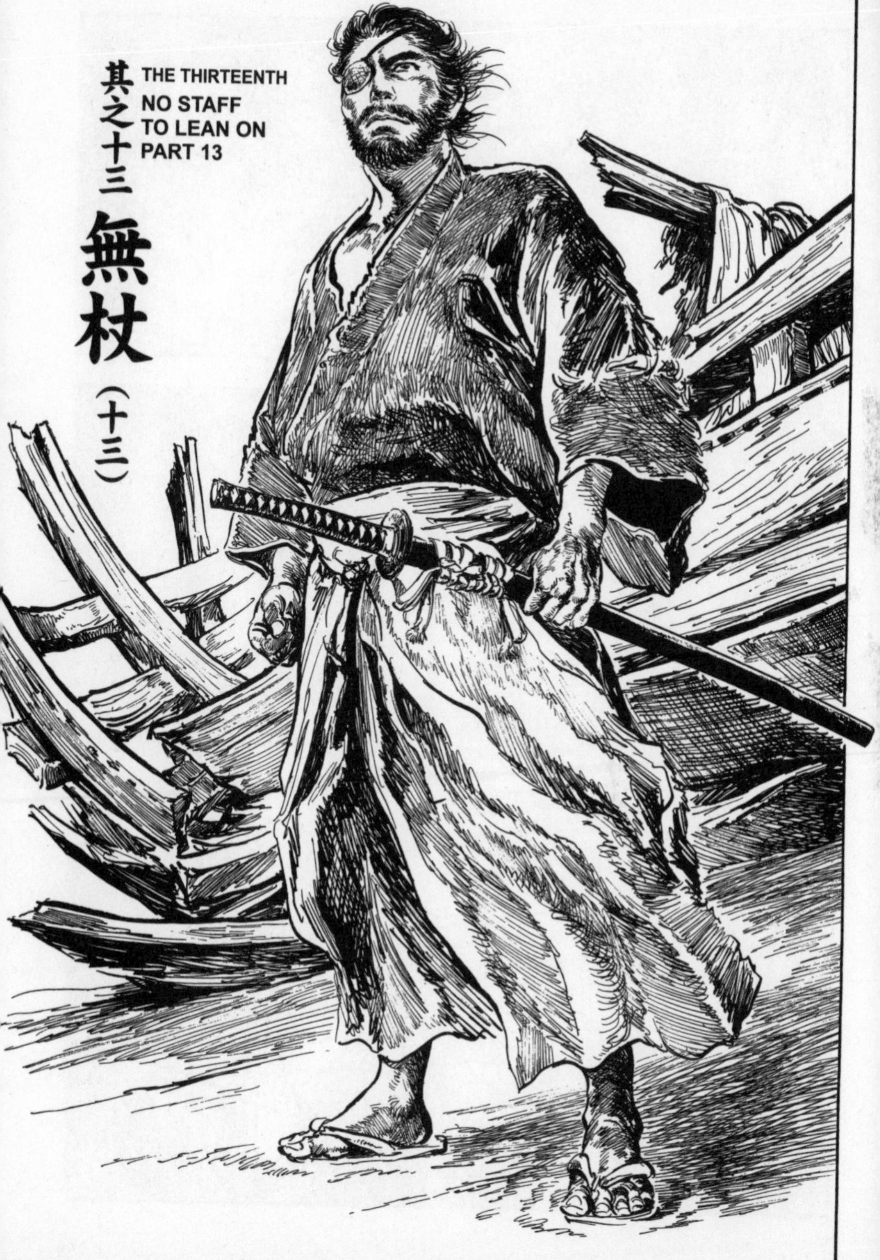
其之十三
無杖
（十三）
THE THIRTEENTH
NO STAFF
TO LEAN ON
PART 13

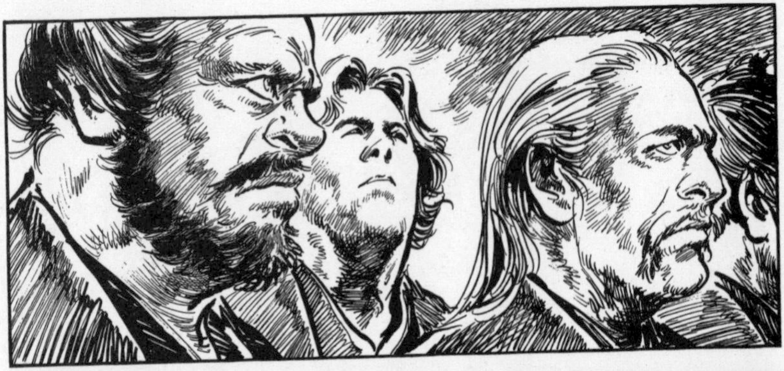

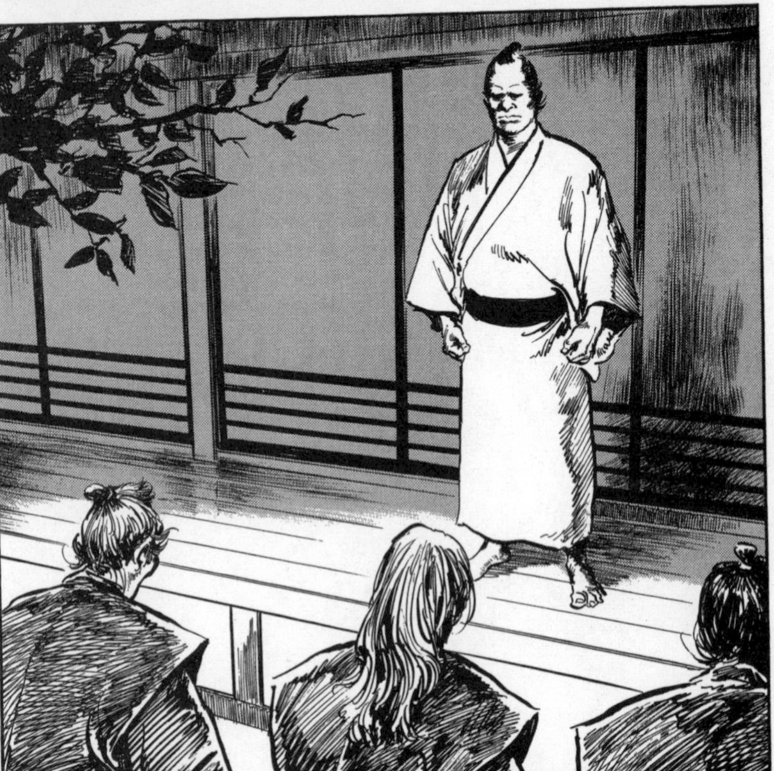

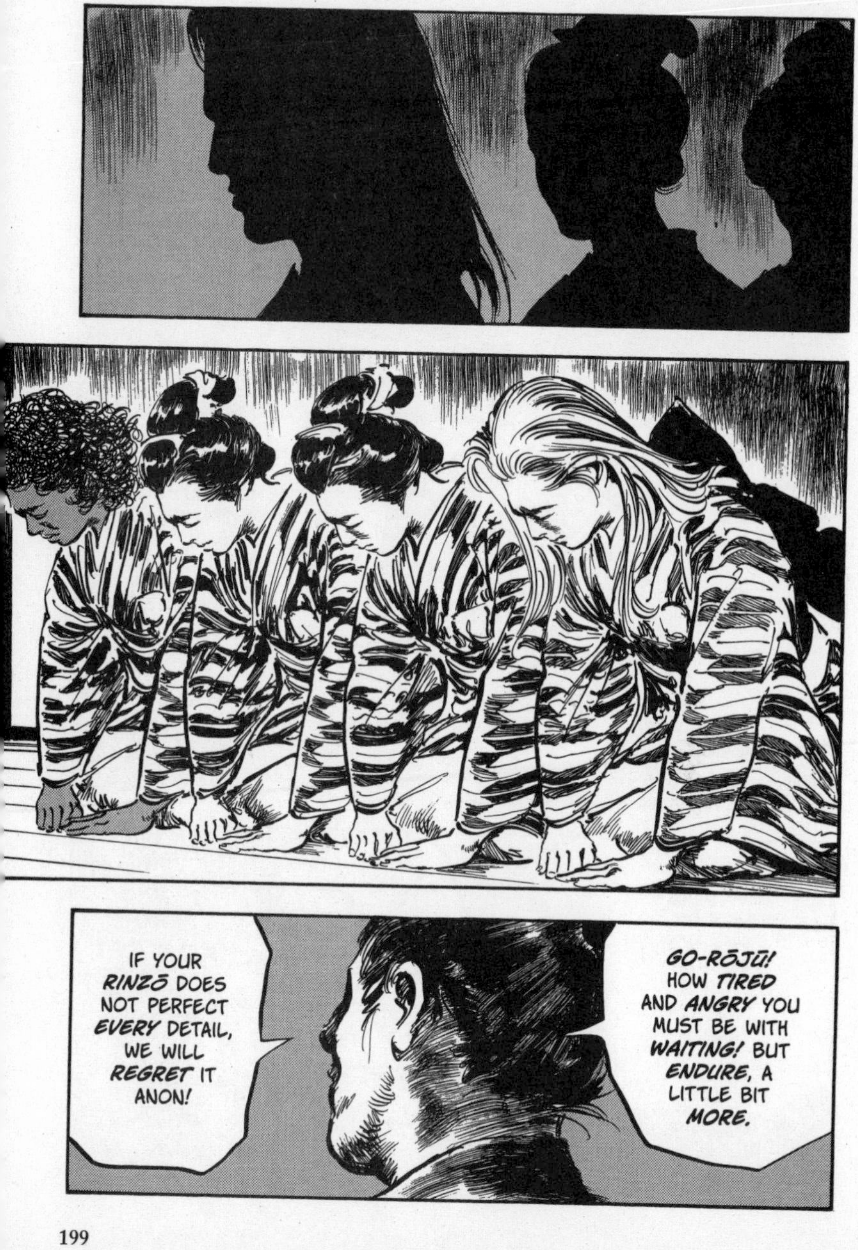
GO-RŌJŪ! HOW TIRED AND ANGRY YOU MUST BE WITH WAITING! BUT ENDURE, A LITTLE BIT MORE.
IF YOUR RINZŌ DOES NOT PERFECT EVERY DETAIL, WE WILL REGRET IT ANON!

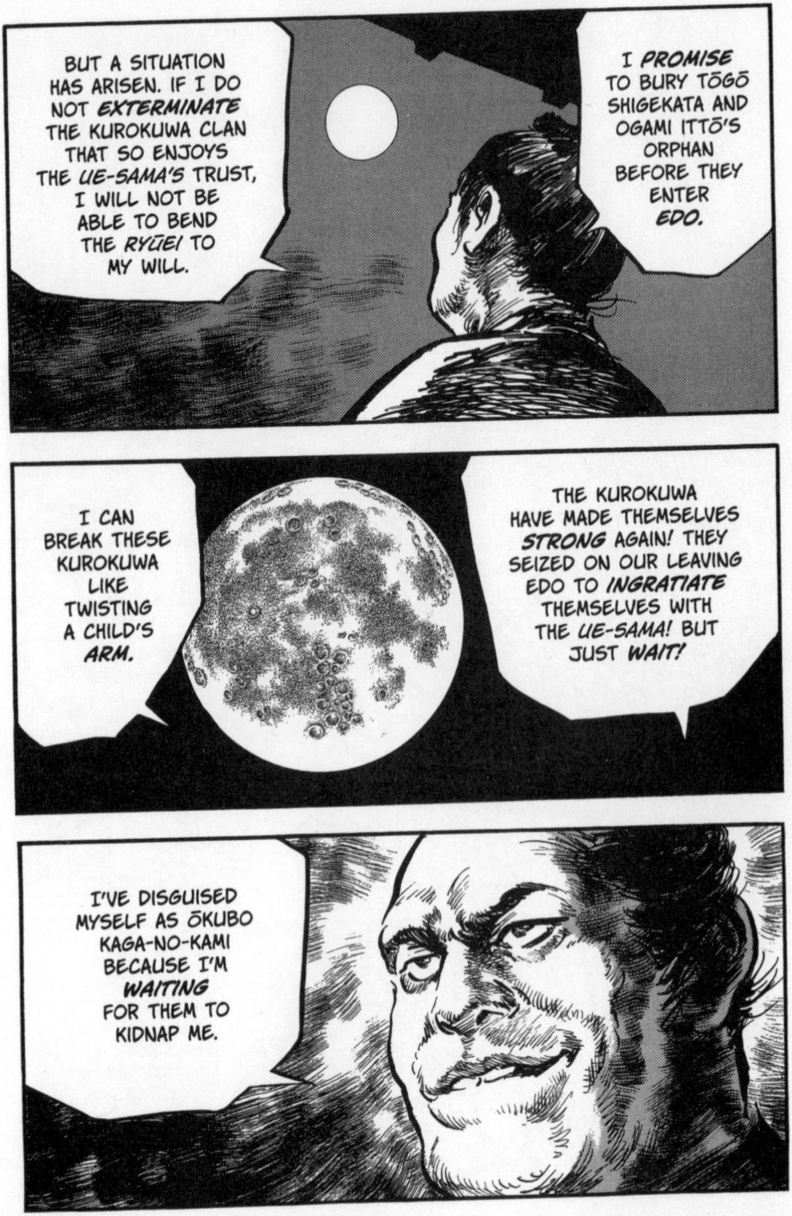
I PROMISE TO BURY TŌGŌ SHIGEKATA AND OGAMI ITTŌ'S ORPHAN BEFORE THEY ENTER EDO.
BUT A SITUATION HAS ARISEN. IF I DO NOT EXTERMINATE THE KUROKUWA CLAN THAT SO ENJOYS THE UE-SAMA'S TRUST, I WILL NOT BE ABLE TO BEND THE RYŪEI TO MY WILL.
THE KUROKUWA HAVE MADE THEMSELVES STRONG AGAIN! THEY SEIZED ON OUR LEAVING EDO TO INGRATIATE THEMSELVES WITH THE UE-SAMA! BUT JUST WAIT!
I CAN BREAK THESE KUROKUWA LIKE TWISTING A CHILD'S ARM.
I'VE DISGUISED MYSELF AS ŌKUBO KAGA-NO-KAMI BECAUSE I'M WAITING FOR THEM TO KIDNAP ME.

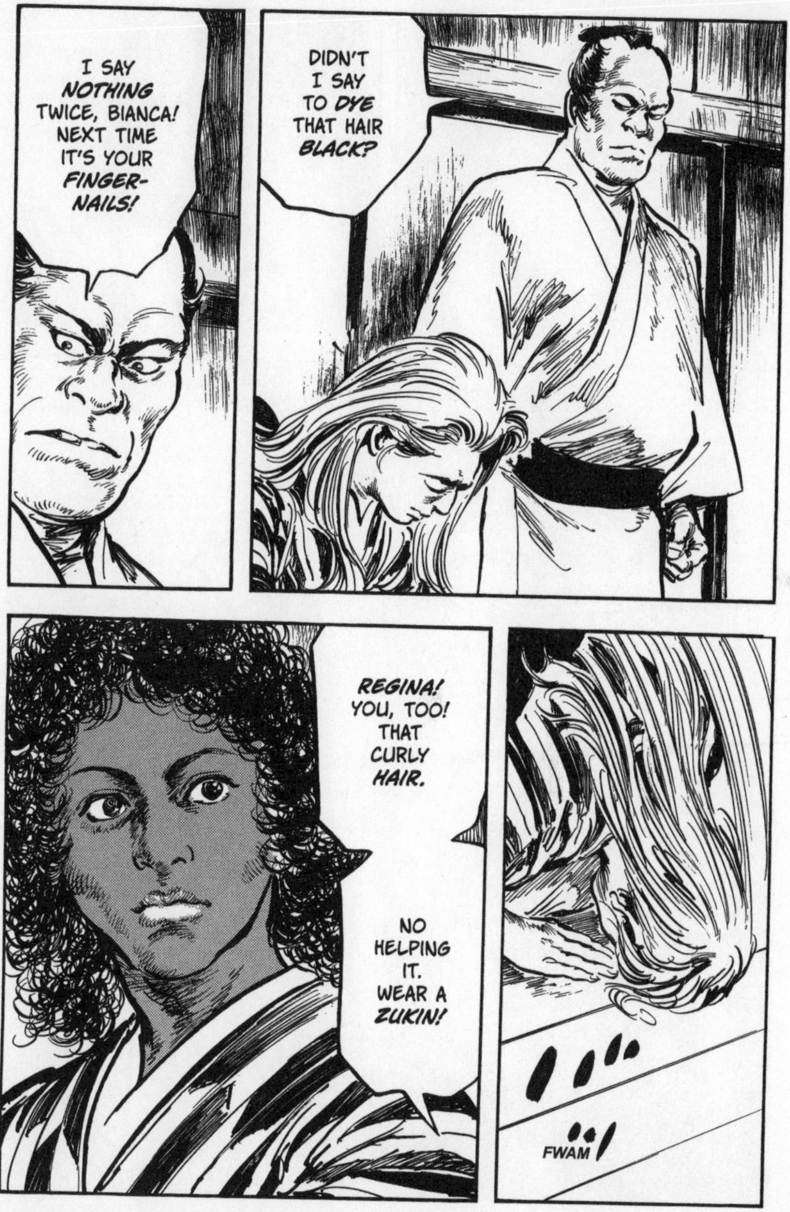
DIDN'T I SAY TO DYE THAT HAIR BLACK?
I SAY NOTHING TWICE, BIANCA! NEXT TIME IT'S YOUR FINGER-NAILS!
FWAM
REGINA! YOU, TOO! THAT CURLY HAIR.
NO HELPING IT. WEAR A ZUKIN!

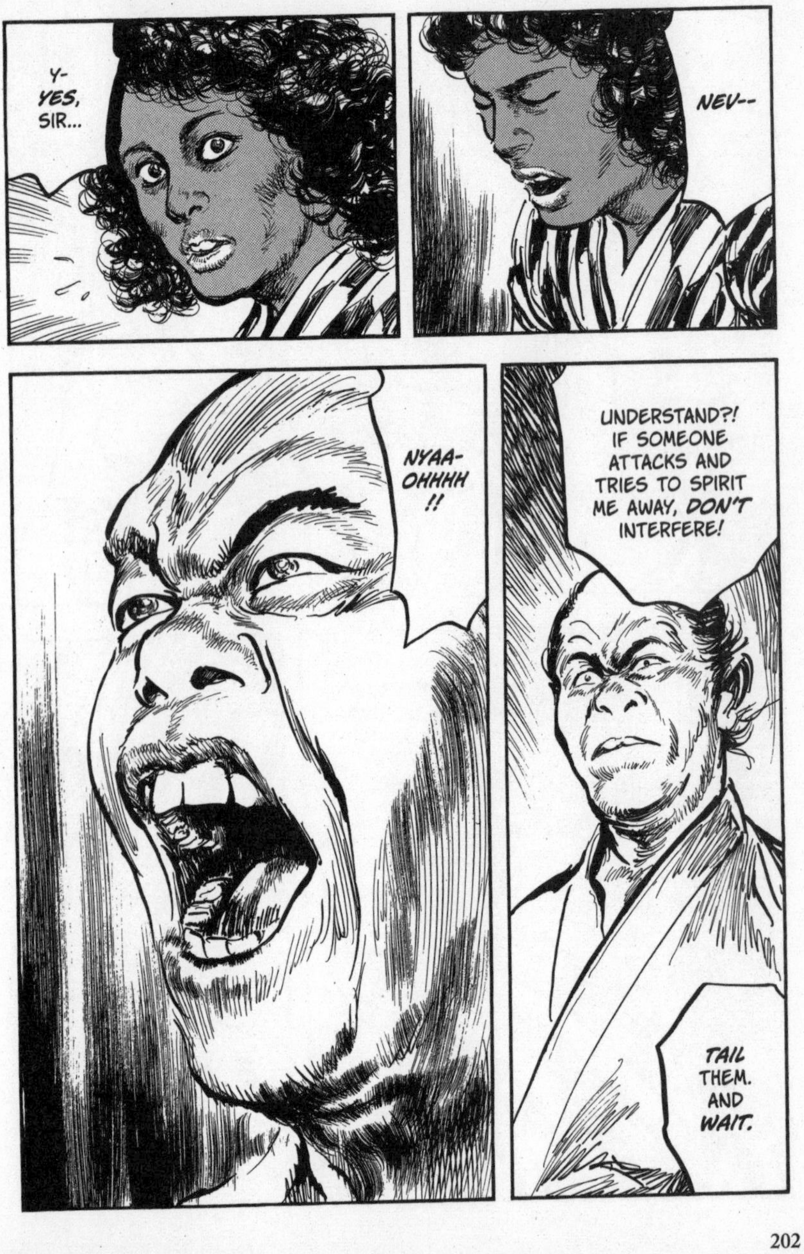
NEV--
Y- YES, SIR...
UNDERSTAND?! IF SOMEONE ATTACKS AND TRIES TO SPIRIT ME AWAY, DON'T INTERFERE!
TAIL THEM. AND WAIT.
NYAA-OHHHH !!

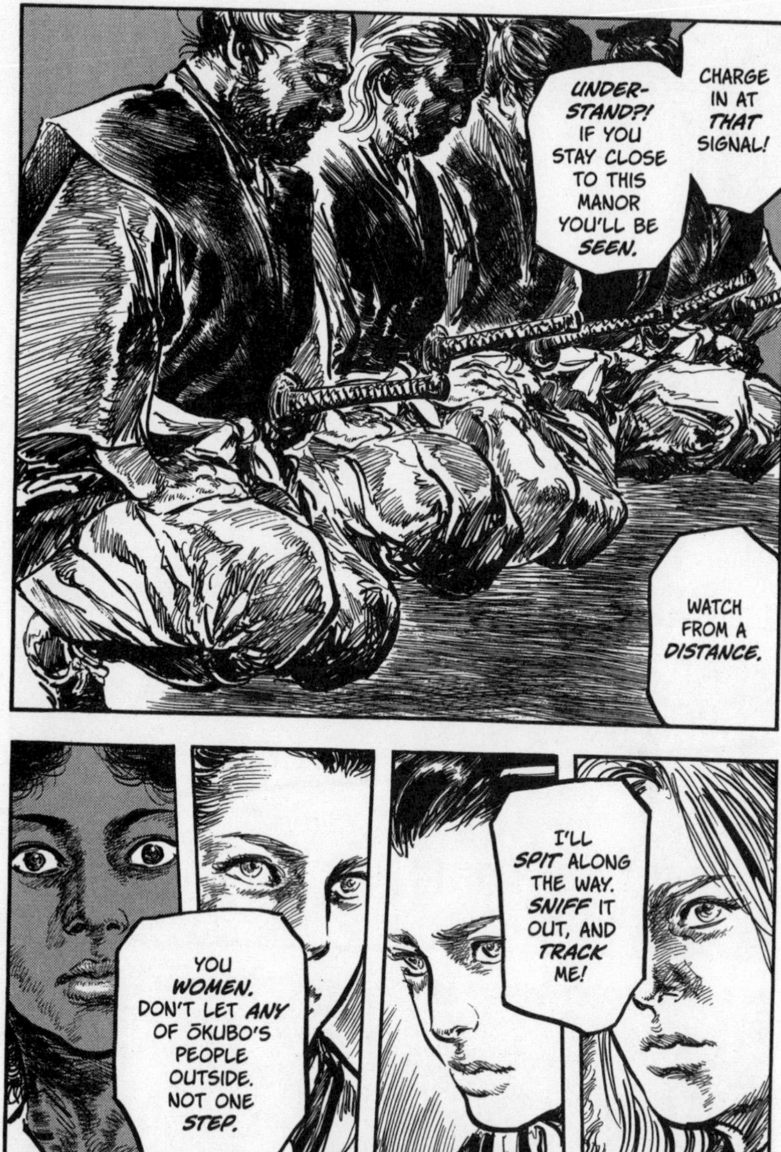
CHARGE IN AT *THAT* SIGNAL!
UNDERSTAND?! IF YOU STAY CLOSE TO THIS MANOR YOU'LL BE *SEEN.*
WATCH FROM A *DISTANCE.*
I'LL *SPIT* ALONG THE WAY. *SNIFF* IT OUT, AND *TRACK* ME!
YOU *WOMEN.* DON'T LET *ANY* OF ŌKUBO'S PEOPLE OUTSIDE. NOT ONE *STEP.*

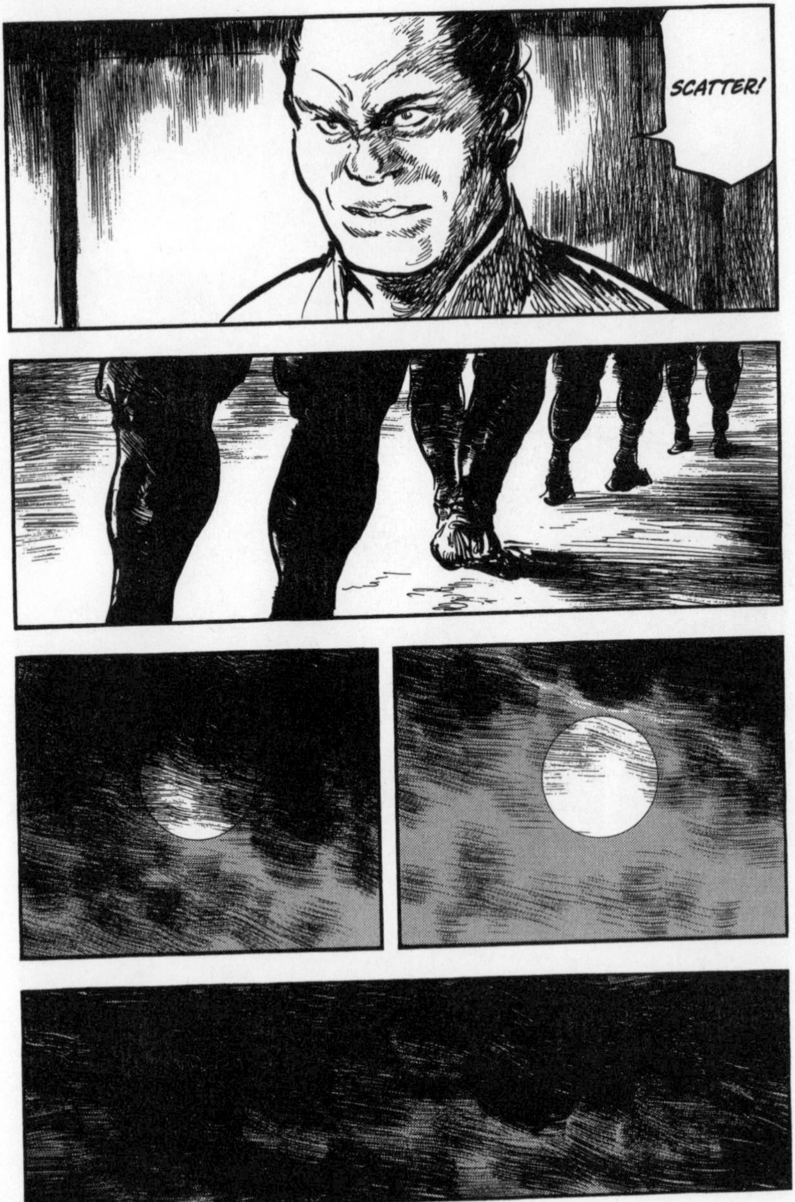
SCATTER!

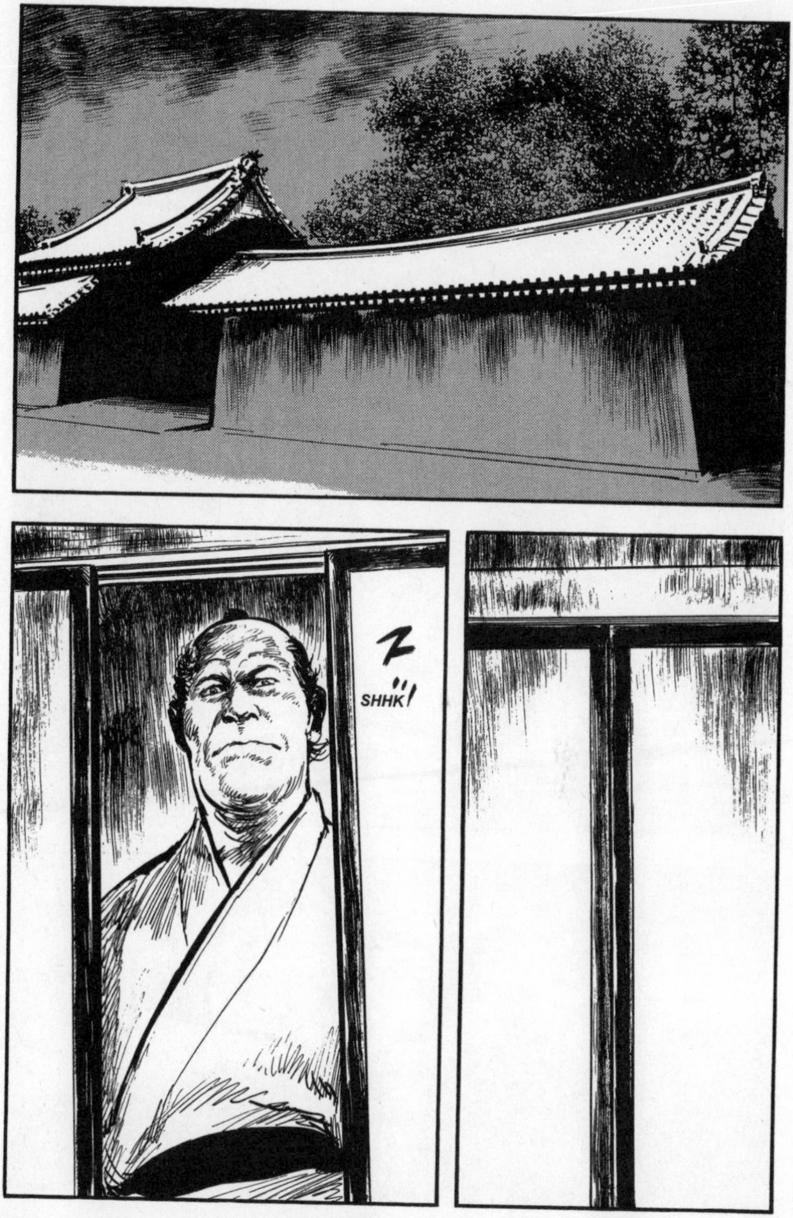
SHHK!

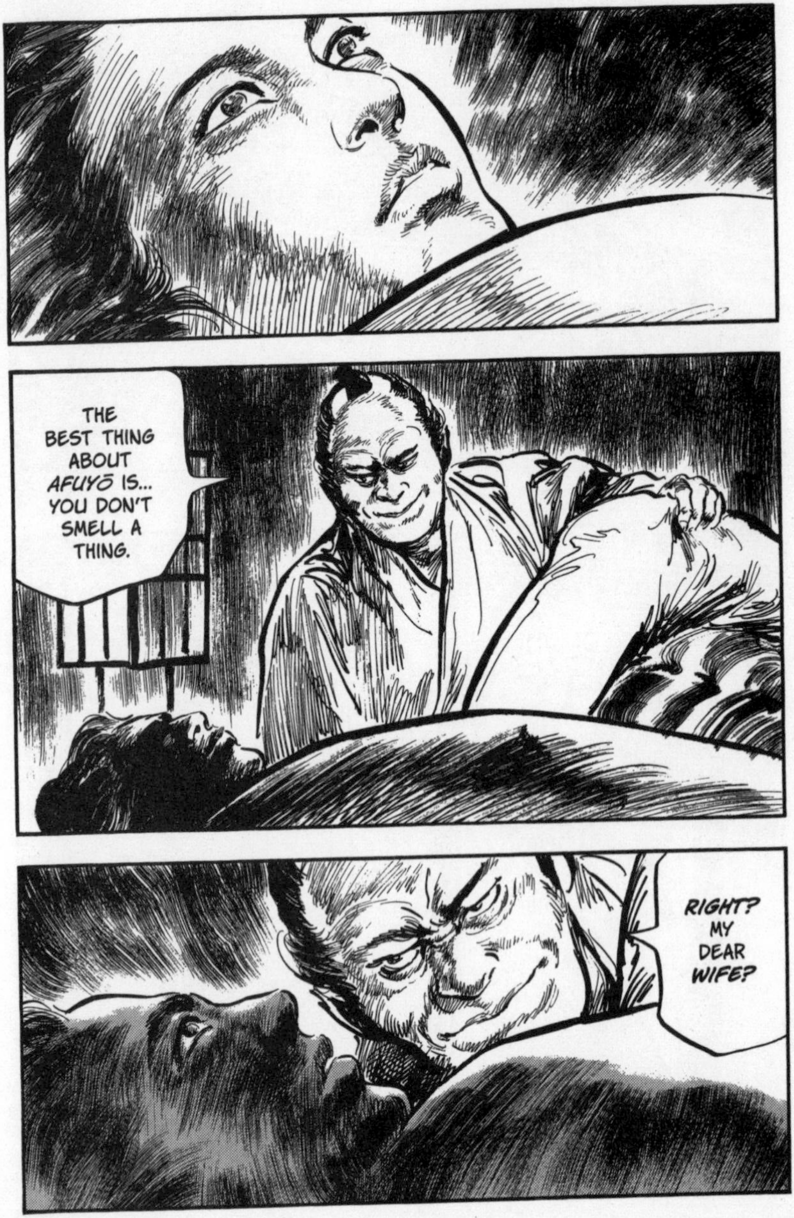
THE BEST THING ABOUT AFUYŌ IS... YOU DON'T SMELL A THING.
RIGHT? MY DEAR WIFE?

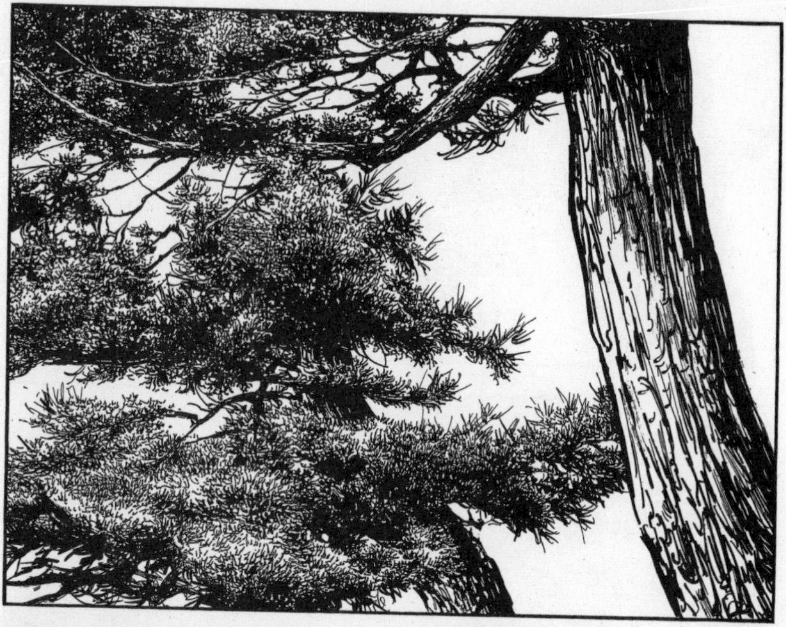

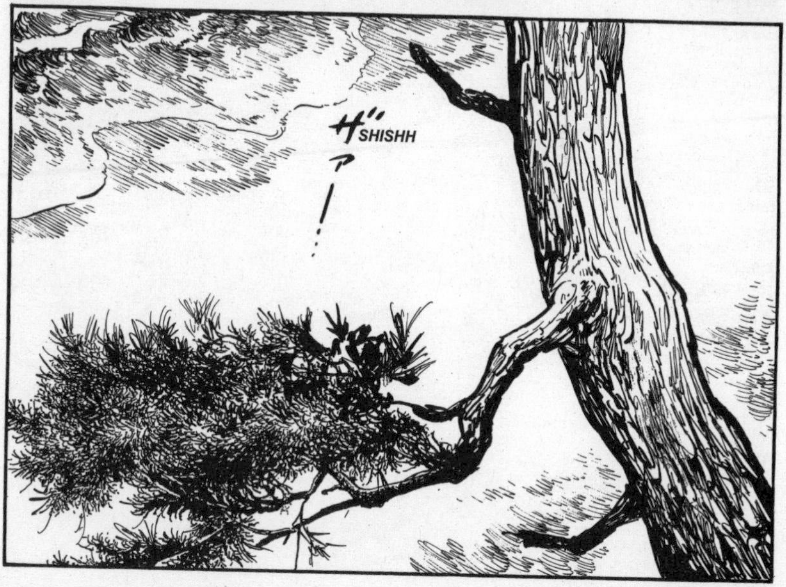
ザァー…
SHISHH

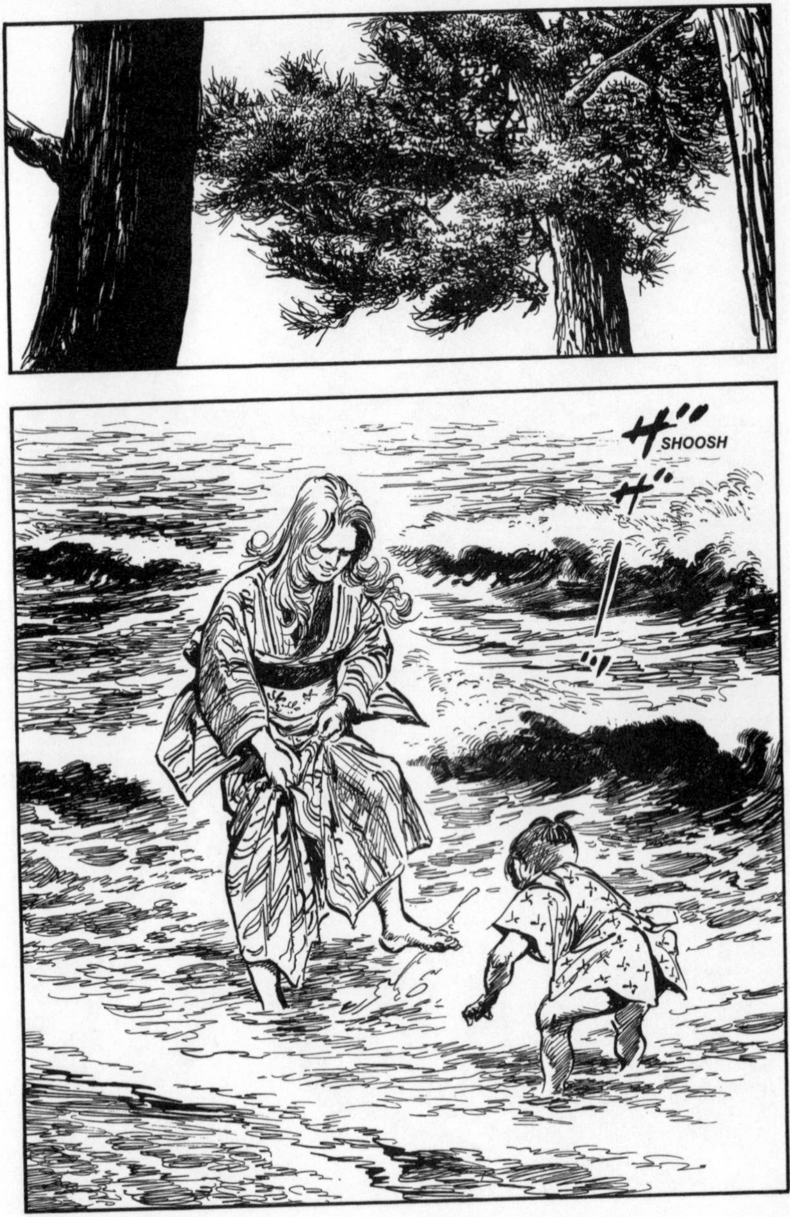
SHOOSH

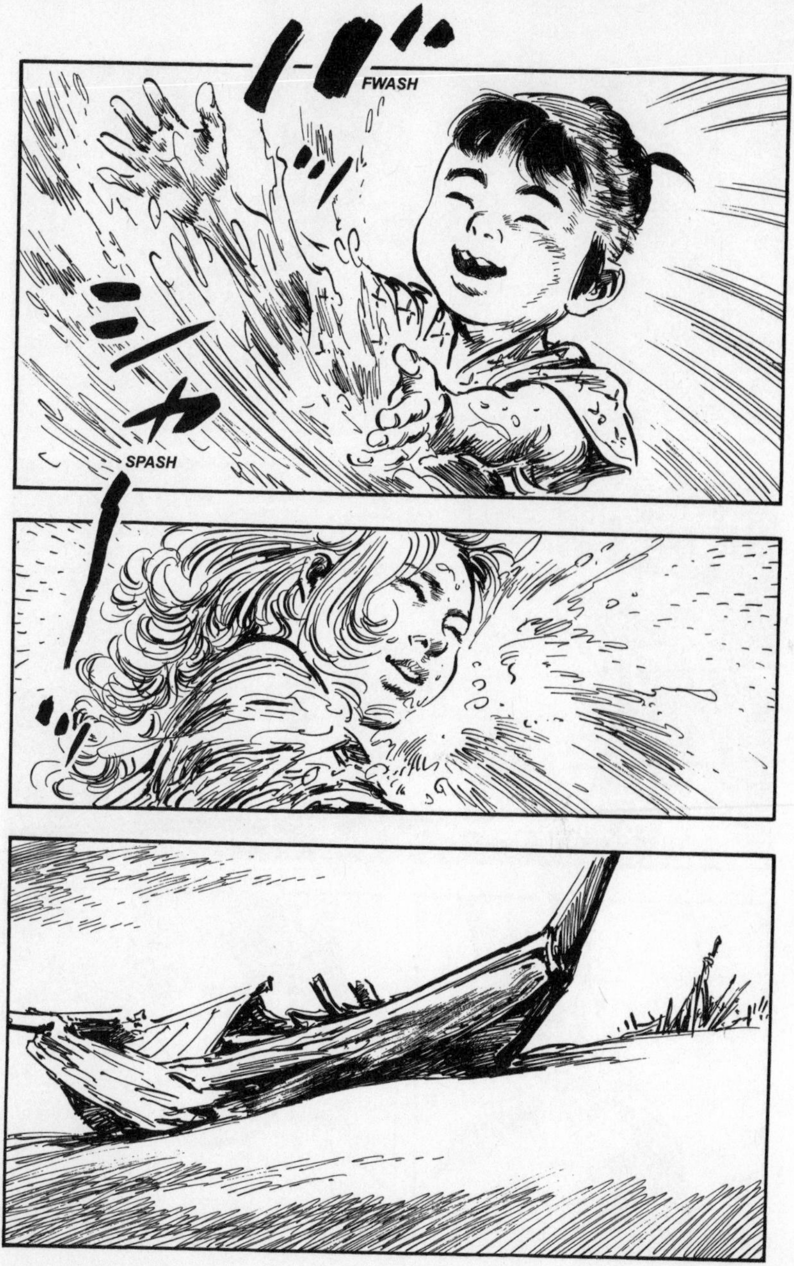
FWASH
SPASH

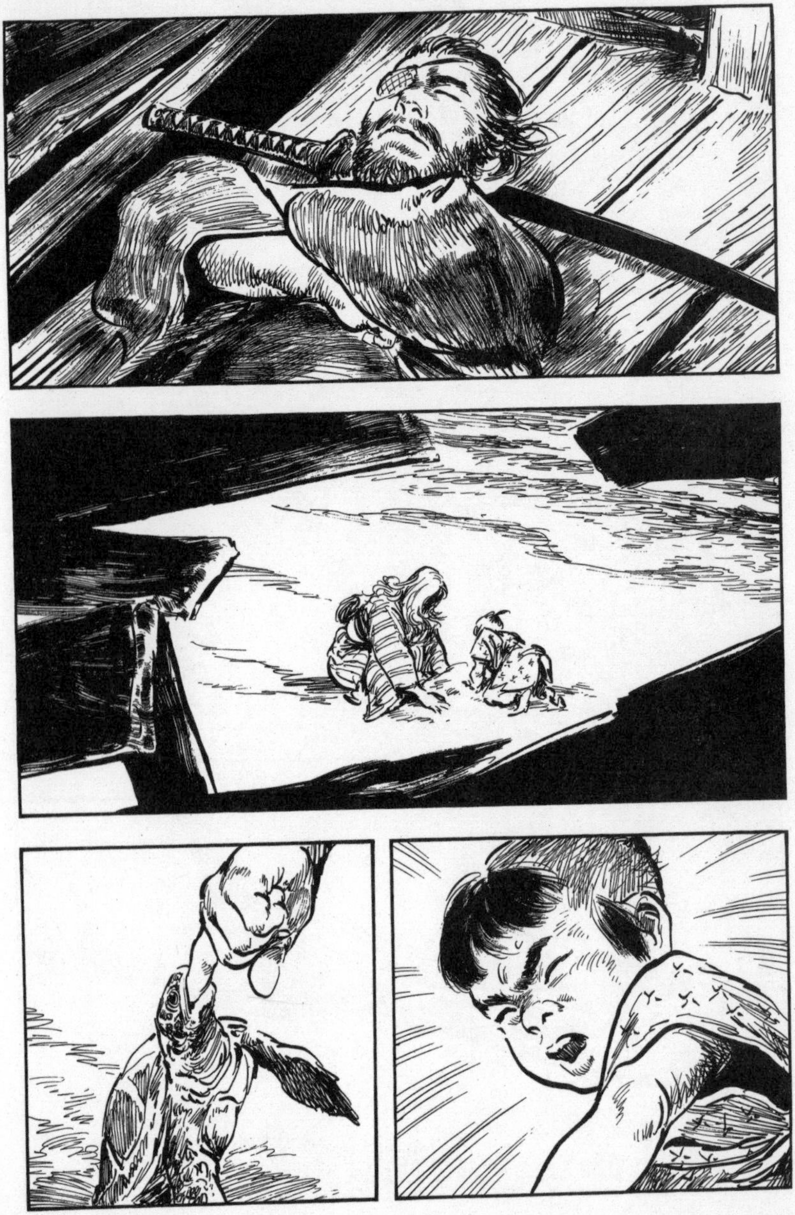

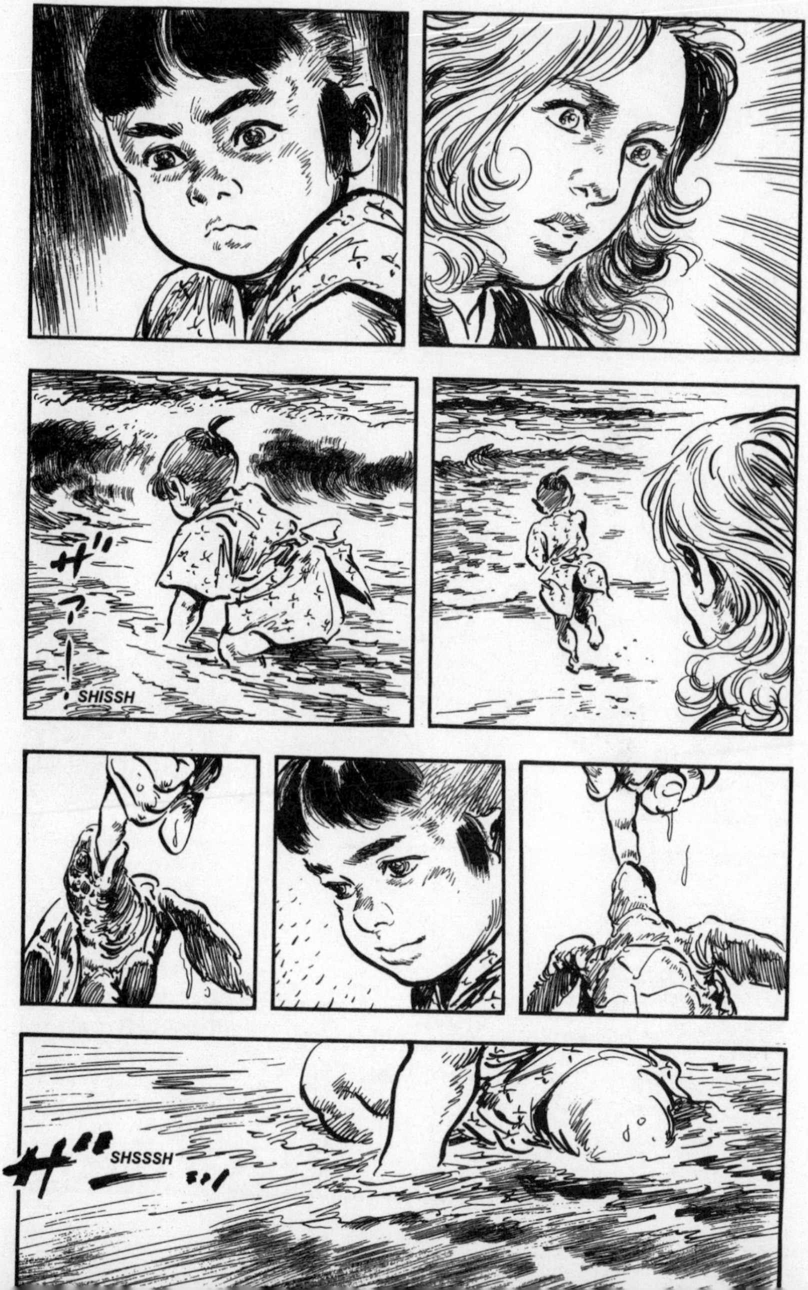
ザァー！
SHISSH
ザーー
SHSSSH

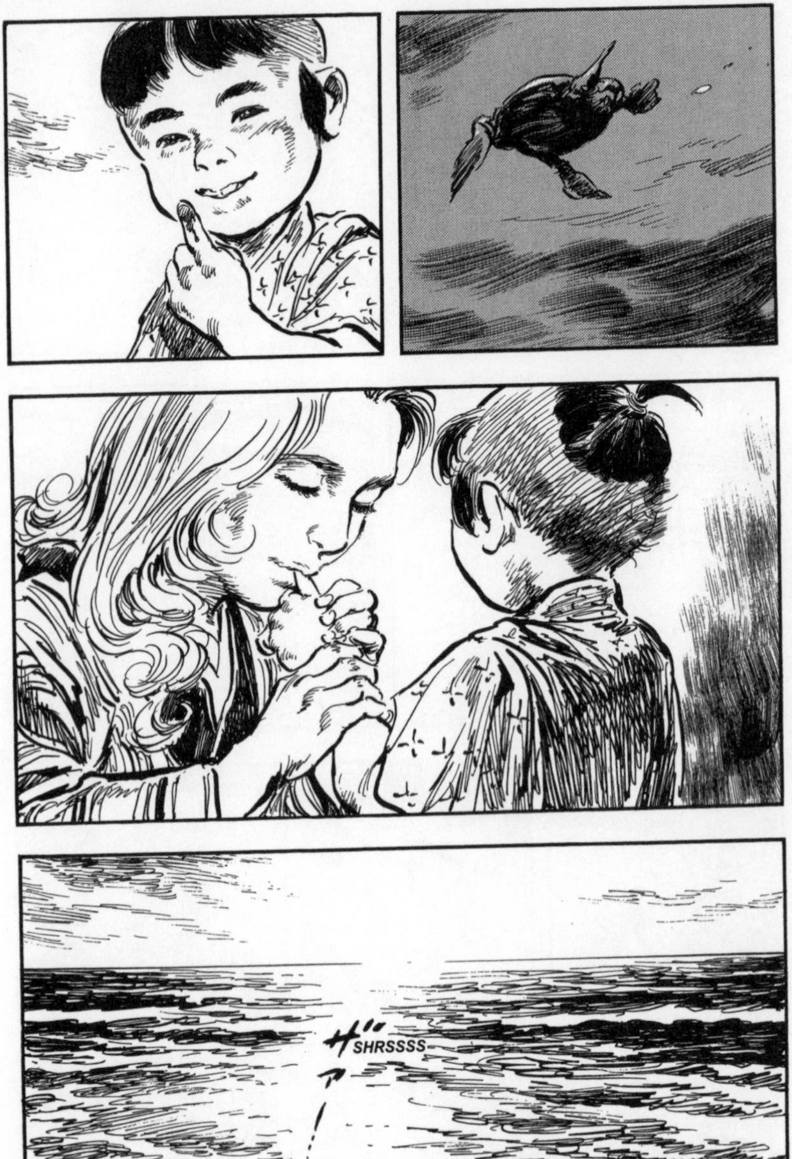
SHRSSSS

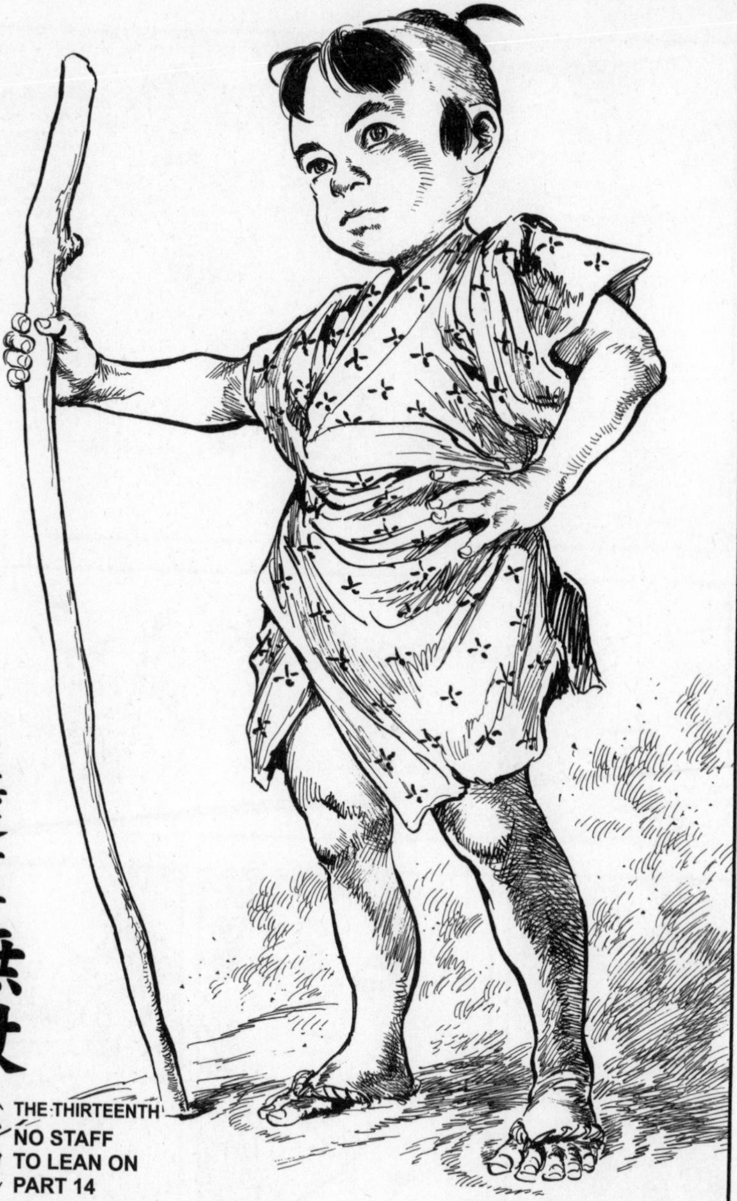

其之十三 無杖（十四）

THE THIRTEENTH NO STAFF TO LEAN ON PART 14

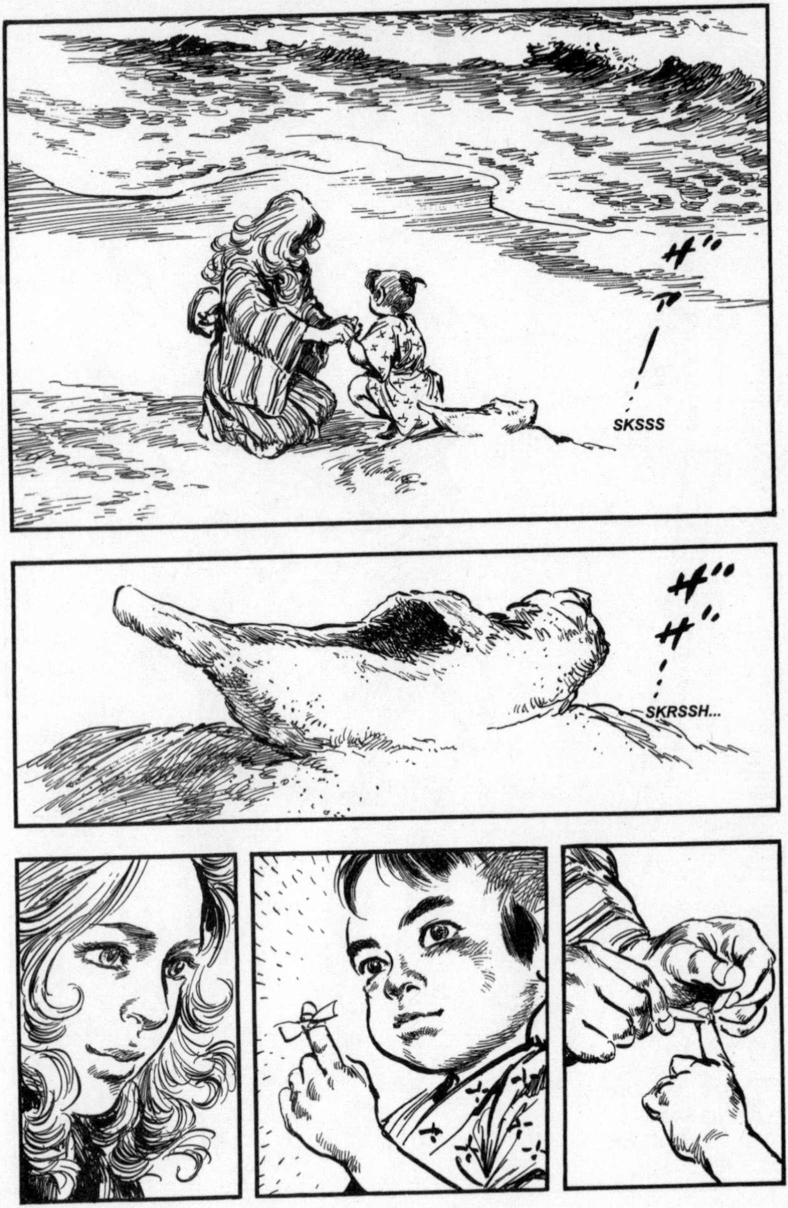
ザァー
SKSSS
ザザ
SKRSSH...

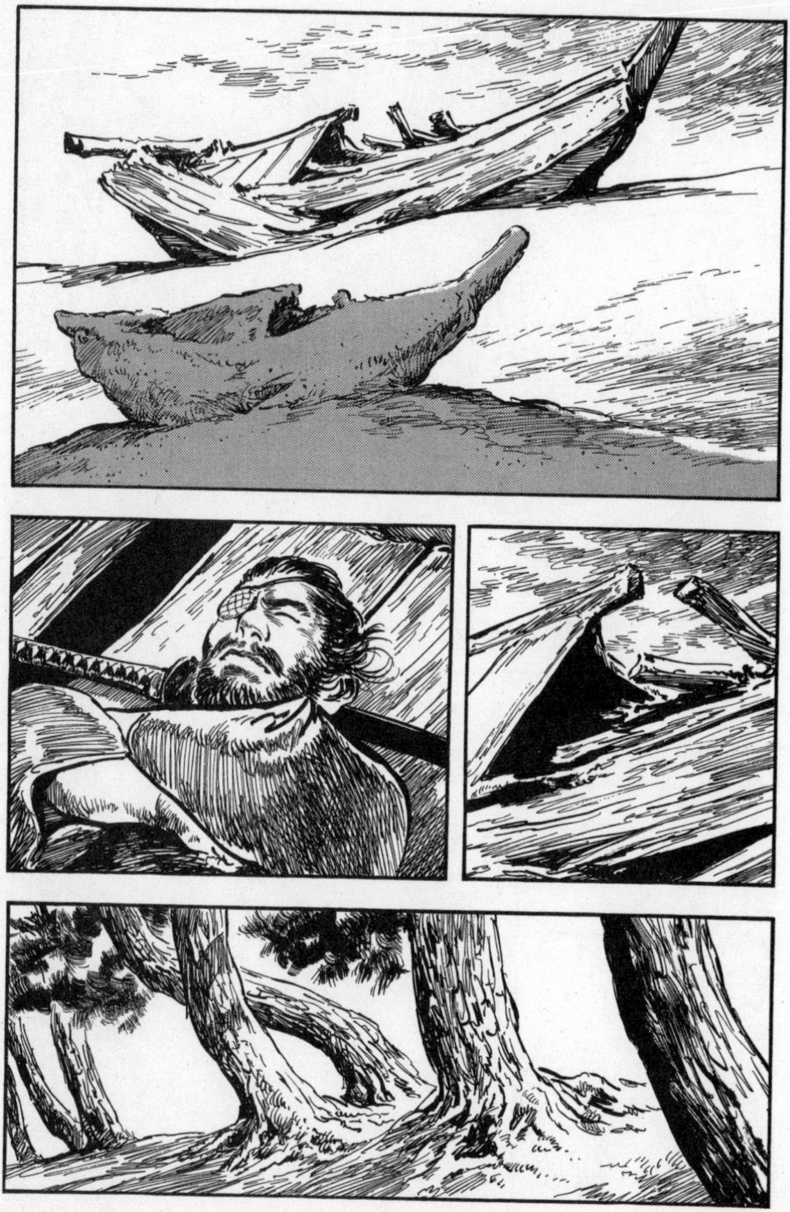

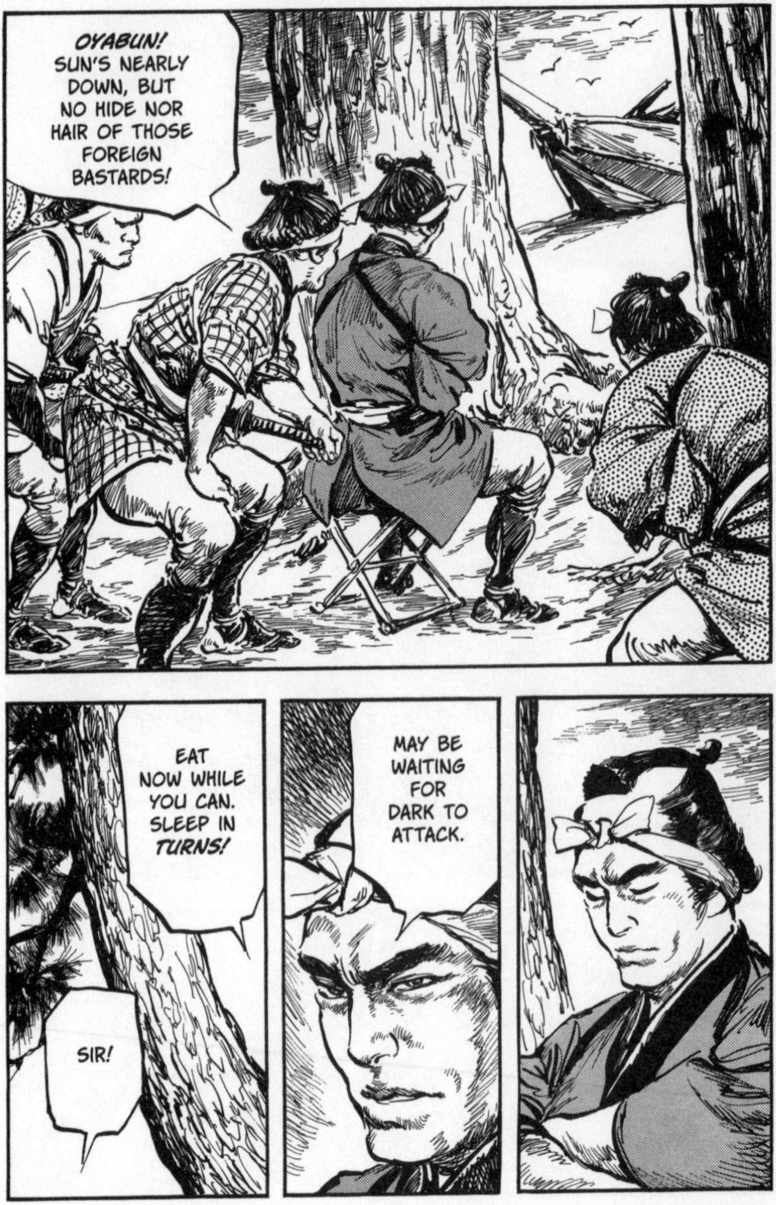

OYABUN! SUN'S NEARLY DOWN, BUT NO HIDE NOR HAIR OF THOSE FOREIGN BASTARDS!
MAY BE WAITING FOR DARK TO ATTACK.
EAT NOW WHILE YOU CAN. SLEEP IN TURNS!
SIR!

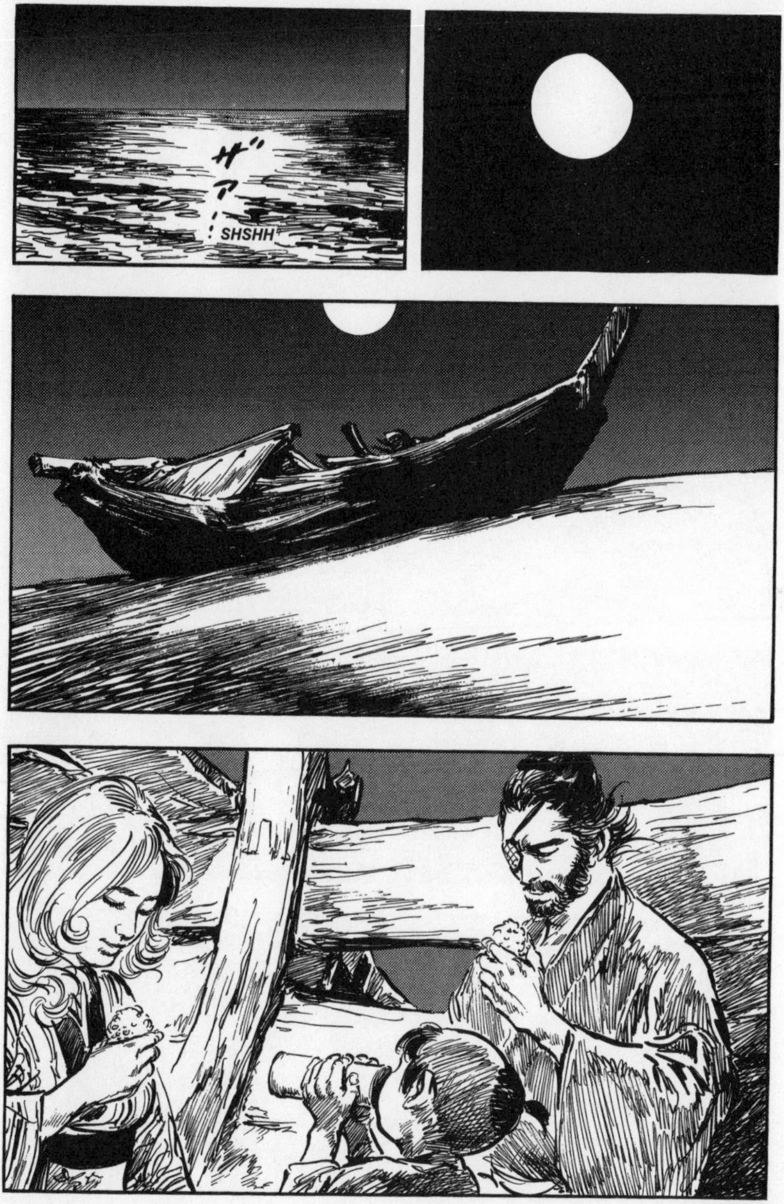
ザァ!
SHSHH

ザ
SHOOSH
ア…

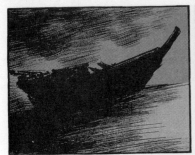

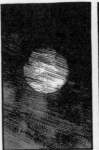

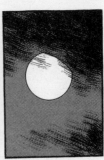

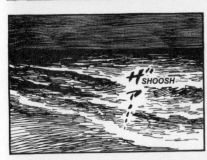

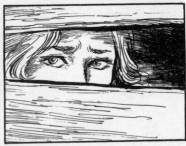

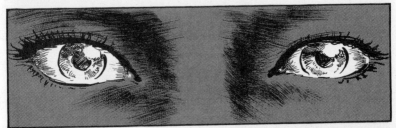

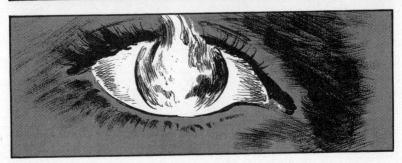

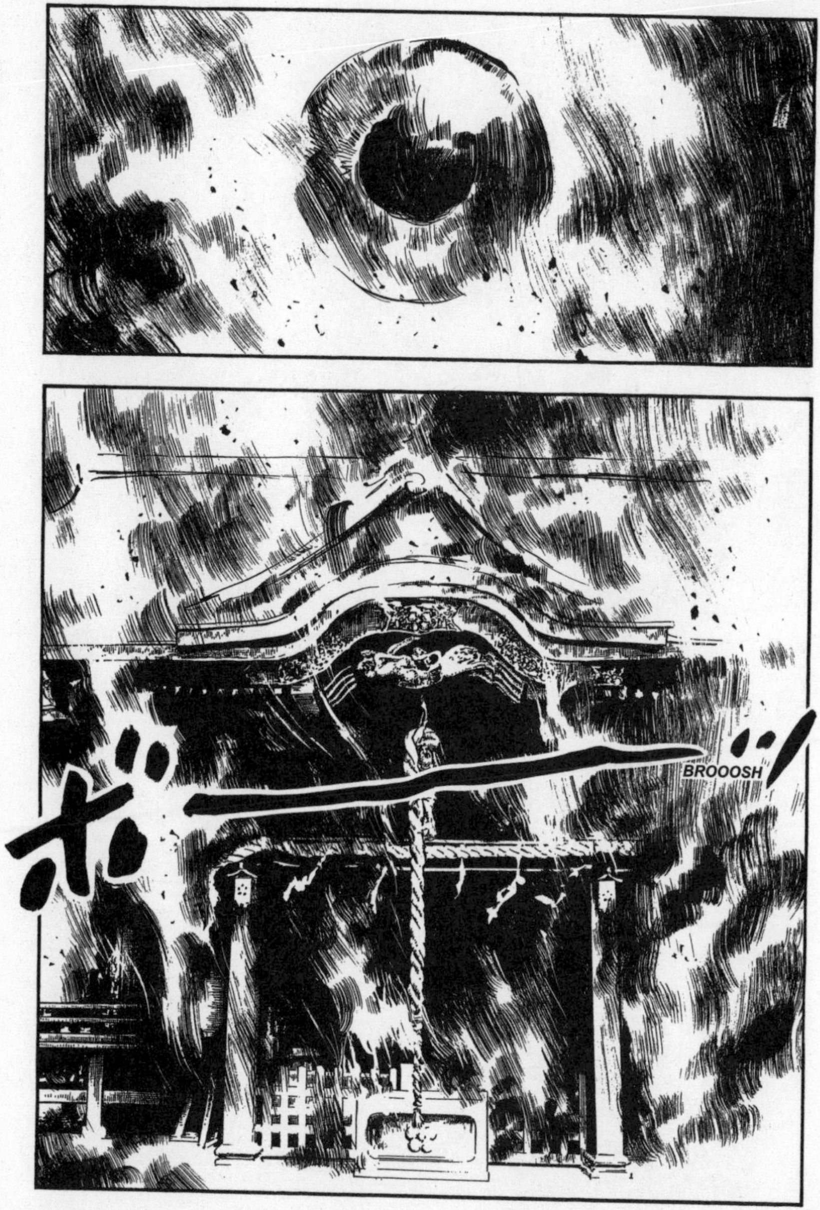
ボーーッ!
BROOOSH

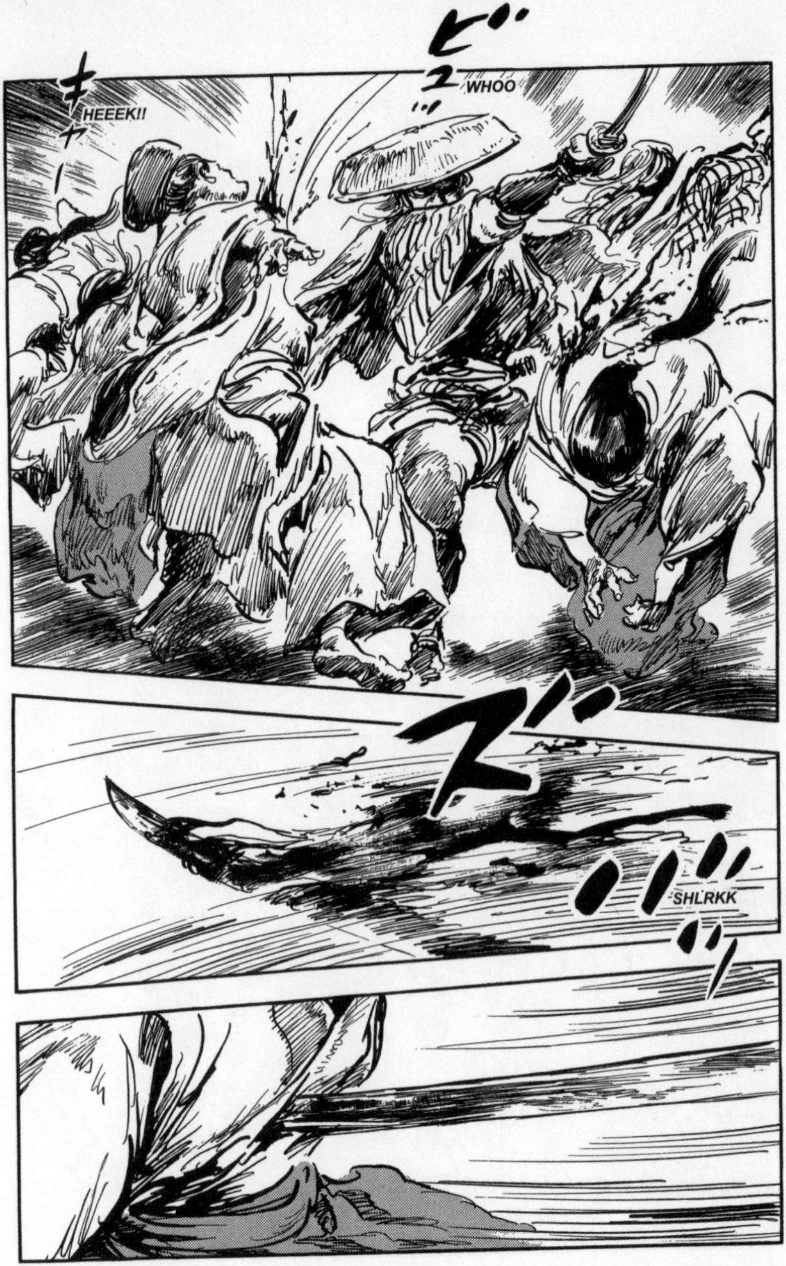
ビュッ
WHOO
キャー
HEEEK!!
SHLRKK

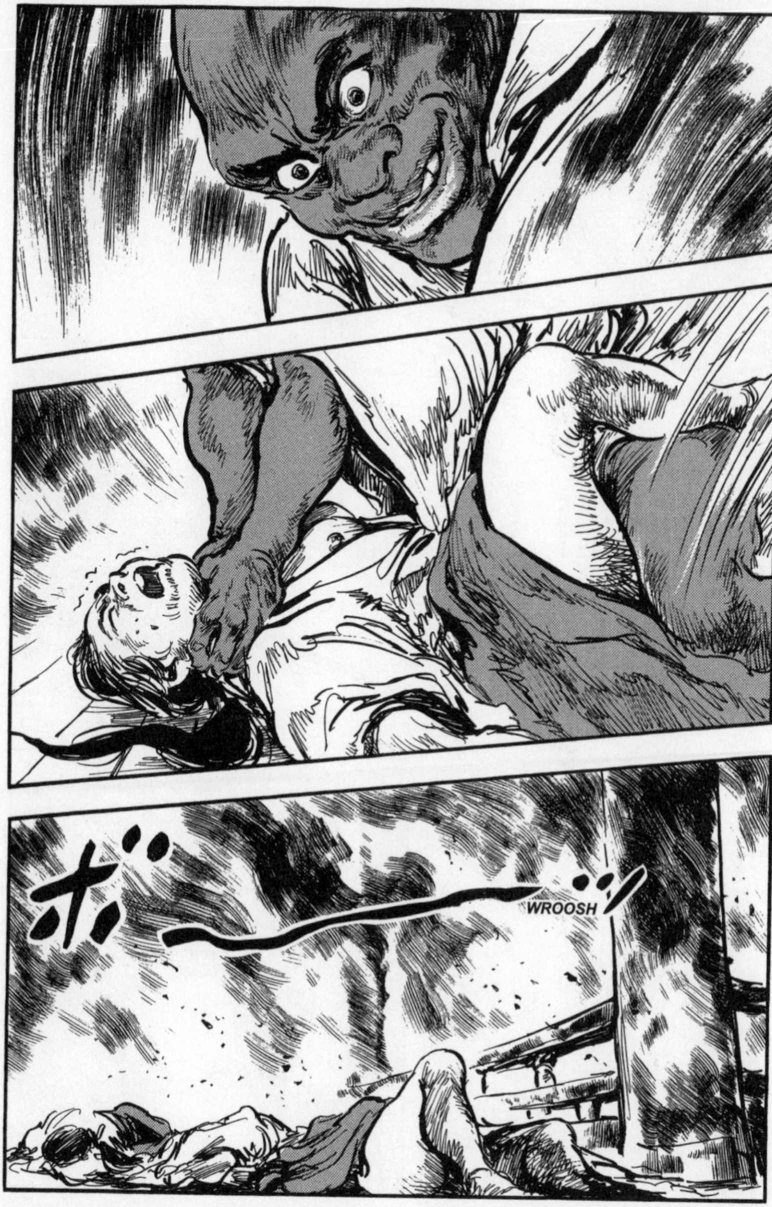
ボ―――ッ
WROOSH

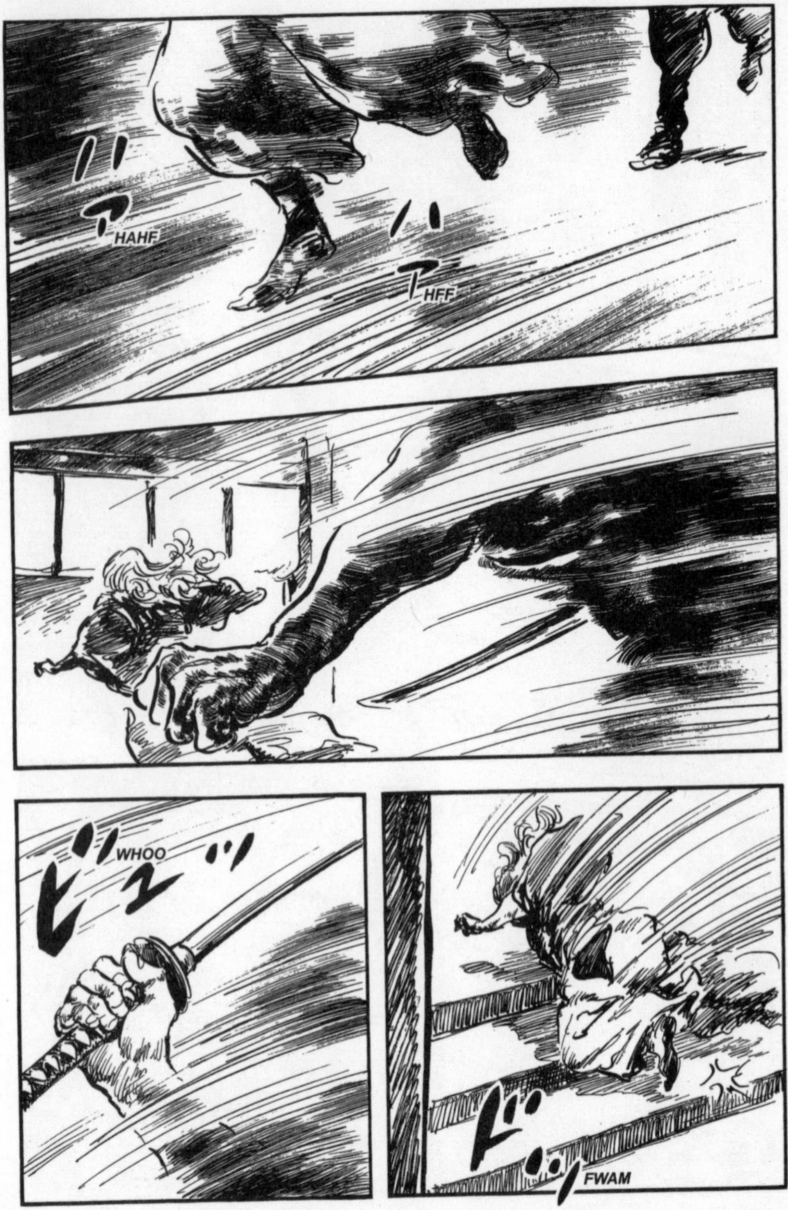
HAHF
HFF
FWAM
WHOO

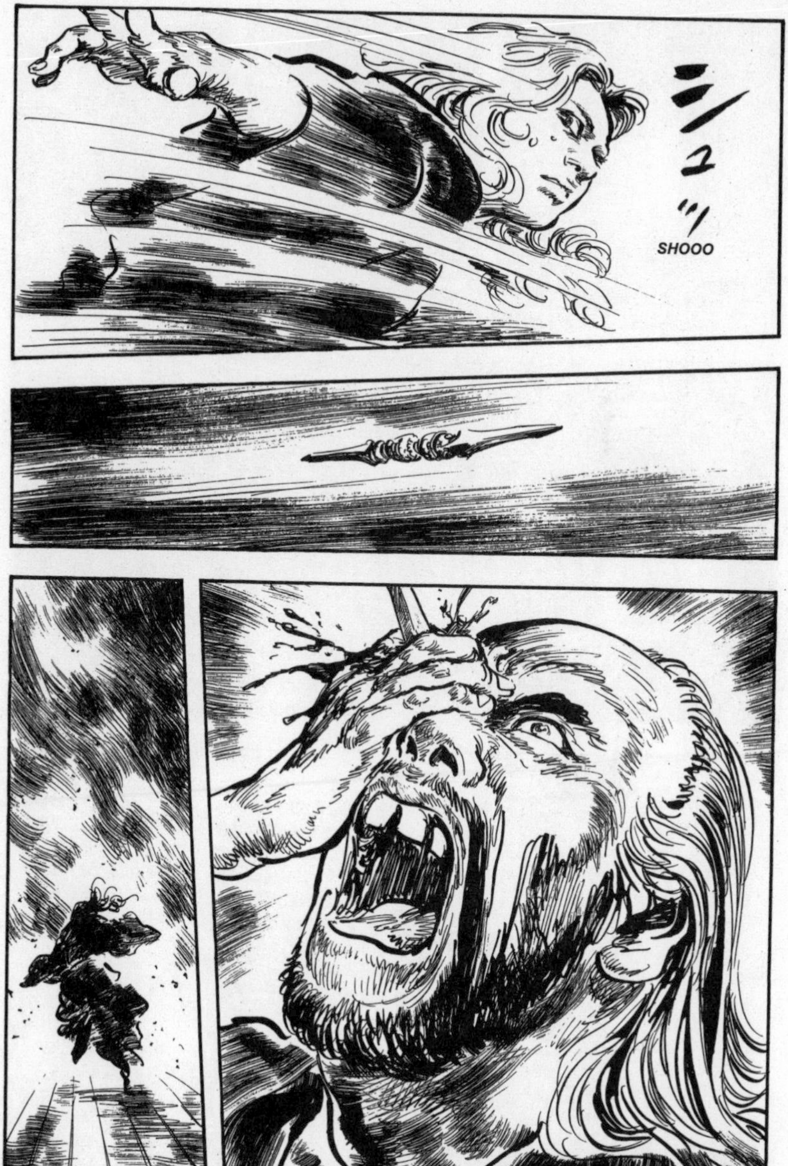
シュッ
SHOOO

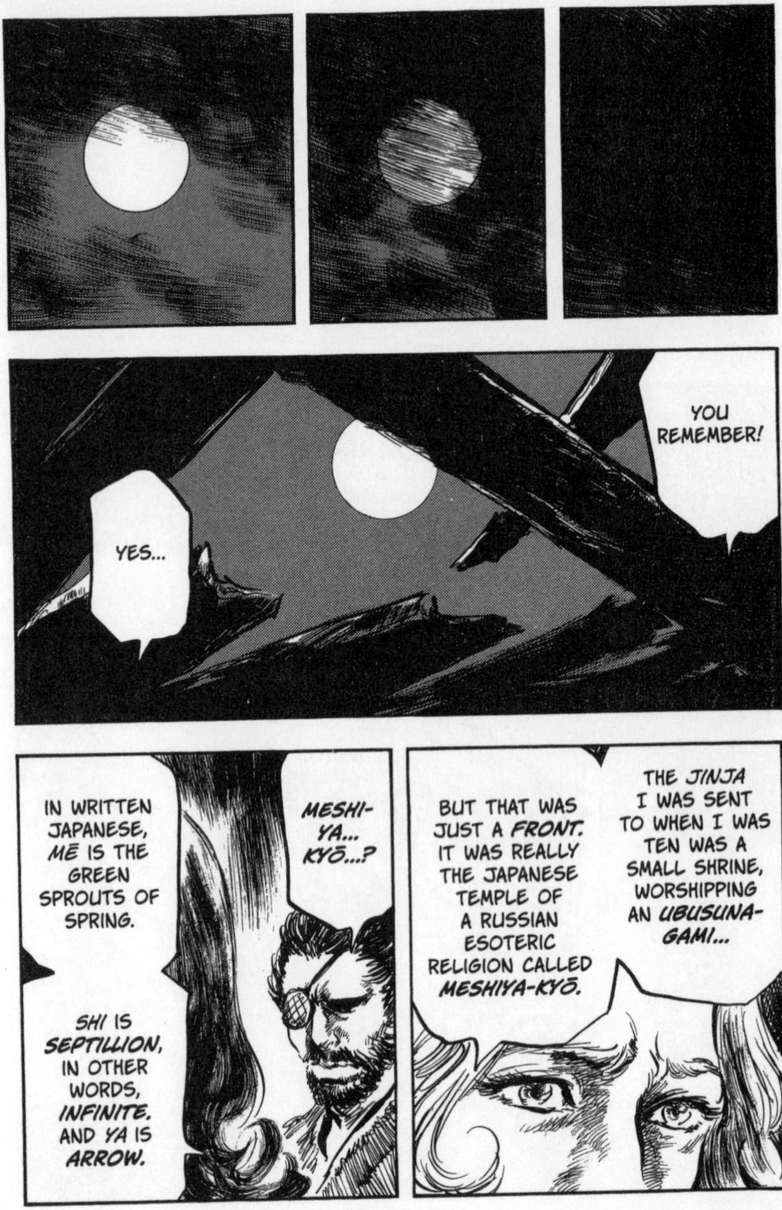
YOU REMEMBER!
YES...
THE *JINJA* I WAS SENT TO WHEN I WAS TEN WAS A SMALL SHRINE, WORSHIPPING AN *UBUSUNA-GAMI...*
BUT THAT WAS JUST A *FRONT.* IT WAS REALLY THE JAPANESE TEMPLE OF A RUSSIAN ESOTERIC RELIGION CALLED *MESHIYA-KYŌ.*
MESHI-YA... KYŌ...?
IN WRITTEN JAPANESE, *MĒ* IS THE GREEN SPROUTS OF SPRING.
SHI IS *SEPTILLION,* IN OTHER WORDS, *INFINITE.* AND *YA* IS *ARROW.*

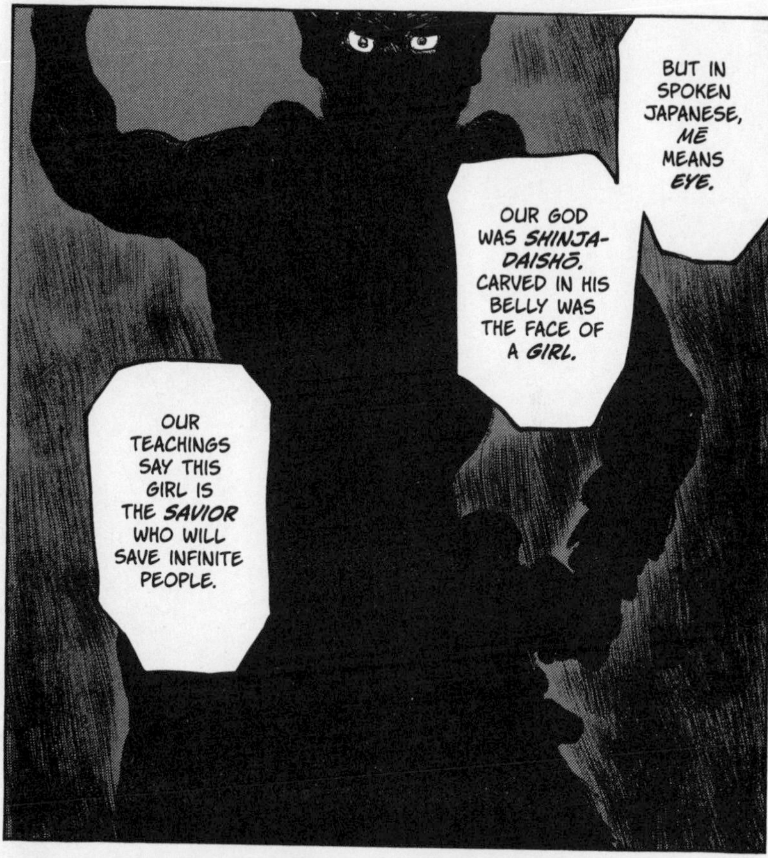
BUT IN SPOKEN JAPANESE, *MĒ* MEANS *EYE.*
OUR GOD WAS *SHINJA-DAISHŌ.* CARVED IN HIS BELLY WAS THE FACE OF A *GIRL.*
OUR TEACHINGS SAY THIS GIRL IS THE *SAVIOR* WHO WILL SAVE INFINITE PEOPLE.

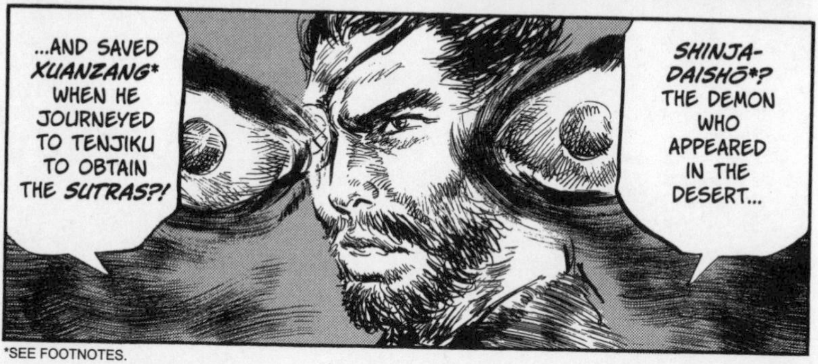
*SHINJA-DAISHŌ**? THE DEMON WHO APPEARED IN THE DESERT...
...AND SAVED *XUANZANG** WHEN HE JOURNEYED TO TENJIKU TO OBTAIN THE *SUTRAS?!*

*SEE FOOTNOTES.

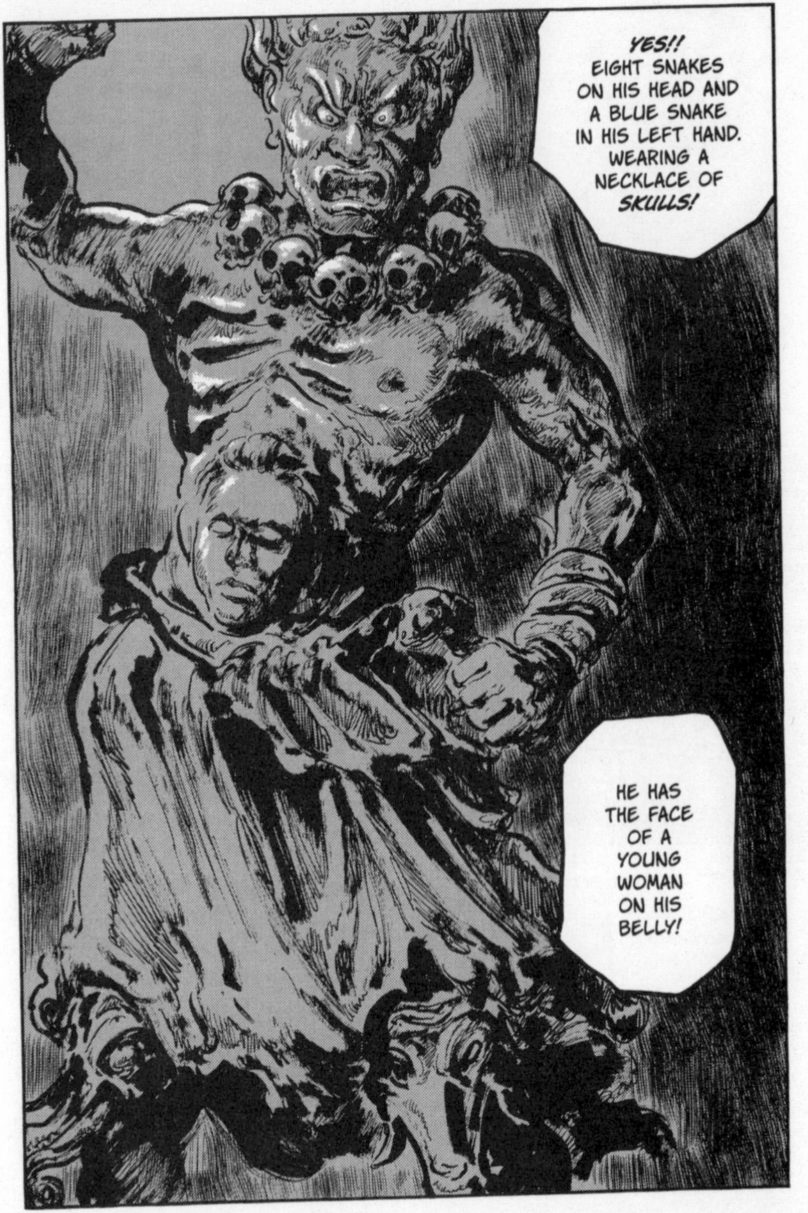
YES!! EIGHT SNAKES ON HIS HEAD AND A BLUE SNAKE IN HIS LEFT HAND. WEARING A NECKLACE OF SKULLS!
HE HAS THE FACE OF A YOUNG WOMAN ON HIS BELLY!

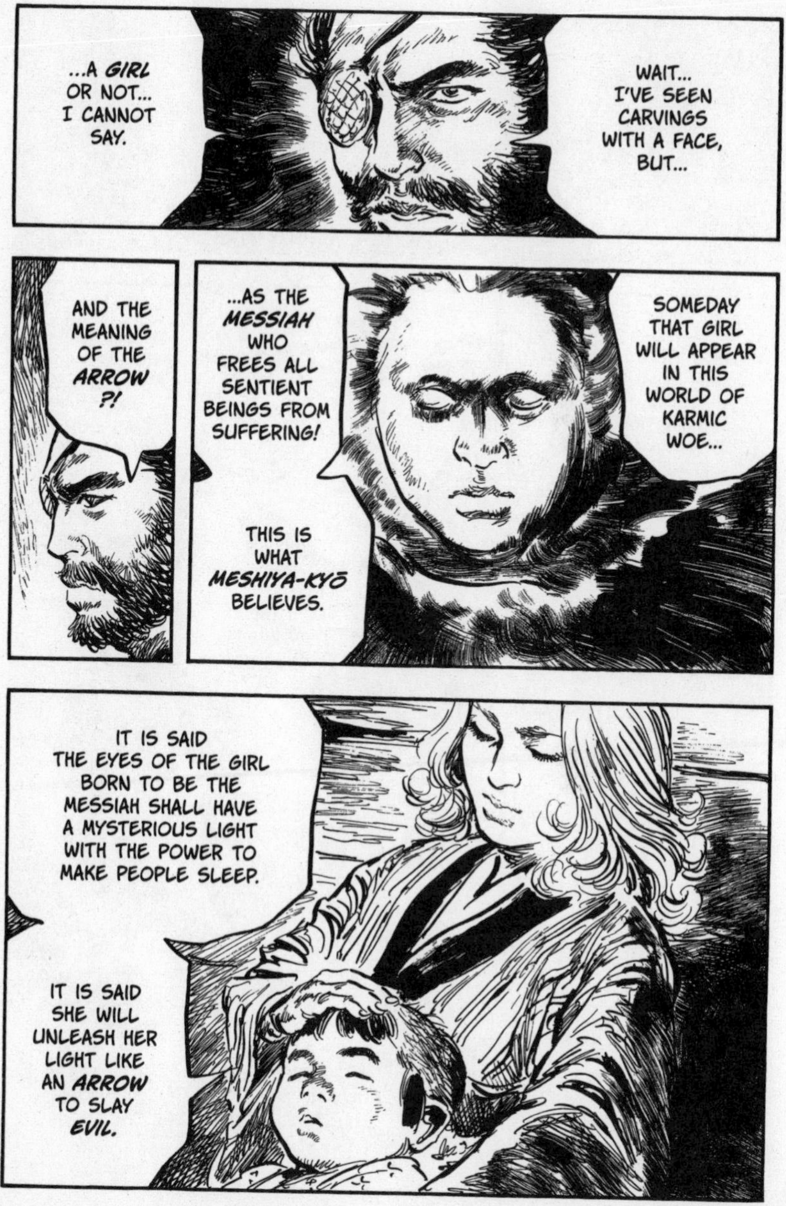
WAIT... I'VE SEEN CARVINGS WITH A FACE, BUT...
...A GIRL OR NOT... I CANNOT SAY.
SOMEDAY THAT GIRL WILL APPEAR IN THIS WORLD OF KARMIC WOE...
...AS THE MESSIAH WHO FREES ALL SENTIENT BEINGS FROM SUFFERING!
THIS IS WHAT MESHIYA-KYŌ BELIEVES.
AND THE MEANING OF THE ARROW ?!
IT IS SAID THE EYES OF THE GIRL BORN TO BE THE MESSIAH SHALL HAVE A MYSTERIOUS LIGHT WITH THE POWER TO MAKE PEOPLE SLEEP.
IT IS SAID SHE WILL UNLEASH HER LIGHT LIKE AN ARROW TO SLAY EVIL.

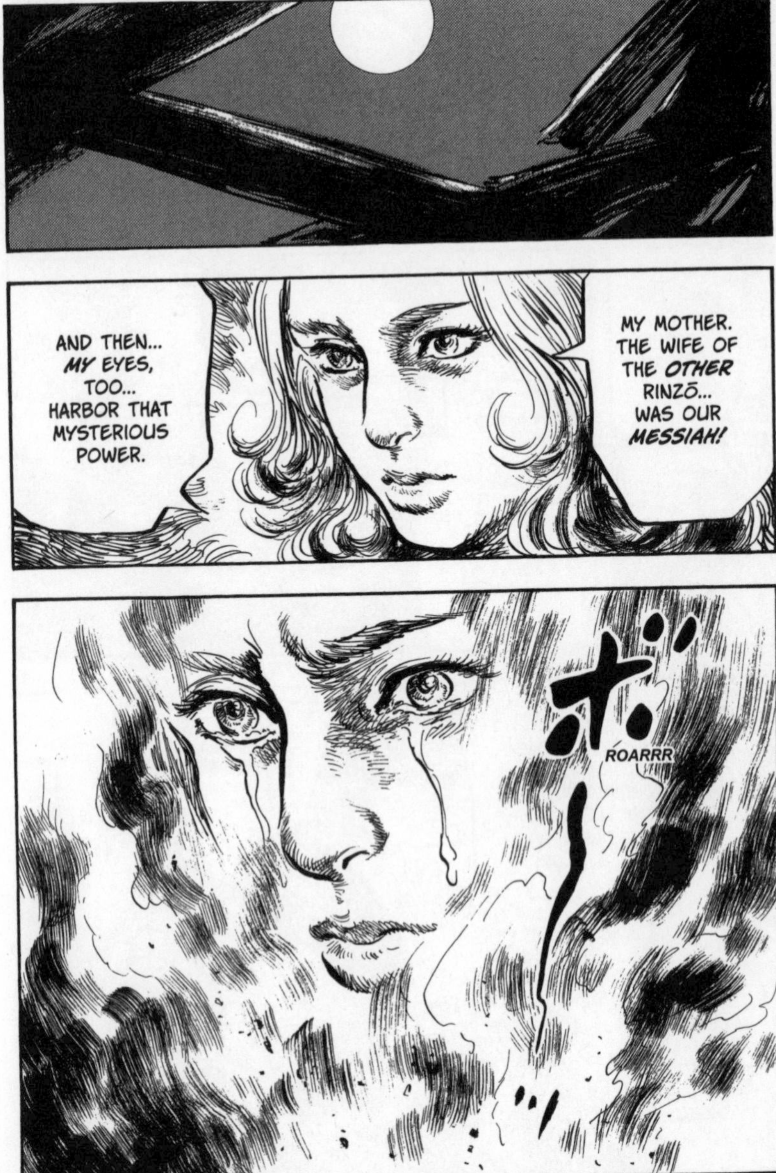
MY MOTHER. THE WIFE OF THE *OTHER* RINZŌ... WAS OUR *MESSIAH!*
AND THEN... *MY* EYES, TOO... HARBOR THAT MYSTERIOUS POWER.
ボ
ROARRR

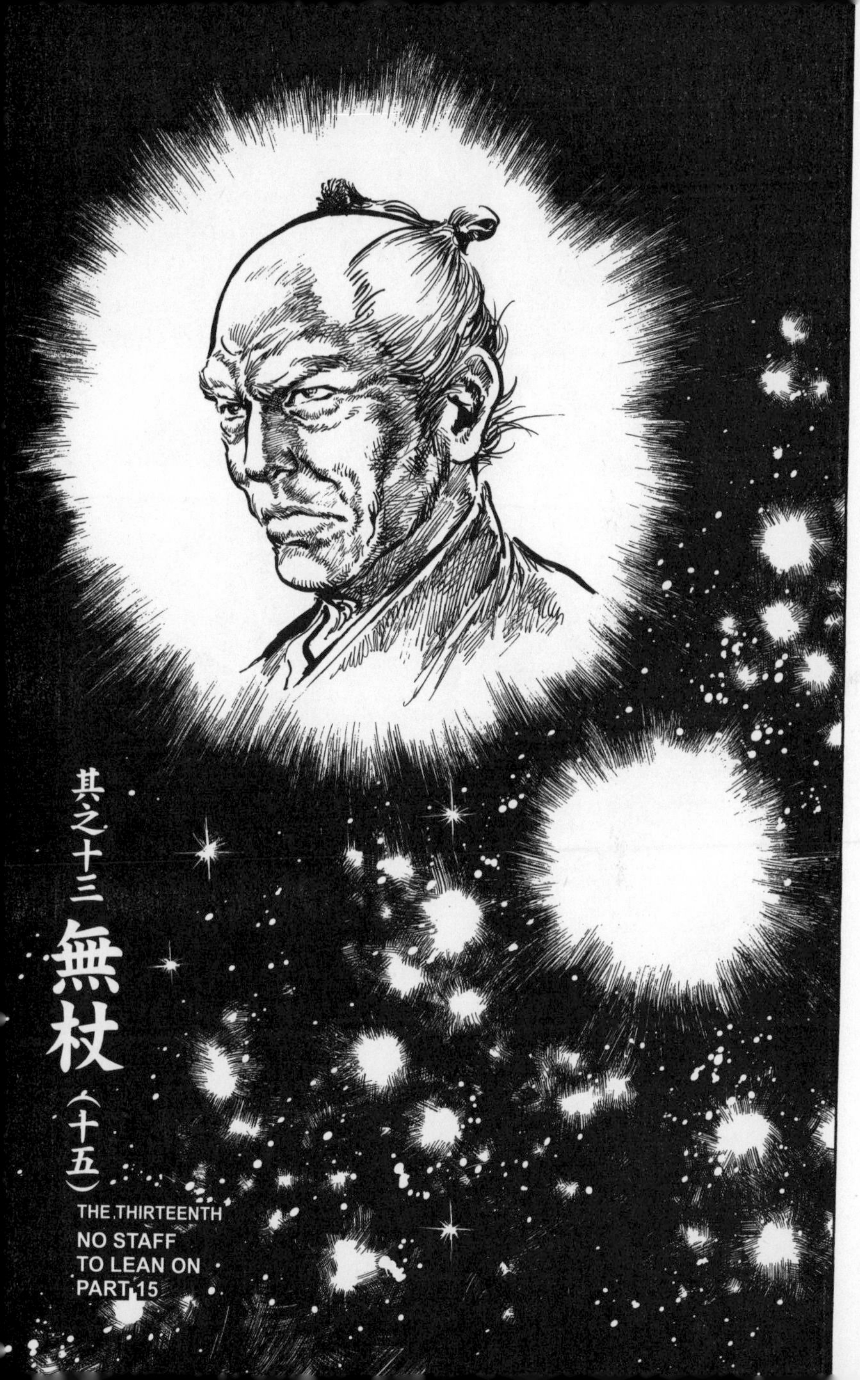
其之十三
無杖（十五）
THE THIRTEENTH
NO STAFF
TO LEAN ON
PART 15

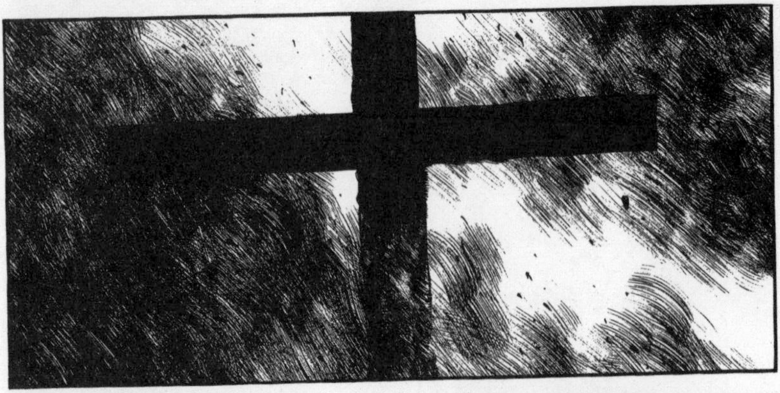
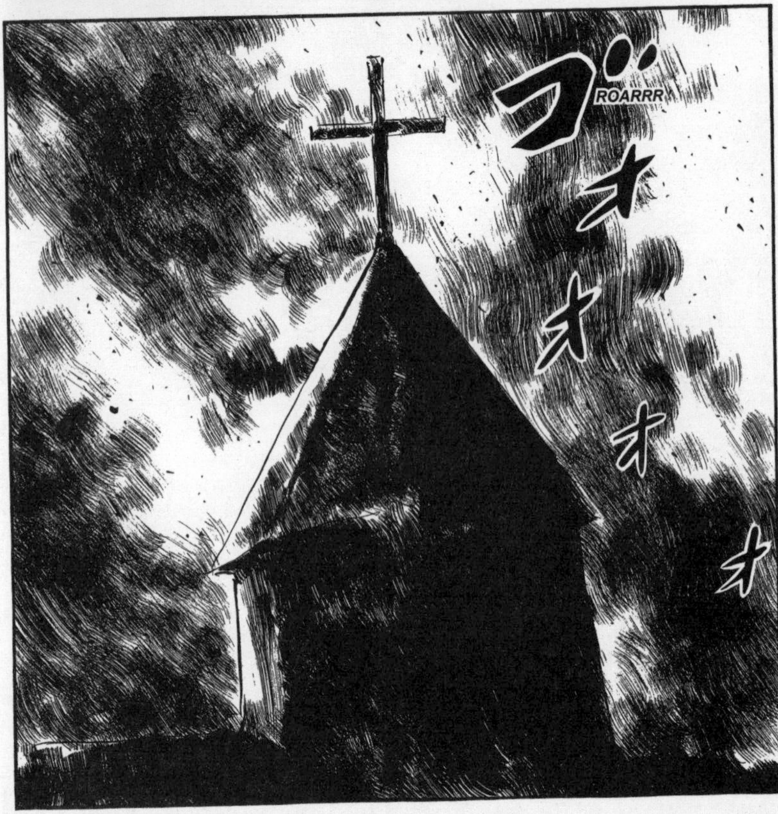
ゴオオオオ
ROARRR

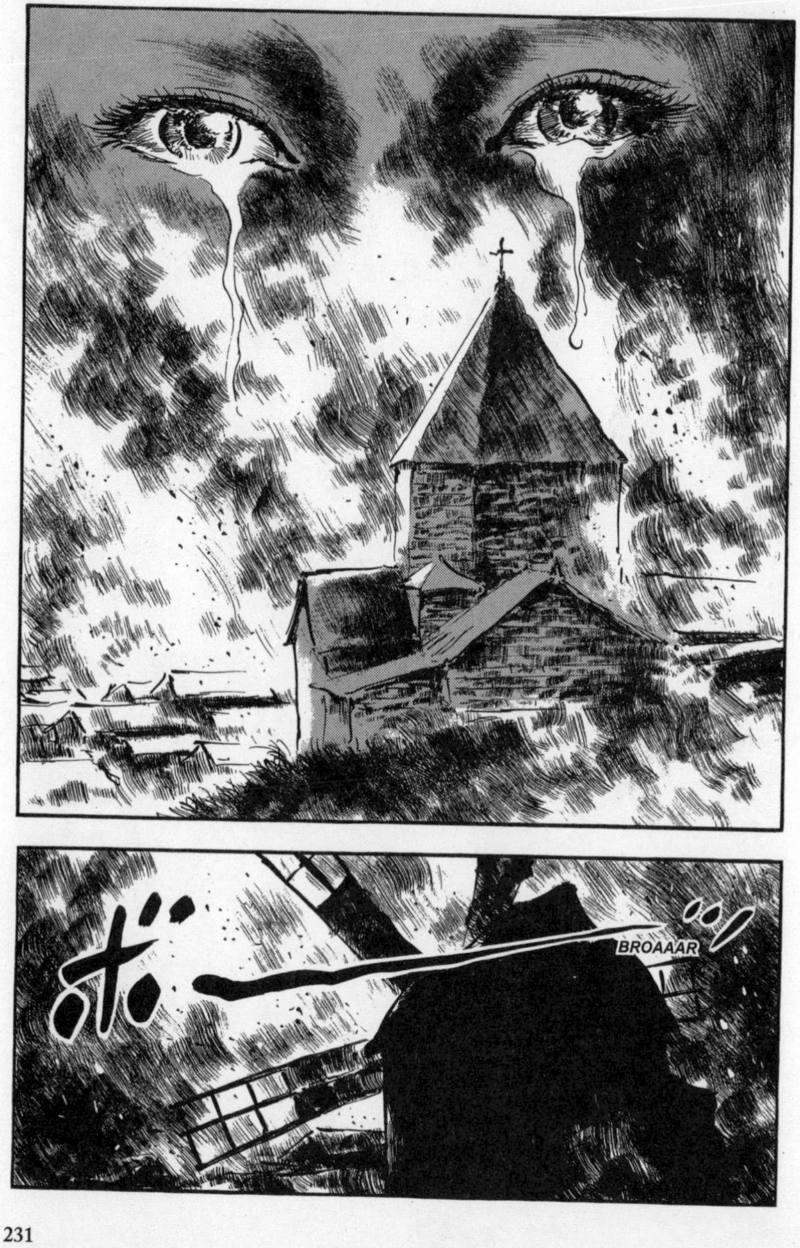
BROAAAR

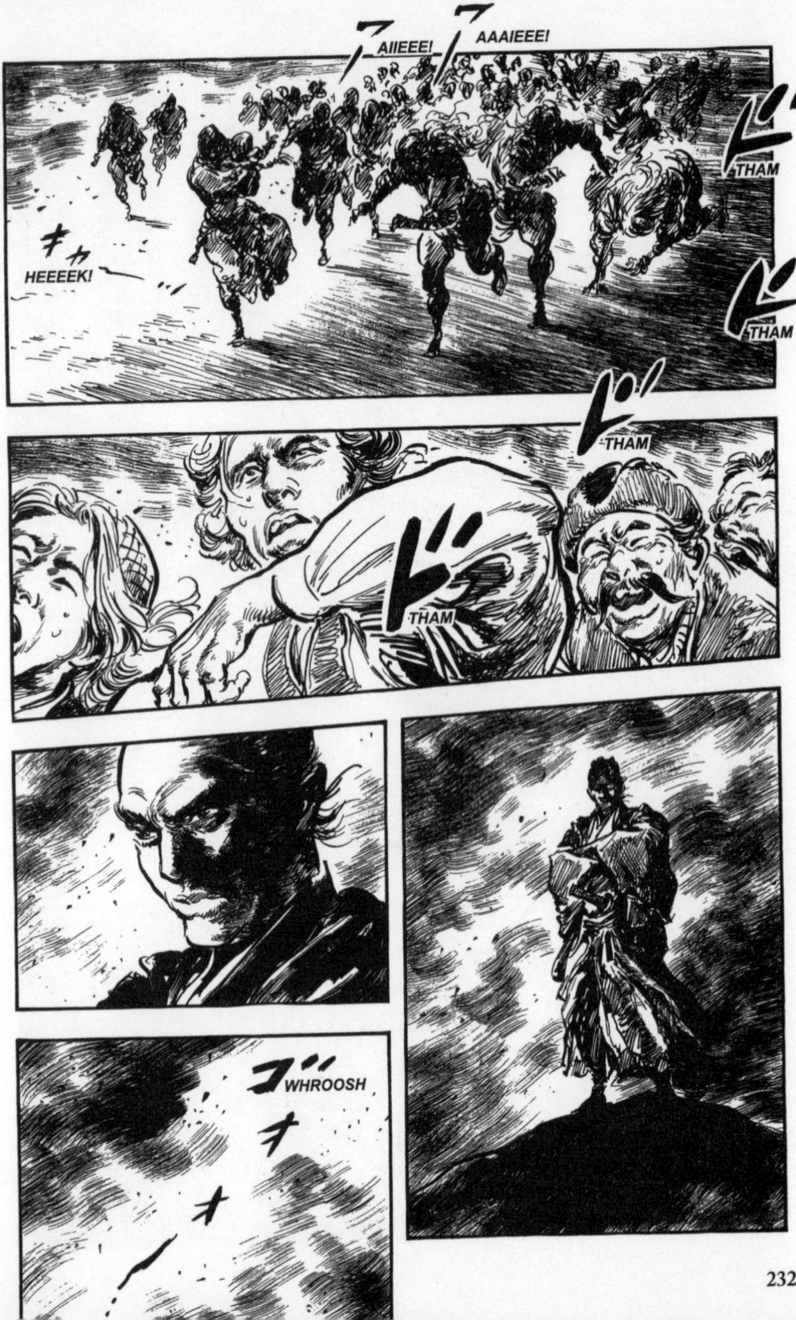
AAAIEEE!
AIIEEE!
THAM
THAM
HEEEEK!
THAM
THAM
WHROOSH

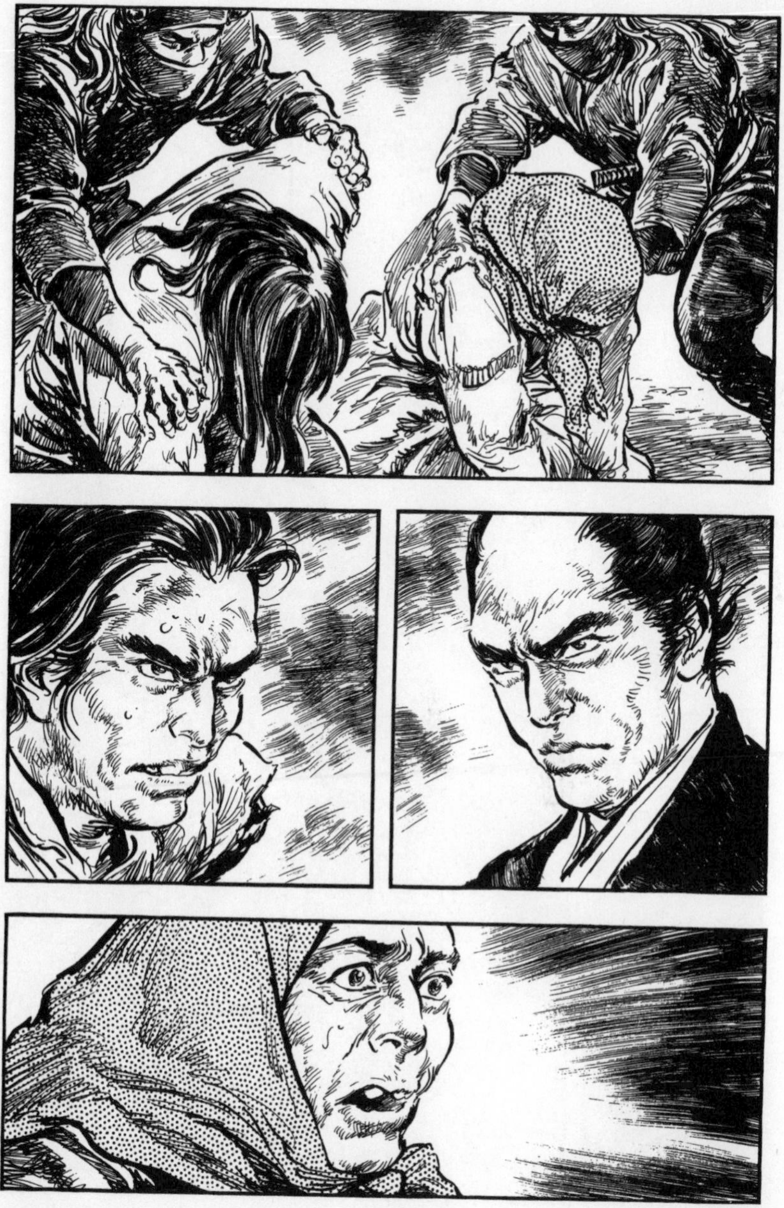

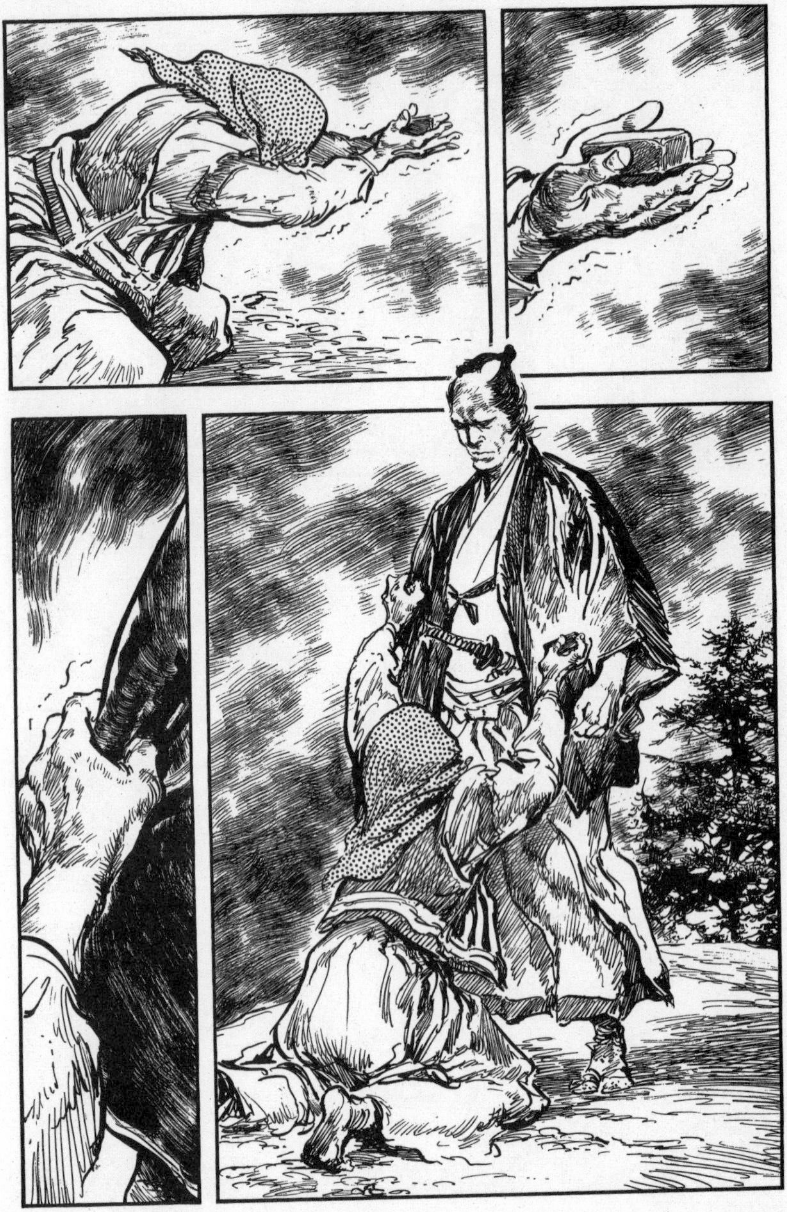

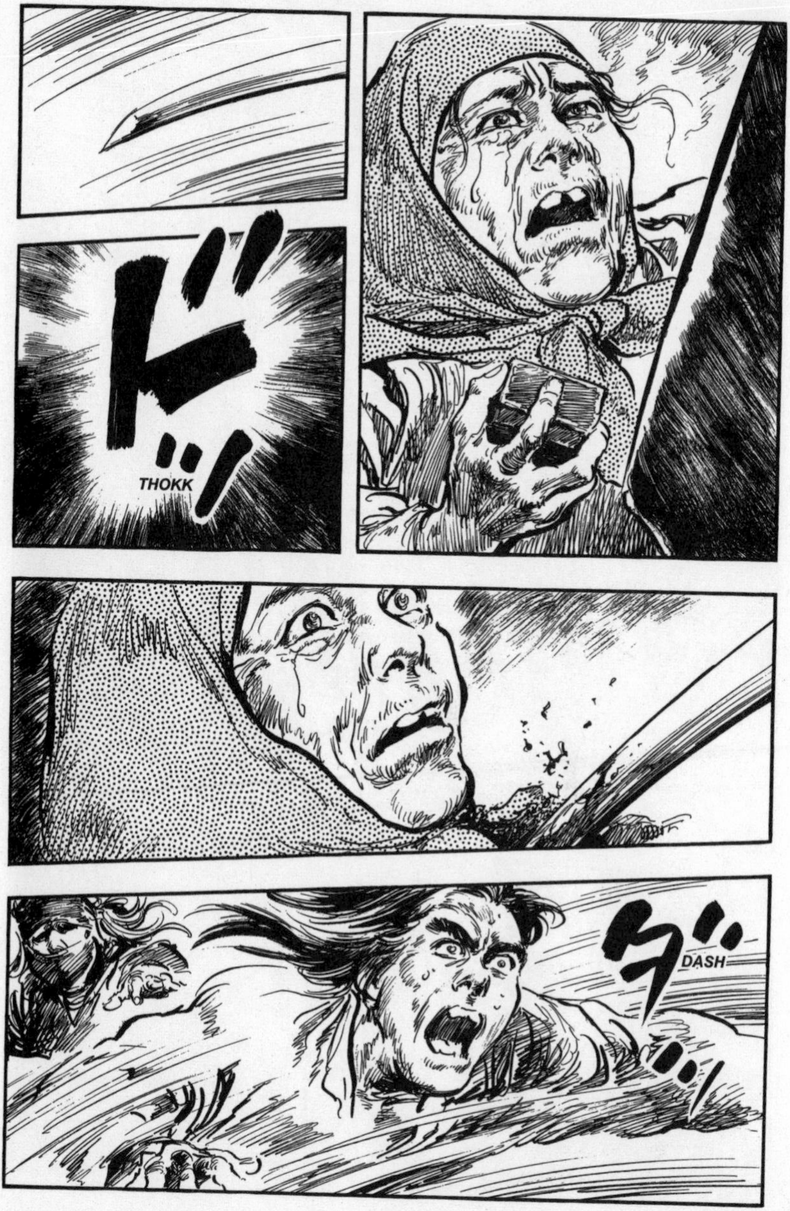
ド
THOKK
ダッ
DASH

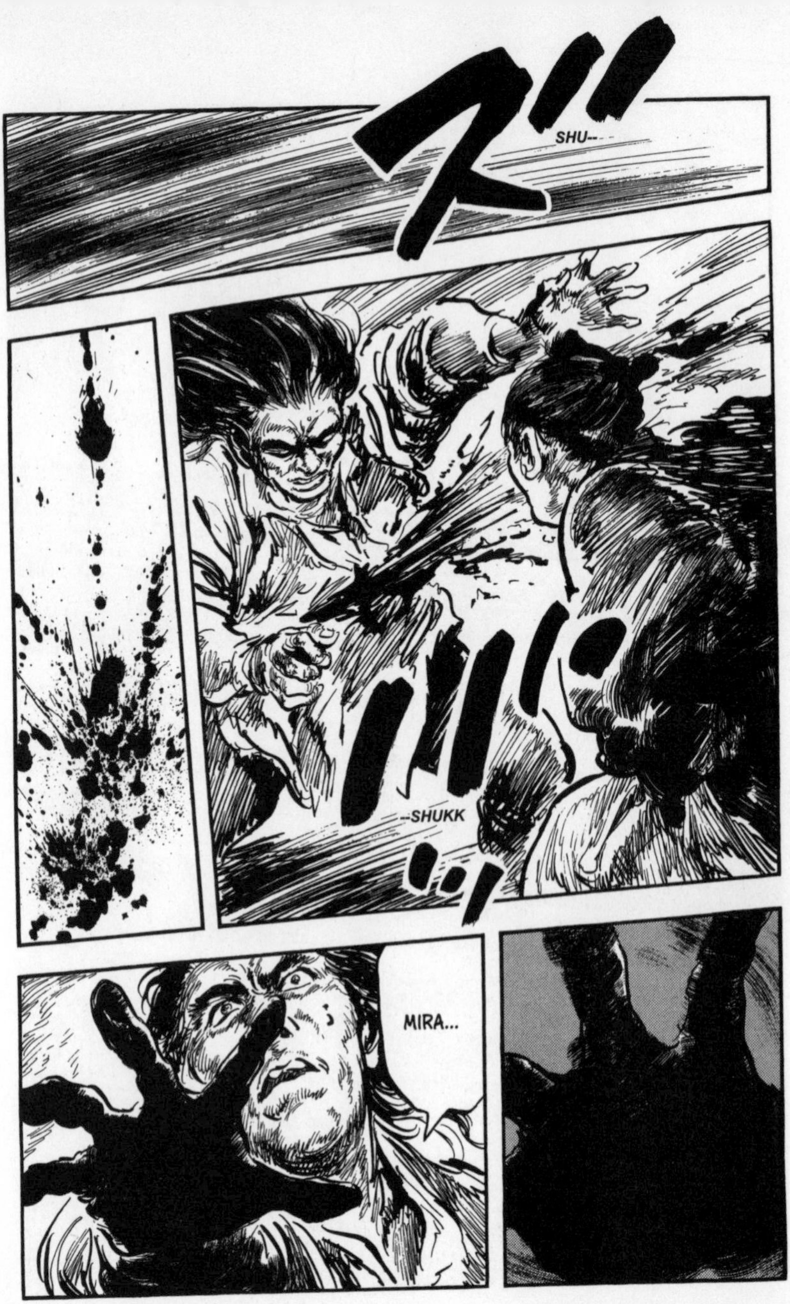
SHU--
--SHUKK
MIRA...

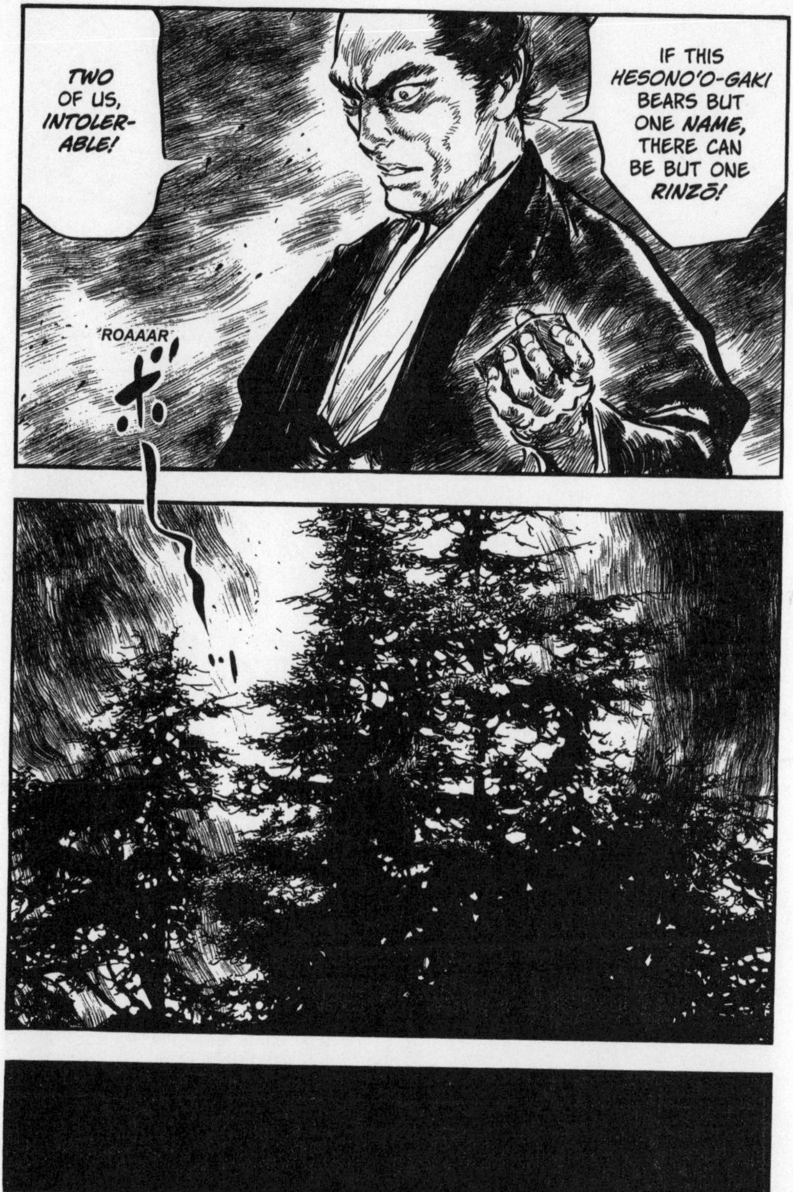
IF THIS *HESONO'O-GAKI* BEARS BUT ONE *NAME*, THERE CAN BE BUT ONE *RINZŌ!*
TWO OF US, *INTOLERABLE!*
ROAAAR
ボッ

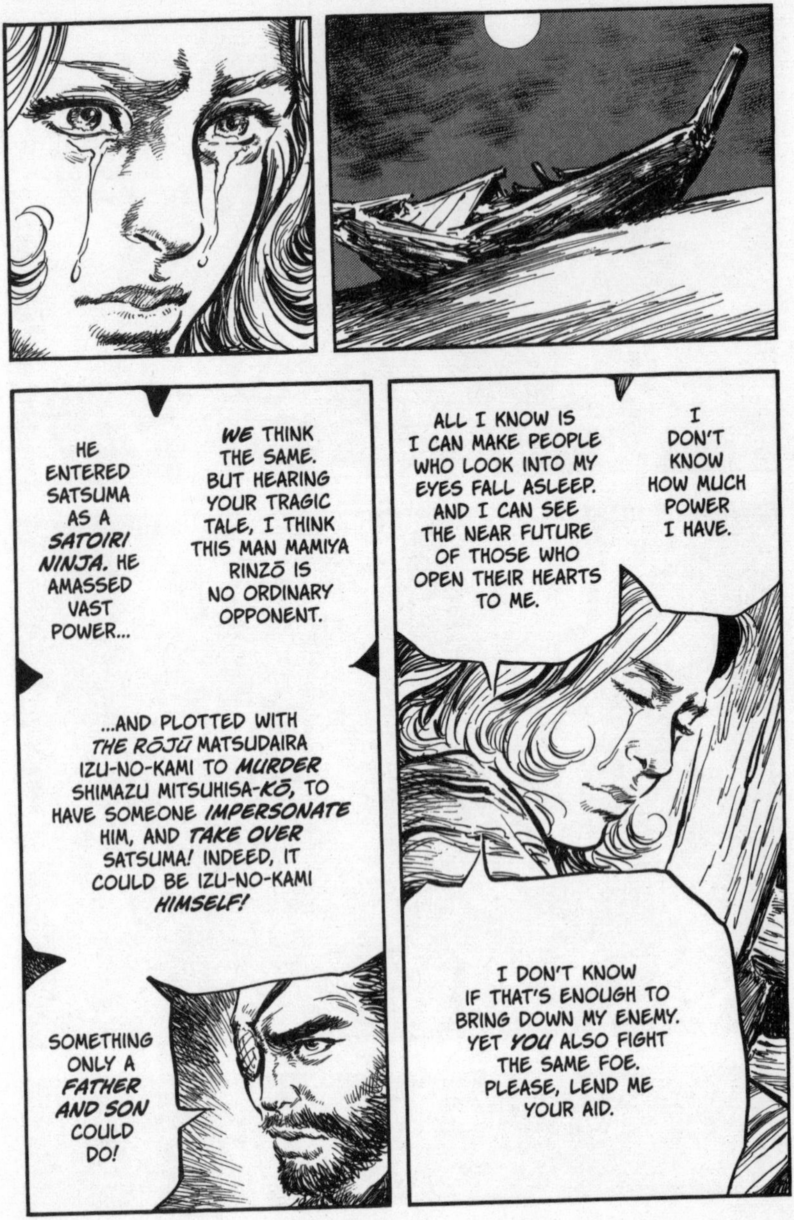
I DON'T KNOW HOW MUCH POWER I HAVE.
ALL I KNOW IS I CAN MAKE PEOPLE WHO LOOK INTO MY EYES FALL ASLEEP. AND I CAN SEE THE NEAR FUTURE OF THOSE WHO OPEN THEIR HEARTS TO ME.
I DON'T KNOW IF THAT'S ENOUGH TO BRING DOWN MY ENEMY. YET *YOU* ALSO FIGHT THE SAME FOE. PLEASE, LEND ME YOUR AID.
WE THINK THE SAME. BUT HEARING YOUR TRAGIC TALE, I THINK THIS MAN MAMIYA RINZŌ IS NO ORDINARY OPPONENT.
HE ENTERED SATSUMA AS A *SATOIRI NINJA.* HE AMASSED VAST POWER...
...AND PLOTTED WITH *THE RŌJŪ* MATSUDAIRA IZU-NO-KAMI TO *MURDER* SHIMAZU MITSUHISA-*KŌ,* TO HAVE SOMEONE *IMPERSONATE* HIM, AND *TAKE OVER* SATSUMA! INDEED, IT COULD BE IZU-NO-KAMI *HIMSELF!*
SOMETHING ONLY A *FATHER AND SON* COULD DO!

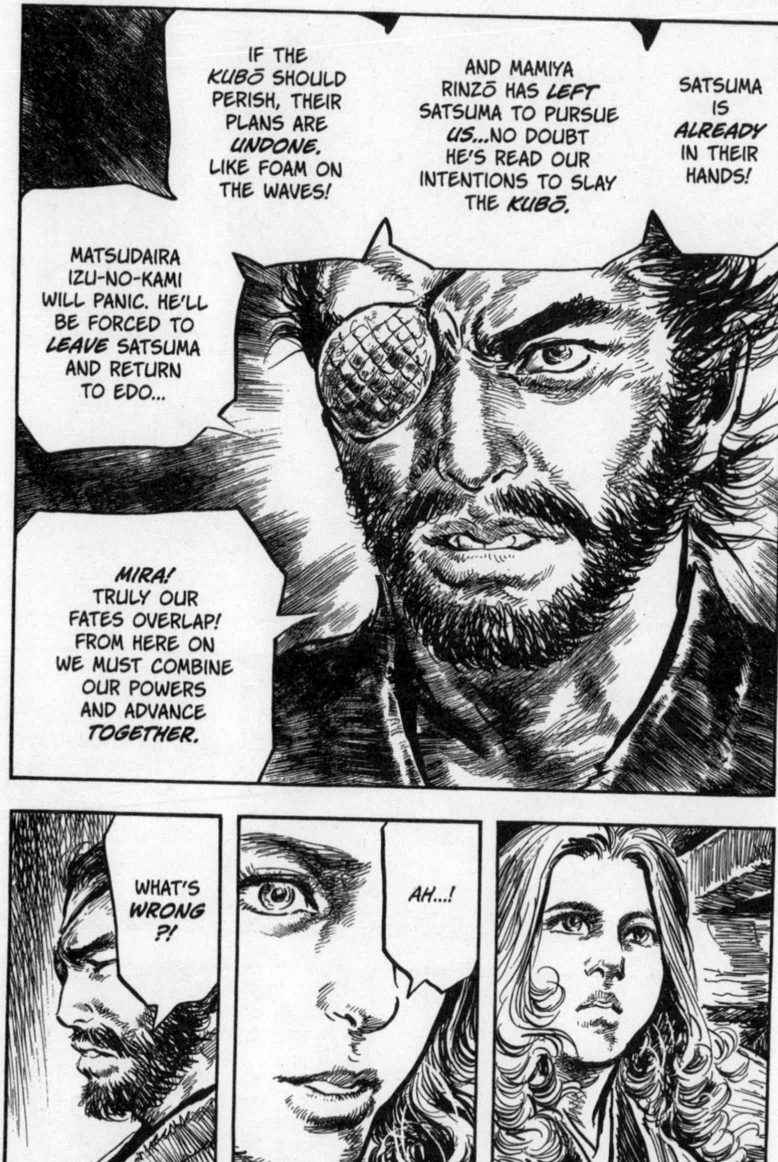
SATSUMA IS ALREADY IN THEIR HANDS!
AND MAMIYA RINZŌ HAS LEFT SATSUMA TO PURSUE US...NO DOUBT HE'S READ OUR INTENTIONS TO SLAY THE KUBŌ.
IF THE KUBŌ SHOULD PERISH, THEIR PLANS ARE UNDONE. LIKE FOAM ON THE WAVES!
MATSUDAIRA IZU-NO-KAMI WILL PANIC. HE'LL BE FORCED TO LEAVE SATSUMA AND RETURN TO EDO...
MIRA! TRULY OUR FATES OVERLAP! FROM HERE ON WE MUST COMBINE OUR POWERS AND ADVANCE TOGETHER.
AH...!
WHAT'S WRONG ?!

THIS "*KU-BŌ*"... IS HE THE *SHŌGUN*?!

YOU "*SAW*" SOME-THING?!

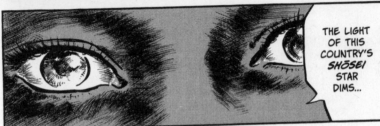

THE LIGHT OF THIS COUNTRY'S *SHŌSEI* STAR DIMS...

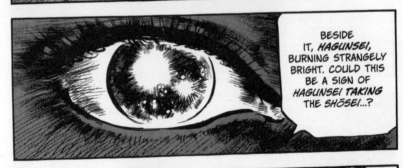

BESIDE IT, *HAGUNSEI*, BURNING STRANGELY BRIGHT. COULD THIS BE A SIGN OF *HAGUNSEI TAKING* THE *SHŌSEI*...?

RINZŌ SHALL *KILL* THE *KUBŌ*?! THAT--THAT *CANNOT* BE!

240

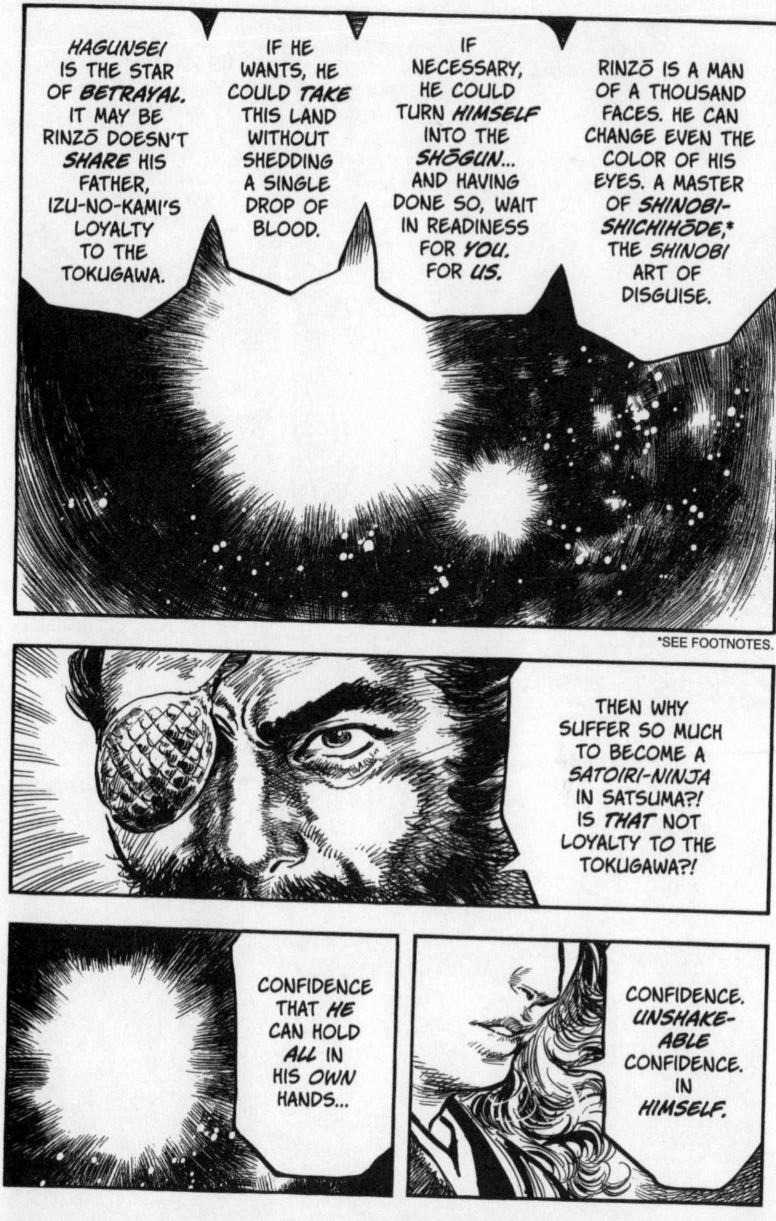
RINZŌ IS A MAN OF A THOUSAND FACES. HE CAN CHANGE EVEN THE COLOR OF HIS EYES. A MASTER OF *SHINOBI-SHICHIHŌDE*,* THE *SHINOBI* ART OF DISGUISE.
IF NECESSARY, HE COULD TURN *HIMSELF* INTO THE *SHŌGUN*... AND HAVING DONE SO, WAIT IN READINESS FOR *YOU*. FOR *US*.
IF HE WANTS, HE COULD *TAKE* THIS LAND WITHOUT SHEDDING A SINGLE DROP OF BLOOD.
HAGUNSEI IS THE STAR OF *BETRAYAL*. IT MAY BE RINZŌ DOESN'T *SHARE* HIS FATHER, IZU-NO-KAMI'S LOYALTY TO THE TOKUGAWA.
THEN WHY SUFFER SO MUCH TO BECOME A *SATOIRI-NINJA* IN SATSUMA?! IS *THAT* NOT LOYALTY TO THE TOKUGAWA?!
CONFIDENCE. *UNSHAKE-ABLE* CONFIDENCE. IN *HIMSELF*.
CONFIDENCE THAT *HE* CAN HOLD *ALL* IN HIS *OWN* HANDS...

*SEE FOOTNOTES.

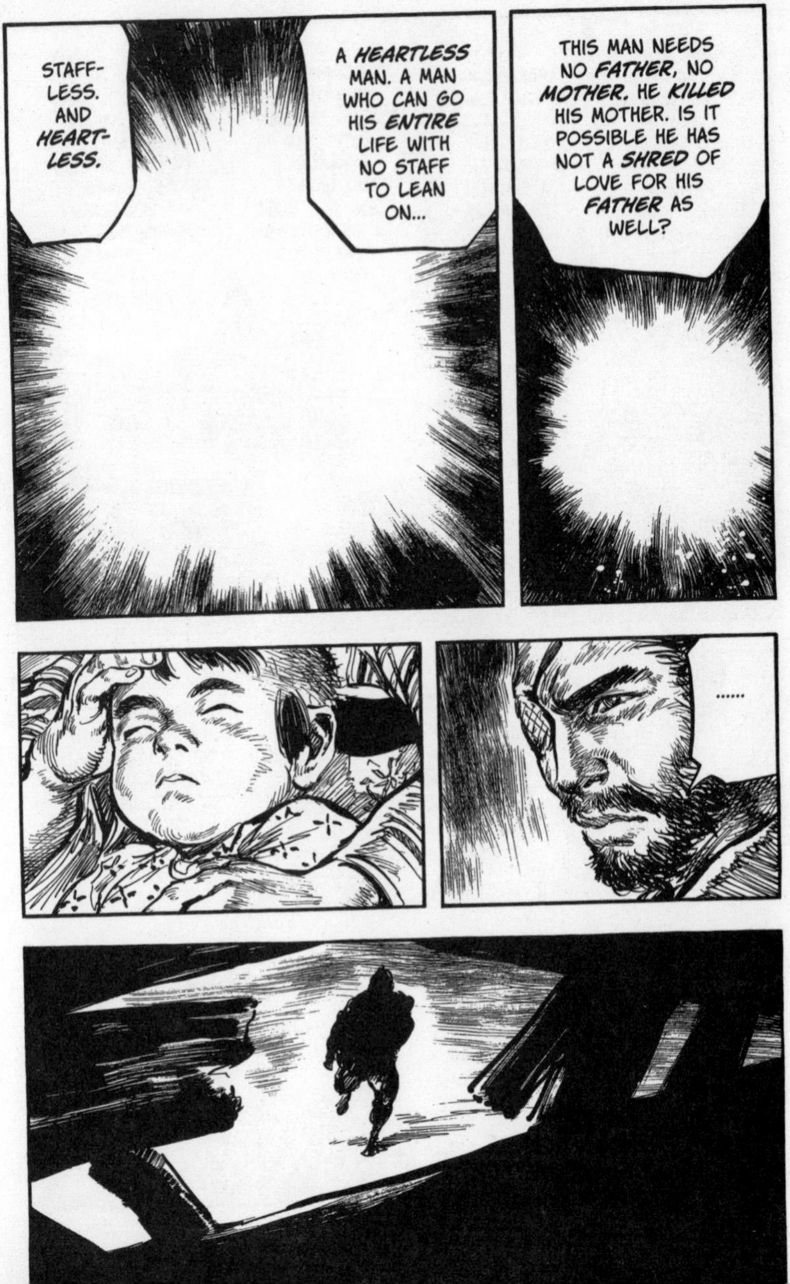
THIS MAN NEEDS NO FATHER, NO MOTHER. HE KILLED HIS MOTHER. IS IT POSSIBLE HE HAS NOT A SHRED OF LOVE FOR HIS FATHER AS WELL?
A HEARTLESS MAN. A MAN WHO CAN GO HIS ENTIRE LIFE WITH NO STAFF TO LEAN ON...
STAFF-LESS. AND HEART-LESS.
......

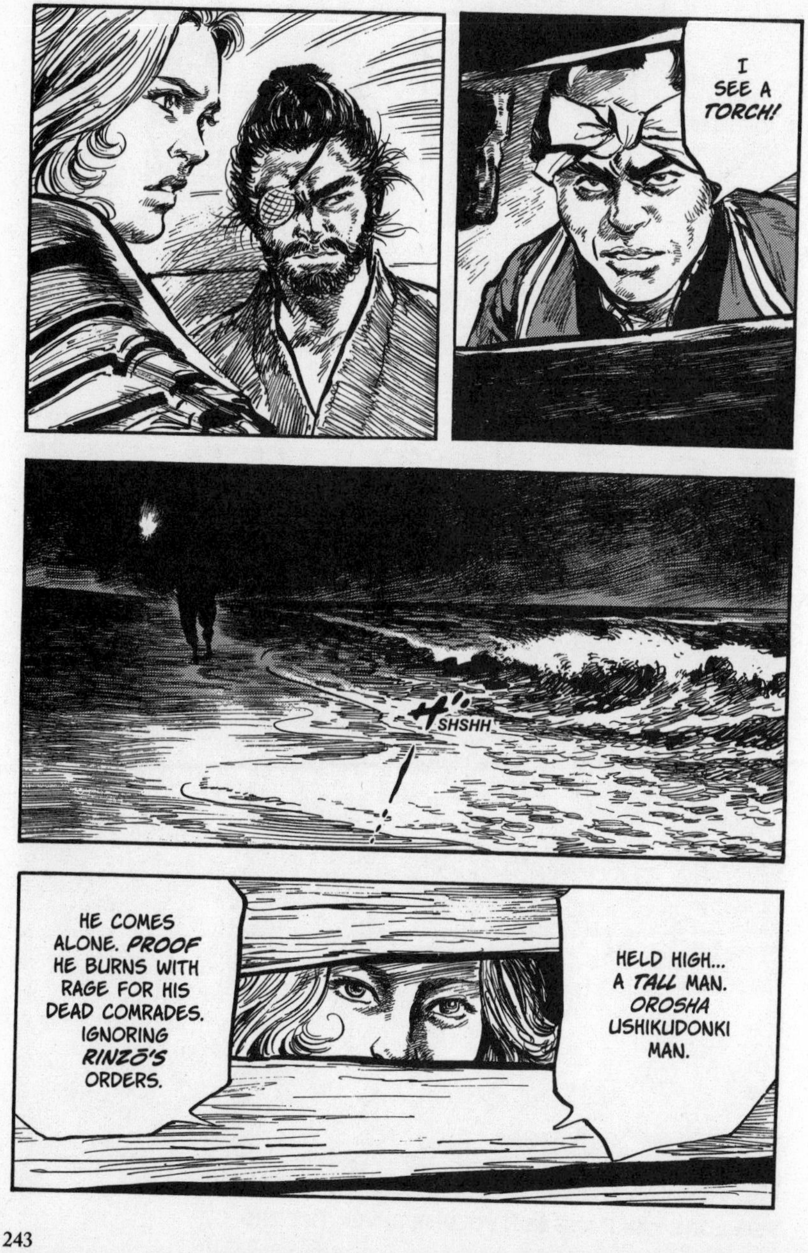
I SEE A TORCH!
SHSHH
HELD HIGH... A TALL MAN. OROSHA USHIKUDONKI MAN.
HE COMES ALONE. PROOF HE BURNS WITH RAGE FOR HIS DEAD COMRADES. IGNORING RINZŌ'S ORDERS.

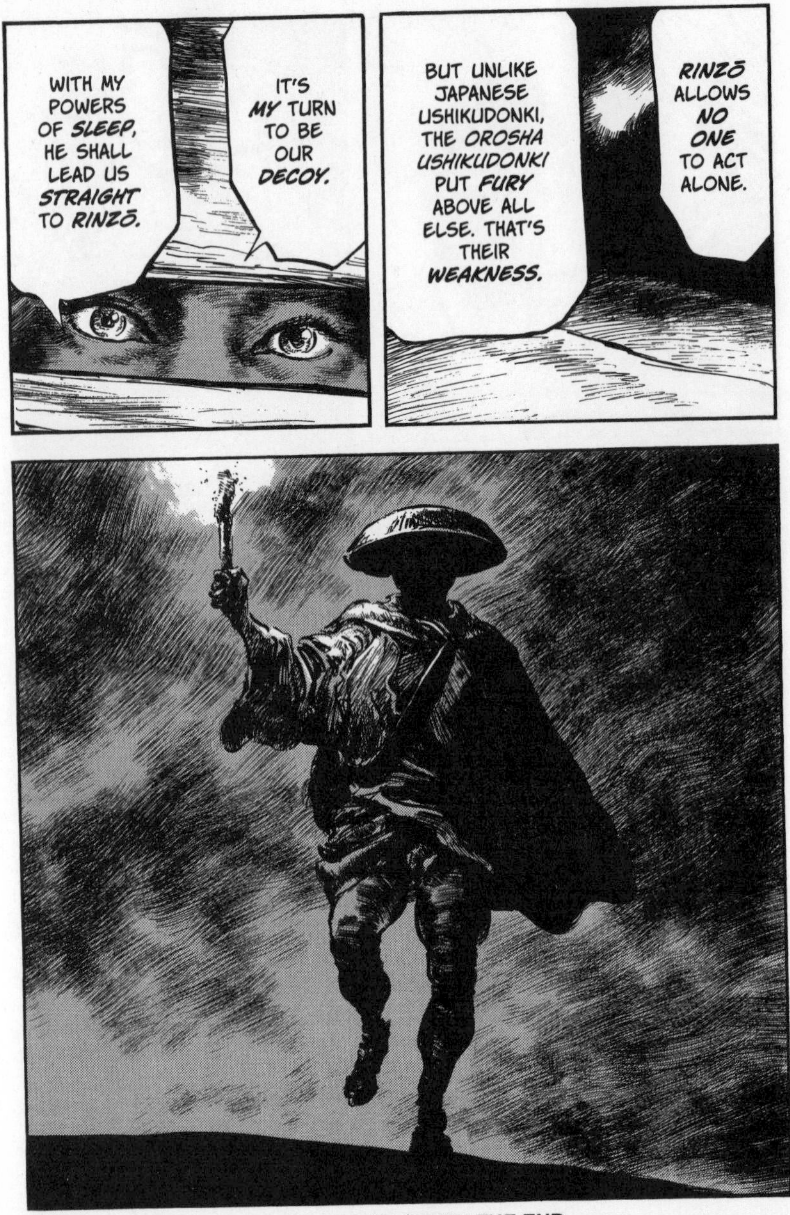
RINZŌ ALLOWS NO ONE TO ACT ALONE.
BUT UNLIKE JAPANESE USHIKUDONKI, THE OROSHA USHIKUDONKI PUT FURY ABOVE ALL ELSE. THAT'S THEIR WEAKNESS.
IT'S MY TURN TO BE OUR DECOY.
WITH MY POWERS OF SLEEP, HE SHALL LEAD US STRAIGHT TO RINZŌ.

NEW LONE WOLF AND CUB VOLUME SEVEN THE END

GLOSSARY

afuyō An Edo-period term for opium. The modern Japanese term is *ahen*.

bōjutsu A traditional Japanese martial art using a staff weapon roughly six feet in length called a *bō*.

bushi A samurai. A member of the warrior class.

bushidō The way of the warrior. Also known as *shidō*.

bushoku-tosei A *yakuza* gambler; literally, "jobless wanderer."

Edo The capital of medieval Japan and the seat of the shogunate. The site of modern-day Tokyo.

Ezo An indigenous people of northern Japan, Hokkaido, and Russia, today known as the Ainu.

Ezochi Literally, "Land of the Ezo." Today's northern island of Hokkaido and other small islands inhabited by northern Japan's indigenous Ezo people.

gempuku A traditional coming-of-age ceremony that lasted into the Edo period. Between the ages of ten and sixteen, a young man would adopt an adult name, hairstyle, and dress, and thereafter be considered ready to perform adult duties and to marry.

go-rōjū The inner circle of councilors directly advising the *shōgun*. The *rōjū* were the ultimate advisory body to the Tokugawa shogunate's national government. (*Go* is an honorific prefix, a marker of respect.)

Hagunsei Alkaid, the seventh star of the handle of the Big Dipper, at its left tip. In Japanese *onmyōdō* divination, it is a star leading all toward destruction.

han A feudal domain.

hanshu A lord of a *han*.

hesono'o-gaki A tradition in Japan of saving the dried umbilical cord after birth and place it in a small box together with written proof of the child's name and date of birth.

Jigen-ryū A traditional school of Japanese martial arts founded in the sixteenth century by the historical Tōgō Shigekata in Satsuma Province. Jigen-ryū focuses mainly on swordsmanship and is known for its emphasis on the first strike.

jinja A place of worship for Japan's indigenous Shinto religion.

jōjutsu A traditional Japanese martial art, similar to *bōjutsu*, using a short staff weapon roughly four feet in length called a *jō*.

kami-yashiki During the Edo period, the lords of feudal *han* across Japan were required to spend every other year in Edo, serving under the *shōgun*. This was done to increase surveillance over the *han* and to weaken them financially. *Han* maintained their own lavish *yashiki* mansions near Edo Castle for when their *hanshu* was living in the capital, and wealthy *han* would build several: one for the *hanshu* and his family and the others for lower-ranked vassals. The *kami-yashiki* (upper mansion) was the mansion closest to Edo Castle, home to the *hanshu* when he was in the capital.

kanji Adopted logographic Chinese characters used in the modern Japanese writing system.

▰TO PAGE 248

kaō A personal monogram based on the writer's full signature. Before the vermilion *inkan* stamps used in modern Japan, the *kaō* was an essential way of authenticating a document.

kenjutsu The way of the sword. Fencing as a martial art and spiritual practice. The progenitor of today's *kendō*.

ki Energy. The fundamental mind-body energy of Eastern medicine.

kō A respectful term for a *daimyō* or senior leader.

kubō An alternative term for the *shōgun*. Originally used to refer to the emperor, it came to be used for the *shōgun* during the Tokugawa shogunate. It was often used by samurai when speaking of the *shōgun*.

kunoichi A female ninja.

o-niwaban Ninja; literally, "one in the garden."

Orosha Russia.

osa A chieftain or head of a group or band.

oyabun The boss of a *yakuza* gang. Literally, "father status."

rōjū The inner circle of councilors directly advising the *shōgun*. The *rōjū* were the ultimate advisory body to the Tokugawa shogunate's national government.

ryūei Another word for the shogunate. Refers particularly to the officials running the government.

sakki Blood lust. It was believed that skilled warriors or ninja could feel the hatred directed at them by their foes, even through walls. It is written with the characters for *satsu* (to kill) and *ki* (energy).

-sama An honorific suffix, a marker of respect used for superiors.

satoiri ninja Ninja of the *sato* (homeland). In addition to the ninja based in Edo, the shogunate placed ninja undercover in the various *han* of rival lords. These moles would monitor dissident *han* and gather evidence that could be used to blackmail or dissolve a *han* when it stepped out of line.

shinobi A generic term for ninja, meaning "one who moves in secrecy."

shishōgan The eyes of life and death. The eyes of a master swordsman who has survived countless battles and achieved *muga*, freedom from the self.

shōgun One of Japan's military governors from the twelfth to nineteenth centuries.

Shōsei In Chinese astrology, the "General" or "Commander Star." In Japan the same Chinese characters were used both in their astrological sense and as an alternative term for the *shōgun* himself.

ubusunagami In Japan's indigenous Shintō religion, a deity that protects the people born in a given locality. The deity's protection follows them even if they move away.

ue-sama Literally, "one who is above." Used for the Tokugawa *shōgun* at this time in Japanese history.

wakadoshiyori Junior councilors. The highest advisory body to the *shōgun* on matters affecting the clan, rather than the nation as a whole.

zukin A hood that covers the head, with an opening for the eyes.